Words and Intelligence I

Text, Speech and Language Technology

VOLUME 35

Words and Intelligence I
Selected Papers by Yorick Wilks

Edited by

Khurshid Ahmad
Trinity College, Dublin, Ireland

Christopher Brewster
University of Sheffield, UK

Mark Stevenson
University of Sheffield, UK

 Springer

A C.I.P. Catalogue record for this book is available from the Library of Congress.

ISBN-13 978-90-481-7330-3
ISBN-10 1-4020-5285-5 (e-book)
ISBN-13 978-1-4020-5285-9 (e-book)

Published by Springer,
P.O. Box 17, 3300 AA Dordrecht, The Netherlands.

www.springer.com

Printed on acid-free paper

Contents

Preface

Professor Yorick Wilks has contributed to a wide range of academic fields including philosophy, linguistics and artificial intelligence. The main focus of his work has been the fields of computational linguistics and natural language processing where his work has advanced an unusually wide range of areas such as machine translation, word sense disambiguation, belief modelling, computational lexicons and dialogue modelling. One of the distinguishing features of his work has been his ability to link the engineering of practical text processing systems with more theoretical issues about language, particularly semantics. A number of themes have run through his work and one of the aims of this volume is to show how a body of work on such a diverse range of topics also forms a coherent program of inquiry. A comprehensive record of the range and diversity of Yorick's output is beyond the scope of this volume. Rather, as part of the Festschrift organized to honour his retirement from teaching, we chose this volume to contain a selection of representative pieces including some less accessible papers.

The first paper we have chosen to include ("Text Searching with Templates") is surely one few will be familiar with. This was published as a technical report in 1964 at the Cambridge Language Research Unit, where Yorick first worked on Computational Linguistics. In this paper Yorick outlines an approach in which texts are represented using template structures and world knowledge, in the form of an interlingua, used to define the elements which could be combined into meaningful units. Later these ideas were developed and incorporated into his work on Preference Semantics.

The next paper ("Decidability and Natural Language"), published in the philosophy journal Mind, is a theoretical discussion of whether it is possible to represent the semantics of natural language in any computable way. Here Yorick argues against the accepted belief at the time that the syntax and semantics of natural language utterances should be treated independently, proposing that semantics is not an extensions of syntax but rather the other way round. He also addresses the question of whether a deterministic procedure could ever be developed to decide whether a sentence is meaningful and suggests that a suitable criterion might be whether a single interpretation of the sentence can be identified. In this paper, Yorick discusses a theme which he returns to several times: that the possible meanings of a particular word can only be defined relative to a particular sense inventory and cannot be thought of as abstract, Platonic entities.

The next paper ("The Stanford Machine Translation and Understanding Project") represents Yorick's important contribution to Machine Translation and provides detail of the English-French translation system he worked on at Stanford University. Yorick discusses how the latest advances in linguistics, particularly semantic analysis, could be used to justify another attempt at the MT problem (this paper was written only a few years after the 1966 ALPAC report damning machine translation). He also shows how these ideas could be implemented in a practical way by describing a system which made use of an interlingua approach and analysed the input text by transforming it into template structures similar to those introduced in the first paper.

One of the main outcomes of the Stanford project was Yorick's influential Preference Semantic system, various aspects of which are detailed in three of the papers ("An Intelligent Analyser and Understander of English", "A Preferential, Pattern Seeking, Semantics for Natural Language Inference" and "Making Preferences More Active"). The first paper provides an introduction and shows that, contrary to standard approaches of the day, syntactic and semantic analysis could be carried out in parallel. Preference Semantics is based on the use of selectional restrictions but, rather than treating them as constraints which must be satisfied, they were interpreted as paradigm cases, indicating normal or prototypical word usages which may be expected but could be adapted if necessary. The system represented the preferences using a set of semantic primitives which were also used to represent the possible meanings of each word (called "formulas"). These were combined, and their preferences examined to choose the correct meaning, resulting in a template representing the meaning of the text. The next paper explains how Preference Semantics can be extended to carry out reasoning about texts to perform anaphora resolution. In keeping with one of the main motivations behind Preference Semantics, that a language understanding system should always attempt to provide a usable interpretation, the approach attempted to resolve a wide range of anaphora. The system would make a best guess about the meaning of an utterance, as a human does, and act accordingly. Further experience, gained through additional knowledge about the situation, may suggest a change in interpretation but to carry out many language understanding tasks, including machine translation, requires some commitment to a preferred interpretation. The final paper on Preference Semantics provides more details about how the flexibility of the system can be used to interpret a wide range of usages. Yorick points out that word usages which are often thought of as metaphorical are common in everyday language and that the burden of interpretation should be placed on the language understanding system. Yorick argues that formal theories proposed by linguists were not flexible enough to describe the sort of language used in everyday situations. Yorick motivates this with the now famous example: "My car drinks gasoline". Yorick advocates the use of world knowledge to interpret metaphorical language, in this case we need to know that cars require the insertion of a liquid (petrol or gasoline) to run.

Preference Semantics relied on a set of semantic primitives to denote the typical, or preferred, usages although their use had been questioned. In the next paper ("Good and Bad Arguments about Semantic Primitives"), Yorick replies to these criticisms.

The main questions posed were what semantic primitives actually meant, and where these semantics derived from. Yorick proposes a position where primitives can be though of as part of the language whose semantics they represent. They form a set of building blocks within the language from which more complex statements can be formed by combination. Once again, Yorick argues that the meaning of language is found within the language itself.

Yorick's position in that paper is a theoretical one which is made practical in the next paper we selected ("Providing Machine Tractable Dictionary Tools"). This paper introduces Yorick's extensive work with Machine Readable Dictionaries (MRD) by describing several methods for exploiting the information they contain which had been developed while he led the Computer Research Lab of New Mexico State University. The first technique, the use of co-occurrence statistics within dictionary definitions, is a very different approach from Yorick's previous work on Preference Semantics and allows meaning to emerge from the dictionary definitions in an automated way. Another technique described in this paper concerns the conversion of a MRD into a full Machine Tractable Dictionary, that is a resource in which the terms used to define word senses are unambiguous and so can be readily understood by a computer. This represents a computational implementation of Yorick's view of semantic primitives. One of the main goals of this project is to identify a core set of basic terms which can be used to provide definitions and these were also identified through automatic dictionary analysis. A final application for the dictionary was to automatically generate lexical entries for a Preference Semantics system which provided a method for avoiding the bottleneck caused by the previous reliance on hand coded formulas.

The next paper ("Belief Ascription, Metaphor and Intensional Identification") represents Yorick's work on belief modeling and dialogue understanding which were implemented in the ViewGen system. His work on this area builds upon the techniques developed for understanding metaphors within the Preference Semantics framework.

In the paper entitled "Stone Soup and the French Room" Yorick returns to the topic of Machine Translation to discuss IBM's statistical approach. He is characteristically skeptical of the claims being made and controversially suggests that purely data-driven approaches could not rival mature AI-based techniques since the later represent language using symbolic structures. Yorick makes sure to point out that he does not oppose empirical approaches to language processing by reminding us that "we are all empricists" and also suggests that the roots of the statistical approach to translation could be traced back to some of the earliest work on computational linguistics. The collective memory in language processing is often short and it is important for researchers to be able to be reminded of earlier work may have been forgotten all too quickly. To a great extent Yoricks claims have been proved by recent work on statistical machine translation. During the decade or so since this paper was published work on statistical machine translation has gradually moved towards the use of increasingly rich linguistic structures combined with data derived from text.

In the final paper ("Senses and Texts") Yorick discusses recent work on semantic analysis, specifically two contradictory claims: that the word sense disambiguation problem cannot be solved since it is not well formed and another that suggested the problem had, to a large extent, been solved. Yorick points out that the notion of what is meant by "word sense" is central to these arguments but that it has not yet been adequately defined and, besides, is only meaningful relative to some specific lexicon. One of the claims Yorick discusses rests on the assumption that Computational Linguists had made naïve assumptions about the nature of meaning and he, once again, reminds us to looked to the past; "In general, it is probably wise to believe, even if it not always true, that authors in the past were no more naïve than those now working, and were probably writing programs, however primate and ineffective, that carry out the same tasks as now." Yorick points to one of the motivations behind Preference Semantics, namely that any adequate language understanding system must accommodate usages which are different from the meanings listed in the lexicon but somehow related, as in metaphorical utterances.

Khurshid Ahmad
Christopher Brewster
Mark Stevenson

Origin of the Essays

All permissions granted for the previously published essays by their respective copyright holders are most gratefully acknowledged.

1. Wilks, Y. (1964) "Text Searching with Templates" Cambridge Language Research Unit Memo, ML. 156
2. Wilks, Y. (1971) "Decidability and Natural Language" *Mind.* vol. LXXX pp. 497–520.
3. Wilks, Y. (1973) "The Stanford Machine Translation and Understanding Project" In R. Rustin (ed.) *Natural Language Processing*, pages 243–290. Algorithmics Press, New York.
4. Wilks, Y. (1975) "An Intelligent Analyser and Understander of English" *Communications of the ACM* 18(5):264–274.
5. Wilks, Y. (1975) "A Preferential, Pattern Seeking, Semantics for Natural Language Inference" *Artificial Intelligence* 6:53–74.
6. Wilks, Y. (1977) "Good and Bad Arguments about Semantic Primitives" *Communication and Cognition* 10(3/4):181–221.
7. Wilks, Y. (1979) "Making Preferences More Active" *Artificial Intelligence* 11:197–223.
8. Wilks, Y., Fass, D., Guo, C-M., McDonald, JE., Plate, T., Slator, BM. (1990) "Providing Machine Tractable Dictionary Tools" *Machine Translation*, 5(2):99–151.
9. Ballim, A, Wilks, Y., Barnden, J. (1991) "Belief Ascription, Metaphor and Intensional Identity" *Cognitive Science*, 15(1):133–171.
10. Wilks, Y. (1994) "Stone soup and the French Room" In A. Zampoli, N. Calzolari, and M. Palmer (eds.) *Current Issues in Natural Language Processing: In Honour of Don Walker* pp. 585–595.
11. Wilks, Y. (1997) "Senses and Texts" *Computers and the Humanities* 31(2):77–90.

1

Text Searching with Templates

Yorick Wilks
Cambridge Language Research Unit

1.1 Introduction

A 'template' (to be abbreviated as 'T') is a sequence of atomic marks which are either

(1) a left-hand *bracket* or a right-hand *bracket*
(2) a connective written ":" or "/"
(3) an *element* which is a member of one of the lists (p. 6) of elements selected from the elements of the C.L.R.U. interlingua "Nub"

and which are combined in the form

$$(X : p) : (m \ v \ / \ n \ (Y : q)1)$$

where p, v, q are elements chosen from given lists. X, Y, l, m, n are variables whose substitution values are *formulae* of the interlingua. A formula is defined recursively in the following manner;

(1) every element is a formula
(2) every formula not itself an element is of the form X b Y where X, Y are formulae and b is a connective.

l, m, n are only mentioned here for completeness, in that we may require their presence in the basic formula above when considering more complexities than we do now. They will not be mentioned again here, and we will therefore consider the basic formula in the simpler form.

$$(X : p) : (v \ / \ (Y : q))$$

This is itself a formula on the above recursive definition. We shall refer to X and Y as *text* variables, and p, v and q as *template* variables.

K. Ahmad, C. Brewster and M. Stevenson (eds.), Words and Intelligence 1, 1–7.
© 2007 *Springer.*

We give as section (1.5) of this note mutually exclusive lists of plausible inter-lingual elements as substitution values for p and/or q and for v respectively. Not all the values of the above formula, which are obtained by substituting each of the members of its appropriate list for each of p, q and v in turn, are T's.

We give next in (1.5) a table showing which of the concatenated pairs (p q), formed from this class of values for p and q, can form part of a 'permitted' T.

These lists are preceded by an outline of a preprogram (section (1.4)). This would operate upon a text coded in the interlingua, which we shall call the datum-text. A digression is required at this point on the construction of this datum-text.

1.2 The Participation of the Interlingual-dictionary Entries in the Datum-text

It is assumed that the text is provided in structured interlingual form (whether of nubs[1] or of full entries, for all the words of the original message or only for certain 'key' words is discussed below).

i) The interlingual dictionary is made by giving more than one formula, in general, for each English word; which of these are we to insert in the datum-text; since the interlingual syntax allows for only one?

In general I think we must hope for a large enough computer to be able to insert each of the formulae in turn and subsequently to choose the 'best' output. We shall require some criterion for the best output even without this – at least, we shall until the T's are far less crude than they are at present.

ii) The question then arises as to which *part* of these formulae "participate" in the datum-text?

If we insert only the 'nubs' we will presumably not then be able to read off semantically satisfactory values of the 'text-variables' (see below) from the processed data text. However, providing we *can* re-associate each nub with the appropriate natural language word we could leave the 'non-nub' part of each formula in the store and change the present syntactic form of a T by dropping the "bracket and connective restrictions". On the other hand it has yet to be shown that inserting the whole formula does produce *unmanageably many* contours.

(i) and (ii) are independent in so far as ambiguity is part-of-speech ambiguity (in which case interlingual entries for an English word have, in general, different nubs, and *this* ambiguity can be resolved fairly simply by syntactic considerations), which is to say that if we insert only nubs in the data text problem (i) *will not arise* at this stage.

---

[1] "nub" is defined in the interlingua "Nub" (a variant of "Nude") now being constructed by J. Burns. Essentially a nub is the last element of the interlingual formula for a word which also fixes some of its syntactic properties.

1.3 Contours

The program outlined in (1.4) first divides the datum-text into *strings*. A string contains the formulae corresponding to a phrase or clause in the natural language text, and the latter is divided into phrases and clauses by a modified form of the C.L.R.U. Syntax-Bracketting program. Within each string the constituent formulae are re-ordered, if necessary, to make the syntax of the string conform to the rules of the interlingua. It should be possible to stipulate a maximum length for such strings in terms of interlingual elements. The aim of the program is to match each of the strings on the datum-text with the inventory of T's that is stored in the machine as concatenated triples of elements. Output for each string is given as a list of "matched and augmented (i.e. X & Y made explicit) T's" or "*contours*". A contour is a T in which X and Y are replaced either by formulae or by nothing at all (in which case the connectives preceding the 'p' and 'q' elements are deleted also). We say there is a contour in a given string if the following marks occur in it in left-right order:-

$$p): v/q) \qquad\qquad (1)$$

where p, v, q represent any of the elements in the appropriate lists (p. 6). Each pair of marks in the contour, except those forming part of the values of X or Y, may occur in the string in such a way as to be separated by other marks except that;

the 'p' element must be immediately followed by the '):'
the 'v' element must be immediately followed by the '/'
the 'q' element must be immediately followed by the ')'.

The list 1 above does not represent a necessary condition since we shall recognize cases in which the marks corresponding to values for the X, Y, v, /, marks do not occur. We actually *define* the occurrence of a *contour* in terms of a subset of the marks 1, as follows. We shall say that there is a contour in a string if it contains a substitution value for a "p):" mark followed, but not immediately followed, by a substitution value for a "q)" mark i.e. by a *pair* not a *triple*. This last stipulation requires some justification.

When searching for contours we might *treat as T's* the list of permitted concatenated triples (p v q) which we will call *full templates* by contrast with the (smaller) set of permitted concatenated pairs, or blank templates (p q). But there are troubles about this which can be readily illustrated by using the symbol '↔' (whose negation is '↮') to mean 'can be written for' which can be roughly interpreted as 'means the same as' i.e. it denotes a symmetrical relation.

Now it is clear from the structure of the given basic T, (and will be quite transparent from the lists of suggested values for p, v, & q below), that the T's are intended to have a 'sentential feel', (though we cannot of course assume in advance that the *strings* will correspond to sentences in the text), p corresponding roughly to a subject, v to a verb, and q to an object or complement.

Generally, *in Anglo-Nude*, given values from the appropriate classes for p, q & v it is the case that

a. (p v q) ↔ (p q v) *but*
b. (p v q) ↮ (v p q) [2]
c. (p v q) ↮ (v q p)
d. (p v q) ↮ (q p v)
e. (p v q) ↮ (q v p)

Any doubt about (a) interpreted as a true statement about English word-order can be laid by *making it a necessary condition* that for a given (p′ v′ q′) to be admitted as a full template that (a) be true for *those* values of p, v, or q.

Now when a matching program is given a definite form, since the string must be searched from either the left hand end or right hand end in written order, and since the class of possible values is to be the same for p and q, equivalences rejected by (c), (d), and (e) can never arise. Since the program as given cannot distinguish such forms from forms occurring in (a) or (b). So it will be seen from (a) and (b) that the set of permitted triples is a subset of the set of possible triples, it is in fact that subset in which the 'v' separates or follows the members of the pair. We may then (having located the pair), look for a 'v' element to make it a *full template*, searching first between the elements of the pair, (since such an ordering is the more common construction in English), than after the pair in the given string. This means no more than that each triple may be considered as being written twice in the inventory, but in two forms. If no 'v' element appears in the search we record the result as a pair or '*blank contour*'.

When such a pair has been located in a string we say that the string has a substructure; we can then *read off* the values of the text variables X, Y as those elements bracketed with the p and q elements so located.

Two other things should be noted at this point. It will be seen that there may be many potential contours 'in' any given string which satisfy these requirements, and we shall require that the program locates all the contours in it.

1.4 The Form of the Program

A program to locate a single contour in a given string would operate as follows. Each element in the string would be examined in turn starting from the 'left-hand end'. In each case the examination would consist in enquiring whether the element occurred on the "p or q" list, if not we pass on to the next element (moving right on the paper); if it does so occur, we examine the next elements to the right in turn to see if one of them also occurs on this list, if one does i.e. *this* pair is designated '1' in the table on p.6 we say we have a *blank template*, if not we pass on. *For*

---

[2] We might refer to (b) as the "re-ordering function Q" for 'question-templates', though we shall not make use of this feature here.

each such blank template a further search for a "v" element is made as follows: the elements between the "p" and the "q" element in question are examined in *left to right* (reverse) order to see if they occur on the "v" list, if one does, *and* the triple is on the T list (p.7), we have a full template, if not we proceed to examine (again in "left to right" order) these elements in the string to the left of the "q" element and match with the 'T' list as before.

A program to extract *all* the contours would be one that continued in this way i.e. proceeding as before but *as if* the *matching* triple just found did not so match, after registering each success. It is not difficult to see that for an exhaustive search of a string of n elements the total number of comparison operations with the T list is:

$$\sum_{r=1}^{n} (n-r)\,(n-r-1)$$

which is:

$$n^2 \; - \; 1 \; + \; \sum_{r=1}^{n} r^2 \; + \; (1-2n) \sum_{r=1}^{n} r$$

or:

$$\frac{n^3 + 6n^2 + 2n - 3}{3}$$

i.e. for a string with 12 elements the number is 871.

A routine would be needed to ensure that the "same" contour, even if located many times, was only recorded once.

Each T may be negated by placing a 'NOT' element before its 'v' element. (In this context we ignore the logical distinction between internal and external negation, which requires separate discussion).

In order to record this in the output we should have a routine which enquired in the case of each 'accepted' "v" element whether or not the preceding element was a "NOT".

If *all* the T's are extracted it might turn out that one of them in a given string corresponded to *textual* features that could be said to be "contained in" the text corresponding to another T. But it would, I think be misleading to think of this as one template "being a value of another" or anything like that.

It must be emphasized that we cannot complain of such a program that it locates the *wrong* contours. What we *can* ask of any output are answers to the following questions:

1. Are the located contours useful for some defined purpose?
2. Is the list of templates used intuitively adequate?
3. Does it correspond with, or at least include, the list of templates found by other methods; from say, a list of contours located by phonetic stress-point analysis?

A separate note is required to indicate how this program might be achieved with punched cards, and what the appropriate method of coding both of the interlingua-word entries and of the template forms would be.

1.5 The Template List

The T's on this list are for some part wholly arbitrary, but this need not prevent the program being carried through and the value of the output assessed. The list of templates will require ultimate justification in much the same way as the choice of the basic elements and the individual word formulae. The two lists or the values of p or q, and v form a restricted sub-interlingua so that some of the elements in the templates above have idiosyneratic, though consistent, senses. These might well repay further study.

Values for p or q	Values for v
DO	PLEASE
FOLK	SENSE
KIND	BE
MAN	FEEL
PART	HAVE
WHOLE	USE
THING	WANT
STUFF	CAUSE
GRAIN	CHANGE
WORLD	PAIR
SIGN	

We may thus display the 121 possibilities of ordered pairs in the following table.

In it the elements written on the left hand side of the page represent the occurrence of the first element of the pair considered, those written vertically the second. An "O" indicates that the pair represented by that position is not a permitted pair; a "1" indicates that it is.

	DO	FOLK	KIND	MAN	PART	WHOLE	THING	STUFF	GRAIN	WORLD	SIGN
DO	1	1	0	1	0	0	1	1	1	0	1
FOLK	1	1	0	1	0	1	1	1	0	1	1
KIND	1	1	1	1	1	1	1	1	1	1	1
MAN	1	1	0	1	1	1	1	0	1	1	1
PART	0	1	1	1	1	1	1	1	0	1	1
WHOLE	0	0	1	1	1	1	1	0	0	1	1
THING	1	1	0	1	0	1	1	1	1	1	1
STUFF	1	1	0	1	1	1	1	1	1	1	1
GRAIN	0	1	1	1	1	1	1	1	1	1	1
WORLD	1	1	0	1	1	1	1	1	0	1	1
SIGN	1	1	1	1	1	1	1	1	1	1	1

We need to give no justification in terms of 'logical impossibility' or what not for the above exclusion of 21 of the 121 possibilities. We can keep which we like and simply judge the acceptability of the corresponding results. (Note that all 'double elements' (qq) remain at present).

2

Decidability and Natural Language

Yorick Wilks
Stanford University

2.1 Grammaticality and Decidability

It would be absurd to try to construct a procedure that could, formally and generally, decide whether English sentences were true or false. If that could be done then, at the very least, there would be no need of scientific experiment wherever English was spoken. But the absurdity of that possibility should not cause anyone to dismiss two other, more interesting, questions: one about what are usually called grammatical English sentences, and the other about meaningful English sentences. Are either of these sets of sentences decidable? Could there be procedures that would determine whether a string of English words was, or was not, either grammatical or meaningful?

Attempts have been made to construct both sorts of procedure: in the case of meaningfulness there is Carnap's theory of Logical Syntax [1]: and in the case of "grammaticality" there is Chomsky's more recent work in the field of linguistics [2]. Carnap's work rested upon an analogy between the ungrammaticality of sentences like "Caesar is and" and the apparent meaninglessness of such sentences as "Caesar is triangular". Carnap thought that, if the rules of grammar were supplemented and extended by "rules of logical grammar", then the meaninglessness of "Caesar is triangular" could be shown by the same procedures as dealt with the more obviously odd "Caesar is and". Carnap's work in this area was largely programmatic: he did not construct such a system of rules in any detail and then apply it to actual texts.

Chomsky's work in linguistics is a natural and proper successor to Carnap's. His original suggestion was that a set of "transformational grammar rules" could produce all and only the grammatical sentences of English from a number of initial "kernel sentences", that were themselves produced by rules of a different sort called "phrase structure rules". Chomsky's paradigm of a transformational rule [2:43] was one which would convert an English sentence into its "equivalent passive": *i.e.* "John loves Mary" into "Mary is loved by John".

Chomsky's work is even closer to Carnap's than is generally realised, in that it too is an attempt to "explicate" or produce, the class of *meaningful* sentences, in spite of Chomsky's initial intention to dispense with meaning and concentrate on

9

K. Ahmad, C. Brewster and M. Stevenson (eds.), Words and Intelligence 1, 9–27.

grammar. My claim here is not a mystical one about Chomsky's intentions. It can be supported by drawing attention to the greatly extended sense in which he has used "grammar" in the last few years: he has introduced what he calls a "semantic component" [3] into his grammars, so that grammaticality is now for him a notion quite different from syntactically correct. But to demonstrate this point in detail would be a narrowly linguistic enterprise. In this first part of this paper I want to argue that, whether or not Chomsky is now explicating meaningfulness, he cannot be explicating grammaticality as he originally set out to do, because grammaticality lacks the necessary properties for that to be possible. I shall then go on to argue that meaningfulness differs somewhat from grammaticality in this respect.

One further point: it might be objected at the outset that considerations about decidability are of a purely syntactic nature in the sense of "syntactic" in which Gödel's theorem is said to be a purely syntactic theorem, and so they can have nothing to do with questions of meaningfulness, or "grammaticality" in a linguistic sense. The premise is perfectly true, but I am not trying to introduce meaning, truth or grammaticality where it cannot belong. I am simply raising the question as to how one might interpret the notion of theoremhood in certain canonical languages of the kind described by Post [4, 5]. Chomsky himself has observed [6] that his own system of transformational rules can be viewed as a system of production rules for a canonical language in Post's sense. A canonical language has a finite alphabet, a finite number of productions, or inference rules, and a finite number of axioms. The axioms are concatenated strings of items in the alphabet, and any string which can be produced from these axioms by means of a finite number of applications of the production rules can be called a theorem. The decision problem for the language is determining whether any given string is a theorem or not. The analogy between generative grammars and this formulation of proof theory depends upon considering as "theorems" the strings produced by the operation of grammar rules, or "rules of inference". Only the last, or what Chomsky calls the terminal, string of a production is interpreted as having the property associated with theoremhood, namely, "grammaticality". The only "axiom" in Chomsky's system is then the string 'S', for "Sentence", with which all productions begin.

Chomsky does not claim that transformational grammars are complete, in that they produce all and only the grammatically correct sentences of English. Nor does he claim that they are decidable, in that their rules decide of an arbitrary string of English words whether or not it is grammatically correct. However, he is presumably trying to construct a system having either or both these properties; for that is the programme he originally set himself, whatever his subsequent disclaimers about decision procedures [2:55].

In the case of transformational grammars it is not easy to be clear about their decidability, or otherwise, because Chomsky is unwilling to give them any general form. But it does seem generally agreed that a set of transformational rules of the sort Chomsky has described characterizes a recursively enumerable set of sentences, but not necessarily a recursive set. That is to say, you can generate as many sentences as you like with the rules, but you may not be in a position to decide whether or not a given, ungenerated, sentence can be generated [7].

In this respect transformational rules differ from phrase structure rules, which are known to be decidable in a number of cases [8]. In almost all his writings Chomsky has included a number of arguments against the use of phrase structure grammars which, he contends, can produce only the sort of "surface grammatical structure" to be found in, say, school grammar books.

Yet, in this important respect of the decidability of the formal system, phrase structure grammars seem *to start with a distinct advantage*; for, whatever the practical advances made using heuristic transformational parsers (e.g.[9][10]) programmed on computers, it can never be known for certain whether or not a given transformational grammar can analyse a given sentence.

Chomsky also argues against what are called finite state [2:21] grammars, and again, by implication, for transformational grammars, on the ground that there are grammatical English sentences that no finite state grammar of a certain class can produce [11]. That is to say finite state grammars are incomplete *in the sense that* they do not cover the known "theorems". I do not want to go in detail into this linguistic dispute, for what is important here for my purposes is to point out the assumption behind Chomsky's argument; namely, that there *is* some survey of what it is to be a "theorem to be covered" by a generative grammar, which is to say, a grammatical sentence. My contention is that, on the contrary, there is not *as a matter of fact* a survey of the set of sentences Chomsky has in mind, and it is not a class of sentences about which native speakers can take reasonable decisions, in the way they can about meaningful sentences. If one asks an informant "Is 'Colourless green ideas sleep furiously' a grammatical sentence?", one tends to provoke only puzzlement; though linguists, philosophers and logicians are less unwilling to decide the question, and the diversity of their answers is an argument against Putnam's view [9:38-39] that speakers broadly agree on such questions, and hence the grammatical sentences of a language are probably a recursive set. Curry [12] thinks such sentences are grammatical; Ziff [13] thinks they are ungrammatical but not nonsensical; Jakobson thinks that they are grammatical but false [14]; Putnam [9] thinks they are at least ungrammatical, and certainly not false. Chomsky's view has, as I said, changed on this question: in the original formulation of his views, he contrasted such sentences with ungrammatical ones, but in *Current Issues in Linguistic Theory* [3:25] he argued for the existence of a set of grammatical sentences to be "explicated", and that it was a set not dependent on notions like "meaning" for its characterisation:

> "...the notion 'grammatical' cannot be identified with 'meaningful' or 'significant' in any semantic sense. Sentences (1) and (2) are equally nonsensical, but any speaker of English will recognize that only the former is grammatical.
>
> (1) Colourless green ideas sleep furiously.
> (2) Furiously sleep ideas green colourless."

Chomsky later refers to this quoted passage as a demonstration of the independence of "grammar" and "meaning", though there is no demonstration here in any strong sense, but simply an appeal to observe the difference between two sentences.

I do see a difference between the two sentences, in that I can think of a number of things that sentence (1) might mean, whereas I find it less easy to see what sentence (2) could be about. But even that might be only a question of effort: I could probably work out an interpretation for "Furiously fought men tired weary", and might well be able to do something similar for (2). I can see no other difference between (1) and (2) unless I am provided with specific grammar rules that (1) abides by and (2) breaks. By "work out an interpretation" I refer to the ability native speakers of a language have to explain what they mean by a piece of language embedding it in a larger explanatory text or conversation. In the case of sentence (1), one might try to show that it was meaningful by embedding it in some improbable story about the nature of the brain's activity during sleep, and its effect on the sleeper's behaviour. The story might also make it clear that "green" was being used in the sense of "new or untried".

This ability to explain the meaning of something, and so to show that it is meaningful, is part of the ability to write or speak a language. One thinks of Wittgenstein's "words have those meanings which we give them; and we give them meanings by explanations" [15]. Not so, however, with Chomsky's intuitions about grammaticality: I do not share his intuitions about the difference between sentences (1) and (2), yet I remain unrepentantly a native speaker of English. But in the case of grammaticality there is no such explanatory, or elucidatory, *procedure* that Chomsky can employ in order to convince anyone who fails to share his intuition of the difference between sentences (1) and (2).

Grammatical knowledge is no part of what it is to speak and understand a language, for, on the contrary, grammatical explanations and manipulations are what people *who do not speak a language well* fall back on. That is not to deny that for any actual grammar there is a set of sentences well formed with respect to it. But saying that is quite different from what Chomsky says, for it does not imply that there is such a set prior to the construction and use of the grammar, nor does it imply that there are "grammatical mistakes" except in so far as some "rule" is specified with respect to which they are mistakes.

Since he wrote the passage quoted Chomsky [3:9] has changed his view, and now considers sentences like (2) above to be "deviant" in that they should *not* be produced by a good grammar. Hence, such sentences are now considered to be ungrammatical by Chomsky. So he might seem to be in some doubt about what is and what is not a grammatical sentence; yet his whole task of explicating the set of such sentences depends on there being some independent survey or characterisation of what it is to be a grammatical sentence. Without such a survey or characterisation there is no notion of what it is to be a "theorem" for his, or any other, system of derivations to produce. Putnam [7:191] has argued that the grammatical sentences of a language *are* surveyable in that there is general agreement about the membership of the set, and that this justifies us in considering them a recursive set capable of being produced by a decidable generative grammar. The plausibility of his case comes from examples like "Mary goed home", about which there would be general agreement that it is ungrammatical. But there is not this agreement, even among experts, about interesting cases of odd, or deviant, sentences such as "Colourless green ideas sleep furiously". Thus Putnam's case is not made.

I may have laid myself open to the charge of simply punning on the words "decision procedure" by introducing them into a discussion of natural language. Let me try to get at the main point slightly differently: as is well known, the Propositional Calculus has a decision procedure; namely, certain computations on *truth tables*. However, there is also a partial survey of what it is to be a theorem independent of the truth tables, for they are not required in order to know that "p ⊃ p" is true in the Propositional Calculus. If that were not so one could not discuss completeness or decision procedures at all. For example, when expressing Gödel's [16] theorem in the form "no consistent language can be adequate for the expression of mathematics, and at the same time be capable of proving all true propositions in elementary number theory", it is implied that there is some survey of what it is to be a true proposition in elementary number theory independent of an axiomatisation and a decision procedure. Otherwise Gödel's theorem loses its point. Yet this kind of survey is utterly lacking in the case of grammatical sentences.

Logical truths, then, can be surveyed prior to the construction of any system of explication, and, moreover, the notion of logical truth can itself be characterised in terms of other concepts. These characterisations, such as Leibniz's "true in all possible worlds", are ultimately unsatisfying but it is an important fact about logical truth that they can be proposed and sustained by argument. Similarly the notion of meaningfulness has been characterised in terms of many other concepts, and another possible characterisation of it is explored in a tentative fashion in the last section of this paper. But it is not easy to see how the notion of grammaticality can be characterised in any similar fashion. "What speakers admit as grammatical" does not seem quite good enough for, whatever the inadequacies of "those sentences that are true in all possible worlds" as a characterisation of logical truths, it is certainly better than "those sentences that speakers (or logicians) admit as logical truths".

Chomsky [11], and more recently Ziff [13], have suggested characterisations of grammaticality independent of the acceptance of sentences by some particular set of grammatical rules. Chomsky has suggested that an ungrammatical utterance is read with a falling tone on every word, and Ziff has suggested that an ungrammatical utterance is one that a native speaker "balks at". It needs no concentrated analysis to see that those suggestions will not do, and for the same reasons in each case.

On the one hand perfectly comprehensible sentences like "Mary goed home" would almost certainly be read by a speaker with the same intonation, and as little balking, as the more conventional "Mary went home", even though both Chomsky and Ziff would consider the first sentence ungrammatical and the second grammatical. On the other hand, even intelligent and well-disposed speakers balk at sentences that are perfectly grammatical by our authors' standards, but which express some particularly striking falsehood such as "An elephant isn't really an animal you know".

My conclusion from these arguments is not that many mathematical linguists are wasting their time, or are engaged in some form of linguistic circle squaring. It is rather that if their enterprise is, as it is usually, one of testing a given string of words to see if it has a given property or not, then it would be better to call the property "meaningfulness" than "grammaticality", since the latter property does not admit of being attached to that procedure. Whereas, as I shall try and show below, meaningfulness is at least a starter in that respect. The relabelling would be quite appropriate to Chomsky's changing notion of "grammatical", which once included "Colourless green ideas sleep furiously" but now excludes it, and has at present an extension very like many people's notion of "meaningful".

If the arguments of these first and second sections are correct, then meaningfulness is not a poor relation of grammaticality, but rather the other way round. If grammaticality is to have a sense as well as an extension then it must, if it is to be anything, be a rather more general notion of meaningfulness. And that view is, I think, consistent with the traditional notion of grammar, though this is not the place to argue for that. Alice saw the point when she detected a very general meaning, or message, in the poem Jabberwocky, which has been taken to be a paradigm of "grammatical nonsense": "Somebody killed something, that's clear, at any rate".

2.2 Characterising Meaningfulness

I have discussed how one might characterise the notion of grammaticality in terms of other concepts. In this section I want to suggest a characterisation of the notion of meaningfulness: one that may seem both odd, and at the same time, obvious. I suggest that we call an utterance meaningful, in some primary sense, if and only if we can decide which of a number of things that it might mean it actually does mean. Or to put the suggestion another way: to be meaningful is to have one and only one of a number of possible interpretations.

If these two apparently different concepts, meaningfulness and sense-resolution, can be brought together then some light might be thrown on an old puzzle about meaningfulness: when grammarians deem a sentence meaningless, or when Carnap deemed a metaphysical sentence [17] meaningless on the grounds of its incorrect logical syntax, then it might not have been that the sentences *had no meaning*, but rather that each had several meanings or interpretations; though taken as single sentences in isolation from others they could not be resolved as having some particular interpretation, and so they were deemed meaningless. However, had they been put back into the context from which they came, or had other suitable context been constructed around them, each might have admitted of one and only one interpretation, as in the case of "Colourless green ideas sleep furiously" embedded in the simple story I suggested for it.

It is a trivial observation that many words have a number of meanings or senses, and that without adequate context they cannot be resolved, in the sense of being attached to one and only one dictionary explanation. If I say "I must go down to the post with these letters" then that sentence can be resolved because it constitutes adequate context to show that, for example, by "post" I mean "place for depositing mail", and not "thing to which horses may be hitched". But if I say "I found I hadn't got a jack" it cannot be resolved, because a hearer cannot resolve "jack" without knowing whether the sentence belongs to, say, a card-playing story or a car-breakdown story. What I am maintaining is that, in some primary sense of "meaningful", the sentence "I found I hadn't got a jack" is meaningless apart from some context, or context-substitute, in just the way that "Colourless green ideas sleep furiously" is.

Before answering charges that what I have just claimed is either absurd or straightforwardly wrong, I want to say a little more to support the claim that primary meaningfulness is of resolved segments of language. I think some general justification can be constructed along the lines of Quine's discussions of synonymy where, in the course of a detailed examination and criticism of the assumptions of descriptive linguistics [18, 19, 20], he describes a situation of possible confrontation with a speaker we do not understand at all. Quine begins by distinguishing what he calls the activity of the grammarian from that of the lexicographer: the former seeks to catalogue significant sequences in a language, the latter to catalogue the synonym pairs within a language, or between languages. Quine points out that their enterprises are intimately related in that one is concerned with what it is to have meaning, while the other is concerned with what it is to have the same meaning.

Quine then directs his attention to the lexicographer's problem, which he discusses in the conventional terms of substitutions of putative synonyms within larger contexts that remain synonymous as wholes. That way of discussing "having the same meaning" is not a referential one at all, where by "referential" is meant all sense, designation and Fregean dualist theories of meaning. For on any of those theories one should determine whether or not words are synonymous by inspecting the objects or concepts (or both) to which they refer, and seeing whether or not they are the same. Quine's view is essentially a monistic, intra-linguistic, view of meaning and it concerns only relations between strings of words. I see no real difference on Quine's view of things, between saying that two utterances have the same meaning and saying that each is a meaning, interpretation, or paraphrase of the other. The problem then immediately arises of *which* of a number of possible strings of other words is the meaning under discussion, and it is here that substitution, or what Quine calls "a retreat to longer segments", comes in:

> "...a retreat to longer segments tends to overcome the problem of ambiguity or homonymity. Homonymy gets in the way of the law that if a is synonymous with b and b with c, then a is synonymous with c. For, if b has two meanings (to revert to the ordinary parlance of meanings), a may be synonymous with b in one sense of b and b with c in the other sense of b. This difficulty is sometimes dealt with by treating an ambiguous form as two forms, but this expedient has the drawback of making the concept of form dependent on that of synonymy.
>
> We may continue to characterize the lexicographer's domain squarely as synonymy, but only by recognizing synonymy as primarily a relation of sufficiently long segments of discourse."

But what other function for a "retreat to longer segments" can there be than an overcoming of sense ambiguity? What is a "sufficiently long segment" other than one that resolves such ambiguity? Quine does not say explicitly, but I think one can reasonably infer from the quoted passage that he means a segment sufficiently long to resolve word-sense ambiguity and in particular the ambiguity of the members of a synonym pair when either of them is substituted in the segment. Quine goes on: "So we may view the lexicographer as interested, ultimately, only in cataloguing sequences of sufficient length to admit of synonymy in some primary sense" [21:58]. So the difference between Quine's primary synonymy of resolved segments and the non-primary synonymy of their parts is that the former synonymy is a context independent one. No question arises of substituting resolved segments in anything longer, for there is no more to make clear. "Resolved" means simply that all sense ambiguity has been cleared up.

Let us return to the grammarian, who was said by Quine to have the same problem as the lexicographer. If that is so, then the grammarian, too, will "retreat to longer segments". Corresponding to Quine's remark about "primary synonymy" we might expect another to the effect that "primary significance is of resolved sequences". I do not think that Quine draws this inference in the course of his arguments, but it seems to me a correct one, and a way of stating the necessary condition involved in the characterisation of meaningfulness I suggested earlier.

What is one to make of this necessary condition: the claim that a piece of language is meaningful only if it has one, and only one, interpretation, and hence that it fails to be meaningful if it has none, or two or more? The claim may sound reasonable enough for utterances whose meaningfulness is in dispute, where, as with "Colourless green ideas sleep furiously", the procedure used to show that the utterance is meaningful usually consists in constructing a narrative round the sentence so that it does have a single interpretation. I am using the terms "interpretation" loosely here, and will do something to make it more precise later on, but I think the general idea is sufficiently clear if we assume some notion of paraphrase, interpretation or synonymy between utterances. For the moment let us assume it to be Quine's "primary synonymy" of resolved utterances.

There may well be an important distinction to be made between "being ambiguous, and so meaningless, because of two interpretations" and "being ambiguous, and so meaningless, because of more than two interpretations". Poetry can often preserve two, though not usually more, interpretations over considerable lengths of text which are properly considered meaningful. But for the moment I want to consider poetry, allegories and jokes as special cases.

So then, if the utterance "He fell while getting to the ball" is embedded in a football narrative, then all proper paraphrases of it will be equivalent to "A man fell to the ground while trying to reach the object in play in the game". And the assertion that the second mentioned sentence is a paraphrase of the first would resolve the first in just the way that inserting it into a football narrative would. In the case of either procedure, inserting or giving a paraphrase, we would then know that "ball" was not being used in the sense of a "formal dance". It is also important to notice that resolving an utterance by giving a paraphrase or interpretation is not the same thing as resolving the constituent words. To know that the two sentences just mentioned are possible paraphrases or interpretations of each other is also to know that, for example, "ball" is being used in its "round object" sense. But the converse is not necessarily true, since the interpretations of sentences are not simply computed from the interpretations of their constituent words, as anyone knows who has tried to make himself understood in a foreign language with the aid of only a dictionary, or even with a foreign grammar book as well.

But aside from sentences whose meaningfulness is *in dispute*, how reasonable is the application of the necessary condition to an everyday sentence such as "He fell while getting to the ball"? Is it not absurd to say that the sentence is meaningless just because, taken in isolation, we do not happen to know which of two likely interpretations it bears? However, if challenged to show that, or how, the sentence is meaningful, a speaker who cannot make use of gestures, and so go outside language, will certainly embed the sentence in some story or anecdote so as to give it one of its two more obvious interpretations. And that is the same procedure as the one adopted by the defenders of the meaningfulness of "Colourless green ideas sleep furiously". In other words, use is made of a procedure that does give the questioned utterance some particular interpretation. I am not taking refuge here in some highly general view such as "meaningfulness can only be discussed with respect to an entire language", or anything like that. I am calling attention to a particular *procedure* of sense resolution, in which a particular interpretation is assigned to a questioned utterance by means of telling a surrounding story, uncovering more of a surrounding book page, or perhaps simply by producing utterances with the form of dictionary entries, such as "ball means round object".

But even if the necessary condition is plausible in itself it does not shed any light on the "primary significance" that only resolved segments can have. In Quine's discussion of a "primary synonymy" he gave a quite different explication of that notion in behavioural terms. But here I think we can push the characterisation in terms of sense-resolubility a little further, and get something like a sufficient condition for primary meaningfulness as well.

The sufficient condition for meaningfulness would be that a text was meaningful if it had one and not more than one interpretation. But in virtue of what can a text be said to have a single interpretation? Why does one want to say that "I must take these letters to the post" has a single interpretation, though "He fell while getting to the ball" has two? The difference cannot be simply that "ball" has two senses while "post" has one, for "post" usually has more senses listed in a dictionary than "ball".

If an English speaker is asked to explain, in informal terms, how he knows that "I must take these letters to the post" has only one interpretation, he will probably say that the notion of "letters" is connected to only one sense of the notion "post", and so if the word "letters" is present in an utterance then it can only be the "mail" sense of "post" that is intended. But in the case of "He fell while getting to the ball" there is no such overlap of coherence of notions to disqualify either of the two natural interpretations of the utterance.

This common-sense explanation can be put in linguistic terms quite straight-forwardly: if classifiers, or markers, can be attached to the senses of words so as to distinguish the senses from each other, then it is a technical matter to specify coherence rules, operating on the markers, that select certain word senses in preference to others. So for example, if there was a marker MAIL in use, then we would expect to find it in a table of linguistic information attached to only one sense of "letters" (not the "alphabetic items" sense) and to only one sense of "post". We might then examine the sentence "He took the letters to the post" armed with the rule "if the marker MAIL is attached to senses of *more than one word* in the sentence, then select those senses". That rule would be a very simple-minded one, though it would work in this case. However, such rules can be made as complicated as necessary (e.g.[22]) and there is no more mystery about the attachment of suitable markers to word-senses than there is to the construction of the conventional entries in an English dictionary that distinguish the senses of words from one another.

Moreover, the operation of such rules as the simple one involving the marker MAIL can be equivalent, in effect, to the provision of an interpretation, or paraphrase, for the utterance under examination. If the marker MAIL pins down, or selects, one particular sense of "letters", we can suppose that sense to be expressed as a conventional dictionary entry such as "letters as papers that are mailed". That expression of the sense would be entered, in tables specifying the rules of a possible linguistic system, along with the marker MAIL, but "letters as items in an alphabet" would not. Part of the dictionary entry tagged to MAIL, namely "papers that are mailed", could then be substituted for "letters" in the original utterance. If this procedure were repeated for each word of the utterance we would end up with a new, resolved, utterance that was a paraphrase of the original one. In that sense, the operation of this sort of rule also provides paraphrases.

Now consider a different example, which I shall call a pseudo-text: "Do you like my car. I always wear a flower. The seats are leather". An utterance like that would almost certainly be said to be meaningless, even though it is not inconceivable that an ingenious person could embed it within some intelligible story, perhaps as an entry for a literary competition. It is not easy to say why the pseudo-text seems meaningless. The simplest way of putting the matter is to say that there is nothing that it is about, in that the ideas the utterance expresses do not cohere together sufficiently for there to be an interpretation that is not identical with the utterance itself.

What is claimed here by the sufficient criterion of meaningfulness, given above, is that the pseudo-text *would be* meaningful if there were sufficient coherence between its constituent concepts, of the sort expressed earlier in linguistic terms by means of the MAIL marker. Rules specifying such occurrences of markers can be as complex as necessary, and the specification is a technical matter for linguistics. What is important for the present discussion is that the meaningfulness criterion, expressed in terms of "having one and only interpretation", should refer to an overall interpretation, located by means of coherence rules of the sort I have discussed. It cannot refer simply to the sense-resolubility of the individual words of the utterance under scrutiny.

This last point can be made by looking again at the pseudo-text. Each of its three constituent sub-sentences is such that one can see, for each word in it, in which of its senses it is being used. That remains true whether the three sentences are considered separately or as parts of the pseudo-text. So there is no problem about word-sense ambiguity in the pseudo-text, and hence, if the meaningfulness criterion were expressed simply in terms of word-sense ambiguity resolution, then the pseudo-text would satisfy the condition, and so be meaningful in terms of it.

I have given only the crudest example of the way in which a vague notion like "conceptual coherence" can be operationally expressed by means of procedures involving linguistic markers. In fact such procedures are almost always more complex than the simple co-occurrence of a single marker, and it is easy to see that a simple "threshold" notion of coherence will usually not suffice to establish meaningfulness. Consider another pseudo-text: "All kings wear crowns. All crowns are coins. All kings wear coins". That pseudo-text is like the earlier one in that each sub-sentence is resolved as regards word-sense ambiguity, although the whole pseudo-text does not seem to admit of a single interpretation. Yet, unlike the last example, it is not that there seems to be *no* interpretation, but rather an oscillation between two alternative ones, depending on the sense of "crown" selected. But this example would satisfy the very crudest standards of conceptual coherence, in that each sub-sentence would have an overlap of markers, given any reasonable choice of markers, with either of the other two sentences comprising the whole pseudo-text. Hence, any rules applying to such markers would have to be more structured than the simple one applying to MAIL that I gave earlier.

I have been defending the suggested characterisation of meaningfulness against charges of absurdity and wrongness, but is it nonetheless vague? After all, *what* precisely is being characterised as meaningful? Earlier in this paper, I described a procedure used when the meaningfulness of an utterance is challenged: a speaker defending its meaningfulness attempts to embed the utterance in a story or narrative whose overall meaning is clear. But, in terms of the characterisation, the utterance so embedded is properly deemed meaningless if it does not have one clear interpretation in isolation; and, if the whole story containing it is clear and unambiguous, then it is that whole that is shown to be meaningful by the embedding procedure. Further-more, no inference can be made from the meaningfulness of the whole story to that of the embedded utterance, any more than one can infer that p is a theorem because it is a proper part of the theorem $p \supset p$.

If the last point is correct, then it is not proper to speak, as I did earlier in the paper, of the procedure of embedding an utterance whose meaningfulness is questioned as one giving a survey of meaningful utterances. What that discovery brings out is that the present formulation of the characterisation is incomplete: it requires an addendum "…one and only one interpretation with respect to some dictionary, or dictionary substitute". Consider again the utterance "He fell while getting to the ball". My claim was that that is meaningless in isolation, in that one could not decide whether its proper interpretation contained the "round object" or the "formal dance" sense of "ball". But that judgement assumed a conventional dictionary containing those two senses of the word "ball", even though a considerable proportion of English speakers do not know that "ball" can be used to mean "formal dance", and so to them the utterance might be said to be unambiguous and so perfectly meaningful.

What I am saying here can be put as a series of assertions in which X stands for the utterance "He fell while getting to the ball" and Y stands for what I shall call the "dance text": a story about a dance and containing the sentence X. Then, in terms of the augmented characterisation, X is meaningful with respect to Y; X is meaningful with respect to the contracted dictionary containing "ball as round object" but not "ball as formal dance"; X is meaningful with respect to a text containing the sentence "a ball is a round object" and X; X is meaningless with respect to a conventional dictionary containing "ball as round object" and "ball as formal dance"; Y is meaningful with respect to one contracted dictionary and with respect to the conventional dictionary.

The words "with respect to" are being used in two different ways here: in "with respect to a dictionary" they mean considered in regard to such-and-such possible senses explanations; but in "with respect to a text" the words naturally mean considered as properly embedded in such a text as proper parts of it. The main point made is a simple one: the sentence X is not meaningful with respect to a conventional dictionary; the dance text Y, in virtue of its presumed internal coherence discussed earlier, is meaningful with respect to the same dictionary. This extension of the characterisation removes the *prima facie* absurdity of saying that X is meaningless, since it is now proper to say that X is meaningful with respect to any text or dictionary that does duty for Y.

However, if nothing is specified after "with respect to", then one has to assume that it is a conventional dictionary that is intended, and in that case the utterance X remains meaningless. In those terms the rejection of metaphysical sentences by Carnap was perfectly correct: if sentences of the sort he rejected have, as I think they can be shown to have, more than one interpretation with respect to a conventional dictionary, then they are properly rejected when so considered in isolation. But, and this is the important proviso, why consider such utterances in isolation in the first place if one's aim is to understand what is being read. If the present characterisation is at all correct, then there is no proper inference from such a judgement of meaning-lessness to "there is no text Y with respect to which this X is meaningful". Yet that is precisely the inference that Carnap wanted his readers to draw.

2.3 Meaningfulness and Decidability

If meaningful utterances can be surveyed and meaningfulness characterised, then it is possible to ask the important question, is it possible to decide formally of any utterance whether it is meaningful or not; which is to decide whether any given arbitrary string of words can be placed into one and only one of two classes, the meaningful and the meaningless.

There is no general theoretical problem about deciding meaningfulness that can be expressed in the same form as truth-decision problems. Discussions of Gödel's theorem often include informal paradoxes of the following sort: given a table of named statements, consider the following two items in the table:

m ..."The sentence n is false"

n ..."The sentence m is true"

Examples of that sort cannot be produced for the case of meaning, for, if "true" and "false" in the example are replaced by "meaningful" and "meaningless" respectively, then there is no paradox. Nor is there any paradox if only one such replacement is carried out: the result is a pair of statements of the same truth value. The same goes for Tarski's example, the one he considered to be an informal representation of Gödel's theorem:

> The sentence in this square is false.

If "false" is replaced by "meaningless" then again there is no paradox, only a false statement. It is true, on the other hand, that "The sentence in this square is meaningless" in the square implies that the same sentence is meaningful, since all true sentences are meaningful. Thus its truth implies its falsity. But the converse is not true, and hence there is no paradox in any strong sense.

But the absence of any real "paradoxes of meaning", and the argued possibility of characterising the notion of meaningfulness, do not, of course, suffice to show that meaningfulness is a decidable property. When drawn out, the implication of the earlier discussion about characterisation is that meaningfulness is not a decidable property, and that meaningful utterances do not form a recursive set.

Consider again the tentative claim, made earlier, that meaningful utterances can be surveyed. A parallel was drawn with the Propositional Calculus where some survey of theorems is possible prior to any particular axiomatisation. However, in a survey of the Propositional Calculus one also knows, again prior to any axiomatisation, that $p \supset \sim p$ is not a theorem. Is there any parallel in the case of meaningfulness, in that there are utterances known in advance to be meaningless? In terms of the characterisation discussed, the answer must be no. In the course of the earlier discussion, two kinds of paradigms of meaninglessness were produced: those with no interpretations, like the pseudo-text, and those with more than one, like "He fell while getting to the ball". But, as became clear in the discussion, those utterances were deemed meaningless with respect to some particular dictionary, or surrounding context equivalent to such a dictionary. There is no way of knowing that those same utterances would not be meaningful with respect to some other, unconventional, dictionary or context, and in the case of such examples as "He fell while getting to the ball" it was trivially easy to construct the dictionary required.

And in terms of the presently proposed characterisation there can be no real survey of meaningful utterances either, other than with respect to particular dictionaries or contexts, since any paradigm of meaningfulness might be ambiguous, and so meaningless, with respect to another dictionary. For example, one with an arbitrary word-sense added to it. The normally unambiguous "I must take these letters to the post" would be ambiguous with respect to a conventional dictionary *plus* the entry "post means franking machine". The fact that this entry does not describe a use of "post" in contemporary English is neither here nor there.

This feature of natural language is quite independent of the particular characterisation of meaningfulness proposed here, for, given any characterisation of the notion, we can never know of any given string of words that human ingenuity cannot render it meaningful with the aid of sufficient assumptions of the form "X means Y" where X is a word in the string, and Y is some other, suitably chosen, word. Any suggested boundary to meaningfulness defined by means of any set of rules only constitutes a challenge to that ingenuity. One thinks of Wittgenstein's "If someone were to draw a sharp boundary I could not acknowledge it as the one I too had always wanted to draw, or had drawn in my mind. For I did not want to draw one at all" [23].

If there can be no true paradigms of meaninglessness, then there can be no proper survey of meaningful utterances, and hence no reason to expect them to form a recursive set. The paradigms of meaninglessness discussed earlier were therefore in something of the same position as the paradigms of ungrammaticalness discussed in section 1. They were ungrammatical, I argued, only with respect to some particular set of grammatical rules in each case, and so there was no survey of such grammatical utterances independent of particular sets of rules.

However, the characterisation of the meaningfulness of utterances with respect to particular dictionaries or texts, as having one and only one interpretation, can lead to some formal assessment of meaningfulness. It can, I think, though this suggestion and what follows is highly tentative, lead to some formal assessment of *degree* of meaningfulness of utterances or texts. That would be a quite different matter from any attempt to divide utterances into the meaningful and the meaningless, in the way that a decidable logic divides putative theorems into theorems and non-theorems. It would be quite possible, in principle, to order utterances by degree of meaningfulness while admitting that any utterance whatever might find a place at the far end of the scale.

Now consider a possible linguistic system for deciding meaningfulness. Let us suppose it consists of a system of production rules starting with an initial symbol, just as generative grammars do. Suppose, too, the rules are of a straightforwardly decidable sort, like simple phrase structure [8] rules. This stipulation cannot, of course, make meaningfulness decidable in any sense. It is simply a property of the formal system used that, for any string, the system either produces it or shows that it cannot be produced. Now suppose that there is an additional procedure, let us call it *Expand*, outside this system of rules, and having the following property: given an utterance X which the rules certainly cannot produce, *Expand* produces an additional rule which, when added to the existing system of rules, allows the augmented system to generate X. Let us suppose that *Expand* can be applied recursively in such a way that we can know that, after some finite number of such applications, the system of rules attained by that time *will* be able to produce X.

What can one say about such a constructible series of rule systems? The metamathematical analogy has now been almost entirely jettisoned, for the procedure for adding a rule so as to produce a meaningful but rejected X is not at all related to the procedure Gödel discussed for adding a true, but undecidable, sentence to the axioms of a logical system. In the present case what is added is not the recalcitrant item itself but a different one, namely a fresh rule of inference. In any case, Gödel's point was that to add such a sentence to the axioms is useless because there would always be *at least one more* true but undecidable sentence. But in the present case I do not think the procedure I have described need be useless.

Each particular set of rules is decidable and if each is thought of as an explication of the characterisation of primary meaningfulness proposed here, namely having and only one interpretation, then rejection by any particular set, in that the rules cannot produce that utterance, gives no assurance that *Expand* cannot add sufficient rules so as to yield a set of rules that does produce the utterance in question. Since any particular set of rules expresses, among other things, the dictionary with respect to which meaningfulness is being assessed, then it is quite in accordance with the proposed characterisation that meaningfulness with respect to any particular set of rules should be decidable.

However, what is to be said about the whole series of rule systems, constructible from some initial set of such rules plus the *Expand* procedure? The set of utterances that can be produced by the whole series of such systems might possibly explicate the other, non-primary and more shadowy, sense of "meaningful" that has been discussed in this paper. In that other sense of meaningfulness, any utterance whatever might be meaningful, in that it could conceivably be used, or be made sense of, with respect to some possible dictionary. It was part of the definition of the *Expand* procedure that it could add sufficient rules so as to yield a system of rules capable of producing any utterance whatever. But if there can be no real boundary to meaningfulness, then that is precisely the sort of explication of the concept one would expect. It is this non-primary concept of meaningfulness, it will be remembered, that can be characterised by the ability of speakers to embed any utterance whatever in some suitable story.

The series of constructible systems of rules could then explicate meaningfulness usefully only as a matter of degree; in that an utterance X might be said to be more meaningful than an utterance Y if it required less applications of the *Expand* procedure to yield a system of rules capable of producing it. That feature would save the important intuition that some utterances are undoubtedly more meaningful than others, even though with sufficient effort and imagination any utterance whatever might be made meaningful.

All this is very tentative indeed, yet if some procedural and linguistic flesh can be put on these rather bare bones, it would have another philosophical implication. It could be argued that all that has been said in the last section of this paper is merely an elaborate restatement of the contemporary philosophical platitude that all meaningfulness is with respect to some presupposed area of discourse, or within some language game. Defences of particular language games, such as theology or aesthetics, along these lines have become commonplace. However, if some concrete expression could be given to the constructible series of rules systems sketched here, then they might also give a hint as to how it is possible to pass, as it were, from one language game to another. For it is surely an ultimately unsatisfactory view that human language games, whatever they may be, are wholly separate and unconnected structures.

It is not hard to see how, in principle, a system of phrase structure rules could express the characterisation of primary meaningfulness argued for here: namely, having one and only one interpretation. Phrase structure rules are simply rules which allow one item to be rewritten as a string of items. So in a phrase structure grammar, of the sort discussed in section 2.1, we might expect to find a rule $N \rightarrow A + N$, which simply means that in the course of producing a grammatical representation of a sentence, a noun symbol "N" can be replaced by an adjective symbol "A" followed by a noun symbol "N". It can be seen right away that a conventional dictionary entry can be put in this form. For example, two different entries for "post" could be written in phrase structure form as post $\rightarrow$ items + that + can + be + mailed, and post $\rightarrow$ a + stake + fixed + in + the + ground.

Rules of that sort, constituting a grammar, can produce from some starting symbol a representation of a sentence as a structured string of part-of-speech symbols. A string of such symbols that might well be produced would be $D + A + N + V + A$. Then, with the aid of a grammar dictionary of rules like D (determiner) $\rightarrow$ the, $A \rightarrow$ old, $V \rightarrow$ is, and so on, the sentence "the old man is dead" could be produced from that symbol string. The inferences in common sense terms, would be that in that sentence "old" is used as an adjective, "man" as a noun and so on. That sort of inference is not always trivial matter, as can be seen by considering the parsing of "The old dog the footsteps of the young". In a sentence like that, just looking at the odd word or two will not do. The part of speech determination can only be done reading it off from some representation of the whole sentence.

So much, by way of analogy, for grammar. It is not a considerable step farther to conceive of similar rules that produce, not structured grammar codes, but structurings of the semantic markers that I discussed earlier. If one can attach markers like MAN to the dictionary entries for word senses indicating human beings, and STUFF to the dictionary entries for word senses indicating substances, then one could interpret strings of such markers directly: MAN + BE + KIND, for example could be interpreted "a man is of a certain sort" and would be involved in any "semantic parsing" of a sentence like "The Pope is Italian". So, with a clearly ambiguous sentence like "The old salt is damp" one would expect to produce two structurings for it, MAN + BE + KIND and STUFF + BE + KIND. Such a "semantic parsing" would be in rather the same position as a grammatical parsing of a sentence like "They are eating apples", where it is usually said that two quite different strings of grammar codes can be produced for that sentence with the same phrase structure grammar.

This is where the characterisation of primary meaningfulness I argued for would come in: meaningfulness with respect to a given set of such rules would be translated naturally as "can be produced by the set of rules in one and only one way". Thus the sentence "the old salt is damp" would not pass that test and so would be rejected by the set of rules. But, of course, if it were produced as part of either a sea story, or, alternatively, as part of a grocery shop story, then the whole story might well have a single interpretation, provided there are also rules that produce only certain combinations of the strings of markers. Just as with the recurrence of the MAIL marker in the example discussed earlier, there would be rules opting for either the MAN + BE + KIND or the STUFF + BE + KIND structure on the basis of the markers to be found elsewhere in the grocery or sea story. To choose either of these two structures is to impose a single interpretation on the sentence and hence to render it meaningful with respect to the story of which it happens to form a part.

If all this seems over optimistic it is because I have simplified considerably by assuming the attachment of only a single marker to a word, such as MAN to the "sailor" sense of "salt", in the way that "N" suffices to pin down the noun part-of-speech of any word. The dictionary must in fact be more complex than that, as it also has to be for a realistic grammar parsing, and the structurings of markers attached to the senses of words have to be as complex as is needed to distinguish each word-sense from every sense of every other word in the dictionary. But that is again a matter of linguistic detail, and the principles are not affected. It cannot be in principle difficult to select, say, the "sailor" sense of "salt" in a sea story because any English speaker, reading the story and encountering the example sentence, makes the required inference immediately. Unless this inference is made by occult means it is reasonable to assume it is done on the basis of the other words occurring in the story. If the reader also sees "ships", then he's pretty sure that it is the "sailor" sense of "salt" that is in question.

It is equally easy to see how, in principle, the *Expand* procedure might work. Suppose a given set of rules fails to produce a representation for some text, and suppose, too, that it is possible to examine the attempts to produce a representation with the rules, and to find the word that is holding up the process, as it were, in that the markers in the dictionary entries for that word do not cohere sufficiently with the other words of the text for a representation to be produced. Suppose now that, having found such a recalcitrant word A, *Expand* can look at the dictionary entries for all the words in the text and find b, the word-sense of word B which is closest in meaning, in terms of some defined procedure, to the recalcitrant word in question. *Expand* could then add a rule to the system which is equivalent to adding that close sense b to the possible senses of the recalcitrant word A. With the new rule added we have a larger rule system and the analysis can be tried again to see if a representation can now be produced for the text. A reasonable inference, if the new augmented system *does* succeed in producing a representation, is that "yes, this text can be meaningful if A can mean B in it".

This is not a fanciful suggestion but is, I suggest, how people may actually cope with difficult texts, especially those, like philosophical texts, that use ordinary words in new and apparently improbable ways that no one would expect to find in any conventional dictionary. In a very real sense Spinoza's *Ethic* becomes comprehensible only when such a new possibility has been considered: one might say that the key-sense extension that a reader must consider is that "substance" in that work means "the whole Universe". The interesting question, if one were to analyse such difficult texts with the aid of a linguistic system [24] based on the one sketched here, is *how many* applications of a procedure like *Expand* would have to be made in order to resolve any particular text. The *Expand* procedure must eventually allow an interpretation to be produced for any text because, after a sufficiently great number of applications of the procedure, so many word senses in the text will have been mutually identified that some trivial resolution will be produced.

In order to sketch out this small piece of possible experimental philosophy I have had to make some highly questionable assumptions. There are three assumptions that I have not mentioned in the body of the paper, and which are assumptions not made generally by linguists at the present time. Firstly, I have assumed that it makes sense to talk of senses of words, in that there can be an exclusive classification of the occurrences of the tokens of any word into sense-classes. Secondly, I have assumed that it is not just a contingent fact about our language that most words have more than one sense. Lastly, I have assumed that there can be a generally agreed starting place in the way of dictionaries: that it can be agreed that such-and-such a dictionary is a conventional one for some purpose. Without some such assumption the enterprise sketched in the last section of the paper could never begin. These are large assumptions, but I feel justified in avoiding discussion of them here, not only for reasons of space, but because they are assumptions also made by the makers of an English dictionary. And it would undoubtedly have been a pity if such enterprises as the Oxford English Dictionary had never begun because of the nature of these particular assumptions.

Acknowledgement

I am indebted to Mr. D. S. Linney for helpful criticisms and suggestions during the writing of the first two sections of this paper.

References

[1] R. Carnap, *The Logical Syntax of Language*, London, 1937.

[2] N. Chomsky, *Syntactic Structures*, The Hague, 1957.

[3] N. Chomsky, *Current Issues in Linguistic Theory*, The Hague, 1964.

[4] E. Post, "Recursively enumerable set of positive integers and their decision problems", *Bull. Am. Math. Soc.*, 1944.

[5] E. Post, "Finite Combinatory Processes", *J.S.L.*, 1936.

[6] N. Chomsky, *Aspects of the Theory of Syntax* (1966), p. 9.

[7] H. Putnam, "Some issues in the theory of grammar" in *Symposia in Applied Mathematics*, vol. xii, p. 48, American Math. Soc.

[8] Bar-Hillel, Perles and Shamir, *On the formal properties of simple phrase structure grammars*, Univ. of Jerusalem, 1960.

[9] R. Walker *et al.*, "Recent developments in The MITRE Syntactic analysis procedure", *Proc. AMTCL*, 1966.

[10] D. Liberman *et al.*, "Specification and utilization of a transformational grammar", *IBM Project 4641*, 1966.

[11] N. Chomsky, "Three models for the description of language", *Proc. I.E.E.E.*, (1956), p. 20.

[12] H. Curry, "Logical Aspects of Syntactic Structure", in *Symposia in Applied Mathematics*, vol. xii, p. 60, Amer. Math. Soc.

[13] P. Ziff, "About ungrammaticalness", *Mind*, 1964.

[14] R. Jakobson, "Boas' view of grammatical meaning", *American Anthropologist*, p. 144, 1959.

[15] L. Wittgenstein, *The Blue and Brown Books* (Oxford, 1958), p. 26.

[16] K. Gödel, *On formally undecidable propositions of P.M. and related systems,* tr. Meltzer, Edinburgh, 1962.

[17] R. Carnap, "The Elimination of Metaphysics", in A. J. Ayer (ed.), *Logical Positivism*, New York, 1959.

[18] W.V.O. Quine "Two dogmas of empiricism" and "The problem of meaning in linguistics" in [21].

[19] W.V.O. Quine "Meaning and Translation", in Brower (ed.), *On Translation*, Cambridge, Mass., 1959.

[20] W.V.O. Quine *Word and Object*, M.I.T. Press, 1964.

[21] W.V.O. Quine *From a Logical Point of View*, Cambridge, Mass.19 p. 58.

[22] J. J. Katz,"Semantic Theory and the meaning of 'Grammatical'", *Journal of Philosophy*, 1964.

[23] L. Wittgenstein, *Philosophical Investigations* (§76), Oxford, 1953.

[24] Y. Wilks "On-line semantic analysis of English texts" in the *Proceedings of the International Conference on Computational Linguistics*, Stockholm, 1969.

3

The Stanford Machine Translation Project

Yorick Wilks
Stanford University

Abstract: This paper describes a system of semantic analysis and generation, programmed in LISP 1.5 and designed to pass from paragraph-length input in English to French via an interlingual representation. A wide class of English input forms is covered, with a vocabulary initially restricted to a few hundred words. The distinguishing features of the translation system are:

It translates phrase by phrase, with facilities for reordering phrases and establishing essential semantic connectivities between them. These constitute the interlingual representation to be translated. This matching is done without the explicit use of a conventional syntax analysis.

The French output strings are generated without the explicit use of a generative grammar. This is done by means of stereotypes: strings of French words, and functions evaluating to French words, which are attached to English word senses in the dictionary and built into the interlingual representation by the analysis routines

3.1 Introduction

The on-going project to be described here aims to translate from English to French, using a reasonably wide vocabulary and paragraph-length texts, and at a later stage to "understand" the translated material, in the sense of being able to answer questions about it in an on-line context. The method to be used is a non-standard semantic analysis that has been applied to English texts of some length and complexity [13, 15].

It is the semantic approach that is intended to answer the question: "Why start Machine Translation (MT) again at all?" The generally negative surveys produced after the demise of most of the MT research of the Fifties in no way established that a new approach was foredoomed to failure. At this time, it is easy to be unfair to the memory of that early MT work and to exaggerate the simplicity of its assumptions about language. But the fact remains that almost all of it was done on the basis of naive syntactic analysis and without the use of any of the developments in semantic structuring and description that have been noteworthy features of recent linguistic advances.

At this point a word of warning is appropriate about the semantic method used here. This is intended to be a practical talk, concerned with describing what is being done in a particular system not with arguing abstractly for the advantages of

29

K. Ahmad, C. Brewster and M. Stevenson (eds.), Words and Intelligence 1, 29–59.
© 2007 *Springer.*

systems based on conceptual connections over other contemporary but better-known approaches: this has been done elsewhere by writers such as Simmons [12], Quillian [9], Klein [3], Schank [11], as well as myself. I am not concerned, therefore, with arguing for a general method, nor shall I set out much in the way of the now familiar graph structures linking the items of example sentences in order to display their "real structure." I am concerned more with displaying the information structure I use, and how the system applies to certain linguistic examples to get them into the prescribed form for translation. The display of conceptual or dependency connections between items of real text will only be made in cases where unnecessary obscurity or complexity would be introduced by displaying the same connections between items of the interlingual representation.

This project is intended to produce a working artifact, not to settle general questions. However, because the territory has been gone over so heavily in the past years and because the questions still at issue seem to cause the adoption of very definite points of view, it is necessary to make certain remarks before beginning. In particular, different views are held at the present time on the question of whether the intermediate representation between two languages for MT should be logical or linguistic in form.

What the words in the last sentence, "logical" and "linguistic," actually mean is not as clear as might appear; for example, they are almost certainly not mutually exclusive; any "logical coding" of text will require a good deal of what is best called linguistic analysis in order to get the text into the required logical form: this could include coping with sense ambiguity, clause dependency, and so on. On the other hand, few linguistically oriented people would deny the need for some analysis of the logical relations present in the discourse to be analyzed. However, for the purposes of the present project certain assumptions may safely be made:

1. Whatever linguists and philosophers may say to the contrary, it has never been shown that there are linguistic forms whose meaning cannot be represented in some logical system. Linguists often produce kinds of inferences properly made but not catered for in conventional existing calculi: for example, the "and so" inference in "I felt tired and went home;" but nothing follows to the effect that such an inference could not be coped with by means of a simple and appropriate adjustment in rules of inference.

2. Whatever logicians may believe to the contrary, it has never been shown that human beings perform logical transformations when they translate sentences from one language to another, nor has it ever been shown that it is necessary to do so in order to translate mechanically. To take a trivial example, if one wants to translate the English "is," then for an adequate logical translation one will almost certainly want to know whether the particular use of "is" in question is best rendered into logic by identity, set membership, or set inclusion; yet for the purposes of translating an English sentence containing "is" into a closely related language like French, it is highly unlikely that one would ever want to make any such distinction for the purpose immediately at hand.

The above assumptions in no way close off discussion of the questions outstanding: they merely allow constructive work to proceed. In particular, discussion should be continued on: (a) exactly what the linguist is trying to say when he says that there are linguistic forms and common sense inferences beyond the scope of any logic, and (b) exactly what the logician is trying to say when he holds in a strong form the thesis that logical form is the basis of brain coding, or is the appropriate basis for computing over natural language.

On this subject we note the present conjunction of hitherto separate work: the extended set logic of Montague [7] that he claims copes with linguistic structure better than does MIT linguistics, and, the work of G. Lakoff [4] which claims that the transformationalists in general and Chomsky in particular were always seeking for some quite conventional notion of logical form. However, these problems have not affected the development of our system which is designed to translate from one natural language to another and is potentially capable of question-answering and the additional "understanding" that implies.

The coexistence of the two forms of coding, logical and linguistic, within a single system might preclude a way of testing the logicist and linguistic hypotheses about MT against each other. Such a test would be precluded because any translation into logic within such a system would have much of the work done by linguistic analysis; so there could be no real comparison of the two paths.

ENGLISH → PREDICATE CALCULUS REPRESENTATION → FRENCH

ENGLISH → LINGUISTIC CONCEPTUALIZATION → FRENCH

However, it might be possible to get translated output by each of the two paths in a single system and so give some rein to the notion of experimental comparison; I discuss this below.

3.2 The Structure of the Translation and Organization System

The diagram below represents the overall structure of the system under construction.

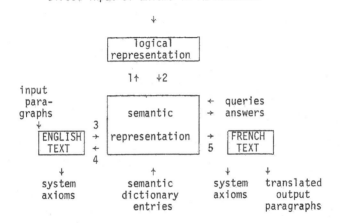

I assume in what follows that processes 2, 4, and 5 are the relatively easy tasks — in that they involve throwing away information — while 1 and 3 are the harder tasks in that they involve making information explicit with the aid of dictionaries and rules.

With all the parts to the diagram and the facilities they imply (including not only translation of small texts via a semantic representation but also the translation of axioms in the predicate calculus (PC) into both natural languages) it is clear that input to the system must be rather restricted. However, there clearly are ways of restricting input that would destroy the point of the whole activity; for example, if we restricted ourselves to the translation of isolated sentences rather than going for the translation of paragraph-length texts. Whatever Bar-Hillel says to the contrary about MT being essentially concerned with utterances [1], I am assuming that the only sort of MT of interest here will be the translation of text.

The general strategy of translation is to segment the text in some acceptable way, produce a semantic representation as directly as possible, and generate an output French form from it. This involves mapping what I call semantic templates directly onto the clauses and phrases of English, and trying to map directly from the templates into French clauses and phrases, though with their relative order changed where necessary. I also assume that no strong syntax analysis is necessary for this purpose and that all that is necessary can be done with a good semantic representation — which leaves us with the question: what is in the semantic box, and how is it different from what is in the logic box?

I am using "semantic representation" narrowly to mean whatever degree of representation is necessary for MT — not necessarily for question-answering (that's what the logic box is for) or for theories of how the brain works. For this we may well not need the refinements of "is" mentioned earlier, nor, say, existential quantification or the analysis of presuppositions given by translation of definite descriptions. My main assumption here about the difference between the two boxes, logical and linguistic, is that an "adequate" logical translation makes all such matters explicit, and that is why it is so much more difficult to translate into the top box than the bottom one. But the difference between the two remains a pragmatic one, intended to correspond to two "levels of understanding" in the human being.

3.3 The Processing of English Text

The aim of the text-processing sections of the overall program is to derive from an English text an interlingual representation that has adequate expressivity as a representation from which: (1) output in another natural language can be computed, and (2) it can serve as an analysandum of predicate calculus statements about some particular universe.

The first pass made of the English input text is the fragmentation and reordering procedure, whose function is to partition and repack texts of some length and sentential complexity into the form most suitable for matching with the template forms mentioned above. This stage is necessary because, like all proposed coding schemes, logical, linguistic, or whatever, the template format is a more-or-less rigid one and the variety of natural language must be made to fit, if the system is to analyze anything more than simple example sentences.

The principal item of semantic structure used to analyze and express input text is the *template*. Templates are semantic frames, intended to express the messages or "gists" of the sentences and parts of sentences used in normal discourse. The system has an inventory of these templates available to it and seeks to match them with the fragments of the input text.

The template is of the basic form, subject-verb-object — or in semantic terms, actor-act-object — such as MAN HAVE THING, to be interpreted as "some human being possesses some object," and which would be matched as the bare template name of any sentence such as "John owns a car." MAN, HAVE, and THING are interlingual elements, and MAN, for example, would be expected to be the principal, or head, element for any semantic formula representing the English word "John" in the dictionary. Similarly, HAVE would be the head element in the appropriate semantic formula for "owns," and so on. A simple matching algorithm would then be able to match the acceptable sequence of head elements from the template, MAN HAVE THING, onto a sequence of formulas drawn from the dictionary for the words of "John owns a car."

The details of the matching algorithm are not a matter of concern here; what is important to see is that an algorithm for matching a bare three-element template onto a piece of language by inspecting just the head elements of formulas and searching for acceptable sequences of them will, in the course of making the match, select not only the head element of the word formula, but with it the whole formula of which it was the head, where "whole formula" is to be understood at this point as a coded form that expresses the whole content of the word sense in question. In the present case "John," being a mere name, has no sense other than that it refers to a human being, and its whole formula would be simply (THIS MAN), which says no more than that.

One of the hypotheses at work here is that there is a finite inventory of templates adequate for the analysis of ordinary language — a useable list of the messages that people want to convey with ordinary language — and that in selecting those sequences of formulas for a fragment that are also template sequences (as regards their head elements) we pick up the formulas corresponding to the appropriate senses of the words of the fragment. This description is highly general; the details of the application of this method of analysis to complicated text appear in [15].

Moreover, it is assumed that any fragment of natural language can be named by (that is to say, matched with) at least one such bare template, and that the name will serve as a basic core of meaning for the purpose of translating the fragment. In other words, we translate from the complex interlingual representation of which the bare template MAN HAVE THING is the name simply because we know how to express as an algorithm the message "a person has a thing" in French. The template is thus an item, or unit, of meaning to be translated.

An example might help to give the general idea of what ties are established between text items by the matching routines described. Suppose we apply the above template to the sentence: "My brother owns a large car." Let us suppose, furthermore, that we are not concerned with the problem of selecting the *correct* sense formulas, one corresponding to each word as it is used in the sentence. We shall make the simplifying assumption that each of those six words has only one sense entry in the dictionary, and that we are considering the relationships set up indirectly among the words by matching an interlingual representation onto the sentence.

From the point of view of the matching routine, the initial representation of the sentence is a string of six semantic formulas, whose details I shall discuss later. What matters at the moment is that the formula for "brother" has the head element MAN, just as did the one for "John," and so on for "owns" and "car." The formulas for "my" and "large" have the conventional head element KIND, since they specify what kind of thing is in question. The template-matching routine scans the formula string from left to right and is able to match the bare template MAN HAVE THING from the template inventory onto the formulas for "brother," "owns," and "car," respectively, since those elements, in that order, are the heads of those formulas. Those three words are, as it were, the points in the sentence at which the template puts its three feet down.

So far, at the word level, ties that can be written as follows have been established:

brother ↔ owns ↔ car

These are much the same sort of ties that would be established at the word level by any system of conceptual semantic analysis applied to that sentence [11]. However, given that all realistically coded words in the dictionary would have many sense formulas attached to them, only certain selections of formulas would admit of being matched by an item in the template inventory. For example, in the sentence "This green bicycle is a winner," the semantic formula for "winner" that has MAN as its head and means "one who wins" is never picked up by the matching routine simple because there is no bare template THING BE MAN in the inventory.

To return to the sentence "My brother owns a large car;" having matched on the bare template, the system looks at the three formulas it has tied together by means of their heads to see if it can extend the representation, top-down, by attaching other formulas and so create a fuller representation. In this case it looks from the formula for "brother" to the one that preceded it, the formula for "my." This, it sees, can indeed qualify the formula for "brother," and so it opens a list of formulas that can be tied onto this "brother" formula. Repeating this process, we end up with an interlingual representation for the sentence in the following schematic form (which I shall call a *full template* — though we shall see later that the tied items are not simply formulas):

$$F[\text{brother}] \leftrightarrow F[\text{owns}] \leftrightarrow F[\text{car}]$$
$$\uparrow \qquad\qquad\qquad\qquad \uparrow$$
$$(F[\text{my}]) \qquad\qquad\qquad (F[\text{large}])$$

where both the horizontal and vertical directions represent dependency ties of the sort I have described, and F[x] stands simply for the interlingual formula for the

English word x. Thus, the upwards vertical dependency is that of a list of qualifying formulas (empty in the case of "owns") on the main formula.

The corresponding ties between the text words themselves established by this method are:

$$\text{brother} \leftrightarrow \text{owns} \leftrightarrow \text{car} \leftrightarrow \text{a}$$
$$\uparrow \qquad\qquad\qquad \uparrow$$
$$\text{my} \qquad\qquad\qquad \text{large}$$

A point that cannot have escaped the reader is that by having a rigid actor-action-object format for templates, one ignores the fact that many fragments of natural language are not of this form, regardless of how the initial input text is partitioned. This is indeed the case, but by using the notion of dummy parts of templates one can in fact put any text construction into this very general format. Since the analysis has no conventional syntactic base, the standard examples of syntactic homonymity, such as the various interpretations that can be thought up for "they are eating apples," are represented only as differing message interpretations. So for that sentence we would expect to match at least the bare templates MAN DO THING and THING BE THING.

3.3.1 Fragmentation and Isolation

The fragmentation routine partitions input sentences at punctuation marks and at the occurrence of any of an extensive list of key words. This list contains almost all subjunctions, conjunctions, and prepositions. Thus the sentence "John is in the house" would be returned by such a routine as two fragments (John is) and (in the house). With the first fragment the system would match MAN BE DTHIS, where the D of DTHIS indicates that, having failed to find any predicate after "is," the system has supplied a dummy THIS to produce the canonical form of template.

If there is more than one available template to choose from, the preferrence is to the representation with the most conceptual connections (which can be thought of simply as the number of →s in the word diagrams) and the minimum number of dummys. For the fragment "in the house," the matching routine finds itself confronted with a string of formulas, starting with one for "in," that has PDO as its head. Prepositions are, in general, assimilated to actions and so have the P in the PDO of their heads to distinguish them from straightforward action formulas. In this case the matching routine inserts a dummy THIS as the left-most member of the bare template, since it first encounters an action formula — headed by a PDO — as it scans the formula string from left to right, and "in the house" is finally matched with the bare template DTHIS PDO POINT. Thus the sentence "John is in the house" is partitioned into two fragments and matched with a semantic representation consisting of a string of two templates whose bare template names are MAN BE DTHIS and DTHIS PDO POINT.

Another example of fragmenting and matching is presented by what might conventionally be called noun phrases. If, after fragmenting, the system is presented with "The old black man" as a single fragment, it can supply two such dummies during the match and end up with a representation named by the bare template MAN DBE DTHIS.

The semantic connectivities described so far have been between formulas that correspond to words occurring in the same fragment of text. But not all semantic ties in a complex sentence will be internal to fragments — many will be between items occurring in different, and maybe not even textually contiguous, fragments. At a later point I shall discuss TIE routines whose function is to provide, in the full interlingual representation, those inter-fragment dependencies necessary for translation. However, the major simplifying role of the fragmentation must not be lost in all this; it allows a complex sentence to be represented by a linear sequence of templates with ties between them, rather than by a far more complex hierarchical representation as is usual in linguistics.

The fragmentation, then, is done on the basis of the superficial punctuation of the input text and a finite list of keywords and keyword sequences, whose occurrence produces a text partition. Difficult but important cases of two kinds must then be considered. First, those where a text string is NOT fragmented even though a key word is encountered. Two intuitively obvious cases are non-subordinating uses of "that," as in "I like that wine," and prepositions functioning as "post verbs" as in "He gave up his post." In these cases there would be no fragmentation before the key words. In other cases text strings are fragmented even though a key word is NOT present. Four cases are worth mentioning:

1. "I want him to go" is fragmented as (I want) (him to go). A boundary is inserted after any form of the words "say" and "want," and a further boundary is inhibited before the following "to." This seems intuitively acceptable, since "want" in fact subjoins the whole of what follows it in the sentence. We shall expect to match onto these fragments bare templates of the form MAN WANT DTHIS and MAN MOVE DTHIS. respectively, where the first dummy THIS stands for the whole of the next template. The fragmentation functions operate at the lowest possible level of analysis; they inspect the semantic formulas given for a word in the dictionary, but they cannot assume that the choice among the formulas has been made.

A verb like "advise," on the other hand, is not of this sort, since we can interpret "I advise him" in a way in which we cannot interpret "I want him" in the earlier case. So we would expect "I advise him to go" to receive no special treatment and to be fragmented as (I advise him) (to go), on a key word basis.

2. Relative clauses beginning with "that" or "which" are located and isolated and then inserted back into the string of fragments at a new point. For example, "The girl that I like left" is fragmented as (The girl left) (that I like PD), where the final period, PD, of the sentence is also moved to close off the sentence at a new point. Thus, the partition after "like" is made in the absence of any key word.

3. "The old man in the corner left" is, naturally enough, fragmented as (The old man) (in the corner) (left). The breach made here between the actor and act of the sentence is replaced later by a tie (see below).

4. The sentences "John likes eating fish," "John likes eating," and "John began eating fish," are all fragmented before "eating," so that these forms are all assimilated to "John likes to eat fish" (which is synonymous with the first sentence above), rather than to "John is eating fish," which would not be fragmented at all. In template terms "John is eating fish" is to be thought of as MAN DO THING, while "John likes fish" is MAN FEEL DTHIS + DTHIS DO THING, where the first DTHIS refers to the whole of the next template, and the second DTHIS stands in place of MAN (i.e., John).

"Of" is a key word that receives rather special treatment, and is not used to make a partition when it introduces a possessive noun phrase. After fragmentation, each fragment is passed through an ISOLATE function, which looks within each fragment and seeks for the right-hand boundaries of "of" phrases and marks them off by inserting a character "FO" into the text. Thus, "He has a book of mine" would be returned from the ISOLATE function as "He has a book of mine FO." This is done in all cases except those like "I don't want to speak of him," where "of" effectively functions as a post verb.

It may seem obvious enough why "of" phrases should remain within the fragment, since "of John" functions as does "John's," but the demarcation of the phrase with the "FO" character can only be explained by considering the PICKUP and EXTEND routines.

3.3.2 Pickup and Extend

The PICKUP routines match bare templates onto the string of formulas for a text fragment. As the routines move through the string of formulas, those contained between an OF and a FO are ignored for the purpose of the initial match. This ensures that "of phrases" are only treated as qualifiers. Thus, in the sentence "The father of my friend FO is called Jack," the match would never try to make the head of the formula for "friend" into the root of a template matching the sentence, since it is sealed between an "of-fo" pair. To illustrate the results of applying PICKUP, I shall set down the bare templates that would be expected to match onto Nida & Taber's [8] suggested seven basic forms of the English indicative sentence. (In this talk I describe only the indicative mood as it is implemented in the trial version of this system. Queries and imperatives, like passives, are dealt with by the appropriate manipulation of the template order.)

In each case I give the basic sentence, the bare template, and a diagramatic representation of the corresponding dependencies implied between the text items, where "↔" again links those words on which the bare template is rooted or based, and "→" links a dependent word to its governor.

A natural question at this point is, what exactly *is* this inventory of bare templates to be used in the analysis of input languages? No detailed defense is offered of the inventory used, nor, I believe, can one be given. The fact is that one uses the inventory that seems empirically right, revises it when necessary, and concludes that that, alas, is how things must be in the real world of practical language analysis.

(1) John   ran   quickly   John ↔ ran ↔ [DTHIS]
     MAN   MOVE   DTHIS   ↑
                                                quickly

(2) John   hit   Bill   John ↔ hit ↔ Bill
     MAN   DO   MAN

(3) John   gave Bill   a ball   John ↔ gave ↔ ball
     MAN   GIVE   THING   ↑   ↑
                                            (to)Bill   a

(The establishment of this dependency by EXTEND is discussed below.)

(4) John   is   in   the   house.
     MAN   BE   DTHIS DTHIS   PBE   THING

     John   ↔   is   ↔   [DTHIS][DTHIS]   ↔   in   ↔   house
                                                                 ↑
                                                                the

(5) John   is   sick   John ↔ is ↔ sick
     MAN   BE   KIND

(6) John   is   a boy   John ↔ is ↔ boy
     MAN   BE   MAN   ↑
                                              a

(7) John   is   my   father   John ↔ is ↔ father
     MAN   BE   MAN   ↑
                                              my

The inventory used can be reconstructed from the table of rules set out below in Backus-Naur Form. It is set out in terms of the action designating semantic elements, such as FORCE, and the classes of substantive designating elements (such as *SOFT meaning STUFF, WHOLE, PART, GRAN, and SPREAD) that can precede such an action as a subject, and follow it as an object to create a three-element bare template.

```
<bare template> : := <*PO><DO><*EN> | <*PO><CAUSE><*EN>|
<*PO><CHANGE><*EN> | <*AN><FEEL><*MA>| <*EN><HAVE><*EN>|
<*AL><PLEASE><*AN>|<*AL><PAIR><*EN>|
<*PO><SENSE><*EN>|<*PO><WANT><*EN>|<*PO><USE><*EN>|
<*PO><TELL><*MA>|<*PO><DROP><*EN>|<*PO><FORCE><*EN>|
<*EN><MOVE><DTHIS>  |<*PO><GIVE><*EN>|<*AL><WRAP><*EN>|
<*AN><THINK><*AM>|<*SO><FLOW><DTHIS>|<*PO><PICK><*EN>|
<*PO><MAKE><*EN>|<*AL><BE><same member of *AL as last
   occurrence>

<*AL>::=<DTHIS|THIS|MAN|FOLK|GRAIN|PART|WORLD|STUFF|
   THING|BEAST|PLANT|SPREAD|LINE|ACT|STATE>
   (*AL means all substantive elements)
```

```
<*EN>::=<DTHIS|THIS|MAN|FOLK|GRAIN|PART|STUFF|THING|
   BEAST|PLANT|SPREAD|LINE>
   (*EN means elements that are entities)
```

```
<*AN> ::=<MAN|FOLK|BEAST|GRAIN>
   <*AN means animate entities, GRAIN is used as
      the main element for social organizations,
      like the Red Cross)
```

```
<*PO>::=<DTHIS|THIS|MAN|FOLK|GRAIN|PART|STUFF|THING|
   ACT|BEAST|PLANT|STATE>
   (*PO means potent elements, those that can
   designate actors. The class cannot be restricted
   to *AN since rain wets the grass and the wind
   opens doors)
```

```
<*SO>::=<STUFF|PART|GRAIN|SPREAD>
```

```
<*MA>::=<ACT|SIGN|STATE>
   (*MA designates mark elements, those that can
   designate items that themselves designate like
   thoughts and writings)
```

I have distorted BNF very slightly to write the bare templates containing BE in a convenient and perspicuous form. The forms containing MOVE and FLOW also contain a DTHIS (i.e., they are "dummy templates") indicating that there cannot be objects in those bare templates. Thus, MOVE is used only in the coding of intransitive actions and not to deal with such sentences as "I moved all the furniture round the room."

There are dummy templates not included in this list — several occur in the description of the Nida and Taber sentences above. The remaining rules specifying them are intuitively obvious, but may be found in detail in [15], with important ancillary rules which specify when dummies are to be generated in matching sentences. Naturally, a dummy MAN BE DTHIS is generated for the first fragment of (John is) (in the house) simply because a proper three-element bare template cannot be fitted onto the information available. But in other cases, where a three-element template can be fitted, dummies are generated as well, since subsequent routines to be described may prefer the dummy to the bare template. For example, in the analysis of the first fragment of (The old transport system) (which I loved) (in my youth) (has been found uneconomic), a reasonably full dictionary will contain formulas for the substantive sense of "old" and the action sense of "transport." Thus, the actor-action-object template FOLK CAUSE GRAIN can be fitted on here but will be incorrect. The dummy GRAIN DBE DTHIS will also be fitted on and will be preferred by the EXTEND procedures described below. Such slight complexity of the basic template notion is necessary if so simple a concept is to deal with the realities of language. This matter is described in greater detail in [15].

The matching by PICKUP will still, in general, leave a number of bare templates attached to a text fragment. It is the EXTEND routines, working out from the three points at which the bare template attaches to the fragment, that try to create the densest dependency network possible for the fragment, and thus reduce the number of templates matching a fragment.

In order to show more clearly how EXTEND does this, it is necessary to say more about the semantic formulas which make up the full template. A semantic formula expresses the meaning of one sense of a natural language word in the dictionary. It is made up of left and right parentheses and of semantic elements. The latter include THING, STUFF, MAN, etc., for basic items in the world; FORCE, CAUSE, DROP, CHANGE to describe basic kinds of actions; and so on. The formulas are binarily bracketed pairs of whatever depth of nesting is necessary to express the meaning of a particular word sense. The formulas are made up, and interpreted, with a dependency of the left element, or bracket group, upon the corresponding right-hand element or bracket group in every case.

So, (MAN KIND) would be interpreted as "of a human sort;" it is a formula for "human" used as a qualifier. In ((MAN FEEL) CAUSE) the dependency within the inner bracket is of an actor-act type, whereas that within the outer bracket — of (MAN DO) on CAUSE — is of the object-of-action on act type. So the whole sub-formula is to be interpreted as "causes a person to feel something," and we would therefor expect to find this sub-formula within any formula for, say, "torment." (There are restrictions on the ways in which the elements can combine contained in a table of "scope notes" for the system of coding: for example, CAUSE cannot be anything but an action, so ((MAN DROP) CAUSE) could not be the specification of a sort of cause, but only the causing of something. The most important element in a formula is its rightmost one, or head, with which PICKUP connects formulas for words to templates for whole fragments.)

Formulas that can qualify any other substantive formula have the head KIND, and those that can qualify actions have the head HOW. Most action formulas have as head DO, BE, MOVE ("run," for example), or GIVE. GIVE verbs are important in that they can function in the representation of action constructions like "He left John his watch," where an indirect object of an action can appear without any preceding preposition. GIVE verbs function in much the same way as TRANS verbs in Schank's analysis [11], and the appearance of GIVE as a formula head for, say, the action "left" primes the system to expect such an indirect object. The verb "tell" also has GIVE as the head of its principal formula, since it can participate in such indirect object constructions as "John tells me a story." The lack of necessary connection between the English word "tell" and the interlingual element TELL is brought out by the fact that the formula head of "tell" is not TELL but GIVE. In the case of "say," on the other hand, the head of its main formula is TELL, since it cannot occur in the GIVE-type constructions.

Most substantive formulas have as their heads such elements as MAN, STUFF, THING, ACT (for abstract substantives which are the result of action, such as "adjustment"), STATE (abstract substantives such as "friendship," "happiness"), GRAIN (abstract substantives any sort of structure such as "system") and so on. A formula for a substantive is assumed to be singular unless the element MUCH is its first item at the top level.

Action formulas can specify a preferred class of actors, or of objects of the action, or both. Preferred actors are specified by FOR and preferred objects by TO. So then the formula for the action "talk" will contain the pair (MAN FOR), since most things that talk are human, and if there is a possibility of setting up a dependency with a human actor, the system will take it. The restriction cannot be absolute in this, or most other cases, since machines and dogs talk, in fable if not in fact. The important facility is to be able to PREFER the usual, if a representation for it is available, but to be able to accept the unusual if necessary.

The syntax of the action formula is as follows: (X FOR) or (X TO) appears as the first item at the top level of the action formula if appropriate — in LISP terminology the pair is simply CONS'd onto the verb formula. If both are appropriate, as in a formula for "interrogate," then the (X TO), for the objects, is CONS'd first, and appears at one level lower in the nesting of the formula than the (X FOR), specifying the preferred actors. Thus the formula for "interrogate" would read:

$$((MAN\ FOR)\ ((MAN\ TO)\ (TELL\ FORCE))).$$

The preferred substantives, or classes of them, for qualifiers are indicated in an extension of this notation, by including (X FOR) as the first item at the top level in the formula for a qualifier.

In order to keep a small useable set of interlingual semantic elements, and to avoid arbitrary extensions of the list of elements, many notions are coded by conventional sub-formulas: (FLOW STUFF) is used to designate liquids, for example, and (WHERE SPREAD) to code spatial area of any sort.

The role of EXTEND was discussed in general terms above: it inspects the strings of formulas that replace a fragment, and seeks to set up dependencies of formulas on each other. It keeps a score as it does so, and in the end selects the structuring of formulas with the most dependencies, on the assumption that it is the right one (or ones, if two or more structurings of formulas have the same dependency score).

The dependencies that can be set up are of two sorts: (1) those between formulas whose heads are part of the bare template, and (2) those of formulas whose heads are not in the bare template upon those formulas whose heads are in the bare template.

Consider the sentence "John talked quickly," for which the bare template would be MAN TELL DTHIS, thus establishing, at the word level, the dependency John↔talked↔[DTHIS]. Now suppose we expand out from each of the elements constituting the bare template in turn. In the formula for "talked" there is the preference for an actor formula whose head is MAN — since talking is generally done by people. This preference is satisfied here; we can think of it as establishing a word dependency of "John" on "talked," which is a type (1) dependency. Expanding again from the element TELL, we have a formula for "quickly" whose head is

HOW, and HOW-headed formulas are proper qualifiers for actions. Hence we have been able to set up the following diagramatic dependency at the word level:

$$\text{John} \leftrightarrow \text{talked} \leftrightarrow \text{[DTHIS]}$$
$$\rightarrow \quad \uparrow$$
$$\text{quickly}$$

(where "$\leftrightarrow$" indicates a bare template connectivity strengthened by a direct semantic dependency — springing from the preference of "talked" for a human actor in this case), and we would score two for such a representation. Furthermore, the formulas having type (B) dependence would be tied in a list to the main formula on which they depend. The subtypes of dependence are as follows:

(A) Among the formulas whose heads constitute the bare template
  (1) preferred subjects on actions
      "John talked"
  (2) preferred objects of actions on actions
      "interrogated a prisoner"
(B) Of formulas not constituting bare templates on those that do
  (1) qualifiers of substantives on substantives
      "red door"
  (2) qualifiers of actions on actions
      "opened quickly"
  (3) articles on substantives
      "a book"
  (4) of — fo phrases on substantives
      "the house of my father fo"
  (5) qualifiers of actions on qualifiers of substantives
      "very much"
  (6) post verbs on actions
      "give up"
  (7) indirect objects on actions
      "gave John a..."
  (8) auxiliaries on actions
      "was going"
  (9) "to" on infinitive form of action
      "to relax"

The searches for type (B) dependencies are all directed in the formula string in an intuitively obvious manner: 1, 3, 4, 5, and 8 go leftwards only; 6 and 7 go rightwards only; and 2 goes rightwards and leftwards.

The purpose of the score of dependencies established will become clear if we consider an example of (B) (7): the indirect object construction. Let us take the sentence "John gave Mary the book," onto which the matching routine PICKUP will have matched two bare templates as follows, since it has no reason to prefer one to the other:

```
John    gave   Mary    the    book
MAN     GIVE   MAN
MAN     GIVE                   THING
```

EXTEND now seeks for dependencies, and since the formula for "gave" has no preferred actors or objects, the top bare template cannot be extended at all, and so scores zero. In the case of the lower bare template, then, a GIVE action can be expanded by any substantive formula to its immediate right which is not already part of the bare template. Again, "book" is qualified by an article, which fact is not noticed by the top bare template. So then, by EXTENDing we have established in the second case the following dependencies at the word level and scored two (of the "→" dependencies).

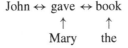

Thus the second representation is preferred. This is an application of the general rule referred to earlier as "pick the most connected representation from the fragment."

The auxiliary of an action also has its formula made dependent on that of the appropriate action and the fact scored, but the auxiliary formulas are not listed as dependent formulas either. They are picked up by EXTEND and examined to determine the tense of the action. They are then forgotten and an element indicating the tense is CONS'd onto the action formula. In its initial state the system will recognize only four tenses of complex actions:

```
PRES:   does hide/is hiding/did hide/are hiding/am hiding
IMPE:   was hiding/were hiding
PAST:   did hide/had hidden
FUTU:   will hide/will be hiding/shall hide/shall be hiding
```

In the case of the negative of any of these tenses the word "not" is forgotten, and an atom NPRES, NIMPE, NPAST, or NFUTU attached to the appropriate action formula instead. At present the system does not deal with passives, though I indicate later how they are dealt with within the template format.

Even when the representation with the densest dependency has been found, there may still be more than one representation with that score for a given fragment. So, in the case of "The man lost his leg" there may well be two representations of this sentence with the same dependency score, one corresponding to each of two different senses of "leg" — one as a part of a body, and one as an inanimate thing that supports some other thing (as in "piano leg"). There is a further routine in EXTEND, called into play in such cases, that attempts to establish additional "semantic overlap" of content both between the actor and object formulas of the template, and between each of the three main formulas of the template and its qualifiers. If any can be found, the additional dependencies are used to choose among representations that have achieved the same score in the EXTEND routines described earlier. So, in the present case, the formula for "leg of a person" would be expected to contain the sub-formula (MAN PART), whereas the formula for "piano leg" would not, and this connectivity with the initial formula of the template, whose head was MAN, would suffice for one representation to be chosen in preference to the other, again on the principle of preferring the most connected representation.

The third and last pass of the text applies the TIE routines, which establish dependencies between the representations of different fragments. Each text fragment has been tied by the routines described so far to one or more full templates, each consisting of three main formulas to each of which a list of dependent formulas may be tied. The interlingual representation consists, for each text fragment, of one full template together with up to four additional items of information called *key*, *mark*, *case*, and *phase* respectively. The interlingual representation also contains the English name of the fragment itself.

The *key* is simply the first word of the fragment, if it occurs on the list of key words; or, in the cases of "that" and "which" a key *use* of the word.

The *mark* for a given key is the text word to which the key word ties the whole fragment of which it is the key. So, in (He came home) (from the war), the mark of the second fragment is "came" and the second fragment is tied in a relation of dependence to that mark by the key "from." Every key has a corresponding mark, found by TIE, unless (a) the key is "and" or "but" or (b) the fragment introduced by the key is itself a complete sentence, not dependent on anything outside itself. The notion will become clearer from examining the example paragraph set out below.

From the point of view of the present system of analysis, the *case* of a fragment, if any, generally expresses the role of that fragment in relation to its key and mark: it specifies the sort of dependence the fragment has upon its mark. In general, case markers are attached to fragments on the basis of the key and the mark. It may be that no case is finally assigned to a fragment, though it will be if a fragment is introduced by a preposition. The cases are, in a sense, a cross classification of prepositions, whose correct rendering into, say, French is so vital for adequate translation

The provisional working list of cases and the English prepositions that can introduce them is as follows:

RECEIVER: to, from, for
INSTRUMENTAL: with, by
DIRECTION: to, from, towards, outof, for
POSSESSION: with
LOCATION (space and time): at, by, near, after, in, during, before
CONTAINMENT: in
SOURCE: outof, from
GOAL: to, at
OBJECT (as in (I want) (her to leave)): no key word necessary

The case analysis routines in TIE work by considering the above classification of prepositions in reverse, as it were: thus, in (He struck the boy) (with a stick), TIE locates the "with" and finds in the stereotypes for "with" that "with" can introduce either a POSSESSIVE or INSTRUMENTAL fragment. If, for example, an INSTRUMENTAL case is in question it will expect a preceding action whose head is DO, CAUSE, or FORCE, and will also expect a substantive in the fragment it introduces whose head is THING. In the case mentioned, it finds these conditions satisfied, since the head of the appropriate formula for "stick" is THING, and so it ties the second fragment to the mark "hit" and assigns the INSTRUMENTAL case to the second fragment as a description of that tie.

In any other situation, where these criteria are not satisfied, the fragment introduced by "with" is tied to the immediately preceding substantive, and the case POSSESSIVE is assigned to the tie, as in (He struck the boy) (with long hair). In one special class of cases, the POSSESSIVE case is assigned even though a THING substantive is found in the "object position" of the second template following a DO, CAUSE or FORCE action in a preceding template. These are the cases where the object is a part of the substantive previously mentioned. For, even though a leg is a THING, we would want to assign a POSSESSIVE case to the second template of the pair (He hit the boy) (with the wooden leg). How this TIE is obtained algorithmically is discussed in detail in the section after the description of STEREOTYPES.

This procedure can be thought of as an ambiguity resolution of the prepositions, which has not been dealt with at all by the PICKUP routines, since prepositions are inserted into the formula strings as a single formula and are never considered ambiguous at that stage. The TIE routines also resolve other semantic ambiguity not dealt with by the PICKUP routines. If our last example had been (He struck the boy) (with a bar) we would have expected there to be at least two formulas for "bar" still in play: corresponding to the heads THING and POINT — the latter corresponding to the place sense of "bar." Hence, there would still be two full templates matching the latter fragment at this stage, both considered by TIE, which would prefer the template containing the sense of "bar" coded with the head THING, since only in that case could a dependency tie be made (to "hit" in another fragment, in this case) on the basis of information extracted from the formulas.

Phase notation is merely a code to indicate in a very general way to the subsequent generation routines where in the "progress of the whole sentence" one is at a given fragment. A phase number is attached to each fragment on the following basis by TIE, where the stage referred to applies at the BEGINNING of the fragment to which the number attaches.

0: main subject not yet reached
1: subject reached but not main verb
2: main verb reached but not complement or object
3: complement or object reached or not expected

3.3.3 The Interlingual Representation

What follows is a version of the interlingual representation for a paragraph, designed to illustrate the four forms of information – key, mark, case, and phase. The schema below gives only the bare template form of the semantic information attached to each fragment – the semantic formulas and their pendant lists of formulas that make up the full template structure are all omitted.

```
(LATER CM) → (PLUS TARD VG)
nil:nil:nil:0:No Template

(DURING THE WAR CM) → (PENDANT LA GUERRE VG)
DURING:GAVEUP:location:0:DTHIS PBE ACT

(HITLER GAVE UP THE EVENING SHOWINGS CM) →
(HITLER RENONCA AUX REPRESENTATIONS DU SOIR VG)
nil:nil:nil:0:MAN DROP ACT

(SAYING) → (DISTANT)
nil:HITLER:nil:3:DTHIS DO DTHIS

(THAT HE WANTED) → (QU'IL VOULAIT)
THAT:SAYING:object:3:MAN WANT DTHIS

(TO RENOUNCE HIS FAVORITE ENTERTAINMENT) →
(RENONCER A SA DISTRACTION FAVORITE)
TO:WANT:object:3:DTHIS DROP ACT

(OUTOF SYMPATHY) → (PAR SYMPATHIE)
OUTOF:RENOUNCE:source:3:DTHIS PDO SIGN

(FOR THE PRIVATIONS OF THE SOLDIERS PD) →
(POUR LES PRIVATIONS DES SOLDATS PT)
FOR:SYMPATHY:recipient:3:DTHIS PBE ACT

(INSTEAD RECORDS WERE PLAYED PD) →
(A LA PLACE ON PASSA DES DISQUES PT)
INSTEAD:nil:nil:0:MAN USE THING (comment:template active)

(BUT) → (MAIS)
BUT:nil:nil:0:No Template

(ALTHOUGH THE RECORD COLLECTION WAS EXCELLENT CM) →
(BIEN QUE LA COLLECTION DE DISQUES FUT EXCELLENTE VG)
ALTHOUGH:PREFERRED:nil:0:GRAIN BE KIND
```

(HITLER ALWAYS PREFERRED THE SAME MUSIC PD) →
(HITLER PREFERAIT TOUJOURS LA MEME MUSIQUE PT)
nil:nil:nil:0:MAN WANT GRAIN

(NEITHER BAROQUE) → (NI LA MUSIQUE BAROQUE)
NEITHER:MUSIC:qualifier:0:DTHIS DBE KIND

(NOR CLASSICAL MUSIC CM) → (NI CLASSIQUE VG)
NOR:INTERESTED:nil:0:GRAIN DBE DTHIS

(NEITHER CHAMBER MUSIC) → (NI LA MUSIQUE DE CHAMBRE)
NEITHER:INTERESTED:nil:0:GRAIN DBE DTHIS

(NOR SYMPHONIES CM) → (NI LES SYMPHONIES VG)
NOR:INTERESTED:nil:0:GRAIN DBE DTHIS

(INTERESTED HIM PD) → (NE L'INTERESSAIENT PT)
nil:nil:nil:1:DTHIS CHANGE MAN

(BEFORELONG THE ORDER OF THE RECORDS BECAME VIRTUALLY
FIXED PD) →
(BIENTOT L'ORDRE DES DISQUES DEVINT VIRTUELLEMENT FIXE PT)
BEFORELONG:nil:nil:0:GRAIN BE KIND

(FIRST HE WANTED A FEW BRAVURA SELECTIONS) →
(D'ABORD IL VOULAIT QUELQUES SELECTIONS DE BRAVOURE)
nil:nil:nil:0:MAN WANT PART

(FROM WAGNERIAN OPERAS CM) → (D'OPERAS WAGNERIENS VG)
FROM:SELECTIONS:source:3:DTHIS PDO GRAIN

(TO BE FOLLOWED PROMPTLY) →
(QUE DEVAIENT ETRE SUIVIES RAPIDEMENT)
TO:OPERAS:nil:3:MAN DO DTHIS (comment: shift to active
template again may give a different but not incorrect
translation)

(WITH OPERETTAS PD) → (PAR DES OPERETTAS PT)
WITH:FOLLOWED:nil:3:DTHIS PBE GRAIN

(THAT REMAINED THE PATTERN PD) → (CELA DEVINT LA REGLE PT)
nil:nil:nil:0:THAT BE GRAIN (comment: no mark because "that"
ties to a whole sentence)

(HITLER MADE A POINT OF TRYING) →
(HITLER SE FAISAIT UNE REGLE D'ESSAYER)

```
nil:nil:nil:0:MAN DO DTHIS (comment: some idiom
recognition essential to cope with this)
```

```
(TO GUESS THE NAMES OF THE SOPRANOS) →
(DE DEVINER LES NOMS DES SOPRANOS)
TO:TRYING:object:2:DTHIS DO SIGN
```

```
(AND WAS PLEASED) → (ET ETAIT CONTENT)
AND:HITLER:nil:3:DTHIS BE KIND
```

```
(WHEN HE GUESSED RIGHT CM) → (QUAND IL DEVINAIT JUSTE VG)
WHEN:PLEASED:location:3:MAN DO DTHIS
```

```
(AS HE FREQUENTLY DID PD) →
(COMME IL LE FAISAIT FREQUEMENT PT)
AS:GUESSED:manner:3:MAN DO DTHIS
```

It is assumed that those fragments that have no template attached to them, such as (LATER), can be translated adequately word-for-word. Were it not for the difficulty involved in reading it, we could lay out the above text so as to display the dependencies implied by the assignment of cases and marks at the word level. These would all be of dependencies of whole fragments on particular words. For example, the relation of just the first two fragments appears as:

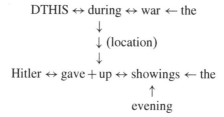

This intermediate stage is an arbitrary one in the English-French processing that is useful to examine at the surface level. It is often supposed that an intermediate stage like the present interlingual representation must contain "all possible semantic information" in some explicit form if it is to be adequate. But the quoted words are not, and cannot be, well-defined with respect to any coding scheme. What is the case is that the interlingual representation must contain sufficient information to admit of the formal manipulations, adequate for producing translations in natural or formal languages. The IR need not contain any particular *explicit* information about a text. The real restriction is that in its creating no information should have been thrown away that will later turn out to be important; one of the difficulties of English-French MT is the need to EXTEND and make explicit in the French things that are not so in the English.

Consider the sentence "The house I live in is collapsing," which contains no subjunction "that," though in French it *must* be expressed explicitly, as by "dans laquelle." There need not be any representation of "that" anywhere in the IR. All that is necessary is that the subordination of the second fragment to the mark "house" be coded, and generation procedures which know that in such cases of subordination an appropriate subjunction must occur in the French output. It is the need for such procedures that constitutes the sometimes awkward expansion of English into French, but the need for them in no way dictates the explicit content of the IR.

3.3.4 The Dictionary Format

The dictionary is essentially a list of pairs of semantic formulas (each corresponding to one sense of an English word), and of explanations of that sense. By "explanation" I mean not simply an English word or phrase, such as was used in earlier versions of this system of analysis [15], but what I shall call a French *stereotype*. For example, one sense of the English word "colorless" might have appeared in the dictionary as:

(((((WHERE SPREAD) (SENSE SIGN)) NOTHAVE) KIND)
(COLORLESS AS NOT HAVING THE PROPERTY OF COLOR))

The first half of the pair, the formula, expresses the fact that being colorless means not having a spatial (WHERE SPREAD) sensory property (SENSE SIGN). The second half of the pair is a sense explanation in English that contains the name of the word and serves to distinguish that particular sense of "colorless" from other senses — such as one about human character.

But the senses of the English words may equally well be explained and distinguished by means of their French equivalents, at least in cases where the notion of "a French equivalent to an English word" is an appropriate one. So, for example, the French words "rouge" and "socialiste" might be said to distinguish two senses of the English word "red," and we might code these two senses of "red" in the dictionary by means of the sense pairs:

(((WHERE SPREAD) KIND) (RED (ROUGE)))
((((WORLD CHANGE) WANT) MAN) (RED (SOCIALISTE)))

The French words "rouge" and "socialiste" are enclosed in list parentheses because they need not have been, as in this case, single French words. They could be French word-strings of any length: for example, the qualifier sense of "hunting" as it occurs in a "a hunting gun" is rendered in French as "de chasse;" hence, we would expect (HUNTING (DE CHASSE)) as the right-hand member of one sense pair for "hunting."

This simplified notion of stereotype is adequate for the representation of most qualifiers and substantives. Below I shall generalize to the notion of a *full stereotype* adequate for the representation of prepositions and actions, in which there may be more than one list after the English word name in the right-hand member of the sense pair. Moreover, they will be lists in which functions will occur as well as the names of French words.

We should pause at this point to see what the notions of *sense pair* and stereotype are doing for us in the system. Earlier I described the structure of a full template as made up of formulas and lists of formulas. But these would more accurately have been described as sense pairs and lists of sense pairs; the analysis routines, in fact, build into the template not just the formulas, but the *whole sense pairs*, of which the formulas are the lefthand members. Hence, the full template already contains the French equivalents of the English words in the fragment. Moreover, the stereotypes for actions and prepositions contain not only French equivalents but implicit rules for assembling these equivalents to generate French output: the generation routines never need consult an English-French dictionary. The full template may appear to be a complex and cumbrous item of information, containing as it does not only a conceptual semantic representation of English text, but also French output forms and implicit generation rules; still, the avoidance of repeated consultation of a large dictionary of forms and rules in LISP format is no small compensation.

The full stereotype, then, may contain not only French words but also predicates and functions of interlingual items whose values are always French word strings, or a blank item, or NIL. The notion of "interlingual item" here covers not only the interlingual elements that make up the formulas, but also the names of the cases abbreviated to a standard four-letter format, for example; RECE, INST, DIRE, POSS, LOCA, CONT, SOUR, GOAL, OBJE, QUAL (see the list of cases given earlier).

The general form of the stereotype is a list of predicates, followed by a string of French words and functions that evaluate to French words, or to NIL (in which case the stereotype fails). The functions may also evaluate to blank symbols for reasons to be described.

The predicates, which occur only in preposition stereotypes, normally refer, respectively, to the case of the fragment containing the word and to its mark. If both these predicates are satisfied the program continues on through the stereotype to the French output.

Let us consider the verb "advise," rendered in its most straightforward sense by the French word "conseiller." It is likely to be followed by two different constructions, as in the English: (1) I advise John to have patience, and (2) I advise patience.

Verb stereotypes contain no predicates, so we might expect the most usual sense pair for "advise" to contain a formula followed by

(ADVISE (CONSEILLER A (FN1 FOLK MAN))
(CONSEILLER (FN2 ACT STATE STUFF)))

The role of the stereotypes should by now be becoming clear: in generating from, in this case an action, the system looks down a list of stereotypes tied to the sense of the action in the full template. If any of the functions it now encounters evaluate to NIL, the whole stereotype containing the function fails and the next is tried. If the functions evaluate to French words, they are generated along with the French words that appear as their own names, like "conseiller."

The stereotypes do more than simply avoid the explicit use of a conventional generative grammar; they also direct the production of the French translation by providing complex context-sensitive rules at the required point without any search of a large rule inventory. This method is, in principle, extendable to the production of reasonably complex implicit rephrasings and expansions, as in the derivation of "si intelligent soit-il" from the second fragment of (No man) (however intelligent) (can survive death), given the appropriate stereotype for "however."

Preposition stereotypes are, in general, more complex, than those for actions, but before illustrating them I should mention a point that arises in connection with stereotypes and their relation to the enumeration of the senses of the input. As I have described the dictionary so far, many output stereotypes may be attached to one sense of an English word, that is to a single semantic formula. In the example sentences above, "advise" is taken as being used in the same sense in the two sentences, even though different constructions follow the word in the two cases. So the notion of stereotype in no way corresponds to that of word sense, Indeed, the notion of word-sense is extremely unclear and resistant to any formal analysis.

In the case of prepositions, I take them as having only a single sense each, even though that sense may give rise to a great number of stereotypes. Let us consider, by way of example, "outof" (considered as a single word) in the three sentences:

(1) (It was made) (outof wood)
(2) (He killed him) (outof hatred)
(3) (I live) (outof town)

It seems to me unhelpful to say that here are three senses of "outof," even though its occurrence in these examples requires translation into French by "de," "par," and "en dehors de," respectively, and other contexts would require "parmi" or "dans." Given the convention for stereotypes described earlier for actions, let us set down stereotypes that would enable us to deal with these cases:

(S1) ((PRCASE SOUR) (PRMARK *DO) DE (FN1 STUFF THING))
(S2) ((PRCASE SOUR) (PRMARK *DO) PAR (FN2 FEEL))
(S3) ((PRCASE LOCA) EN DEHORS DE (FN1 POINT SPREAD))

Here *DO indicates a wide class of action formulas: any, in fact, whose heads are not PDO, DBE, or BE.

When the program enters the second fragment of (It was made) (outof wood) it knows from the whole interlingual representation described earlier that the case of that fragment is SOURCE and its mark is "made." The mark word has DO as its head, and so the case and mark predicates PRCASE and PRMARK in the first stereotype are both satisfied. Thus, "de" is tentatively generated from the first stereotype and FN1 is applied, because of its definition, to the object formula in this template, the one for "wood." The arguments of FN1 are STUFF and THING, and the function finds STUFF as the head of the formula for "wood" in the full template, is satisfied, and generates "bois" from the stereotype for "wood."

In the case of the second fragment of (He killed him) (outof hatred), the two predicates of the first stereotype for "outof" would again be satisfied, but (FN1 THING STUFF) would fail with the formula for "hatred," whose head is STATE. The next stereotype (S2) would be tried; the same two predicates would be satisfied, and now (FN2 FEEL) would be applied to (NOTPLEASE(FEEL STATE)), the formula for "hatred." But FN2 by its definition does not examine formula heads, but rather seeks for the containment of one of its arguments within the formula. Here it finds FEEL within the formula and so generates the French word stereotype for "hatred."

Similar considerations apply to the third example sentence involving the LOCATION case, though in that case there would be no need to work through the two SOURCE stereotypes already discussed, since, when a case is assigned to a fragment during analysis, the only stereotypes left in the interlingual representation are those that correspond to the assigned case.

In the case of fragments with a key, TIE routines search the stereotypes for the key until they find one that matches the fragment and its mark except with respect to case. So in the sentence (I live) (outof town), the analysis routines assign LOCATION to the second fragment in the first place, because they locate in the third stereotype for "outof" a formula for the object of the preposition whose head is POINT.

3.3.5 The Generation of French

Much of the heart of the French generation has been described in outline in the last section, since it was impossible to describe the dictionary and its stereotypes without describing the generative role of the stereotypes.

To complete this sketch we need some description of the way in which generations from the stereotype of a key and of the mark for the same fragment interlock — the mark being in a different fragment — as control flows backwards and forwards between the stereotypes of different words in search of a satisfactory French output. There is not space available here for description of the bottom level of the generation program — the concord and number routines — which in even the simplest cases needs access to mark information (e.g., in locating the gender of "heureux" in (John seems) (to be happy) translated as "Jean semble etre heureux").

Again, much of the detailed content of the generation is to be found in the functions evaluating to French words that I have arbitrarily named FN1, ..., etc. Some of these seek detail down to gender markers. For example, one would expect to get the correct translations "Je voyageais en France" but "...au Canada" with the aid of functions, say, FNF and FNM that seek not only specific formula heads but genders as well. So, among the stereotypes for the English "in" we would expect to find (given that formulas for land areas have SPREAD as their heads): ...A (FNM SPREAD)) and ...EN (FNF SPREAD)).

It is not expected that there will be more than twenty or so of these inner stereotype functions in all, though it should be noted at this point that there is no level of generation that does not require quite complicated semantic information processing. I have in mind here what one might call the bottom level of generation, the addition and compression of articles. An MT program has to get "Je bois DU vin" for "I drink wine," but "J'aime LE vin" for "I like wine." Now there is no analog for this distinction in English and nothing about the meanings of "like" and "drink" that accounts for the difference in the French in a way intuitively acceptable to the English speaker. At present we are expecting to generate the difference by means of stereotypes that seek the notion USE in the semantic codings — which will be located in "drink" but not in "like," and to use this to generate the "de" where appropriate.

The overall control function of the generation expects five different types of template names to occur:

(1) *THIS *DO *ANY where:
    *THIS is any substantive head (not DTHIS)
    *DO is any real action head (not BE, PDO, DBE) and
    *ANY is any of *DO or KIND or DTHIS

With this type of template the number, person, and gender of the verb are deduced from the French stereotype for the subject part.

(2) type *THIS BE KIND is treated with type 1.

(3) DTHIS *DO *ANY These templates arise when a subject has been split from its action by fragmentation. The mark of the fragment is then the subject. Or the template may represent an object action phrase, such as a simple infinitive with an implicit subject to be determined from the mark.

(4) *THIS DBE DTHIS Templates of this type represent the subject split off from its action, represented by a type (2) template, above. The translation is simply generated from the stereotype of the subject formula, since the rest is dummies, though there may arise cases of the form DTHIS DBE KIND where generation is only possible from a qualifier, as in the second fragment of (I like tall CM) (blond CM) (and blue-eyed Germans).

(5) DTHIS PDO *REAL
    Templates of this type represent preposition phrases, and the translation is generated as described from the key stereotype, after which the translation for the template object is added (*REAL denotes any head in *THIS or is KIND).

The general strategy for the final stages of the program is to generate French word strings directly from the template structure assigned to a fragment of English text. The first move is to find out which of the five major types of template distinguished above is the one attached to the fragment under examination.

For a fragment as simple as "John already owns a big red car," the program would notice that the fragment has no mark or key, hence, by default, the generation is to proceed from a stereotype which is a function of the general type of the template attaching to the fragment. The bare name of the template for this one fragment sentence is MAN HAVE THING, and inspection of the types above will show this to be a member of type (1). The stereotype is a function, let us say FTEMP, of that template type and, to conform with the general format for stereotypes described earlier, this can be thought of as being one of the stereotypes for the "null word."

In this case, in the generation of French, function FTEMP evaluates to a French word string whose order is that of the stereotypes of the English words of the fragment. This order is directed by the presence of the first type of template, comprising an elementary sequence subject-action-object. This is done recursively so that, along with the French words generated for those English words whose formulas constitute the bare template (i.e., "John," "own," and "car"), formulas are generated that are merely dependent on the main formulas of the template — in this case the formulas for "already," "big," and "red."

If complex stereotypes are located while generating for any of the words of the fragment, then generation from these newly found stereotypes immediately takes precedence over further generation from the last stereotype at the level above ("complex" simply means full stereotypes which have constituents that are functions as well as French words).

Now suppose we consider the two-fragment sentence "I order John to leave." The fragments will be presented to the generation program in the form described earlier: with key, mark, case, and phase information attached to each fragment:

> (I order John)   nil:nil:nil:0
> (to leave)   to:order:OBJE:2

Also attached to the fragments will be full templates whose bare template names in this case will be MAN TELL MAN and DTHIS MOVE DTHIS, respectively.

The generation program enters the first fragment, which has no mark or key; so it starts to generate, as before, from a stereotype for the null word, which again is one for the first template type. This gets the subject right: "je" from the stereotype for "I," later to be modified to "j" by the concord routine. It then enters the stereotypes for the action, the first being

> (ORDONNER A (FN1 MAN FOLK)).

The head of the formula for "John" is MAN. FN1 here is an arbitrary name for a function that looks into the formula for the object place of a template and, if the head of that formula is any of the function's arguments, it returns the stereotype value of that formula. In this case FN1 is satisfied by "John," thus that stereotype for "order" is satisfied. The program generates from it the sequence "ordonner à Jean," giving the correct sequence "Je\$ ordonner\$ à Jean" (where \$ indicates the need for further minor processing by the concord routine). The stereotype has now been exhausted — nothing in it remains unevaluated or ungenerated; similarly, the fragment is exhausted, since no words remain whose stereotypes have not been generated, either directly or via the stereotype for some other word, and so the program passes on to the second fragment.

The program enters the second fragment and finds that it has a mark, namely "order." It then consults the stereotype in hand for "order" in the first fragment to see if it was exhausted. It was, and so the program turns to the stereotypes for "to," the key of the second fragment. Among those whose first predicate has the argument OBJE will be the stereotype.

> ((PRCASE OBJE) (PRMARK FORCE TELL) DE (FNINF *DO))

The head of the current formula for "order," the mark of the second fragment is FORCE, and PRMARK seeks and compares its arguments with the head of the mark formula. The predicates are seen to be satisfied and the program generates "de" after seeing that FNINF is satisfied, since an action formula for "leave" follows, whose head, MOVE, is in the class *DO.

FNINF on evaluation finds the implicit subject of the infinitive. That is unnecessary here, but would be essential in examples only slightly more complex, such as "Marie regrette de s'etre rejouié trop tôt." Finally, FNINF itself evaluates to the French stereotype selected for "leave." This might give rise to more searching if the use of "leave" dictated its own sequents, as in "I order John to leave by the first train." Here, however, the evaluation terminates immediately to "partir," since the sentence stops. Thus the correct French string "Je$ ordonne$ à Jean de partir" has been generated.

The last example was little more than a more detailed redescription of the processes described in the dictionary Section, (3.3.4), in connection with the example "I advise John to have patience." However, now that we have dealt fully with a fairly standard case and shown the recursive use of stereotypes in the generation of French on a fragment-by-fragment basis, we can discuss a final pair of examples in which a more powerful stereotype can dictate and take over the generation of other fragments.

If we were to consider in detail the generation of French for the two-fragment sentence (I throw the ball) (outof the window), we should find the process almost identical to that used in the last example. In this case, too, the main stereotype used to generate the French for the first fragment is that of the action — "throw" in this case — and the stereotype for "throw" is exhausted by the first fragment, so that nothing in that stereotype causes the program to inspect the second fragment.

Now consider, in the same format, (I drink wine) (outof a glass). Following the same procedures as before, we shall find ourselves processing the stereotype for "drink," which reads (BOIRE (FN1 (FLOW STUFF))) (FNX1 SOUR PDO THING) ↑ DANS (FNX2 THING)), where "↑" indicates a *halt-point*. The program begins to generate tentatively, evaluating the functions left to right and being prepared to cancel the whole stereotype if any one of them fails. FN1 is applied to the formula for "wine" and specifies the inclusion in its formula, not of one of two elements, but of the whole conventional sub-formula for liquids (FLOW STUFF). This, it finds, is satisfied, and so evaluates to "vin," to be modified by concord to "du vin."

The program now encounters FNX1, a function which by definition applies to the full template for some following fragment. At this point the program evaluates FNX1 which returns a blank symbol if and only if it finds a following fragment with a SOURCE case and a template, the last two elements. of whose bare name are PDO THING, i.e., it is a preposition-type fragment with a physical object as object. This situation would not obtain if the sentence were "I drink the wine outof politeness." If FNX1 is satisfied, as in this case, it causes the generation from this stereotype to halt after generating a blank symbol. Halting in an evaluation is to be taken as quite different from both *exhausting* (all functions evaluated to French word strings or a blank) and *failing* (at least one function evaluates to NIL).

The main control program now passes to the next fragment, in this case "outof a glass." It asks first if it has a mark, which it has, namely "drink," and looks at the stereotype in hand for the mark to see if it is exhausted, which it is not, merely halted. The program therefore continues to generate from the same stereotype, for "drink," producing "du vin," then "dans," followed by the value of FNX2, namely "verre," thus giving the correct tanslation "Je *bois* du vin dans un verre."

The important point here is that the stereotypes for the key to the second fragment, "outof," are never consulted at all. The translations for all the words of the second fragment will have been entered via a stereotype for the previous fragment, the one for "drink." The advantage of this method will be clear: because it would be very difficult, conceptually and within the framework described, to obtain the translation of "outof" as "dans" in this context from the stereotype for "outof," since that translation is specific to the occurrence of certain French words, such as "boire," rather than to the application of certain concepts. In this way the stereotypes can cope with linguistic idiosyncrasy as well as with conceptual regularity. It should be noted, too, that since "dans" is not generated until after the halted stereotype restarts, there is no requirement that the two example fragments be contiguous. The method I have described could cope just as well with (I drink the wine) (I like most) (outof a silver goblet).

For clarification about what words are generated through the stereotypes for what other words, a diagram follows in which lines connect the English word through whose stereotype a generation is done to the word, for which output is generated. All generations conventionally start from ϕ, the null word mentioned above; it is, by convention, the word for which the five basic stereotypes are the stereotype. The more straightforward case (I threw the ball) (outof the window) would be generated as follows:

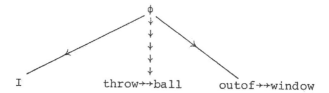

Articles are omitted for simplicity. In this case the new fragment starting with "outof" returns to ϕ to begin generating again. In the more complex case (I drink wine) (outof a glass), the generation pattern would be as follows:

The general rule with action stereotypes, then, is that the more irregular the action, the more information goes into its stereotype and the less is needed in the stereotypes for its sequents. So, for example, there is no need for a stereotype for "outof" to contain DANS at all. Again, just as the regular case "I order John to leave" produced the translation "J'ordonne à Jean de partir" by using the stereotype

for the key "to," the less regular case "I urge John to leave," which requries the quite different construction "J'exhorte Jean à partir," would be dealt with by a halting stereotype for "urge" whose form would be

(EXHORTER(FN1 MAN FOLK) (FNX1 OBJE *DO) ↑ A(FNXINF *DO))

In this case, the stereotype for "to" would never be consulted at all.

Finally, it should be admitted that in the actual analysis and generation system, two items described, "case" and "mark," shrink in importance, though by no means disappear. Their role has been overstressed in this paper, in order to make a clear distinction between the analysis and generation routines and so present a clear interlingual representation whose format is independent of the algorithmic techniques employed. What I sought to avoid was any reference to a "seamless computational whole" all of whose levels seem to presuppose all of the other levels, and which even if it works, cannot be inspected or discussed in any way.

The assignment of the case and mark information demands access to the French stereotypes. It would clearly be absurd to consult the stereotypes to assign this information and then, later, consult them again in order to make use of it in the generation of French. In fact, the analysis and generation of French. In fact, the analysis and generation routines fuse at this point, and the case and mark are located during the generation of the French output. The change in the format that this requires is that the mark predicate PRMARK is not now simply a predicate that checks whether the *already assigned* mark for the fragment in hand meets the specification: it is a predicate that at the same time actively seeks for a mark meeting that specification. And, as with the stereotype functions already described, the failure to find such a mark fails the whole stereotype containing it. There will now be a number of mark predicates fulfilling different roles. The case predicate, conversely, is not diversified but vestigial, because there is now no *previously assigned* case to a fragment for the predicate to check, and the case is now just a label in the dictionary of stereotypes to aid the reader.

A last, quick look at a previous example should make all this clear. Consider again (He hit the boy) (with the wooden leg) as contrasted with the alternative second fragments (with a stick) and (with long hair). Let us consider the analysis routines terminating with the provision of full templates for fragments (and phase information), and let us consider everything that follows that a French generation.

Let us now consider the generation program entering the second fragment, armed with the following list of stereotypes for "with:"

((PRMKOB *ENT) (POSS) A (FN *ENT))
((PRMARK *DO) (INST) AVEC (FN THING))
(PRMARK *ENT) (POSS) A (FN *REAL))

PRMKOB is a directed predicate that seeks for a mark in a preceding fragment (within a range of two fragments). It looks only at candidates whose heads are in the class *ENT, that is, THING, MAN, FOLK, BEAST, or WORLD; entities that can in some sense have parts. In the same sense the heads ACT, STATE, POINT, etc., are not attached to word senses that we can speak of as having parts. PRMKOB compares the formulas for potential marks in the third, object, template position of preceding fragments with the formula for the object in the template for the fragment in hand. And it is true if and only if the latter formula indicates that it ties to a word sense that can be a part of the entity tied to the "candidate mark" formula.

So, in the case of (He hit the boy) (with the wooden leg) PRMKOB finds itself comparing the formulas for "boy" (head MAN) and "leg" (which contains the sub-formula (MAN PART)). In this case PRMKOB is satisfied and the generation continues through the first stereotype, correctly generating "à" for "with" and then the output for "wooden leg." The *REAL in the function in the first stereotype merely indicates that any object in that fragment should then have its stereotype generated (any substantive head is in the class *REAL), because its appropriateness has already been established by the satisfaction of PRMKOB.

Following exactly the procedures described in other examples, it will be seen that (with a stick) fails the first but is translated by the second stereotype, while (with long hair) fails the first two but is correctly generated by the third.

References

[1] Bar-Hillel, Y., "Some Reflections on the Present Outlook for High-Quality Machine Translation," Mimeo, University of Texas, 1970.
[2] Bierwisch, M., "Semantics," in *New Horizons in Linguistics*, Lyons, J., (Ed.), London, 1970.
[3] Klein, S., et al., *The Autoling System*, Tech. Report. #43, Computer Science Dept., University of Wisconsin, 1968.
[4] Lakoff, G., "Linguistics and Natural Logic," *Studies in Generative Semantics #1*, University of Michigan, Ann Arbor, 1970.
[5] McCarthy, J., and Hayes, P., "Some Philosophical Problems from the Standpoint of Artificial Intelligence," in *Machine Intelligence 4*, Edinburgh, 1969.
[6] Michie, D., *On Not Seeing Things*, Experimental Programming Reports #22, University of Edinburgh, 1971.
[7] Montague, R., "English as a Formal Language," in *Linguaggi nella Societa e nella Tecnica*, Milan, 1970.
[8] Nida, E., and Taber, C., *The Theory and Practice of Translation*, Leiden, 1969.
[9] Quillian, R., "The Teachable Language Comprehender," *CACM* (1969).
[10] Sandewall, E., "Representing Natural Language Information in Predicate Calculus," *Machine Intelligence 6*, Edinburgh, 1971.

[11] Schank, R., "Finding the Conceptual Content and Intention of an Utterance in Natural Language Conversation," *Proceedings of the 2nd Joint International Conference on Artificial Intelligence*, London, 1971.

[12] Simmons, R., *Some Semantic Structures for Representing English Meanings*, Tech. Report #NL-1, University of Texas at Austin, 1970.

[13] Wilks, Y., "On-Line Semantic Analysis of English Texts," *Machine Translation and Comp. Linguistics*, 1968.

[14] ———, "Decidability and Natural Language," *Mind*, 1971.

[15] ———, *Grammar, Meaning and the Machine Analysis of Natural Language*, London, 1972.

[16] Winograd, T., *Procedures as a Representation for Data in a Computer Program for Understanding Natural Language*, Project MAC Memo #MAC TR-84, Massachusetts Institute of Technology, 1971.

4

An Intelligent Analyzer and Understander of English

Yorick Wilks
Stanford University

Abstract: *The paper describes a working analysis and generation program for natural language, which handles paragraph length input. Its core is a system of preferential choice between deep semantic patterns, based on what we call "semantic density." The system is contrasted: (1) with syntax oriented linguistic approaches, and (2) with theorem proving approaches to the understanding problem*

4.1 Introduction

After the unhappy conclusions of most early attempts at machine translation, some justification is required for presenting it again as a reasonable computational task. Minsky [4], among others, argued that there could be no machine translation without a system that, in an adequate sense, understood what it was trying to translate. The meaning structures and inference forms that constitute the present system are intended as an understanding system in the required sense, and as such, justify a new attack on an old but important problem.

Machine translation is an important practical task; furthermore, it has a certain theoretical significance for a model of language understanding. For it provides a clear test of the rightness or wrongness of a proposed system for representing meaning, since the output in a second language can be assessed by people unfamiliar with the internal formalism and methods employed. Few other settings for a theory of language analysis leave room for such objective tests. Dialog systems are notoriously difficult to assess; and command systems are restricted to worlds in which commands are relevant, e.g. those of physical objects and the directions for picking them up, which domain excludes the world of real nonimperative discourse about such subjects as friendship, the United Nations, and the problems of juvenile delinquency. On the other hand, conventional systems of linguistics produce only complex representations that can be disputed only on internal grounds. They are never used to produce objective, discussable output, like a sentence in another language that would test the adequacy of the whole representation.

K. Ahmad, C. Brewster and M. Stevenson (eds.), Words and Intelligence 1, 61–82.
© *2007 Springer.*

It should be added here that although the present system is cast in the role of a machine translation system, the popular forms of example to test "understanding"— i.e. finding the correct reference of a pronoun on the basis of knowledge of and inferences about the real world—can all be reconstructed within it, as will be shown.

Since the early machine translation work there has been a considerable development in formal linguistics, in particular, the creation of the school of transformational grammatical analysis. This form of analysis of natural language has little relation to the work described here, and for three reasons.

Firstly, Transformational Grammar was set up to be quite independent of all considerations of meaning, context, and inference, which constitutes something of a disqualification for the present task, namely understanding language. Consider such an even apparently structural-grammatical matter as the ambiguity of prepositions; "out of," for example, is highly ambiguous, which can be seen from any reflection on such sentences as: I live out of town. I hit her out of anger. I threw the ball out of the window. The statue is made out of marble. An objective measure of the ambiguity is that the occurrences of "out of" in those sentences would be translated into French in three different ways. Yet, even in such a basic structural area, Transformational Grammar makes no suggestions whatever as to how the choice should be made. Whereas in the Preference Semantics system, described below, the choice is made in a simple and natural manner. Such defects as this have been to some extent remedied in a recent development of the Transformational Grammar system, Generative Semantics. However, for our purposes Generative Semantics, like Transformational Grammar, suffers from the other two defects below.

Secondly, it is a matter of practical experience, that Transformational Grammar systems have been extremely resistant to computational application. This practical difficulty is in part due to theoretical difficulties concerning the definition and computability of Transformational Grammar systems.

Thirdly, Transformational Grammar and Generative Semantics systems suffer one overwhelming defect, from the point of view of understanding natural language. Both have a "derivational paradigm," which is to say, both envisage a system which constructs a derivation by running from an initial symbol to a language sentence. Such derivations have the function of either accepting a sentence or rejecting it because no such derivation can "reach" the sentence from the starting symbol. Thus all sentences are sorted into two groups by such systems—the acceptable and the unacceptable—and by doing this they claim to define the notion of an "acceptable," "meaningful," or "grammatical" sentence.

One can see how far such a task is from the one of understanding language, for sorting in this way is exactly what human beings do not do when they hear a sentence. They endeavor to interpret it, changing their rules if necessary as they do so. Yet, within the Transformational Grammar and Generative Semantics derivational paradigm, it makes no sense to talk of changing the rules and trying another set, even though that is just what any "intelligent" understanding system must do. For example, most conventional grammatical systems are armed with some rule equivalent to "only animate things perform tasks of acertain class," which compels them to reject such perfectly comprehensible utterances as those which speak of the wind opening doors and cars drinking gas. (It is unimportant here whether any particular system employs such a particular rule. The point here is a general one about behavior in the face of rule failure.) Only an "intelligent" system, outside the derivational paradigm and able to reconsider its own steps, can overcome this defect. The limitations of Transformational Grammar and Generative Semantics systems, from the point of view of this project, have been discussed in detail in [12 and 13].

The proper comparisons for the present work are with systems of analysis orginating from within either artificial intelligence or computational linguistics, none of which (except the work of Woods [17]) owes any strong debt to the Trans-formational Grammar tradition all of which, in differing degrees, make the concept of meaning representation central, such as the work of Simmons [11], Winograd [16], Schank [8], and Sandewall [7].

Some points of difference between these systems and Preference Semantics may be mentioned briefly.

(i) Preference Semantics is very much oriented toward processing realistic text sentences of some complexity and of up to 20 to 30 words long. This difference of emphasis, and the sentence fragmentation and large-scale conceptual linkages its implementation requires, distinguishes Preference Semantics from all the approaches mentioned.

(ii) Preference Semantics copes with the words of a normal vocabulary, and with many senses of them, rather than with single senses of simple object words and actions. It is not wholly clear that the methods of [16] could, even in principle, be extended in that way.

(iii) Preference Semantics contains no conventional grammar for analysis or generation: its task is performed by a strong semantics. This contrasts with Winograd's use of a linguistic grammar and simple marker system, and to some extent with Simmons' use of case grammar.

(iv) Preference Semantics does not take theorem proving techniques, of whichever major type, to be the core manipulations for an understanding system, but rather sees them as techniques to be brought in where appropriate. In this respect it differs most strongly from Sandewall, whose work assumes some form of theorem prover of a resolution type, into which his predicate calculus representations of natural language sentences can be plugged. Preference Semantics also differs here from Winograd, whose PLANNER-based system is far more oriented to the proving of truths than the Preference Semantics system described below. Another major difference between Preference Semantics and these two other systems is that Preference Semantics inference rules operate on higher level items, structures of semantic concepts and cases representing whole sentences and paragraphs of text, rather than on items at the level of text words and facts (or predicates and features that replace such items one to one in grammatically parsed structures). The latter approach leads to an enormous multiplication of axioms/inference rules, with all the subsequent difficulty of searching among them.

Nothing here, of course, denies the need for knowledge of the physical world, and inferences based upon it, for understanding and translation. What is being argued for here is nondeductive, common sense inference expressed in a formalism that is a natural extension of the meaning representation itself.

A simple case will establish the need for such inference: consider the sentence "The soldiers fired at the women, and we saw several of them fall." That sentence will be taken to mean that the women fell, so that when, in analyzing the sentence, the question arises of whether "them" refers to "soldiers" or "women" (a choice which will result in a differently gendered pronoun in French), we will have to be able to infer that things fired at often fall, or at least are much more likely to fall than things doing the firing. Hence there must be access to inferential information here, above and beyond the meanings of the constituent words, from which we could infer that hurt beings tend to fall down.

The deductive approaches mentioned claim to tackle just such examples, of course, but in this paper we will argue for a different approach to them, which we shall call common sense inference rules. These are expressions of "partial information" (in McCarthy's phrase): generalizations, like the one above about hurt things tending to fall down, which (a) are not invariably true and (b) tend to be of a very high degree of generality indeed. It is part of the case being made here that the importance of such apparently obvious truths in natural language understanding is considerable, but also easy to overlook.

4.2 A System of Semantics Based Language Analysis

A fragmented text is to be represented by an interlingual structure, called a *Semantic Block*, which consists of *templates* bound together by *paraplates* and *common sense inferences*. These three items consist of *formulas* (and predicates and functions ranging over them and subformulas), which in turn consist of *elements*.

Some of these semantic items represent text items in a fairly straightforward way as follows:

Items in semantic representation	Corresponding text items
formula	English word sense
template	English clause or simple sentence
semantic block	English paragraph or text

Paraplates and common sense inferences, as we shall see, serve to bind templates together in the semantic block. Semantic elements correspond to nothing in a text, but are the primitives out of which *all* the above complex items are made up.

4.3 Semantic Elements

Elements are 70 primitive semantic units used to express the semantic entities, states, qualities, and actions about which humans speak and write. The elements fall into five classes, which can be illustrated as follows (elements in uppercase, and the approximate concept expressed in lowercase):

(a) Entities: MAN (human being), STUFF (substances), SIGN (verbal and written symbols), THING (physical object), PART (parts of things), FOLK (human groups), ACT (acts), STATE (states of existence), BEAST (animals), etc.
(b) Actions: FORCE (compels), CAUSE (causes to happen), FLOW (moving as liquids do), PICK (choosing), BE (exists), etc.
(c) Type indicators: KIND (being a quality), HOW (being a type of action), etc.
(d) Sorts: CONT (being a container), GOOD (being morally acceptable), THRU (being an aperture), etc.
(e) Cases: TO (direction), SOUR (source), GOAL (goal or end), LOCA (location), SUBJ (actor or agent), OBJE (patient of action), IN (containment), POSS (possessed by), etc.

In addition to these primitive elements, there are *class* elements whose names begin with an asterisk, such as *ANI for the class of animate elements MAN, BEAST, and FOLK; *HUM for human elements MAN and FOLK; *PHYSOB, which denotes the class of elements containing MAN, THING, etc., but not, of course, STUFF. There are also action class elements such as *DO.

The elements are not to be thought of as denotative, even of intensional entities, but as the elements of a micro-language in which more complex concepts are expressed. Thus their justification is wholly in terms of their use to construct semantic *formulas*.

4.4 Semantic Formulas

Formulas are constructed from elements and right and left brackets. They express the senses of English words; one formula to each sense. The formulas are binarily bracketed lists of whatever depth is necessary to express the word sense. Their most important element is always their rightmost, which is called the *head* of the formula, and it expresses the most general category under which the word sense in question falls. However, an element that is used as a head can function within formulas as well. So, for example, CAUSE is the head of the formula for the action sense of "drink" and it may be thought of as a "causing action," but CAUSE can also occur within the formula for a word sense, as it does, for example, within the formula for the action sense of "box," which can be paraphrased in English as "striking a human with the goal of *causing* him pain."

It will help in understanding the formulas to realize that there are conventional two-element subformulas, such as (FLOW STUFF) for liquidity, to avoid the introduction of new primitives. Another such is (THRU PART) to indicate an aperture. Formulas can be thought of, and written out, as binary trees of semantic primitives. In that form they are not unlike the lexical decomposition trees of Lakoff and McCawley. Here is a selection of formulas that will be needed in later examples. In each case I give the formulas as a tree of subformulas, with the head as the rightmost element, then as a table of subformulas, and lastly as a paraphrase in English. The formulas are for the English words "drink" (as an action), "grasp" (as a *physical* action), "fire at." I also give, in a less extended range of forms, the formulas for "policeman," "big," "interrogates," "crook" as a human being and as a physical object, and "singing" as an activity.

Nothing at all depends on these particular codings. What is at issue here is the claim that codings of this degree of complexity, and containing at least this much semantic information, are necessary for doing any interesting degree of linguistic analysis.

"drink" (action) → ((*ANI SUBJ) (((FLOW STUFF) OBJE)
((SELF IN) ((((*ANI (THRU PART)) TO) (BE CAUSE)))))

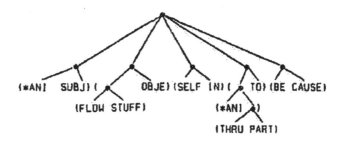

Formulas are best seen as nestings of *subformulas*, each of which is either a case specification or a direct specification on the head itself. Within any subformula there is a dependence at every level of the left half of a binary pair of the right half. This dependence relation is normally to be understood as type subspecification, in the way that *ANI specifies the type of agent in the example above. The mutual relation of the subformulas is not one of dependence, even though all the other subformulas be thought of as dependent on the rightmost subformula containing the head. However, the order of the subformulas is significant, since, for example, an object specification is considered to be the object of *all* actions to its right in the formula, whether they are the head or at some other level in the formula.

Let us now decompose the formula for "drink." It is to be read as an action, preferably done by animate things (*ANI SUB) ; to liquids, or to substances that flow ((FLOW STUFF)OBJE) ; causing the liquid to be in the animate thing (SELF IN); and

Subformula	Case/Act	Value	Explanation
(*ANI SUBJ)	SUBJ	*ANI	the preferred agent is animate
((FLOW STUFF)OBJE)	OBJE	(FLOW STUFF)	preferred object is liquid
(SELF IN)	IN	SELF	the container is the self, the subject
(((* ANI(THRU PART))TO)	TO	(* ANI(THRU PART))	the direction of the action is a human aperture(the mouth)
(BECAUSE)	CAUSE	BE	the action is of causing to be (somewhere else)

via (TO indicating the direction case) a particular aperture of the animate thing, the mouth, of course. It is hard to indicate a notion as specific as "mouth" with such general concepts. But we think that it would be simply irresponsible to suggest adding MOUTH as a semantic primitive, as do semantic systems that simply add an awkward lexeme as a new "primitive."

This notion of "preferring" is important: SUBJ case displays the preferred agents of actions, and OBJE case the preferred objects, or patients. We cannot enter such preferences as stipulations, as many linguistic systems do, such as Fodor and Katz's "selection restrictions." For we can be said to drink gall and wormwood, and cars are said to drink gasoline. It is proper to prefer the normal (quite different from probabilistically expecting it, we shall argue), but it would be absurd, in an intelligent understanding system, not to accept the abnormal if it is described. Not only everyday metaphor but the description of the simplest fiction require it.

A formula expresses the meaning of the word senses to which it is attached. This claim assumes a common sense distinction between explaining the meaning of a word and knowing facts about the thing the word indicates. The formulas are intended only to express the former, to express what we might find in a reasonable dictionary, though in a formal manner.

Now let us consider:

"grasp"(physical action) → ((*ANI SUBJ)((*PHYSOB OBJE)
(((THIS(MAN PART))INST) (TOUCH SENSE)))))

So, grasping in this sense is something preferably done by an animate thing to a physical object, done with the hand as instrument: an action of physical contact with the object. The mental sense of "grasp" is a THINK action.

Now consider:

"fire at" (action) → ((*HUM SUBJ)((*ANI OBJE)
((STRIK GOAL) ((THING MOVE)CAUSE))))

The fact that the bullet is the agent of the moving is implicit, and agents are unmarked except at the top level of the formula, although objects are marked at every level. So then, "firing at" is causing a thing to move so as to strike an animate target.

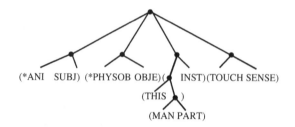

Subformula	Cast/Act	Value	Explanation
(*ANI SUBJ)	SUBJ	*ANI	the preferred agent is animate
(*PHYSOB OBJE)	OBJE	*PHYSOB	the preferred agent is a physical object
((THIS(MAN PART))INST)	INST	((THIS(MAN PART))	the instrument is a human part, the hand
(TOUCH SENSE)	SENSE	TOUCH	the action is of physical contact

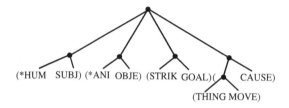

Subformula	Cast/Act	Value	Explanation
(*HUM SUBJ)	SUBJ	*HUM	preferably done by a human
(*ANI OBJE)	OBJE	*ANI	preferably done to an animate thing
(STRIK GOAL)	GOAL	STRIK	the aim being to strike the animate thing
((THING MOVE)CAUSE)	CAUSE	(THING MOVE)	the action is of causing an object (the bullet) to move

Let me now give the remaining formulas, with only an explanation, if the principles of the tree and table representation are now clear.

$$\text{"policeman"} \rightarrow ((\text{FOLK SOUR})(((((\text{NOTGOOD MAN})\text{OBJE})\text{PICK}) \ (\text{SUBJ MAN})))$$

i.e. a person who selects bad persons out of the body of people (FOLK). The case marker SUBJ is the dependent in the last element pair, indicating that the normal "top first" order for subject-entities in formulas has been violated, and necessarily so if the head is also to be the last element in linear order.

$$\text{"big"} \rightarrow ((\text{*PHYSOB POSS}) (\text{MUCH KIND}))$$

i.e. a property preferably possessed by physical objects (substances are not big).

$$\text{"interrogates"} \rightarrow ((\text{MAN SUBJ}) ((\text{MAN OBJE}) (\text{TELL FORCE})))$$

i.e. forcing to tell something, done preferably by humans, to humans.

"crook" → ((((NOTGOOD ACT)OBJE)DO) (SUBJ MAN))

i.e. a man who does bad acts.

"crook" → ((((((THIS BEAST)OBJE)FORCE)(SUBJ
MAN))POSS)(LINE THING))

i.e. a straight object possessed by a man who controls a particular kind of animal.

"singing" → ((*ANI SUBJ)((SIGN OBJE)((MAN
SENSE)CAUSE)))))

which is to say, an act by an animate agent of causing a person to experience a sign, the song.

4.5 Semantic Templates

Just as the semantic elements have been explained by seeing how they functioned within formulas, so formulas, one level higher, are to be explained by describing how they function within *templates*, the third kind of semantic item in the system. The notion of a template is intended to correspond to an intuitive one of message: one not reducible merely to unstructured associations of word-senses.

A template consists of a network of whole formulas, and its connectivity is between an agent-, action-, and object-formula, such that from any one of these members of the basic triple a list of other formulas may depend. In any particular example, one or more of the formulas may be replaced by a dummy. We shall discuss such cases further.

The program sees each clause, phrase, or primitive sentence of text (called its *fragments*) as strings of formulas, drawn, one for each text word, from a dictionary. The program attempts to locate one or more templates in each string of formulas by first looking only at their head elements and seeking for acceptable sequences of heads.

A *bare template* is such an acceptable, or intuitively interpretable, sequence of an agent head, an action head, and an object head (subject again to the proviso about dummies). If there is a sequence of formulas whose heads are identical to such a bare template of elements, then the sequence of *formulas* is a template for that fragment, taken together with any other formulas that may be found to depend on those three main formulas.

(CAUSE is the head of the verbal sense of "father"; "to father" is analyzed as "to cause to have life.")

The first sequence has no underlying bare template because there is no intuitively interpretable element triple there, in the sense in which MAN CAUSE MAN in the

	small	men	sometimes	father	big	sons
	KIND	MAN	HOW	MAN	KIND	MAN
and	KIND	MAN	HOW	CAUSE	KIND	MAN

second sequence is intuitively interpretable as "a human causes another human to exist." Thus we have already disambigulated "father," at the same time as picking up a sequence of three formulas, which is the core of the template for the sentence. It must be emphasized here that the template is the sequence of formulas (which are trees or structured lists) and is not to be confused with the bare template, or triple of elements (heads) used to locate it.

It is a hypothesis of this work that we can build up a finite but useful inventory of bare templates adequate for the analysis of ordinary language: a list that can be interpreted as the messages that people want to convey at some fairly high level of generality (for template matching is not in any sense phrase-matching at the surface level). The bare templates are an attempt to explicate a notion of a nonatomistic linguistic pattern: to be located whole in sentences in the way that human beings appear to when they read or listen.

We would not wish to defend, item by item, the particular template list in use at any given moment. Such lists are always subject to modification by experience, as are the formulas and even the inventory of basic elements. The only defense is that the system using them actually works; and if anyone replies that its working depends on mere inductive generalization, we can only remind them of Garvin's obvious but invaluable remark that all linguistic generalizations are, and must be, inductive.

Let us now illustrate the central processes of expansion and preference, in which the formulas become active items guiding the extension of the template network from a triple of formulas to a full template with preference bonds and dependent formulas. Let us consider the sentence "The big policeman interrogated the crook," for which we already have the appropriate formulas set out above.

The template matching algorithm will see this sentence as a string of formulas, one for each of its words, and will look only at the heads of the formulas. I shall now write [crook(man)] to denote not the English words in the square brackets but *the formula for the word or words*. Then, since MAN FORCE MAN is in the inventory of bare templates, one scan of the string of formulas containing [crook(man)] will pick up the sequence of formulas [policeman][interrogated][crook(man)], in that order. Again, when a string containing the formula [crook(thing)], the shepherd's sense of "crook," is scanned, since MAN FORCE THING is also a proper bare template, the sequence of formulas [policeman][interrogated][crook(thing)] will also be selected as a possible initial structure for the sentence. I should add here that the formula for both *tenses* of "interrogates" is the same, the tense difference being indicated by a tense element put into the formula during the process of expansion now being described.

We now have two possible template representations for the sentence after the initial match; both are triples of formulas in actor-action-object form. Next, the templates are expanded, if possible. This process consists of extending the simple networks we have so far, both by attaching other formulas into the network and by strengthening the bonds between those already in the template, if possible. Qualifier formulas can be attached where appropriate, and so the formula [big] is tied to that for "policeman" in both templates. But now comes a crucial difference between the two representations: one which will resolve the sense of "crook."

The expansion algorithm looks into the subparts of the formulas that express preferences to see if any of the preferences are satisfied: as we saw, the formula [big] prefers to qualify physical objects. A policeman is such, and that additional dependency is marked in both templates: similarly for the preference of "interrogate" for human actors in both representations. The difference comes with preferred objects: only the formula [crook(man)] for human crooks can satisfy that preference for human objects, since the formula [crook(thing)] for shepherd's crooks, cannot. Hence the former template network is denser by one dependency, and is preferred over the latter in all subsequent processing: its connectivity is (ignoring the "the's"): [big] → [policeman] →↔ [interrogates] ↔← [crook(man)] and so that becomes the template for this sentence. The other possible template (one arrow for each preferential dependency established, and a double arrow to mark the standard, nonpreferential, link between the three major formulas of the template) was connected as follows: [big] → [policeman] →↔ [interrogates] ↔ [crook(thing)] and it is now discarded.

Thus the parts of the formulas that express preferences of various sorts are not only used to express the meaning of the corresponding word sense, but they can also be interpreted as implicit procedures for the construction of correct templates. This preference for the greatest semantic density works well, and can be seen as an expression of what Joos calls "semantic axiom number one" [2], that the right meaning is the least meaning, or what Scriven [10] has called "the trick [in meaning analysis] of creating redundancies in the input." As we shall see, this uniform principle works over both the areas that are conventionally distinguished in linguistics as syntax and semantics. There is no such distinction in this system, since all manipulations are of formulas and templates, and these are all constructed out of elements of a single type.

4.6 Templates and Linguistic Syntax

As a further example of linguistic syntax done by preference, let us take the sentence "John gave Mary the book," onto which the matching routine will have matched two bare templates, since it has no reason so far to prefer one to the other, as follows:

The expansion routine now seeks for dependencies between formulas, in addition to those between the three formulas constituting the template itself. In the case of the first bare template, a GIVE action can be expanded by any substantive formula

John	gave	Mary	the book
MAN	GIVE		THING
MAN	GIVE	MAN	

to its immediate right which is not already part of the bare template (which is to say that indirect object formulas can depend on the corresponding action formula). Again "book" is qualified by an article, which fact is not noticed by the second bare template. So then, by expanding the first bare template we have established in the following dependencies at the surface level, where the dependency arrows "→" correspond to *preferential* relations established between formulas for the words linked.

$$\text{John} \leftrightarrow \text{gave} \leftrightarrow \text{book}$$
$$\uparrow \qquad \uparrow$$
$$\text{Mary} \qquad \text{the}$$

But if we try to expand the second bare template by the same method, we find we cannot, because the formula for "Mary" cannot be made dependent on the one for "give," since in that template "Mary" has already been seen, wrongly of course, as a direct object of giving, hence it cannot be an indirect object as well. So then, the template MAN GIVE MAN cannot be expanded to yield any dependency arcs connecting formulas to the template; whereas the template MAN GIVE THING yields two dependency arcs on expansion, and so gives the preferred representation.

This general method can yield virtually all the results of a conventional grammar covering the same range of expressions, while using only relations between semantic elements.

4.7 Case Ambiguity

In the actual implementation of the system, an input text is initially fragmented, and templates are matched with each fragment of the text. As we shall see, there are then complex routines for establishing contextual ties between these templates separated by fragmentation. However, it is claimed here that, for dealing with text containing realistically long and complicated sentences, some such initial fragmentation is both psychologically and computationally important.

The input routine fragments paragraphs at the occurrence of any of an extensive list of *key* words. The list contains all punctuation marks, subjunctions, conjunctions, and prepositions. In difficult cases, described in detail in [14], fragmentations are made even though a key word is not present, as at the slash in "John knows / Mary loves him," while in other cases a fragmentation is not made in the presence of a key word, such as "that" in "John loves that woman."

Let us consider the sentence "John is / in the country," fragmented as shown. It should be clear that the standard agent-act-object form of template cannot be matched onto the fragment "John is." In such a case, a degenerate template MAN

BE DTHIS is matched onto the two items of this sentence; the last item DTHIS being a dummy object, indicated by the D.

With the second fragment "in the country," a dummy subject DTHIS fills out the form to give a degenerate template DTHIS PBE POINT. The PBE is the same as the head of the formula for "in," since formulas for prepositions are assimilated to those for actions and have the head PDO or PBE. The fact that they originate in a preposition is indicated by the P, so distinguishing them from straightforward action formulas with heads DO and BE. POINT (indicates a spatial location that is not a movable physical object) is the head of the formula for "country," so this bare template triple for the fragment only tells us that "something is at a point in space." At a later stage, after the preliminary assignment of template structures to individual fragments, *TIE* routines attach the structures for separated fragments back together. In that process the dummies are tied back to their antecedents. So, in "John is in the country," the DTHIS in the MAN BE DTHIS template for the first fragment of the sentence ties to the whole template for the second fragment, expressing where John is.

It is very important to note that a preference is between alternatives. If the only structure derivable does *not* satisfy a declared preference, then it is accepted anyway. Only in that way can we deal naturally with metaphor.

So, in examples like "I heard an earthquake / singing / in the shower" (fragmentation as indicated by slashes), as contrasted with "I heard / an earthquake sing / in the shower," we shall expect, in the first case, to derive the correct representation because of the preference of notions like singing for animate agents. This is done by a simple extension of the density techniques to relations between structures for different fragments by considering, in this case, alternative connectivities for dummy parts of templates.

Thus, there will be a dummy subject and object template for /singing/, DTHIS CAUSE DTHIS, based on the formula for "singing" given earlier.

Now the overall density will be greater when the agent DTHIS, in the template for "singing," is tied to a formula for "I" in a preceding template, than when it is tied to one for "earthquake," since only the former satisfies the preference for an animate agent, and so the correct interpretation of the whole utterance is made.

But, and here we come to the point of this example, in the second sentence, with "sing" no such exercise of preference is possible, and the system must accept an interpretation in which the earthquake sings, since only that can be meant.

In order to give a rough outline of the system, I have centered our description on the stages of analysis within the individual fragment. After what has been described so far, *TIE* routines are applied to the expanded templates in a context of templates for other fragments of the same sentence or paragraph. The same techniques of dependency and preference are applied between full templates for different fragments of a sentence or paragraph. At that stage, (1) case ties are established between templates (using the same cases as occur within formulas at a lower level); (2) dummies are attached to what they stand for as we indicated with the earthquake example; (3) remaining ambiguities are resolved; and (4) anaphoric ties are settled.

4.8 Paraplates and Case Ambiguity

The first of these tasks is done by applying *paraplates* to the template codings, using the same density techniques one level further up, as it were. Paraplates are complex items having the general form:

$$\langle \text{list of predicates on mark-template} \rangle \langle \text{case} \rangle$$
$$\langle \text{list of predicates on case-template} \rangle$$
$$\langle \text{generation stereotype} \rangle$$

A stereotype is a context sensitive generation pattern which will be described in the section on generation below, and in what follows here I shall give the paraplates *without* the attached stereotypes. The paraplates are essentially patterns that span two templates, which I call the mark and case templates, where the mark template generally precedes, though not necessarily immediately, the case template. If the predicates are all satisfied by the contents of the two templates, then that paraplate is considered to match onto the two templates and the case ambiguity of the preposition that functions as the pseudo-action in the second template is solved. Thus if we were analyzing "He ran the mile in four minutes" and we considered the template for the second fragment "in four minutes," we would find that all the predicates in some paraplate for TIMELOCATION case matched onto the appropriate parts of the templates for the two template fragments, and we would then know that the case of the second template was indeed TIMELOCATION and not, say, CONTAINMENT, as it would be in "He ran the mile in a plastic bag."

The paraplates are attached, as left-right ordered lists, to key words in English, generally prepositions and subjunctions. Consider the following three schematic paraplates for senses of "in" written out in order of preference below. These are presented without generation stereotypes for ease of explanation, but with a description in lowercase of which sense of "in" is in question in each line. The notion of *mark* is the standard intuitive one of the point of dependence of a phrase or clause. Thus, in "He ran the mile in four minutes" the second clause may be said to depend on the action "ran," which is then its mark. Whereas, in "He liked the old man in the corner," the mark of the second fragment is "man."

I will write the three paraplates out, first in linear order as they really are, and then in tabular form for ease of comprehension. The linear order is to be understood as corresponding to that of the six major formulas of the mark and case templates. The predicates in the paraplates may refer to any or all of these. The paraplates are called in on encountering the ambiguous subjunction, or most usually, ambiguous preposition that always functions as the pseudo-action of the second template—the one in hand, as it were. I have put a slash in the paraplate to indicate where the shift is, from predicates on the mark template to those on the case template. Also, where predicates have atomic arguments, like 2OBCAS below, it indicates that those elements are separate arguments of the predicate. Where a predicate, like PRMARK below, has an argument that is a list, that list is a subformula that has to be located whole in the appropriate template formula so as to satisfy the predicate in question.

(1) (PRMARK (MOVE CAUSE))(2OBCAS INST GOAL) /
    (TO into) (PROBJE (CONT THING))
(2) (PRMARK *DO) (2OBHEAD) / (LOCA make part)
(3) (PRMARK (MOVE CAUSE)) / (TO into) ((PROBJE(CONT THING))

What is not made absolutely clear by that form of the paraplates is where, on the six formulas of the two templates, each of the above predicates matches. Let us now set out each paraplate vertically in six lines, corresponding in turn to agent of first template, action of first template, object of first template, and then the same order for the second, case template.

Now consider the sentence "I put the key / in the lock," fragmented at the slash as shown. Let us consider that two templates have been set up for the second fragment: one for "lock" as a fastener, and one for the raising lock on a canal. Both formulas may be expected to refer to the containment case, and so to satisfy (PROBJE CONT). We apply the first paraplate and find that it fits only for the template with the correct (fastener) sense of "lock," since only there will 2OBCAS be satisfied, i.e. where the formulas for "lock" and "key" both have a subformula under GOAL indicating that their purpose is to close something. The third paraplate will fit with the template for the canal sense of "lock," but the first is a more extensive fit (indicated by the order of the paraplates, since the higher up the paraplate list, the more nontrivial template functions a paraplate contains) and is preferred. This preference has simultaneously selected both the right template for the second fragment and the correct paraplate linking the two templates for further generation tasks.

If we now take the sentence "He put the number / in the table," with two different templates for the second fragment (corresponding to the list and flat object senses of "table" respectively) we shall find that the intuitively correct template (the list sense) fails the first paraplate but fits the second, thus giving us the "make part of" sense of "in," and the right (list) sense of "table," since formulas for "number" and (list) "table" have the same head SIGN, though the formula for (flat, wooden) "table" does not.

Conversely, in the case of "He put the fork / in the table," fitting the correct template with the third paraplate will yield "into" sense of "in" (case DIRECTION) and the physical object sense of "table"; and this will be the preferred reading. Here we see the fitting of paraplates, and by choosing the densest preferential fit, which is always selecting the highest paraplate on the list that fits, we determine both word sense ambiguity and the case ambiguity of prepositions at once. Paraplate fitting makes use of deeper nested parts (essentially the case relations other than SUBJ and OBJE) of the formulas than does the template matching.

(1)

	FIRST AGENT
(PRMARK (MOVE CAUSE))	FIRST ACTION
(2OBCAS INST GOAL)	FIRST OBJECT
	SECOND AGENT
(TO into)	SECOND ACTION
(PROBJE (CONT THING))	SECOND OBJECT

(2)

	FIRST AGENT
(PRMARK *DO)	FIRST ACTION
(2OBHEAD)	FIRST OBJECT
	SECOND ACTION
(LOCA make part)	SECOND AGENT

(3)

	SECOND OBJECT
	FIRST AGENT
(PRMARK(MOVE CAUSE))	FIRST ACTION
	FIRST OBJECT
	SECOND AGENT
(TO into)	SECOND ACTION
(PROBJE (CONT THING))	SECOND OBJECT

*DO is a wide class of action heads, TO and LOCA are case markers, 2OBCAS and 2OBHEAD are simply predicates that look at both the object (third) formulas of the current template (the second) and of the preceding template, i.e. at two objects. 2OBHEAD is true iff the two have the same head, and 2OBCAS is true iff they contain the same GOAL or INSTRUMENT subformula. The fact that those two predicates actually apply at two of the six places is a notational weakness in the tabular display above. PRMARK is a predicate on the semantic form of the mark, or a word governing the fragment that the key begins. In all the following examples, the mark is the action in the first fragment, and the predicate is satisfied iff it is a (MOVE CAUSE) action: an action that causes something to move. Similarly, PROBJE is a predicate on the semantic form of the object (third formula) of the current template, and is satisfied if the predicate's argument is found in the formula.

4.9 Anaphora and References

The TIE routines also deal with simple cases of anaphora on a simple preference basis. In cases such as "I bought the wine, / sat on a rock / and drank it," it is easy to see that the last word should be tied by TIE to "wine," and not "rock." This matter is settled by density after considering alternative ties for "it," and seeing which yields the denser representation overall. It will be "wine" in this case since "drink" prefers a liquid object.

In more complex cases of anaphora that require access to more information than is contained in formulas, templates, or paraplates, the system brings down what we referred to earlier as common sense inference rules.[1] Cases that require them will be ones like the sentence: "The soldiers fired at the women and we saw several of them fall." Simple semantic density considerations in *TIE* are inadequate here because both soldiers and women can fall equally easily, yet making the choice correctly is vital for a task like translation became the two alternatives lead to differently gendered pronouns in French. In such cases the Preference Semantics system applies a common sense rule, whose form, using variables and subformulas, would be

$$(1(\text{THIS STRIK})(*\text{ANI } 2)) \leftrightarrow ((*\text{ANI } 2)(\text{NOTUP BE})\text{DTHIS})$$

where the variables are restricted as shown, and the final DTHIS is simply a dummy to fill out the canonical form. This rule can be made more perspicuous by extending the informal [ ] notation to denote the *template form* representation of whatever is in the square brackets, thus: [1 strikes animate2] ↔ [animate2 falls]. The rules are applied to "extractions" from the situations to form chains of templates and template forms, and a rule only ultimately applies if it can function in the shortest, most-preferred, chain.

The way the common sense inferences work is roughly as follows: they are called in at present only when *TIE* is unable to resolve outstanding anaphoras, as in the present example. A process of extraction is then done, and it is to these *extractions*, and the relevant templates, that the common sense rules subsequently apply. The extractions are new template forms inferred from the deep case structure of formulas. So for example, if we were extracting from the template for "John drank the water," then going down into the tree structure of primitive elements in the formula for "drink," given earlier, we would extract that some liquid was now inside an animate thing (from the containment case in the formula for "drink"), and that it went in through an aperture of the animate thing (from the directional case). Moreover, since the extractions are partially confirmed, as it were, by the information about actor and object in the surrounding template, we can, by simple tying of variables, extract new template forms equivalent to, in ordinary language, "the water is in John," etc. These are (when in coded form) the extractions to which the common sense rules apply as the analytical procedure endeavors to build up a chain of extractions and inferences. The preferred chain will, unsurprisingly, be the shortest.

So then in the "women and soldiers" example we extract a coded form, by variable tying in the templates, equivalent to [soldiers strike women], since we can tell from the formula for "fired at" that it is intended to strike the object of the action. We are seeking for partial confirmation of the assertion [X? fall], and such a chain is completed by the rule given, though not by a rule equivalent to, say [something strike X] → [X die], since there is nothing in the sentence as given to

---

[1] The present paper describes the linguistic base, or basic mode, of the system. The extended mode, requiring the rules of partial information and their application to the deep structure of formulas, is described in considerable detail in [15].

partially confirm that particular rule in a chain, and cause it to fit here. Since we are in fact dealing with sub-formulas in the statement of the rules, rather than with words, "fitting" means an "adequate match of sub-formulas."

It is conceivable that there would be another, implausible chain of rules and extractions giving the other result, namely that the soldiers fall: [soldiers fire] ∧ [X fires] → [X fired at] → [X fall], etc. But such a chain would be longer than the one already constructed and would not be preferred.

The most important aspect of this procedure is that it gives a rationale for selecting a preferred interpretation rather than simply rejecting one in favor of another, as other systems do. It can never be right to reject another interpretation irrevocably in cases of this sort, since it may turn out later to be correct, as if the "women" sentence above had been followed by "and after ten minutes hardly a soldier was left standing." After inputting that sentence the relevant preferences in the example might be expected to change. Nonetheless, the present approach is not in any way probabilistic. In the case of someone who utters the "soldiers and women" example sentence, what is to be taken as his meaning is that the women fell. It is of no importance in that decision if it later turns out that he intended to say that the soldiers fell. What was meant by that sentence is a clear, and not merely a likelihood, matter.

It must be emphasized that, in the course of this application, the *common sense* rules are not being interpreted at any point as rules of inference making truth claims about the physical world. It is for this reason that we are not contradicting ourselves in this paper by describing the Preference Semantics approach while arguing implicitly against deductive and theorem proving approaches to language understanding. The clearest way to mark the difference is to see that there is no inconsistency involved in retaining the rule expressed informally as [1 strikes animate2] → [animate2 falls], and at the same time, retaining a description of some situation in which something animate was struck but did not fall or even stagger. There is a clear difference here from any kind of deductive system which, by definition, could not retain such an inconsistent pair of assertions.

4.10 The Generation System for French

Translating into French requires the addition to the system of generation patterns called *stereotypes*. Those patterns are attached to English word senses in the dictionary, both to key and content words, and are carried into the semantic block for the sentence, or paragraph, by the analysis. The block contains all that is necessary for generation, which is then a task of recursively unwrapping the block in the right way. The generation process is described in considerably more detail in [1].

A content word has a list of stereotypes attached to each of its formulas. When a word sense is selected during analysis, this list is carried along with the formula into the block. Thus, for translation purposes, the block is not constructed simply with formulas but with *sense-pairs*. A sense-pair is: ⟨formula for a content word⟩ ⟨list of stereotypes⟩. We saw in the last section that each key paraplate contains a stereotype, which gets built into the block if the corresponding paraplate has been selected by the *TIE* routines. This stereotype is the generation rule to be used for the current fragment, and possibly for some of the fragments that follow it. The simplest form of a stereotype is a French word or phrase standing for the translation of an English word in context, plus a gender marker for nouns. For example:

private (a soldier):   (MASC simple soldat)
odd (for a number):   (impair)
build: (construire)
brandy: (FEMI eau de vie)

Note that, after processing by the analysis routines, all words are already disambiguated. Several stereotypes attached to a formula do not correspond to different senses of the source word but to the different French constructions it can yield.

Complex stereotypes are strings of French words and functions. The functions are of the interlingual context of the sense-pair and always evaluate either to a string of French words, to a blank, or (for content words only) to NIL. Hence such stereotypes are context-sensitive rules, which check upon, and generate from, the sense-pair and its context, possibly including fragments other than the current one. When a function in a content word stereotype evaluates to NIL, then the whole stereotype fails and the next one in the list is tried.

For example, here are the two stereotypes attached to the formula for the ordinary sense of "advise":

(conseiller (PREOB a MAN))
(conseiller)

The first stereotype would be for translating "I advised my children to leave." The analysis routines would have matched the bare template MAN TELL MAN on the words I-advised-children. The function PREOB checks whether the object formula of the template, i.e. the formula for "children" in our example, refers to a human being; if it does, as in this case, the stereotype generates a prepositional group with the French preposition "à," using the object sense-pair and its qualifier list. Here this process yields "à mes enfants," and the value of the whole stereotype is "conseiller à mes enfants." For the sentence "I advise patience," however, whose translation might be "je conseille la patience," this stereotype would fail, because the object head in the template, brought in by the concept of patience, is STATE. The second is simply "(conseiller)," because no prescription on how to translate the object needs to be attached to "conseiller" when the semantic object goes into a French direct object. This is done automatically by the higher level function which constructs French clauses.

Thus we see that content words have complex stereotypes prescribing the translation of their context, when they govern an "irregular" construction: one that is irregular by comparison to a set of rules matching the French syntax onto the semantic block.

The general form of the generation program is a recursive evaluation of the functions contained in stereotypes. Thus, depending on its context of occurrence, a particular word of the French output sentence may have its origin in stereotypes of different levels: content word stereotype, or key word stereotype (or stereotypes) that are part of a set of top level basic functions. The system is formally equivalent to an augmented transition network in the sense of Woods [17].

Some complexity arises from the fragmented structure of the block and from dealing with the problem of integrating complex (i.e. context-sensitive) stereotypes. The program maintains a cursor which points to the fragment which is being generated from; the purpose of certain functions in a stereotype is to move the cursor up and down the block.

Integration of complex stereotypes in some contexts requires the reordering of the stereotype string. Thus, for "I often advised him to leave" going into "Je lui ai souvent conseille de partir," the stereotype: (conseiller (PREOB a MAN)) needs to be rearranged. This is done by a feature which permits the values of designated functions in a stereotype to be lifted and stored in registers. The values of these registers can be used at a higher level of recursive evaluation to construct a new correct French string.

Finally, the integration of complex stereotypes requires the implementation of a system of priorities for regulating the choice of generation rules. Since any word or key can dictate the output syntax for a given piece of the block, there may arise conflicts, which are resolved by having carefully settled priorities. The principle, as in the analysis program, is that a more specific rule has priority over a more general one. Thus, when a content word stereotype prescribes the translation of fragments other than its immediate context, it has priority over any key stereotype. This important process of a stereotype controlling the generation of other fragments than the one to which it attaches is also described in detail in [1].

4.11 Implementation

The system is programmed in LISP 1.6 and MLISP and runs on line on the PDP 6/10 system at Stanford Artificial Intelligence Laboratory where it is the system dump named MT. It runs at present over a vocabulary of about 600 words and takes texts of up to small paragraph length. There is no morphology in the system at present, every input and output word being treated as a separate LISP atom, since morphology presents no substantial research questions to compare with those of semantics. An English sentence is input and a French output, as it might be as follows to show the ambiguities of the preposition "out of":

I PUT THE WINE ON THE TABLE AND JOHN DRINKS IT OUT OF A GLASS. HE OFTEN DRINKS OUT OF DESPAIR AND THROWS THE GLASSES OUT OF THE WINDOW.
JE METS LE VIN SUR LA TABLE ET JEAN LE BOIT DANS UN VERRE. IL BOIT SOUVENT PAR DESESPOIR ET JETTE LES VERRES PAR LA FENETRE

After this follows the usual cpu time declaration and the line (*common sense inferences called*) if the extended anaphora procedures using partial information are required. After that comes the whole semantic block for diagnostic purposes.

The format of the block is a list, each item of which, at the top level, is a text fragment tied to a template, the template being a list of pairs (of formulas and generation stereotypes) and of sublists of such pairs that are dependents on the main nodes of the template in the manner described above. In the lists at the same level as the text fragments are the key generation stereotypes for fragments, as well as paraplate and inference nodes that declare satisfactory preferred ties.

The block is clearly not wholly target-language independent because it contains the generative rules; however, it is very largely so. Moreover, the semantic representation it expresses could easily be adapted as a data base for some quite different task, such as question-answering. Indeed, many of the inferences required to set up the block, like those described in detail above, are equivalent to quite sophisticated question-answering.

4.12 Discussion

I have presented and argued for a nonstandard approach to the computational semantics of natural language and, by implication, against the more conventional linguistic approaches, as well as those from artificial intelligence that assume that natural language is approximated by restricted micro-worlds of simple object words, and the use of theorem proving methods.

In particular, I think the onus is on those who believe in strictly linguistic approaches to show the psychological and computational importance of the structures they impose with considerable difficulty upon even simple sentences. The present work suggests that a well defined semantic structure is the heart of the matter, that the "semi-parsing" of this system may be sufficient to support such structures, and that the heavily hierarchical syntax analyses of yesteryear may not be necessary.[2,3]

---

[2] By the use of nonhierarchical here, I would mean the connected linear structures I have described, each one approximating a notion of nuclear "message."

[3] The common sense reasoning exhibited here is of a quite different sort from other programs in linguistics and artificial intelligence, and the only other systems to use "partial information" of this sort and Schank's and Rieger's [[8] and [9]]. Their systems and this one share far more similarities than differences. The main points of contrast concern: (a) the fact that the Preference Semantics system emphasizes the notion of choice between alternative competing structures for a piece of language; (b) a more general contrast in that the description of this system is weighted more toward the solution of concrete problems and the application of the system to actual text rather than being the description of a static network of concepts; and (c) the clear differences in the notion of "phenomenological level" the other systems employ in describing common sense reasoning: Preference Semantics tries to avoid imposing highly rationalist analyses of cause and mental phenomena that are very hard to justify in terms of common sense—if that is indeed to be the basis for understanding ordinary language.

References

[1] Herskovits, A. The generation of French from a semantic representation. Stanford Artif. Intell. Proj. Memo # 212, Aug. 1973.

[2] Joos, M. Semantic Axiom # 1, *Language* (1972), 193–211.

[3] McCarthy, J., and Hayes, P. Some philosophical questions from the standpoint of artificial intelligence. In Melzer and Michie (Eds.) *Machine Intelligence 4*, American Elsevier, New York, 1969.

[4] Minsky, M. In Minsky (Ed), *Semantic Information Processing*, MIT Press, Cambridge, Mass., 1968.

[5] Minsky, M. Frame systems. Unpublished ms., MIT, Feb. 1974.

[6] Papert, S. *The Romanes Lectures*. U. of California, Berkeley, 1973.

[7] Sandewall, E. Representing natural language information in predicate calculus. In Melzer and Michie (Eds.) *Machine Intelligence 6*, American Elsevier, New York, 1971.

[8] Schank, R. Conceptual dependency. *Cognitive Psychology* (1972), 82–123.

[9] Schank, R., and Rieger, C. Inference and the computer understanding of natural language. Stanford Artif. Intel. Lab. Memo # 197, May 1973.

[10] Scriven, M. The concept of comprehension. In Carroll & Freedle (Eds.), *Language Comprehension*, Washington, D.C., 1972.

[11] Simmons, R., and Bruce, B.C. Some relations between predicate calculus and semantic net representations of discourse. Proc. Second Internat. Joint Conf. on Artif. Intel., London, 1971.

[12] Wilks, Y. Decidability and natural language. *MIND* (1971), 218–239.

[13] Wilks, Y. *Grammar, Meaning and the Machine Analysis of Language*. Routledge & Kegan, London, 1971.

[14] Wilks, Y. An artificial intelligence approach to machine translation. In Schank & Colby (Eds.) *Computer Models of Thought and Language*, San Francisco, 1973.

[15] Wilks, Y. A preferential, pattern seeking, semantics for natura language inference. To appear in *Artif. Intel.*

[16] Winograd, T. *Understanding Natural Language*, Academic Press, New York, 1972.

[17] Woods, W.A., Procedural semantics for a question-answer machine, Proc. AFIPS 1968 FJCC Vol. 33, pp. 457–471. AFIPS Press, Montvale, N.J.

5

A Preferential, Pattern-Seeking, Semantics for Natural Language Inference

Yorick Wilks
Stanford University

Abstract: The paper describes the way in which a Preference Semantics system for natural language analysis and generation tackles a difficult class of anaphoric inference problems: those requiring either analytic (conceptual) knowledge of a complex sort, or requiring weak inductive knowledge of the course of events in the real world. The method employed converts all available knowledge to a canonical template form and endeavors to create chains of non-deductive inferences from the unknowns to the possible referents. Its method for this is consistent with the overall principle of "semantic preference" used to set up the original meaning representation

5.1 Introduction

This paper describes inferential manipulations in a computer system for representing the content of a fragment of English, by which I mean the drawing of inferences about the course of events in the world that are necessary to understand natural language and, in particular, necessary to resolve pronoun references (anaphora), and ambiguities in the senses of words.

To take a simple example: When the system sees the sentences JOHN LEFT THE WINDOW AND DRANK THE WINE ON THE TABLE. IT WAS GOOD, it decides that the pronoun "it" refers to the wine, whereas if it sees JOHN LEFT THE WINDOW AND DRANK THE WINE ON THE TABLE. IT WAS BROWN AND ROUND, it will decide that it is the table being referred to. "Decide" here must be treated with care since earlier or later textual information might correct both the decisions. The point is that a standard hearer or reader, having encountered the amount of text given above, will understand in the way indicated, even if the speaker or writer *intended* something different.

The system is programmed in LISP 1.6 and MLISP, and runs as an analyser of English and a generator of French, on the PDP6/10 at the Stanford AI Laboratory. This provides a very firm context of verification for a natural language

K. Ahmad, C. Brewster and M. Stevenson (eds.), Words and Intelligence 1, 83–102.
© 2007 *Springer.*

understanding program. In the first example above, if "it" emerges as "il" the French masculine pronoun, it can only refer to "wine" since that is the only masculine noun in the sentence. The examples dear to the hearts of those who analyse stories and dialogues can all be reconstructed within a machine translation environment. This system can be run at Stanford as the self-explanatory dump program MT. The distinctive lower level capabilities of this system have been described elsewhere [6–8]: coping with complex sentences without a isolable syntax package; dealing with wide areas of word sense ambiguity, and the case ambiguity of prepositions. All this is assumed here, and not described again in detail. Those "front-end capabilities" set up very complex semantic objects, called "semantic blocks" which are networks of objects called templates, that are themselves complex structures of semantic primitives. The present system is distinguished not only by the complexity of the semantic objects it handles, but by its ability to handle objects representing stretches of discourse longer than simple sentences. The semantic blocks described below, that are these networks of templates, are representations for small paragraphs of text, while the templates represent the meaning of clauses and phrases. These blocks are not merely the result of applying projection rules to dictionaries, as in most contemporary systems, but are built in part from already available, partially filled-in, structures which are the templates and other cognate structures (see [7]) that are "fuzzy matched" onto text chunks as wholes.

In this paper, I am concerned not with the setting up of these complex objects, but with their manipulation in order to draw out semantic information, and with the application of inference rules to that information in order to solve concrete reference problems. It is an assumption of this work, and a point of contrast with that of Minsky and Charniak [1, 2], that these problems cannot be solved independently of a strong representation [1]. The reason for this being simply that the inferences themselves determine the representation, in part at least.

I would not defend the details of the semantic codings given in this paper, nor the particular control structure of the program. What is essential here is (1) the inferential use of partial information; that is, information weaker than that in dictionaries and analytic (logically true) rules. The use of such information constitutes the EXTENDED MODE of the system described below. The second distinguishing feature is (2) the preferring of one representation or inferential chain to another. This is important and a neglected aspect of modern natural language research, where workers often seem to feel that the first representation or inference their system finds MUST be the right one.

The common sense rules of inference used in this system are not deductive consequences about the world, but correspond to likely courses of events which, if and only if they match onto the available explicit and implicit information in the text, may be said to apply, and by applying may enable us to identify mentioned entities and so resolve problems of reference. To deal with the examples above we need to apply at least a rule equivalent to, in ordinary language, IF SOMEONE CAUSES AN ENTITY TO MOVE INTO HIMSELF, HE WILL WANT OR

OTHERWISE JUDGE IT IN SOME WAY. The utility of such a rule is, in this system, in no way contradicted by mention of obvious exceptions, such as someone wanting some object but doing nothing to move or otherwise affect it. The representation of this rule (see below for details) is fuzzy matched onto what we know from the example, and what we know about drinking, including that it is an act of causing a liquid to move. These processes, to be described below, allow the pronoun to be referred correctly in a way consistent with the common sense inferences a person would make, and are finally reducible to non-deductive pragmatic forms such as SOMETHING HERE X's AND FOO X's, THEREFORE THE SOMETHING IS FOO.

Such inferences could, of course, be represented in some much stronger system with deductive machinery, given all the missing frame axioms, quantification, etc. My point is that nothing would be gained by doing so, because such machinery can never improve the reliability of the partial information being handled. It is the content and applicability of inferences like these that should be our concern in natural language analysis at present, and not the finding of strong systems of logic in which to represent them. I have set out that case in more detail in [8].

Secondly, with regard to what I called preference, it is premise of this work that the basic problems of natural language semantics have simply not been solved, either by the linguists or the AI people in the field, and that insights about the structure of language are still needed; needed in the same sense in which Papert [3] has often argued that AI must offer simple rule systems different from the first sledgehammer you thought of. His persuasive example is that of catching a ball, done by a simple algorithm and not at all, as one might have thought, by the solution of complex differential equations. To this end, we avoid the generative grammatical and semantic systems of the linguists, as well as the deductive systems of logicians. The essential part of the present system that aims to offer a little of the missing content is what I call "Preference Semantics".

The key point is that word sense, and structural, ambiguity in natural language will always, in any system, give rise to alternative competing structures, all of which can be said to "represent" whatever chunk of language is under examination. What I mean by "preference" is the use of procedures, at every level of the system, for preferring certain derived structures to others on the basis of their. "semantic density", and in this paper I shall be particularly concerned with preferring some inferential chains to others on that basis.

What I am postulating, speaking psychologically, is that humans interpret language so as to reduce the conceptual density to a minimum; which can be taken to mean "keeping the amount of new information introduced into the system to a minimum". No technical, information theoretic, notion of "information" is intended here, but only a general suggestive analogy with well-known "laziness hypotheses" about language structure, such as Zipf's law. Without some such faculty, however, a language understanding system cannot function. Thus "Pieces of paper lie about the floor", is understood as being about position rather than deception because from the preference information in the system about the concept "lying" we will know that deceptive lying is a concept that prefers an animate agent if it can get it (here it cannot), while a statement about passive position prefers a physical object as the apparent agent, which is available here. The satisfaction of a preference increases the density of the derived representational network and the densest network will be the one ultimately preferred. But, in understanding "My ideas followed hers closely", we want to accept the ideas as the apparent agent, even though our information about the concept of following is that it normally prefers an animate agent if one can be found. Only in that way can the animate sense of "fly" be chosen correctly as the agent in "The fly followed the ladybird into the web". The point is to prefer the normal, but to *accept* the unusual. A little reflection will show that conventional, generative, linguistic rules, with fixed word classes, operating with (unintelligent) derivational rule systems, cannot do this very simple thing.

Preference computations like these, that involve no real world knowledge above and beyond the conceptual knowledge we have about word meanings, I call the BASIC MODE of the sytem. I want to distinguish the basic from the *extended* mode, that I discuss in detail in this paper, in terms of the kinds of anaphora problem the modes can tackle. In the basic mode, the system resolves those anaphoras that depend on the superficial conceptual content of text words. This is done in the course of setting up the initial semantic representation, a process I have not yet described. I shall call these type A anaphoras. For example, in "Give the bananas to the monkeys although they are not ripe, because they are very hungry", the system in its basic mode would decide that the first "they" refers to the bananas and the second to the monkeys. It does that by seeing, in the representation for the concept of hunger, that it prefers to be applied to something animate, and that the concept of ripeness prefers to be applied to something plantlike. If every satisfied preference increases the density of the conceptual network, then we shall get the densest network when the first "they" is correctly tied to "bananas" and the second to "monkeys". The success or failure is clear in the translation mode of the system because the French equivalents for the two words "bananas" and "monkeys" have different genders.

The main part of this paper describes an EXTENDED MODE of the system that tackles two other kinds of anaphora examples I shall call types B and C, respectively. Consider the correct attachment of "it" in "John drank the whisky from the glass, and it felt warm in his stomach". It is clear that the pronoun should be tied to "whisky" rather than to "glass", but how that is to be done is not immediately obvious. Analysis of the example below suggests that the solution requires, among other things, some inference equivalent to "whatever is in a part of X is in X".

Anaphoras like the last I shall call type B, because the inferences required to resolve them are analytic but not superficial. By analytic I simply mean that the quoted sentence above, about parts and wholes, is logically true, and not a fact about the real world, but rather about the meanings of words like "in". What is meant by "superficial" in the distinction between types A and B will become clear below after some discussion of the meaning formalism employed.

Finally and most importantly, I shall discuss type C anaphoras, which require inferences that are not analytic, but weak generalisations (often falsified in experience) about the course of events in the world. Yet their employment here is not in any sense a probabilistic one. In "The dogs chased the cats, and I heard one of them squeal with pain", we shall, in order to resolve the referent of "one" (which I take to be "cat" not "dog"), need a weak generalisation equivalent to "animate beings pursued by other animate beings may be unpleasantly affected". Such expressions are indeed suspiciously vague, and a reader who is worried at this point should ask himself how he would explain (say, to someone who did not know English well) how he knew the referent of "one" in that sentence. It can hardly be in virtue of a particular fact about cats and dogs because the same general inference would be made whatever was chasing and being chased. I shall be surprised if he does not come up with something very like the inference suggested, and it may be the nature of natural language itself that is worrying him.

The inferences for type C, then, are general expressions of partial information (in McCarthy's phrase) and are considered to apply only if they are adequately confirmed by the context, which is to say that both the "antecedent" and the "consequent" of such an inference must match onto the text representation, or onto implicit representations extracted from the original one. What I mean by all that will become clear in what follows, but in no case do these expressions yield deductive consequences about the future course of the world, nor is there any assumption here that the event generalised about ALWAYS happen in such and such a way. Indeed, they would be foolish if they did because the world's course cannot be captured in that way. In the whisky example above, it might have been his earlier dinner that in fact made him feel good. Yet, nonetheless, the solution of the anaphora problem for an understander, derived as just described, is definite, for anyone who writes the sentence about John's stomach will be taken to mean that the whisky was in his stomach, whatever he might have intended in the rare case of a glass swallower.

It is clear that the content of such rules of partial information, like the one above about judging and causing objects to move, is pretty vacuous. One of the theses being advanced here is that we do need these rather empty rules for understanding natural language, that their emptiness is of a quite different sort from logical tautologies like $[a \vee b \supset b \vee a]$, and that their very obviousness is what made it possible to overlook them. There is an analogy here with what Minsky [2] calls "superframes" that are always true, for there is a long philosophical tradition of regarding what is always true as bordering on the vacuous, but not therefore useless!

Wittgenstein expressed something of this notion, of the dependence of our under-standing on *very general* facts of nature [14, para 142]:

> ...if things were quite different from what they actually are—if there were for instance no characteristic expression of pain, of fear, of joy; if the rule became the exception and exception rule; or if both became phenomena of roughly equal frequency—this would make our normal language games lose their point.

5.2 Brief Recap of the System's Basic Mode of Analysis

The heart of the basic mode's representation is the *template* (not to be confused in any way with the usage of that word in visual character recognition to mean a context-free method of analysis using low-level features). This is an active frame of complex concepts that seeks preferred categories of concepts to fill its slots, though if its preferences are not satisfied it will accept whatever it finds in default. What Minsky has recently called [2] frames are good first approximations to templates, though there is some difference in the logic of preference and what Minsky calls the "default values" in frames. For example, the preferences tell you not only what to assume if you cannot find anything, but also what to look for to put into the slot if there is a choice available.

The template can be thought of as expressing the communicated gist of a phrase or clause, or even simple sentence. It is a coherent connectivity of FORMULAS, which in turn are complex concepts expressing the senses of words, one formula to a word sense. If $F1$ etc. stand for formulas, then a template has the following connectivity:

$$F1 \leftrightarrow F2 \leftrightarrow F3$$
$$F11 \quad F12 \quad F13 \quad F21 \quad F31 \quad F32$$

At nodes $F1$, $F2$, $F3$ are the *principal* formulas of the template which are always agent, action and object (in that order), though any of them may be a dummy in any particular example. But to even be a candidate for filling the agent place in a template, a formula must be of the right sort, which in the case of an agent means having a formula *head* of the right category. ($F11$, $F12$, $F13$) is a list of formulas dependent on main formula $F1$, etc. Let me give an example of a template structure at this point by using the following simplifying notation: any English words in square brackets [ ] stand for the meaning representation of those words in the Preference Semantics system. This device is important in that the content of the [ ]-abbreviated forms can be seen immediately, whereas the complex coded forms themselves would be as hard to read as, say, a sentence read a word at a time. But it is important to restate that the rules and formalisms expressed within [ ] are really formulas and subformulas of structured primitives, and that their tasks could not be carried out, in the way some still seem to believe, by massaging English words into standing, as it were, *for their own meaning representation*.

So then, the template connectivity of formulas for "The black horse passed the winning post easily" could be written (ignoring any ambiguity problems for the moment):

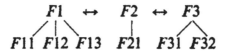

$$[horse] \leftrightarrow [passed] \leftrightarrow [post]$$
$$\uparrow \qquad \uparrow \qquad \uparrow$$
$$[the\ black]\ [easily]\ [the\ winning]$$

When the system runs, input texts are fragmented into clauses, phrases etc. and templates are matched to each of these, probably a number of templates to each text chunk depending on how potentially ambiguous its words are. The first exercise of preference tries to cut this number down and throw away as many templates as possible. To see how this is done, we must realise that the formulas at the nodes of the template network are themselves complex objects. Here, for example, are two formulas for the English action "grasp":

"grasp"(action1) → ((*ANI SUBJ)((*PHYSOB OBJE)(((THIS
(MAN PART))INST)(TOUCH SENSE))))
"grasp"(action2) → ((*HUM SUBJ)((SIGN OBJE)(TRUE THINK)))

There is no space to explain these tree structures of semantic primitives in detail here (see [6–8]), nor is there any need to do so, for the purposes of this paper, beyond giving the feeling that their decomposition and interpretation are well defined. We need only note that the right-most element of each formula is its *head*, or principal, element. Thus, grasp1 is principally a SENSE action, as in grasping a block, while grasp2 is principally a THINK action, as in grasping a theorem. The case subformulas at the left-hand sides of the formulas express the preferences under discussion. The subformula with SUBJ at its right expresses preferred agents (animate things for grasp1, and human things for grasp2), while the subformula with OBJE at its right expresses the preferred objects of the actions, namely physical objects and SIGNs respectively, the latter being thoughts and symbols of thoughts. Element names beginning with a star, *, denote classes of elements. Thus the "class primitive" *ANI, denoting animate things, contains, among others, the primitive elements MAN, denoting human beings, and BEAST, denoting non-human creatures.

This should all become clearer if each formula is thought of as a tree of subformulas. Thus for the first formula above, we have:

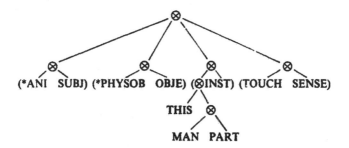

The formula is set out here as a tree of sub-formulas all at the same level, each of which specifies an act or a preferential case restriction of the act. The basic act itself contains the head element, and is the rightmost subformula. This form of display removes the binary bracketing of the formula, which is useful for decomposition purposes, but which introduces too much structure for easy interpretation.

SUBFORMULA	CASE/ACT	VALUE	EXPLANATION
(*ANI SUBJ)	SUBJ	*ANI	the preferred agent is animate
(*PHYSOB OBJE)	OBJE	*PHYSOB	the preferred agent is a physical object
((THIS(MAN PART))INST)	INST	(THIS(MAN PART))	the preferred instrument is a human part, the hand
(TOUCH SENSE)	SENSE	TOUCH	the action is of physical contact

Thus, grasping, in this sense, is an action preferably done by animate beings (*ANI) to physical objects (*PHYSOB), and consists in an act of sensing, by touch, and done with an instrument (INST is the case element) which is a part of the body. When I say "prefers" here, I mean that, if the preferred agent or object cannot be found, a template is constructed with whatever is available. Thus, "The robot grasped the block" would never be rejected; it would only be less preferred than any possible competing interpretation that had an animate agent.

A few other rules will help to clarify the notion of "knowing our way round a formula" when interpreting it: Agents are implicit (need not be specified by SUBJ case) unless (1) they occur at the top level in an action formula as described above, or (2) they attach to the head of a formula, as in:

$$\text{"patient"(entity)} \rightarrow \text{((NOTPLEASE FEEL)(SUBJ MAN))}$$

Here, the normal order, of agents being to the left of (= dependent on) the corresponding action, is violated, since MAN is the agent for FEEL, while at the same time being the head of the whole formula. This violation of order in search is indicated by also violating the order restriction that normally makes the SUBJ case element the governor (right-hand member) of the pair in which it occurs. The corresponding rule of analysis is "On encountering SUBJ as dependent, expect action for the agent to follow to the left".

Objects, however, are never implicit. Moreover, an object is considered an object of all actions to its right. This enables us to express the important notion of real and apparent agents of actions. So, for example, in:

$$\text{"fire + at" (action)} \rightarrow$$
$$\text{((*HUM SUBJ)((*ANI OBJE)((STRIK GOAL)((THING MOVE)CAUSE))))}$$

This action (done preferably by human beings to animate beings) is one of causing a thing to move (the bullet) with the aim (GOAL case) of striking something. Since

*ANI is the object of all actions to its right, it is the object not only of CAUSE, but also of STRIK. Hence the striking is also of the same animate being. Moreover, THING (the bullet) is internally the agent of MOVE, not the object of CAUSE, which is correct as far as the meaning of "fire + at" is concerned.

Let us now return to the construction of templates from formulas. Suppose we are analysing "John grasped the idea". The system will attempt to construct a template corresponding to each "grasp" formula in turn, in both cases inserting the formula at the action node. Both formulas will have their agent preferences satisfied by the formula for "John", at the agent node, because John is both animate and human. But only grasp2 will have its object preference for a SIGN-like entity satisfied by the formula for "idea", at the object node.

So, if we think of each satisfied preference as the strengthening of one of the linking arrows between formulas on the template diagram for this sentence (in the same format as the one given above for the "black horse" sentence), then it is clear that the template with the grasp2 formula at its action node will have the stronger linkage, in virtue of two strengthened links. Thus, that template structure will be preferred and the other, with the grasp1 formula, will be rejected and never considered again.

Conversely, had the sentence under consideration been "John grasped the handrail firmly" the preferences would have been reversed and the template containing the grasp1 formula, preferring *PHYSOB objects, would have been chosen as having the stronger conceptual linkage.

After this process the representation of a text (composed of fragments) is a semantic block, or network of these template networks. The use of "network" here should not lead a reader to think of systems with pre-existing networks, specified in advance. Here they are set up by the process just described and are specific to the phrase or clause they represent.

The templates are interconnected by case ties. The notation of case is discussed in detail in [7], but for the moment a case can be thought of as a type of link tying one template to some particular node in another template. In the sentence "He lost his wallet / in the subway" (fragmented at the stroke) we might say that the second fragment of the sentence depends on "lost" in the first, and that the dependence is of the locative case type. Thus in the representation, the template for the second fragment would be tied to the central, action, node of the first, by a link labelled LOCA. The node on the first template to which the case tie ties is called the *mark* of the second template.

At present we operate with a distinction system of ten cases, which are listed below, together with (in capital letters) the semantic elements that represent them, the questions that define them, and examples of subformulas expressing them. Defining a case is a tricky matter, but the question method is reasonably adequate. Note that the subformula examples are of those parts of a formula that would express that notion as part of the meaning of a word. The subformulas are not, of course, how the system would express the quoted words if encountered in a text, when they would be represented by a template.

recipient: FOR
"for a woman" → ((FEM MAN)FOR)
what/who to? what/who for?

instrument: INST
"with a stick" → ((LINE THING)INST)
what with? by what means?

direction: *DIRE (see below), TO, FROM
"from the top" → ((UP POINT)FROM)
where to? where from? at what? out of where?

possessive: POSS
"owned by a man" → ((MAL MAN)POSS)
who owns the thing mentioned?

location: LOCA
"at that time" → ((THIS(WHEN POINT))LOCA)
when? where? where at? by what? in what time? near what? at what
time? during when? before when?

containment: IN
"in a glass" → (((((FLOW STUFF)OBJE)WRAP)THING)IN) in what?

source: SOUR
"out of wood" → ((PLANT STUFF) SOUR)
out of what? from what?

goal: GOAL
"so as to strike a woman" → ((((FEM MAN)OBJE)STRIK)GOAL)
to what end? for what purpose?

accompaniment: WITH
"without a glass" → (((((FLOW STUFF)OBJE)WRAP)THING)NOTWITH)
accompanied by what/who? with what/whom? without what/whom?

subject: SUBJ
who did this?

object: OBJE
whom/what was this done to?

Certain cases above have negative forms leading to additional elements NOTFOR, NOTPOSS, NOTIN, NOTWITH.

Case elements have two functions and occur in two sorts of constructions: formulas and semantic blocks of templates. In formulas they express part of the meaning of a word sense. Thus in:

"drink"(entity) → (((WRAPTHING)IN)(((FLOW STUFF)SOUR)THING))

---

* DIRE is the name of the class of direction case elements (TO and FROM) and it occurs only as the indicator of the case of a fragment, never in formulas. Conversely, POSS occurs only in formulas, never as the indicator of a fragment case.

we see that a drink has a liquid source (FLOW STUFF), and is in a container (WRAP THING). The other function of these elements is, as already explained, the name of the tie between the template for some fragment and some part of another template.

Case information is only included in a formula when it is specific: when we can say what aspect of the case is involved. In the formula for "pour", for example, we include a direction specification for downwards ((NOTUP POINT)TO). However, in the formula for "move" we do not include the element TO or FROM, even though movement must in fact be in some direction, since we have no reasonable expectation about it as we do with "pour". Sentences containing "move" may very well go on to specify the direction involved, but its association with "move" is conceptually arbitrary and we cannot expect any confirmation of expectations that would, say, resolve ambiguities. In this respect the system differs from other systems that do create case expectations for wide classes of actions, which are essentially unspecific, as in this example, and so we would claim unhelpful semantically.

Enormous gaps have been left in this brief recapitulation of the basic mode: in particular (1) how this last process is done with the aid of dummy templates and highly structured case-locating objects called *paraplates*, (2) how this superficial template matching is converted to a deeper representation, effectively eliminating the dummies, and (3) how the superficial semantic matching and preferring have done the work of a conventional syntactic component (see further in [11]).

I described earlier, with the bananas and monkeys example, how type A anaphoras are resolved in this basic mode of preference. Once resolved, these type A anaphoras also constitute links between templates, from the pronoun variable to its correct referent. Thus the compressed list form of the whole representation obtained, for a single fragment of text, from the basic mode is:

$$(\text{CASE MARK ANAPHORA } F1 \ F2 \ F3$$
$$(F1 \text{ dependents})(F2 \text{ dependents})(F3 \text{ dependents}))$$

The $F1$ etc., and the lists refer to the nodes on the first diagram above, which was the basic template connectivity. The additional nodes (indicated in upper case letters) can be thought of as other pointers tying the whole template connectivity to nodes in other such connectivities. That is, the CASE, MARK and ANAPHORA pointers structure the "semantic block" by defining a network of templates. And it must be remembered throughout that what is actually at the $F1$ node is a complex object containing a formula tree, like the ones for "grasp" illustrated earlier.

So, in the earlier example "John left the window and drank the wine on the table", the compressed list representation for the fragment "on the table" would have a dummy agent formula at $F1$, a pseudo-agent formula for "on" at $F2$ (since prepositions are treated as pseudo-actions) and an object formula for "table" at $F3$. There would be no dependent lists of formulas since "the" is represented along with what it qualifies. The CASE tie would be LOCA, since "on the table" has a location case, and the MARK would be a pointer to the object node in the template for "John drank the wine". The ANAPHORA node is unfilled in this example.

5.3 Quick Sketch of the Extended Mode of Inference

The extended mode of inference, using additional common sense inference rules, is called whenever the basic mode cannot resolve a pronoun anaphora, as between two or more candidate referents, using semantic link density alone. In the above example about John and his stomach, density techniques have no way to decide whether the glass or the whisky is in his stomach. On a basis of preferred agents and objects of actions, what I called superficial conceptual information, both are equally good candidates. The extended inference procedure is called and, if it succeeds, it returns a solution to the basic mode which then continues with its analysis. If it too should fail to reduce the number of candidate referents to one, then the top level of the system tries to solve the problem by default, or what a linguist would call focus. Roughly, that means: assume that whatever was being talked about is still being talked about. So, in "He put the bicycle in the shed and when he came back next week it was gone", neither density criteria, nor the extended inferences to be described here, will help at all. So the system may as well assume, in this limited context, that the bicycle is still the focus of attention, and hence the reference of "it".

Consider again the following sentence after all the basic mode's routines have been applied:

[1: John drank the + whisky / 2 DIRE : DTHIS from a + glass
        /3: and it felt warm / 4 IN: DTHIS in his + stomach]

Since it is in [ ]-abbreviated form, this object is really four successive list-compressed-templates like those described above, one for each of the four fragments of the sentence. The slash marks the fragment boundary and the case names DIRE (direction) and IN (containment) indicate the dependencies of templates 2 on 1, and 4 on 3, respectively. The DTHISs are dummies added to fill out the canonical template triplet in cases of missing agents, objects, etc. Further assume that the "his" has been tied to "John" by the basic mode, and presents no problem of analysis, and that the basic mode provided a list of candidates for the reference of "it" (i.e., "whisky" and "glass").

EXTRACTIONS are then made from each template in turn, if and only if it contains a representation of either a candidate answer word or the variable pronoun itself. An extraction is the unpacking of every possible case tie: both those in the formulas of the template and those labelling a link to other templates. In this example we obtain the following extractions, which are template-like forms as follows (where the first digit of a pair refers to the fragment above, the second to the number of the extraction from a particular fragment, and "+" links words with a single formula):

    11: [whisky (IN in)   John + part],
    12: [whisky (DIRE to)   John + part],
    21: [whisky (DIRE from)   a + glass],
    41: [?it   (IN in)   his + stomach].

We can explain how these extractions were made, even in the absence of detailed knowledge of the structure of formulas: 11, for example, is a new template form derived from the template for "John drank the whisky" because from the structure of the formula for "drink" it follows that the liquid drunk is subsequently inside the drinker. This is because, when making up the formula for the action "drink", we express in it that the action consists in causing a liquid to be inside the agent of the action, as follows:

((*ANI SUBJ)(((FLOW STUFF)OBJE)((SELF IN)
(((WRAP THING)FROM)(((MAN PART)TO)(MOVE CAUSE)))))

This requires no more to be understood than earlier example formulas, except to note that (FLOW STUFF) denotes liquids, the preferred objects of drinking, and that the action causes that liquid to move into the agent's self, and that it is (FROM implies direction case) liquid moved from a container, or (WRAP THING).

Limits of an intuitively obvious sort apply to the process of extraction. For example, from a representation for "A group of women drank beer" we would extract a representation for "Women drank beer". But we would *not* similarly infer "John drank beer" from "The parents of John drank beer". The difference between the examples is easily stated in terms of preference: the extraction is only performed where, as in the first example, the apparent agent does not satisfy the action's agent preference (of "drink" for an animate agent in this case), but the implicitly available agent does satisfy it. In the second example, the apparent agents, the parents, are animate and do satisfy the preference, and so the misleading inference is not extracted.

So, in this informal [ ] representation we have acquired new template-like objects that express, in canonical form, new analytic information extracted from the existing templates, and from which new inferences can be made. It is postulated that the generation of this inexplicit information from the deeper levels of the formulas is essential to the process of understanding. These new forms differ from standard templates only in that their second node, or pseudo-action, has had a case name CONSd onto whatever the node was before. Note here that the form (IN in) is not redundant since the case name IN locates the case precisely as containment, while the English preposition can indicate many cases other than containment, as in "in five minutes".

It will be noticed that not all extractions consist is unpacking the formulas of the template more deeply. Some, such as 21 above, are better called *repackings* for a new template form has not been created, but rather a dummy in an existing template has been filled in. The dummy pseudo-agent of the template based on "from" has been filled in so as to infer "the whisky came in the direction from the glass". It is not appropriate to go into this quite separate matter here, but the criteria for repacking in this way are actually identical with those that decided that this template was tied by the DIREction case to its immediate predecessor 1. These case decisions are made with the aid of structured semantic objects called *paraplates*, described in detail in [7, 8, 11] and in practice flags are set when the case pointers are set, so that in the extended mode the repacking is done without reapplying all the semantic criteria that settled the questions of case.

The extractions, repackings and the templates corresponding to the original text now form an inference pool of canonical template forms upon which the common sense inference rules operate in the extended mode so as to provide a yet deeper understanding and representation of some situation. The template forms are to be thought of active entities, seeking other templates to match. We then try two strategies in turn: first we try a zero-point strategy, which is to try to "fuzzy match" an answer template (or extraction) and a variable template (or extraction) directly, without the use of common sense inference rules [CSIRs].

Another general assumption here, and it is a strong psychological assumption, is that, in order to resolve these painful ambiguities, the understanding system is going to use the shortest possible chain of inferences it can. And a zero-point strategy will, as it were, have no length at all (in terms of a chain of CSIR inferences), since it consists in "fuzzy matching" template forms together directly without intervening rules. And so if it works, it will always provide the shortest chain. This preference for the shortest chain is itself another form of the same psychological "laziness hypothesis", of never introducing more information at any point than necessary, and is consistent with the general principle in use here of always being prepared to complexify, or deepen, a representation, but never doing so unless the problem cannot be solved at a more superficial level. This is a very different overall principle from the wide, forward inference, proposals of Schank [5] and Charniak [1].

The zero-point strategy is adequate for the example under discussion, because we can (under a suitable definition of template and extraction matching) identify extractions 11 and 41, and thus identify "?it" and the whisky, and we are home.

If the zero-point strategy fails, we bring down all the CSIR rules that contain an action subformula occurring in an answer or problem template form in the inference pool, and attempt to find the shortest chain that leads from some answer to some problem variable.

Let us return to the first example of the paper: "John left the window and drank the wine on the table. It was good". Notice already that we can reject all simple solutions based on focus (that the wine is referred to because it is what is being talked about) in view of the contrasting example whose second sentence is "It was brown and round" where clearly it is the table being referred to. Notice that this second sentence pair will be dealt with inside the basic mode, because the preference of concepts of shape for physical object possessors will reject the wine as referent.

Let us now set out that example, using the informal [ ] notation, and label original templates from the representation with T numbers, and label extracted template forms with E numbers. We shall then have after extraction:

    T1: [John left   the + window],
    T3: [John drank   the + wine],
    T3: [wine (LOCA on) the + table],
    E21: [wine (IN in)   John],
    T4: [?it   was   good].

These template forms stay in the inference pool because they contain either the problem variable ?it or one of the possible referents: window, wine or table. The extended mode now accesses those CSIRs which are stored under the main action element of their antecedent and consequent.

Here are two examples rules I shall call I1 and I2 respectively, and give in informal and formal versions, where in both cases the internal natural numbers distinguish variables, restricted as indicated:

I1: ((*ANI 1) (SELF IN)(MOVE CAUSE)) (*REAL 2)) → (1 (£*JUDG) 2)
i.e., [animate-1 cause-to-move-in-self real-object-2] → [1 £*judges 2]
I2: (1 BE £(GOOD KIND)) ↔ ((*ANI 2)(£WANT) 1)
i.e., [1 is £good] ↔ [animate-2 £wants 1]

The pound sign should be ignored for the moment. Its relevance will be clear in the next section on negation. The class *REAL includes all the elements in *PHYSOB as well as STUFF, denoting substances. The class *JUDG includes WANT, FEEL, etc.

The rules are flexible about expression of restrictions on variables by subformulas or elements, and any variable can be restricted as much as necessary. They are to be contrasted with Schank's inference rules [5] which are not so much pattern finders as inferences from a single primitive action head. The idea here is to have far more information in the rules than can be expressed with a single primitive action. It should be noted that, for economy of expression, the variables are only shown restricted on the left-hand side of the rules, but in application the rules are understood as "the right-hand sides can only be satisfied in matching by entities that satisfy the restriction on the corresponding variable on the left-hand side".

The matching and inferring strategy searches from both the problem-variable and from the potential answer template forms, trying chains of length zero first, then of length one, two and so on. At present it will not attempt to construct a chain longer than two. This length limit could be easily extended, but I suspect that understanding of normal situations rarely requires chains longer than three. In a conventional translation into first order logic, the two rules I1 and I2 would appear to be of radically different logical types, but in the matching onto the template pool they are of the same sort, namely, if the "antecedent" has been matched look out for something matching the "consequent".

Again, the consequences drawn are not necessarily true, they resolve ambiguities only where *both* antecedent and consequent match what we already know or can semantically extract. Much of the effort of the program is in the inexact matching of the template forms to the rules. That does not mean the satisfaction of the restrictions on the variables in the rules, that is not fuzzy, but the closeness requirements on subformulas in template forms and rules. This always involves decomposing formulas into case parts, as on the tree diagram earlier, and matching some but not all the branches—this is a process analogous that sketched by Minsky [2] as "matching frames by matching their terminals". It will be clear here that there is a great deal of content of the system in the template matching rules. For example, if the whisky had felt warm in the *hand* then a quite different conclusion would have been appropriate, and so the matching must not make body parts correspond in a random manner. However, this predeliction for short chains with more content between the matching links of the chain, is I believe more perspicuous than the alternative of long chains and weak matching.

In the present example "John left the window and drank the wine on the table and it was £ good", a chain with two inference rules is set up as follows:

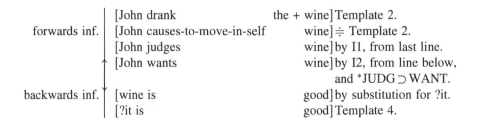

Hence template node [wine] and "?it" are matched, because of the match of the last two lines of the chain, thus referring the pronoun "it". It is virtually certain, as always, that there would be other chains yielding other possible answer-referents, but none with chains shorter than this one.

5.4 A Note on Negation and a Speculation about Further Development

We can see the relative unimportance of negation in the system of inference described in the last section, simply by interpreting the pound sign as NOT, with the proviso that if it is so interpreted on one side of a rule it must also be so interpreted if it occurs on the other. It will then be seen that the last inference chain would do equally well for the sentence "John left the window and drank the wine on the table and it was not good". And indeed, identical inference chains are set up by the system for that sentence with and without the "not".

Notice immediately that this is not a *presuppositional* situation, which can be expressed with an optional not as "I have £ stopped beating my wife" → "I beat my wife". For what we have here is "John drank the wine on the table and it was £ good" → "The wine was £ good". All that is being pointed out here in fact is that in cases like this the matching relevance is more important than the presence of a negation. Nonetheless, it is a useful observation in view of the difficulty of describing a non-deductive system. For this phenomenon could only be described in first-order logic with the aid of rules of the form $(A \rightarrow B \vee \neg B)$ which would be so destructive as to make such a system computationally useless. Yet here such rules function perfectly well. In [2] Minsky calls the frame system he describes *non-deductive*, but it might not be clear to a casual reader in what sense it is non-deductive. After all, mere absence of quantification does not make a system non-deductive. But in the form of rules described here is a concrete suggestion for a non-deductive system.

If we press this notion a little we soon find that negation often is significant in this system. For instance, if we analyse "John drank no gin in his cocktail but it felt warm in his stomach anyway", and we ask the usual questions about the "it", we shall see that the candidature of "gin" is ruled out because we have an extracted template form equivalent to [gin (IN not + in) John], i.e. that the gin is not inside John, and hence [gin] can never match the ?it in some extracted template form [?it (IN IN) Johns + stomach]. Thus negation is significant here in ruling out gin as the referent and leaving us, correctly, with the cocktail.

I cannot pursue this wholly linguistic matter here, but I believe there is no problem about the reconciliation between the treatment of these two types of examples within a single system. My speculation, that I cannot justify here, is that there are reasonably well defined circumstances of match where negation is vital, and where two template forms that differ by a negation element *cannot possibly* match. However, there are other cases, such as direct predications, where a template and its negated form can fuzzy-match, if no preferred non-negated form can be found. In such circumstances a negated form is a better relevance match than nothing.

So, in a rather forced example like "John liked Charles although he was not good" we might wonder about the formal referral of "he", and extract from the first fragment some form equivalent to "Charles was good", using the sort of partial rules about liking that we discussed earlier. We shall then find ourselves wanting to fuzzy match that with the [?he was not + good] of the last fragment, so as to reach what I take to be the correct solution, namely "Charles". What I am speculating is that, unlike the cocktail example, we do not get an exclusion, of Charles, here but a fuzzy match in the absence of anything better, and this other mode of matching is triggered by the presence of a predication of a judgment concept like "good" where relevance matters above logical exclusion of alternatives. But that is a matter for purely linguistic investigation.

5.5 Discussion

The system described cannot be considered in any way adequately tested, partly because no one has any very clear idea of what constitutes a test in this area. But even to qualify, the basic mode must be shown to be stable under a considerable vocabulary and range of senses for words, and the extended mode must be shown to be determinate with a decent sized inventory of CSIRs. The present vocabulary is 500 words yet, though small, it is to my knowledge the largest of any operating deep-structure semantic analyser. At present, the program swaps in two large core images of 46K and 50K respectively, plus two small ones of 5K each, all under control of a SAIL program. A trouble-free paragraph of text is processed in about 6 cpu seconds, while a quite simple sentence requiring inference chaining of the sort just described may require 6 cpu seconds itself. All that has to be shown in the short run is that the inventory of CSIRs is handleable, useable and extensible and open to some conceivable refutation. That would be by the production of alternative chains that reached intuitively correct answers, but which were longer than some other chain that (a) this system would necessarily and wrongly prefer, and which (b) did not resort to the use of implausible phenomenological levels of description. A case of the last would be the writing of some of the common sense rules at an absurd level of primitiveness so as to make the correct chains over-long. This would be done, for example, by writing rules about eating so that they made reference to the motions of the teeth, jaws or digestive muscles (some workers in the area have teetered on the edge of this sort of "primitiveness").

A great number of questions have been ignored here: the extension of these anaphora routines to more general inferential processes for resolving sense ambiguity on the basis of common sense knowledge; the question of wholistic "settings" for discourses, so that we do not have to keep on resolving every occurrence of, say, "bar" when we already know we are discussing a law court. Again, there is the question of how we get outside a pragmatics of local inference, like this one, so as to take account of important facts in a discourse that change all standard interpretations, in the way that a single fact in a detective story can do. No advance will be made there, I am sure, until we have some idea what it is to select out certain salient facts as potential sources of future reinterpretation. It is surely implausible that we search for possibly upsetting information when making every single decision interpreting what is coming in.

I think the use of the shortest possible CSIR chain can be defended as an extension of semantic preference used in setting up the basic representation. That preference was justified as opting for the "semantically densest" interpretation which was, I claimed, the one "with the least meaning" (in the sense in which a string of random words carries the maximum possible information). Similarly, the shortest chain of inferences also minimises the information in play, and introduces the least extraneous inductive information into the system. It is clear that such a simple notion of choice is ultimately inadequate. We only have to consider a sentence like "I was named after my father", where it seems clear that we exclude one interpretation simply because it contains virtually no information at all. This alone shows there must be some qualification to a "minimising information" theory.

The nature of this qualification is reasonably clear in a particular class of anaphora resolutions. Consider the micro-text "John asked Fred to close the window. He did it." The two pronouns in the last sentence are clearly to be resolved together, and we instinctively reject the interpretation where the second sentence merely repeats the first: where "he" is John, and "it" is the asking. The system rejects this interpretation, and we could say that the preference is for the least meaning, *provided it is not zero.*

This last example points up another simplistic feature of the system, in that it does not at present devote the attention to the temporal labelling of asserted events that some systems do. It basically accepts the most primitive iconic feature of language (pointed out to me as such by Dr P. Hayes) that what comes later in reading a text refers to what happened later in the world described. The last example assumed that, and it is a fair assumption provided one has special routines for events described "Before that ...". At the very least, it is a reasonable assumption until a great deal more theoretical work on the problem has been done.

In this paper, and its predecessors, much emphasis has been placed on the template as a device to be parsed onto semantic representations of real text, because the subject investigated in this paper cannot be treated in isolation from an adequate linguistic base system. The inferring of a correct interpretation is intimately related to the systematic exclusion of competing interpretations, and any system that does not allow realistic ambiguity of sense and structure in at the start can hardly appreciate this point. I have developed elsewhere [10] an abstract view of meaning along these lines: that to have meaning is essentially to have one meaning RATHER THAN ANOTHER. Or, put another way, having meaning essentially involves procedures for the exclusion of alternative interpretations. This, I believe, is the residual truth lurking beneath the "procedural view of meaning", a thesis which when taken at face value is patently false.

There has been no space in this paper for comparisons with the work of others (but see [12]), though the similarity of the task described here for the extended mode to the work of Charniak [1] will be obvious. There are overall similarities of aim and assumptions, too, with the work of Schank [5] and Winograd [13]. One main difference of emphasis from both of them is the notion of preference. If there is such a notion in those works it is hidden away in the "hacks" and not brought to the fore where it belongs. To my knowledge the only other author who has emphasised the notion, though in a quite different context, is Quillian [4].

Clear differences from [13, 15] are the use of partial information rules to get outside an unnaturally restricting linguistic micro-world, and the use of a uniform representation and inference system at all stages of operation: there is no conventional division into syntactic, semantic and deductive or knowledge packets.

Some features very familiar in micro-worlds are missing in the present version of the system, as alert readers will have detected already. In an earlier example it is not specified in the notation whether the whisky was, or was not, the Winogradian: WHISKY, which is to say was it or was it not particular whisky, different from other samples of whisky. This is a distinction which makes most sense within a micro-world of inventoried items and samples, and less so outside. A reader in doubt about this should ask himself which words in the sentence he is now reading should have attached colons in a proper representation.

A clear difference from [5] is the emphasis on concrete problems of analysis with definite solutions, and a corresponding description of the system, not abstractly, but in terms of its procedural application to texts.

Acknowledgment

This research was supported by the Advanced Research Projects Agency, Department of Defense (SD 183), USA. An important example in the paper is due to Dr M. Wettler.

References

[1] Charniak, E. Jack and Janet in search of a theory of knowledge. Advanced Papers of the Third International Joint Conference on Artificial Intelligence, Stanford Research Institute, Stanford, Calif. (1973).

[2] Minsky, M. Frame systems. Unpublished manuscript, Massachusetts Institute of Technology, Cambridge, Mass. (February 1974).

[3] Papert, S. *The Romanes Lectures*. Univ. of California Press, Berkeley, Calif. (1973).

[4] Quillian, R. Semantic memory. *Semantic Information Processing*, M. Minsky (ed.), MIT Press, Cambridge, Mass. (1968).

[5] Schank, R. and Rieger, C. Inference and the computer understanding of natural language. Stanford AI Laboratory Memo 197, Stanford University, Stanford, Calif. (May 1973).

[6] Wilks, Y. An artificial intelligence approach to machine translation. Stanford AI Laboratory Memo 161, Stanford University, Stanford, Calif. (March 1971); also in *Computer Models of Thought and Language*, R. Schank and K. Colby (eds.), Freeman, San Francisco, Calif. (1973).

[7] Wilks, Y. Preference semantics. Stanford AI Laboratory Memo 206, Stanford University Stanford, Calif. (July 1973); also in *Formal Semantics of Natural Language*, E. Keenan (ed.), Cambridge Univ. Press, Cambridge (1975).

[8] Wilks, Y. Understanding without proofs. Advanced Papers of the Third International Joint Conference on Artificial Intelligence, Stanford Research Institute, Stanford, Calif. (1973).

[9] Wilks, Y. Natural language inference. Stanford AI Laboratory Memo 211, Stanford University, Stanford, Calif. (October 1973).

[10] Wilks, Y. Decidability and natural language. *Mind* **80** (1971).

[11] Wilks, Y. An intelligent analyser and understander for English. *Comm. ACM* (1975).

[12] Wilks, Y. Natural language understanding systems within the A.I. paradigm—A survey and some comparisons. Stanford AI Laboratory Memo 237, Stanford University, Stanford, Calif. (March 1975).

[13] Winograd, T. *Understanding Natural Language*. Edinburgh Univ. Press, Edinburgh (1972).

[14] Wittgenstein, L. *Philosophical Investigations*. Oxford Univ. Press, Oxford (1953).

[15] Woods, W. Procedural semantics for a question-answer machine. *Proc. FJCC* (1968).

6

Good and Bad Arguments About Semantic Primitives

Yorick Wilks

University of Essex

Abstract: The paper surveys arguments from linguistics, artificial intelligence and philosophy about *semantic primitives*. It concentrates discussion on arguments of Charniak, Hayes, Putnam and Bobrow and Winograd; and suggests that many of the arguments against semantic primitives are based on no clear views about what the defenders are arguing *for*. The proponents of semantic primitives must share blame for this, as well as for supporting these entities by a range of highly specious arguments. However, the paper claims that, provided primitives are supported only by weak and commonsensical hypotheses, they can continue to play a valuable role in the analysis and processing of meaning

6.1 Introduction

This paper is of a heterogeneous nature, but with the single aim of collecting together a number of arguments about semantic primitives in one place. The issues that bear upon 'semantic primitives' are raised in psychology, linguistics and philosophy as well as artificial intelligence (AI) and no comprehensive treatment could be given of them all within the scope of a paper, even though very similar arguments arise in the several fields. Moreover, many of the arguments rest upon minsunderstandings of what advocates of semantic primitives are in fact claiming or *need* to claim, as I shall try to show. Again, one of the peculiarities of the semantic primitives issue is that these entities, whatever they may be, are so open to *bad* defenses by their advocates.

This paper attempts four goals:

(i)   to set out a number of arguments on the issue, and suggest that some are good and some are bad.

(ii)   while passing briefly over a number of well-known arguments on the issue – in particular psychological arguments and those concerned with model-theoretic semantics – to give some detailed attention to arguments of Bobrow and Winograd (in press), Charniak [7], Hayes [13] and Putnam [30], that seem to the author to require some reply in defense of the utility of primitives.

(iii)   to set out a number of weak claims about primitives which constitute a position that either answers or avoids the criticisms discussed.

K. Ahmad, C. Brewster and M. Stevenson (eds.), Words and Intelligence 1, 103–139.
© 2007 *Springer.*

(iv) to set out in an appendix some detailed description of a method of meaning description by means of primitives that has been developed since 1967, to serve as a system in terms of which examples can be given. This description is in a number of ways more detailed than its predecessors [39, 40, 42].

Like most interesting issues, the present one is of great antiquity and can be traced back to the "categories of being" of Aristotle, and more obviously to the Universal Characteristic: the language of universal atoms of meaning with which Seventeenth Century philosophers believed that problems of reasoning could be definitively settled. The same issue underlay the various thesaurus projects – culminating in Rogets Thesaurus to classify the universe in terms of a number of hierarchically organized categories. Again, I would maintain, the same general motivation led Ogden and Richards to specify a limited vocabulary, called 'Basic English', within which, they believed, the whole of literature could be more economically expressed.

However, for practical purposes, the issues can be considered to enter our consideration with the introduction of a semantic component into a Chomskyan generative grammar by Katz and Fodor [22]. This required what they called 'semantic markers': entities like HUMAN which would be attached in a lexicon to the sense of *bachelor* meaning an unmarried man, but *not* to the sense meaning a young seal at a certain phase of its development. Later, and within a group known as 'generative semanticists' entities called 'underlying verbs' were postulated as part of the meaning of verbs: thus STRIKE would be part of the underlying structure for *remind* as it appears in "Max reminds me of Pete" [28].

Thirdly, and simultaneously with the last tendency, Fillmore [11] suggested that verbs should be derived from structures, 'below' the level of the Chomskyan underlying phrase-marker, that incorporated *cases*, like AGENT.

In AI, primitive based systems made their appearance in the sixties, with the system of the Appendix [39] and more recently the system of Schank for verb decomposition (1972) which is also case based. Norman and Rummelhart [27] and Joshi [19]. The criticisms (see below) of Charniak, Hayes and Bobrow and Winograd bear directly upon such systems, as I believe do those of Putnam, although these last were directed against the marker system of Katz.

In what follows I shall not distinguish between such terms as SEMANTIC MARKER, SEMANTIC COMPONENT, SEMANTIC CATEGORY, SEMANTIC PRIMITIVE, CASE, UNDERLYING VERB, UNDERLYING PREDICATE etc. They are distinct in the literature, and defined as such by their authors, but our concern is their *general status*, and at that level the distinctions between them are not fundamental.

6.2 What then is a Primitive?

We can see easily enough *by example* what a primitive is – one of the three above, those in the appendix, or Schank's PTRANS, for example, primitive action underlying actions of physical transfer like *give* – but we clearly need to ask further questions.

The first suggestion to come to mind is that since primitives look like English words, then that is what they are. Zwicky [45] has argued that there are no primitives that do not have obvious 'English translations' (even Schank's PTRANS is evidently a short form of Physical TRANSfer), and that the fact is not due to chance.

However, it is strongly denied by Katz [20:156], Postal [28:113] and Schank [35:8], for example. As Katz puts it "although the semantic markers are given in the orthography of a natural language, they cannot be identified with the words or expressions of the language used to provide them with suggestive labels".

Let us pass over this question temporarily, and return to it after we have considered arguments as to what primitives might be other than the words they certainly appear to be.

Whether or not primitives are words, the question must arise as to whether there are any restrictions on what can be a primitive, and, more generally, whether there are any overall restrictions on the membership of the *set* of primitives used in any system – since primitives are always used within a system or 'language of primitives'.

Katz is perhaps the most obvious example of a system with very specific markers – such as SOMETHING-WITH-A-SEAT as a marker on *chair* – which suggests that, for him at least, any descriptive phrase in English could be, or indicate, a semantic marker.

Certain very general restrictions do suggest themselves, however, on the membership of a natural set of primitives or markers:

a) *finitude:* a marker set should not, for example, contain the names of the natural numbers. More seriously, the set should be considerable smaller than the set of words whose meanings it is to encode.

b) *comprehensiveness:* the set should be adequate to express and distinguish the senses of the word set whose meanings it is to encode.

c) *independence:* there should not be marker X, Y, Z in the set so that there is some function F such that $X = F(Y, Z)$. Though this will not be so easy to achieve if the members are hierarchically organized: if, for example, the set contains ANIMATE *and* HUMAN' for the set would then be non-independent, perhaps, if there were any marker like RATIONAL in it, where one might hold that

$$HUMAN = ANIMATE + RATIONAL.$$

d) *non-circularity:* there should not be such non-independencies such that two markers or primitives can be mutually defined, as in $X = F(Z, Y)$ AND $Z = F'(X, A)$.

e) *primitiveness:* no marker subset should be such that it could plausibly be replaced by a smaller defining set as in $A = F1(P, Q)$, $B = F2(P, Q)$, $C = F3(P, Q)$.

But these desiderata for a marker or primitive set bring us no closer to a definition, even a provisional one, of what a primitive is. Let us state a provisional definition:

> "A PRIMITIVE (or rather a set of primitives plus a syntax etc.) is a reduction device which yields a semantic representation for a natural language via a translation algorithm and which is not plausibly explicated in terms of or reducible to *other entities of the same type*".

This definition leaves open, as it is intended to, the serious question of whether or not primitives are explicable in terms of, or reducible to, entities of some quite other type. This is a serious question because most attacks on the use of primitives take the form of demands that they be explicated in terms of some other type of entity altogether; just as most bad defenses of primitives take the form of offering some very weak equivalence between primitives and other types of entity.

Sampson likened the role of primitives to that of English pound notes with their inscription "I promise to pay the bearer on demand the sum of one pound (i.e. in gold)": in that although the currency promises, in fact one only gets more currency for it at a bank, but never gold. In the same way primitives may seem to promise access to something else, but all one ever gets by way of explanation of their meaning is more primitives – provided that their set is at least somewhat non-independent, so that such an explication of one primitive by others can be given. At the end of this paper, I shall propose the tentative thesis that what Sampson suggests about primitives is true, but that is quite alright. There is no more trouble about that situation than there is in the present financial situation where we happily accept currency for currency at the bank, and just as in dictionaries we accept definitions of words by more words and never hope for more.

In concluding this section, we should note in passing that on the above 'preliminary definition' we shall find there are primitives in many fields: 'Noun' in linguistics, for example, is not further reducible and is not normally considered to be explicatable in terms of entities of any *other* type. Saying "it is that syntactic class whose members refer to physical objects" for example, does not get one far. In the Propositional Calculus, we have a paradigm case of connectives AND, OR, IMPLIES (and perhaps IDENTICALLYEQUAL) which appear to be primitives on the above definition (they are reducible to the single connective "/", the Sheffer stroke, but only with considerable effort and inconvenience). It was only, later, when the truth tables were derived by Wittgenstein and Peirce that the possibility of independent explication of the primitives arose. I.e. only *then* could one ask "What does AND in the Prop. Calc. actually *mean*?". Thus, if one accepts the truth tables as 'giving the meaning' of the connectives then they are no longer primitives in our sense. (We shall return to this point later).

There are examples, too, much closer to home, and in areas of AI generally inimical to the whole notion of 'primitive'. The variable SHOPPER in Charniak's supermarket frames [7], and the Basic Unit PERSON in Bobrow and Winograd's KRL–O language [4] are both primitives. They can be bound as variables to particular shoppers or persons, but nowhere in those systems can one be told *what* a shopper or a person is.

6.3 Escape Arguments

By 'escape arguments' I mean attempts, by both advocates and enemies of primitives, to explicate them in terms of some other kind of entity. In that sense, the claim that semantic primitives were really the words they appear to be and no more (a claim *not* made by Katz, Postal, Schank et al.) would not be an escape argument. Nor would claims (a) that primitives are justified by the overall performance of the linguistic or AI system in which they function, nor that (b) primitives *mean* exactly what the rules of the primitive language allow them to mean, and no more or less. Both these are claims to which we shall return, but for now we shall stay with 'escape arguments', most of which are, in my view, weak arguments.

Katz has given a number of arguments in support of semantic primitives of this general type. In [20:177] he argued that primitives were psychologically real and the content of ideas, in some sense. Later [21:88] he withdrew the claim about psychological reality, and argued instead that primitives referred to abstract concepts. The latter is, if anything, the weaker claim because it offers less for possible refutation. The former can at least be discussed in terms of what people *think* their general ideas are, but the latter cannot.

There has been some ingenious work within psychology proper on the status of semantic primitives, mostly in their support, and this too may reasonably be considered under the general heading of 'escape arguments': [17, 26, 18]. However, the psychological approach might seem to suffer from certain enormous handicaps in that it is very difficult for it, given its assumptions, to eliminate alternative yet pressing hypotheses.[1] So, for example, [17] contains an examination of recall experiments in which subjects correctly recalled the substance, though not the surface form, of sentences. Now this is indeed general supporting evidence for a theory of semantic primitives, but it cannot confirm it over and above, say a hypothesis that meaning is stored in terms of a theory whose primes are, let us say, binary numbers, or some other arbitrary, uninterpretable, *secret primes*.

There are strong considerations suggesting that there cannot be secret primes: the most ingenious of these is Zwicky's 'substance theory' [45] that depends on a projection of notions from chemistry, and in particular the correct view of early chemists that the primes of chemistry were themselves substances in the world (and not secret attributes that did not manifest themselves). This might seem a strong and plausible methodological assumption. There are also general philosophical considerations, adduced in the last section of the present paper, to the effect that there is no reason to believe primitives and words distinct, and that we cannot really conceive of a *secret* reduction language for our natural language. However,

---

[1] Again, in [18] subjects are asked to define words, and it is found that the most primitive words are harder to define, in terms of time taken, than the less primitive. However, it would seem common-sense that there will also be everyday, but not plausibly primitive words, like *unscrew* that will be as hard to define as candidates for primitivity like *move*.

and this is the present point, these considerations are not psychological ones, and I do not see how experimental psychology is to rule out the secret prime hypothesis.

To return to Katz for a moment: he also produces two other, quite different sorts, of argument. One is that primitives function within a linguistic theory as scientific entities, like 'force' or 'neutrino' function in physics [20:181] or as 'number' in mathematics [21:40]. These are *not* escape arguments: quite the opposite, in fact, since they are denials of the possibility of *independent* explication of primitives, since the point about notions like 'neutrino' is that they cannot be explicated independently of the theories in which they function.

The weakness of this argument, of course, is that the procedures of science that indirectly explicate concepts like neutrino, that is *experiments*, are not available to linguistics in any straight forward sense. However, some general *functional* explanation of primitives of this sort – though of an engineering rather than a strictly scientific sort – may well be a reasonable one.

Another persistent strain of argument in Katz is that markers refer not to merely *psychological* entities, but to innate ones, in some stronger sense. As Bierwisch [2:181] puts it "... all semantic structures might finally be reduced to components representing the basic dispositions of the cognitive and perceptual structure of the human organism". Schank, too, has taken a position along these lines, and incorporates explicit symbols, such as Long Term Memory, into his conceptual diagrams as names of psycho-physical entities. In this view there is some stronger commitment to the *universality* of primitives than on the merely psychological view. Moreover, this commitment should be an additional constraint on what can count as a primitive, since, if primitives really refer to entities that are innate or even 'hard wired' into human brains then such notions as the atomic weights of elements would not seem plausible candidates as semantic primitives describing the elements!

The general weakness of this 'escape view' is that it claims that there is some *correct set* of primitives open to discovery. Even if that were true, there is no conceivable way, here and now, of setting up any correlation between that right set and the primitives in actual use in linguistic systems.

And suppose the 'right set' were one day discovered, how would we reconcile that fact with the fact that, as Goodman [12:51] puts it "the terms adopted as primitives of a given system are readily definable in some other system. There is no absolute primitive, and no one correct selection of primitives".

If, say, Schank's primitive actions were located in the brain's hardware, would that necessarily constitute an 'escape justification' of them superior to that of the alternative primitives in terms of which they can easily be expressed: the Schankian PROPEL for example seems to be paraphrasable as Y CAUSE X TO MOVE, and INGEST as Y CAUSE X TO MOVE INTO Y?

But we need not pursue this *choice between* possible escape arguments, since the route via cognitive hardware is no more concrete or real than that via psychological-cum-mental introspection, or even abstract concepts.

6.4 Model Theoretic Semantics

Model theoretic semantics is the paradigm case of what I have called 'escape' theories of semantic primitives. It is also the subject of a great deal of technical and philosophical discussion at present, and no justice can be done to that here".[2] I shall simply mention some criticisms by Lewis, Hayes and Heidrich of three primitive-based systems.

All three criticisms share the assumption that, if primitives are to be used in any linguistic representation system, then they must denote, or refer to, entities of some other type – normally some set-theoretic function of individuals. This denotation is then able (with the aid of technical apparatus derived ultimately from the semantics Tarski constructed for classical logic) to justify the whole primitive-using system and hence the primitives themselves.

Lewis's system [23] is explicitly opposed to that of Katz and Fodor:

> "Semantic markers are symbols; items in the vocabulary of an artificial language we may call *Semantic Markerese*. Semantic interpretation by means of them amounts merely to a translation algorithm ... to the auxiliary language Markerese. But we can know the Markerese translation of an English sentence without knowing the first thing about the meaning of the English sentence.... The Markerese method is attractive in part just because it deals with nothing but symbols".

There is no space here to discuss Lewis's alternative model theoretic semantics (MTS), but it is worth noting that it would be very difficult in principle to provide one that was not open to the criticisms he himself makes here of Katz and Fodor's 'markerese'. A MTS itself turns out to be a translation system to another system of symbols, and to symbols only, for, after all, how could any formal system lead to anything else? One of the most puzzling aspects of this mode of criticism is its persistent belief that it has somehow managed to 'escape' to some other non-symbolic realm. Finally, it is a matter of simple observation that many who master the technical complexities of MTS cannot discern, for any given formal structure, what English sentence it is the structure *for*. Thus it is not clear a priori that Lewis's criticisms will not tell against his own position.

What would it be like to satisfy the demand for a MTS for semantic primitives? Heidrich [15] has attempted to provide one for a fragment of Generative Semantics analysis, and in particular of the analysis of *seek* as *TRY to FIND*, where the two upper case 'underlying verbs' may be considered as primitives for the argument of this paper.

Heidrich gives, as the denotational meaning of *seek*, sets of pairs of seekers and sought things. One of these sets will be that of pairs of humans and the zoological objects they are in fact seeking: a set which can be written

$$((Human)(Zoological\ Object))$$

---

[2] Though see the chapter on "Philosophy of Language" in [9].

If John is in fact seeking a unicorn then the pair (John, Unicorn) will be in that set of pairs. Similarly *find* can also be expressed as a set of pairs of finders and found, of which a subset will be that of the human finders and the zoological objects found and which can also be written as above, although it will not be the *same set of pairs*, because not all things that can be sought can be found – such as unicorns. Lastly, *try* is defined as a mapping from actors (the triers) to actions (the action tried). Thus, *TRY to FIND* will be written

$$((Human)((Human)(Zoological\ Objects)))$$

where the object on the right of this pair is ((Human)(Zoological Object)) i.e. the pairs which are the denotation of *find*. The point of the whole system is to give a *guarantee of the equivalence*:

$$seek = TRY\ to\ FIND$$

by defining an operator 0 such that:

0   ((Human)(Zoological   Object)) = ((Human)((Human)(Zoological   Object)))
which is to say that every seeking of a zoological object by a person is a pair that is also in the pairs that are the meaning of *TRY to FIND*.

The heart of Heidrich's system is the *guarantee* that can be put as the claim that, for any sentence like 'John seeks a unicorn', the corresponding sentence 'John tries to find a unicorn'[3] will be synonymous with it. That is to say, a guarantee that is not given by any pair of *inference rules*:

$$(X)\ (Y)\ (X\,seek\,Y \rightleftarrows X\,try\,to\,find\,Y)$$

The thesis of this paper – and we shall come to an exposition of it in the final section – is that any such guarantees must be misguided, for they are wholly inappropriate to the subject matter, natural language. On the contrary, *seek* and *try to find* are more or less equivalent forms of words, so much so that we might indeed use those on the right as part of a reduction language in the manner of the Generative Semantics. But there is no guaranteed equivalence and our usage does not assume there is – hence no operator like o can guarantee anything, because *there is nothing to guarantee*. It is not merely that we can and do use *seek* so that it is not equivalent to *try to find*, as in "I seek your leader" (which is more like "I want to find"), for my point would hold *even if we could* always use *try to find* where we use seek. The serious point is that the value of such a discovery of equivalence would not be enhanced at all by the postulation of a 0 operator, or by the notion

---

[3] Heidrich's system assumes what Zwicky called 'the substance theory of primes', namely that any primes can necessarily also appear in surface sentences Similarly, Sandeewall [32] criticised Schank's primitive system radically, and argued it did not have a semantics at all in his, Sandewall's, sense, but *at the same time* pointed out that Schank did not distinguish two MAN variables in a particular semantic diagram : a non-radical criticism that Schank was able to remedy immediately.

that the synonymity in practice *rests upon* or requires *any* selection of individuals in another calculus.

Hayes [13, 14] has produced a number of sophisticated arguments against the thesis underlying the present paper. One aspect of these criticisms is not radical Heidrich, too, made such non-radical [4] – in the sense of questioning the very basis of primitives – but is a demand by Hayes that primitive systems give a more explicit account of the rules regulating inferences concerning a primitive for substance, like STUFF. This demand for greater explicitness is a good one, though there is reason to doubt that any coherent and consistent metaphysics of substance can in fact be given. Two and a half millenia of philosophy have failed to provide one, yet throughout that time everyday conversation about substances, such as coal, cil and air goes on unimpeded. It is important to stress this fact, so as to not fall into the error of imagining that language about substances requires such a metaphysics of substances in order to function at all. It clearly does not.

Hayes' demand for the metaphysics of substance in a primitive system – what, he is asking, does STUFF *actually mean* – is also a radical criticism and a demand for an MTS. For him this demand is closely allied to the demand for a MTS of programming languages, a demand that the designers of languages like PLANNER have been slow to meet. In Hayes [14] the two demands are presented in detail in the same paper and as aspects of the same demand. I feel that the two are different in the following ways:

We may properly ask for the MTS of a programming language, and hence for the MTS of any primitive-using natural language understanding program, written in that language, be it LISP, PLANNER or whatever. Such a program semantics will specify the objects and sets whose manipulation is isomorphic to the operation of the program itself. However, and this is my point, there is no reason to suppose that those sets and objects, yielded by the program semantics, will be *the same as the sets and objects that would be the direct denotations of the primitives*, as provided by a standard MTS for the primitive representation system. Hayes seems to argue the need for both, yet never argues that they would yield the same result. But, if they did not, there would be problems for anyone who, like Hayes, believes that such denotations are the "real meanings" of the primitives – for *which set* would then be the real meanings?

The demand for an MTS of a primitive system can be put in one of three analogical ways: as like that of an MTS for a logic, for a programming language, or like that of an axiomatisation of a scientific theory. All three trace back to Tarski's work, but the demands are normally put somewhat differently. However, in all three modes, the system to be analysed is normally considered to have some temporal, if not explanatory, primacy to its axiomatisation of explication: there has to be a Predicate Calculus to have a semantics for it, a LISP to have a semantics at all, and a Quantum theory must exist so as to be axiomatised. In that sense, the original theory cannot be useless without its axiomatisation – the Propositional Calculus

---

[4] Heidrich, too, made such non-radical criticisms when he pointed out that it was unclear whether the Generative Semantics analyses obeyed a commutativity rule or not.

was of great interest before the truth tables provided a semantics for it. But in Hayes' criticisms it is unclear whether he is arguing that the primitive system is 1) *useless without* an MTS or 2) would merely *be better with* it. It seems to me that the analogy from logic, science and programming suggests that he must intend the latter, in which case the author concerned with a primitive system replies; OK but hang on till I have a full system/program for you to explicate. Nonetheless, many of Hayes' criticisms suggest that he actually believes the *former* – in which case the MTS is not just an a posteriori explication, but a creative tool in the construction of the substantive theory, and so should have insights to offer into the subject matter, natural language. But it is a fact of observation that such insights have been very slow in coming (though they have very recently been argued for, in a computational context, by Hobbs and Rosenschein [16]).

6.5 Some Miscellaneous Misunderstandings

Some criticisms of primitives rest only upon misunderstandings; or rather, they result from taking contingent features of some system using primitive representations and imagining that a drawback of primitives *as such* has been found. Let us look at two very briefly.

In [3] Bobrow argues that the primitive expansion or 'paraphrase' requires a more complex match later than does the original English word that the paraphrase is for. The point is not argued in detail, but I feel there are two wrong assumptions behind it: (1) that the whole of a (possibly large) primitive representation must be accessed if any part of it is, and (2) that one has no access to the original 'surface word' after expansion to primitives, and so there must be both a loss of information and a horrible complex match for any process using the expansion.

Now it is true that Schank has, in descriptions of his system, appeared to accept (1), and has denied that any access to the surface word is possible or desirable after a translation to the primitives of conceptual dependency. But primitive-based systems do not have to work that way : in the matcher of Wilks [39, 40, 42] only the head primitives of semantic formulas (see Appendix) are accessed during the initial text match. Again, when that system is operating as a translator, it is most important that it has access, not only to the possible semantic formulas (of primitives) for an input word, but also to the possible French output words to which each formula can lead. Translation would not be possible without this. No representation in primitives could be expected to distinguish by its structure *hammer, mallet* and *axe*, for example, even though their translations into another language may be different and must be got right.

A more serious misunderstanding in [4] occurs when the authors contrast their proposal for 'perspectives' of the representation – perhaps redundantly – of a number of points of view of the same object or action. "In general, we believe that the description of a complex object cannot be broken down into a single set of primitives, but must be expressed through multiple views" (ibid: 5).

Primitives constitute a language of description of meaning and therefore, in principle at least, a language in which alternative descriptions of the same thing can be given. Indeed, it is no accident at all that these who have been concerned with primitives – and this goes for all the movements mentioned at the start of this paper – have also been concerned to emphasise the *ambiguity* of words, surely the paradigm of multiple description.

Bobrow and Winograd's error seems to be in assuming that some of the less defensible claims about primitives, such as their being the absolute and right representation of a word's meaning, must imply that there is also as a matter of fact only *one* such description. But, to the best of my knowledge, not even those who have held the strongest views about primitives have claimed this In Schank [35:264] for example, he argues that *restaurant* must have not only a narrative 'script-like' representation in primitives, but also another representation to express its 'physical sense' as well. In the system of the Appendix, an object like a house can have both a formula with head POINT and one with head SPREAD. The former expresses its aspect as a *location* in space, and that formula should be attached in the representation of "John went to Mary's house", whereas the latter expresses its aspect as a spatially *extended* thing, as in "John lives in a three-bedroomed house". These two formulas need not be thought of as defining two *senses* of house either, merely two ways that *house* is treated in the lexicon.

The criticisms discussed in this section rest, I am sure, on a combination of confused argument, and taking the faults of certain implementations of primitives as abstract criticisms of the general notion.

6.6 Putnam's Argument

It may be of interest to note in passing a version of the primitives-versus-facts dispute within philosophy, or rather as a philosophical attack on the marker system of Katz. Putnam [30] argued that Katz's definition of a word sense as a conjunction of markers is wrong on several grounds. First, because it is simply unrealistic when we look at the ways meanings are actually defined in dictionaries: not only by markers, but by synonyms, facts, and even illustrative quotations etc., a point also made in [6].

Many of Katz's markers are of the type Putnam criticizes, as when (unmarried) appears in the lexical entry for *bachelor*, but many are not, at least in the more developed forms of his work. In the entry for *chair* are forms like (something with legs) and (something with a back) and these have the same content as complex descriptions in ordinary dictionaries. One quite legitimate criticism of Katz is that he never gives either a characterization that determines what would and what would not count as a marker, and that he never gives any syntax, like that of the Appendix or even of Bierwisch [2], that would allow one to characterize such complex markers in terms of an inventory of simple ones. Nonetheless, he certainly does have markers with complex content.

Moreover, it is not the case, as Putnam alleges [30:193] that for Katz the predication, of a marker of the word sense, is *always analytic*. Much of Katz's motivation in all this work, is the provision of an algorithmic explication of the notoriously obscure philosophical notion of analyticity – but, he never claims that "A chair has legs" is analytic[5], in any sense, in virtue of the presence of (has-four-legs) in the lexical entry for *chair*.

The notion of analyticity has to come into our discussion, because it is an important tool – though in quite different ways – for both authors under discussion. This becomes clear when we see that Putnam's alternative proposals are to postulate a *stereotype individual* [30:196], of the kind under discussion and definition, and that meaning 'definitions' should take the form of the statement of *core facts about the stereotype*, as in "A tiger has a striped skin". The opposition to all forms of analyticity is implicit in the use of "fact".

There is a fairly clear similarity between this Katz – Putnam argument, and the opposition of writers like Bobrow and Winograd to primitives discussed in the last section: they even, as it happens, share the terminology of stereotypes and facts.

In the argument under discussion, the opposition is in fact false – although a real disagreement remains, I shall contend – because, as we saw, Katz's notion of marker is so wide that the predication of (something with legs) of *chair* is just a notational variant of a Putnam core fact "A chair has legs" about a stereotype chair. That is to say, not all Katz markers are equivalent to analytic predications, and *many of them are equivalent to the assertion of facts*. Hence the opposition Putnam saw between his proposals and Katz's, was based on the particular examples from Katz he discussed like *bachelor*. Moreover, the notion of stereotype may well have drawbacks that Katz's views do not. A stereotype man, surely has two legs, and therefore "A man has two legs" should be a Putnamian core fact, one that may not be always true, but a reasonable guide to experience. It will have just the same status as "A man is an animal". It is, of course, just the distinction between these two facts that Katz wishes to keep central – and which Putnam cannot – namely that the first 'fact' may let us down from time to time, but the latter almost certainly will not. It was just this distinction – one which may well have its role somewhere in AI systems – that Katz, like all believers in the analytic-synthetic distinction, wished to maintain.

But this is not the issue between Katz and Putnam that really concerns us. If I am right, and Putnam's attack on the nature of Katz's lexical entries fails to take account of their flexibility, is there then any issue remaining between them that is relevant to our concerns here?

I think there is, and that it is our old friend *the reduced language of semantic description*. It is not raised explicitly by Putnam, but there is a clear suggestion that Katz's marker-language is not co-extensive with ordinary English – and that is correct about Katz's intentions – and that the language of core-facts might well be.

---

[5] That is to say, that this sense is true in virtue of meaning, or of logic, or, in any event, independently of the facts of life.

This issue is, of course, independent of the above point about core-facts, that they do not in any way indicate the relative 'factiness' of various facts.

To the reduction point, I would reply, as I did in the last section to Bobrow and Winograd's stereotypes, that they will *in fact* turn out to constitute a restricted, or primitive, language. In KRL, it was clear that certain formal objects were privileged, in the sense of being undefined by others, but in the case of real dictionaries this is not so clear. The statistical study of the contents of Webster's Third International Dictionary[6] have shown that there is use – in the sense of defining words used very frequently to define others, and which incidentally, are very close to the primitives of the Appendix – but, naturally, since these frequent words are also in the dictionary they are precisely not privileged, by being immune from definition themselves. True but, as I shall argue in the last section, the ultimate circularity of dictionaries – in that all words are defined by others, also in the dictionary – does not contradict the 'primitiveness' of real dictionary entries. This is because the key words in the restricted vocabulary or the definitions (like "substance", "size", "animate") are those which, although in the dictionary, have highly unilluminating definitions. The usefulness of the dictionary actually *presupposes* that one knows what those primitive words mean, otherwise it is more or less unusuable.

6.7 Charniak's Argument

Charniak's [8] paper is concerned with the use of the concept of *case* in AI, but it also presents at least one very general argument against the use of primitives, even though its particular target is case primitives.

Charniak is among those who demand some explication of primitives in terms *of something else*, but he is prepared to consider *explicanda* for primitives much more congenial to AI than those proposed by logicians. What he proposes are, in effect, the procedures associated with a particular primitive[7]: [8:19].

"meaning (CASE) = The set of inferences one can make about X, knowing only that X is in case CASE".

where CASE is some primitive such as TO, FROM, INST (instrument) etc. (see list of case primitives in Appendix). He argues that no existing primitive using systems have such inference rules, but that they might well be useful. He proposes one, using the direction primitive TO: (ibid. p. 20)

"TO (LOC, EVENT) IMPLIES that X (where OBJECT (X, EVENT)) is located at LOC".

---

[6] At Systems Development Corporation, Santa Monica, California.

[7] This is precisely the sort of AI-oriented explicandum not taken account of in the anti-primitive arguments of Babrow et al. [5:10].

However, he proposes four conditions that such a rule must satisfy to be useful :

(1) the rule must be independent of the nature of EVENT
(2) that TO must be a case of more than one primitive action for, if it were only to appear with, say, action MOVE, then it would be no more than the name of some argument of MOVE, since MOVE could be written

$$MOVE\ (X,\ Y,\ Z)$$

where, say, Y might be always the "direction towards" argument. In a situation where *only move* had a TO argument, TO would be dispensible in favour of "second argument place in MOVE".

(3) a case primitive in the rule quoted above must not be ridiculously specific, as would be a direction primitive UP–TO–THIRD–FLOOR.
(4) there should not be a better way of doing things that would invalidate any of the above three conditions. Charniak suggests two such better ways:
(4a) having only a single movement primitive in a system (in the system of the Appendix this would involve collapsing MOVE, DROP, FLOW etc.) whose aspects would be distinguished by cases (in that circumstance FLOW, for example, would be replaced be a new more general MOVE, but the mover would always be (FLOW STUFF), a liquid).

Charniak argues that doing this would invalidate condition (2) and so (case) primitives would no longer confer 'benefits' on the system.

(4b) Charniak argues that the result of the proposed TO-inference-rule above could be installed in the representation initially. Thus, in a primitive formula (in the Appendix system) for "move" we could place an additional subformula indicating that the mover ends up at the new location, viz. (a partial formula):

((*PHYSOB SUBJ)(((((WHERE POINT)SAME)SLOCA)(*PHYSOB BE))CAUSE)

THE MOVER   RESULT : LOWER located at same spatial point

((WHERE POINT)TO)MOVE)

DIRECTIONCASE   MAIN PRIMITIVE

Doing this, says Charniak [8:22], would violate condition (3) against *very specific cases*.

There are, I think, a number of misapprehensions and confusions – as well as certain benefits – in Charniak's arguments, and it may be worth examining these briefly.

First, he is quite right to emphasise the value of such rules as his proposed TO-rule, but wrong to suggest that they do not exist in primitive-oriented systems. In the case of my own system, the *extraction rules* are just such rules: that take the case primitives of a formula and make inferences, using the context of the text-template in which that formula is in fact embedded (i.e. its variables are bound to real items). Charniak's TO-rule could serve as one among the extraction rules attached to TO, and these rules programmed in the 1973 version of the associated program [41].

Some of Charniak's conditions for the usefulness of such rules are odd, (1) is unobjectionable, and indeed Charniak adds a useful illustration of the way some systems have confused "TO = movement towards" with "TO = indicating direction", in which case a TO-rule would not be event independent because the rule would not apply to uses of TO coding "change in direction of eyes" since the eyes do not end up at the object they finally point to! So, his condition (1) could be a useful requirement on the level of specificity of case primitives.

However, (2) is a return of a very general argument of Charniak's about the reducibility of case notation to argument place numbering that I have answered elsewhere [43]. But here it should be noticed that *if* case primitives can be reduced to "argument n of action primitive P" descriptions, then it is quite irrelevant whether or not condition (2) holds. Case primitive TO is no less reduced if it is "arg.place n_1 of P_1 *and* arg.place n_2 of P_2" than if it is only the first clause! Reducibility – if it is a vice, and I believe it not to be in this form – is no worse if TO functions only within a *single* action primitive. Thus, condition (2) is idle in conjunction with Charniak's much more general argument.

Condition (3) has the right flavour, but no clear force. We are given no idea of *how* specific a case primitive may be before it becomes ridiculous.

Condition (4) is where Charniak believes the heart of his argument to be, and where he makes use of conditions (2) and (3), but it seems to me to lack all force. Charniak's (4) has value only if suggestions (4a) and (4b) *are* in fact better ways of organizing a primitive using system, but he gives no reasons for believing that they are!

In (4a), with a single movement primitive, we would have a rather restricted system – just as a language with only one movement verb would be (think of baby-talk using only "go"). Suggestion (5b) might violate condition (2) – which is idle anyway as we saw – but so what if (4a) is a very uncomfortable way of organizing a language understanding system?

Much the same applies to (4b), for why would it be better to make all inferences explicit in the initial representation? Discussion of some earlier forms of Schank's system – where he tended towards embodying many inferences in the initial representation – have suggested that is not good procedural sense. Why should Charniak just assume without argument that it is – for his general argument has no force if it is not a benefit. It is well known in logic that rules of inference can be replaced by equivalent axioms – but there are excellent arguments against doing this.

Interestingly enough, even if one did accept Charniak's assumption that (4b) is a benefit, condition (3) is not thereby violated as he claims. The partial formula for "move". that was written above, so as to incorporate suggestion (4b), does not require any more specific cases at all, only repetition of argument names. Charniak is confusing UP–TO–THIRD–FLOOR with UP–TO (third floor).

6.8 Conclusion: Towards a Clearer View of Semantic Primitives

What follows is not intended to be systematic, but only a sketch for a position justifying the use of semantic primitives in an AI system. A position moreover, that avoids the criticisms of their use discussed in this paper, and avoids relying upon bad defences of their use as well.

The first basic claim here is that semantic primitives are a useful *organizing hypothesis* – in Zwicky's [45:471] sense – for an AI natural language system.

They will enable useful generalizations to be made – Charniak's TO-rule will serve as an example, but all primitive advocating papers contain many more complex ones – but this does not require the claim that they lead to universal generalization[8] across language boundaries, nor even that more than one language is translatable into a given primitive system.

We need not expect that such generalizations will lead to conventional linguistic observations at all – only that they will yield a more perspicuous language under-standing system. The linguistic debate over whether or not "kill" can be represented in a system of primitives as CAUSE to DIE or CAUSE to BECOME NOT ALIVE (see [25] and [10] has shown that there is no agreement there over whether or how such proposals can lead to observations of sentences that will settle the matter.

The second basic claim of this paper is that a primitive-using representation language is essentially a natural language. This in no way implies that it is not a suitable language for AI systems, but only that users of primitives should cease to claim (as Katz and Schank, for example, do) that the similarity between primitives like CAUSE and English words like 'cause' is mere chance, and of no theoretical significance.

On the contrary, it is the heart of the matter, because the alternative view – what Yons [24] has called the "conceptual substance" view, that there is a real conceptual substance, *independent of language*, and into which precise and clear conceptual translation can be made – is contrary to commonsense, and the whole weight of Anglo-Saxon philosophical and linguistic tradition.

The counter claim made in this paper is consistent with what Zwicky [45] has called the *Substance Theory of Primes*: that every semantic primitive can appear as a surface word in a natural language[9].

---

[8] Zwicky [45:474] notes that, for him, the "most notable gap in existing treatments of semantic primes is the absence of assertions of formal or substantive universals involving them", but when we see what would count as one such it is not hard to see why no one would assert them as universals, but only as methodological principles, in an AI system or in an underlying linguistic base. Zwicky quotes Chomsky's suggestion of "the condition that artifacts are defined in terms of certain human goals needs and functions instead of solely in terms of physical qualities". This could only be a 'coding postulate' and not anything that could be verified directly by any conceivable linguistic *observations.*

[9] It is unfortunate that 'substance', in the Lyons and Zwicky phrases, occurs in diametrically opposed doctrines.

This does not require that the same 'word' as it appears in the primitive and surface form must, in any definable sense 'have the same meaning'. It is simply a claim that the link between the two cannot be broken[10], even though it is often essential that the two usages do differ, as in the linguistic equation of 'kill" with CAUSE to BECOME NOT ALIVE. The latter can *only* be a representation of 'kill' if CAUSE is taken to mean 'reasonably immediately cause'. For, if it can cover causation at any distance in time, then the non-equivalence of the two forms is obvious[11].

The view being defended is not that the semantic representation system of the Appendix, to take an example close to hand, is really English[12]. It is rather the claim that facts we accept about natural languages are also facts about that primitive language: namely, that it has no *correct* vocabulary, any more than English has; that there may be many adequate alternative vocabularies for it, just as there may be many vocabularies for English. It is not even necessary that the language be a minimal set, with no member definable by the others. As Goodman [12:51], puts it:

> "In general, the terms adopted as primitives of a given system are readily definable in some other system. There is no absolute primitive, and no one correct selection of primitives".

Graham Ritchie (personal communication) has raised the question : if the primitive language is also a natural language, then what set is formed by the union of it and English? The answer is English with some words having senses in addition to those they have in standard English. A more satisfactory analogy than set theory is provided by the elusive Wittgensteinian notion of the game. A form like CAUSE plays different roles in English and the primitive language, just as one rugby player may play both Rugby Union and Rugby League at different times – there is no problem, and he is not required to be a schizophrenic.

The clearest consequence of the thesis, that the primitive language is also a natural language, is that there can be no *direct* justifications of individual primitives (what I called 'escape moves' earlier) any more than there can be direct justifications, or meanings, given for the words of English. There just is no non-linguistic realm into which we can escape from language, and explanations of English words. That is simply fact.

This does not exclude[13] the association of inferential procedures with particular primitives as partial explanations of them – just as we may explain 'cause' in English

---

[10] Prior [29] is the standard argument that the connexion cannot be broken in logic either, for it is not arbitrary that ' ' means 'and'.

[11] Thalberg [36] is another demonstration of the way CAUSE differs from its commonsense meaning in the representations of action- theory.

[12] Hayes [14] has characterized the position of this paper as "Let's pretend it (the primitive language) is English". On the contrary, it is "Let's not pretend that it is unrelated to English", which is a more reasonable view.

[13] Nor does it exclude the association of primitives with complex knowledge structures: of, say. MAN with a 'frame-like' object telling you a lot about humans (see Wilks [44]).

to someone by producing examples of causal inference or, as the Wittgensteinian would say, samples of the proper use of 'cause'.

The third, and final, claim involved in the position of the paper is that we should pay more attention to the structure of real dictionaries when thinking about primitive languages. This point has been put many times[14], in reply for example, to Katz's very rigid views of a semantic dictionary entry, as compared to the function of actual dictionaries.

One final point should be made here about a possible justification of primitives on the grounds that actual statistical analysis of large dictionaries[15] reveals that their definitions are, in fact, in terms of a restricted sub-vocabulary, to a large extent, and that this is close to a natural set of primitives : *cause, human, object, move, substance* and so on. It might be argued that this fact, far from supporting the claims about primitives made in this paper, has the opposite effect: for this 'defining sub-vocabulary' for Webster's Third, say, has all its members actually *in* the dictionary as well, whereas the primitives of the Appendix language, for example, are not, in general, defined in terms of the *other* primitives. Hence, we have a clear difference between the primitive language and English as defined by Webster's Third International Dictionary.

But this difference is mere apparent than real, because it is a fact of observation that the dictionary definitions, in Webster's say, of members of this 'defining sub-vocabulary' are curiously unsatisfactory. Looking up *substance* or *object* in a dictionary (provided you know the language, and are not a foreigner looking up an *unknown* lexeme) is unrevealing, *precisely because* hundreds of entries in the dictionary assume you already know the meaning of the word. In that sense, such words function in very much the way the vocabulary of an explicitly primitive language does. They have a merely organizing role in the dictionary as a whole.

In sum, then, the claim of this paper is that primitives are to be found in all natural language understanding systems – even those like (Bobrow and Winograd, in press) that argue vigourously against them. Explicit use of primitives is preferable, and energy should be concentrated on making the systems that use them *work*, and not on justifying the primitives directly and independently, for that may not be possible, even in principle. However, such systems should be as formal and perspicuous as possible, although it may be necessary at certain stages to take an inductive, or descriptive, approach to the primitive language – to *discover* its generalizations, just as one might with a natural language – rather than attempting to fix all its possible well-formed strings and interpretations *in advance*. Finally, it is most important not to imagine that a useful representational system can only be achieved if certain vexatious philosophical problems – concepts, reference, correctness of the primitive set, etc. – *are cleared up first*. If the analogy with a natural language has any force, then that simply cannot be necessary.

---

[14] Viz. Bolinger [6], Wierzbicka [38], Weinreich [37]. It is also a requirement therefore that a primitive language be as 'readable' or 'habitable' as possible – an interesting proposal to do this for Schank's primitive language is in Shafe [33].

[15] John Olney, Systems Development Corp. (personal communication).

Appendix

The construction of semantic formulas representing word-senses

What follows is a detailed account of how to construct semantic formulas – that represent the senses of English words – from an inventory of semantic primitives. It is not intended to give a *justification* for doing this, that comes elsewhere and from the overall operation of the program using the formulas – but to give the method. Everything i this description simply *assumes* that we are provided with 100 primitives and 7 types of subformulas, and, as I have explained elsewhere [42] I also believe that demands for their independent justification actually rest upon confusions.

Another naive, though almost universal, assumption made here is that a word can be said to have a number of discrete senses – so that we can provide the word with a number of formulas corresponding to these senses. Any careful thought shows that actual usages of words in texts are difficult to assign in practice to one and only one of a set of pre-sorted "senses": it is not just that a usage may cover more than one, but that it may be essentially vague between several. However, discrete senses are a sensible working hypothesis which accords with common sense and, in any case, no one has much idea at the moment of how to capture "vagueness" in a formal manner.

An important feature of the formulas is that they are not diagrammatic. That is to say, they are already in list format, and it does not require a special subtheory to show how to encode them for computation. Moreover, those who prefer to see their sense representations diagrammatically should remember that in a clear sense explanations of word meaning are more natural in a sequential "language-like form". The formulas are intended to provide this, and much of their syntax is part of this effort to produce a "habitable" form (in Watt's sense) readable and writable by the user.

The end product of this process, then, is a list of formulas for any English word, where the formulas may correspond to whatever part of speech in which the word may be used. It is best to begin with a familiar example, that of the action sense of the word "break":

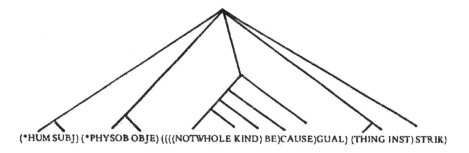

(*HUM SUBJ) (*PHYSOB OBJE) ((((NOTWHOLE KIND) BE)CAUSE)GUAL) (THING INST) STRIK)

The *general* structure of such formulas has been explained in Wilks [39, 40, 41, 42]. They are intended to express the interlingual meaning of the sense of the word, and the primitives that comprise them are intended to be interlingual even though they happen to be mostly Anglo-Saxon monosyllables. Formulas are trees of left right dependencies but the dependence is interpreted differently according to the type of the *subformula*, where a subformula is any left – right pair whose two members are either a primitive or another subformula. Formulas in the dictionary are thus binary trees, though the one above is written so that the four main subformulas (connected directly to the top of the tree) are written *at the same level* as STRIK, the *head* of the formula, that is to say its principal primitive element, which is always the rightmost since the dependencies are always left right. The additional parentheses that make the above tree binary have been left out for perspicuity – I shall return to this point later. Subformulas like the four connected to the top as above, are referred to as the *top level subformulas* of the formula, and are usually *case* subformulas – they have as their principal (rightmost) elements the case primitives SUBJ (Agent), OBJE (Object), GOAL (Purpose) and INST (Instrument) respectively. The whole formula is to be interpreted as explaining the meaning of "break" as a STRIKing, done preferably with an INSTrument that is a THING, with the GOAL of CAUSing a PHYSICALOBJect to BE NOT WHOLE, and the action being preferably done by a HUMan SUBJect. A formal version of such loose explanations will be given below.

The right place to start thinking about the construction of formulas and subformulas is to see them as built up from seven types of subformulas. These are:

I. Adverbial Subformulas

(TRUE HOW)

equivalent to the English "really" in its straightforward sense. The governor (righthand element) is the element HOW, and the dependent lefthand member is always a qualifier element like TRUE, or a *qualifier* subformula (type II, see below) equipollent with a qualifier, or a *case* subformula (type II, see below) as in

((MAN LIKE)HOW)

which is equivalent to (and so could be the formula for) "humanly".

The head must always be HOW if the subformula is also a formula, that is if it is to be in the dictionary as the sense of a word. However, if it occurs *within* formula a type I can have a head that is not HOW – it can be simply be a qualifier element. Thus,

(TRUE TELL)

whose meaning is "speaking truthfully" is a subformula of type V (action groups) where the element TRUE is the dependent, and can be considered a type

I subformula. For an element can be a subformula but not a formula. Later a full list will be given of specific conditions on formulas that *do not apply* to subformulas (such as not being a single element, and requiring a HOW governor in type I etc.). These special conditions are required on the formulas because they not only express meaning but have to participate in higher level structures like *templates* (q.v.).

Since every grouping in a formula is binary and one of the seven types, we should ask what is the interpretation of the left right dependency in each of the types. In a type I subformula, if its governor is HOW then the dependency is just that of an action qualifier on the *name* of a relation (HOW), for HOW is then no more than the name of the relation between the action qualifier, say TRUE and the action qualified, say, TELL.

II. Case Subformulas

These always have a governor that is one of the case elements (see the list in full below). A case subformula is never a formula, which is to say that no type II group is ever listed in the dictionary as the meaning of a word sense. The senses of English surface prepositions which might be thought to have a casetype formulas are in fact formulas with one of the pseudo-action heads PDO and PBE, see below.

A typical case subformula would be the

(THING INST)

occurring in the sample formula for "break" above. The dependent is normally a substantive element or group, or a class element like *HUM which is equivalent to a class of other elements (see the full element list below). The cases WAY (manner)GOAL (purpose) and *TLOCA (time location), however, normally take a depend at which is a full or partial assertion, which is to say groups V, VI and VII. The "syntax of subformulas" is satisfied if the dependent is any of those types, but, and we shall return to this point later, the "semantics of formulas" requires that there be enough information available in the formula so that a "full assertion" (type VII) can be constructed in certain circumstances. So for example, in the "break" formula above, the GOAL (purpose case) subformula is:

((((NOTWHOLE KIND)BE)CAUSE)GOAL)

in which the dependent of GOAL is an action (CAUSE) together with its complement ((NOTWHOLE KIND)BE), i.e. the *dependent* (on GOAL) is type V. However, the agent (*HUM) and object (*PSYSOB) can also be used by later inferences (see below) to create an appropriate *semantic object* of GOAL, because the meaning of the purpose case here is that "breaking" is a causing by humans of physical objects to be not whole. This "semantics of formulas", distinct from their syntax, is discussed below under "trans-group rules".

As with type I, when the governor in type II is a case name (as it always is), the dependency is of an assertion, or an entity, on the case name itself. Since, as we shall see below, type II groups are normally themselves the dependents of actions, the case name is simply the name of the relation of dependency of the case dependent entity on the action in the higher level group. So, in the "break" formula, INST simply names the dependence of THING ON STRIK.

III. Qualifier (or Adjectival) Subformulas

The structure of this type is like that of type I; if the subformula is a formula then its governor is the special element KIND. Thus we have

(LINE KIND)

which is equivalent to the English adjective "linear". If the governor is KIND then the dependent is a qualifier or, as here, a substantive. As can be seen from the

(NOTWHOLE KIND)

subformula in the "break" formula, a subformula of type III can have KIND as a governor while not itself being a formula. In that example it is of that form, rather than merely NOTWHOLE as in

(NOTWHOLE BE)

so as to make clear that the subformula

((NOTWHOLE KIND)BE)

is of type V, which includes forms (III BE), a predication of a quality, and *not* type VI which includes (IV BE), a predication of equivalence. WHOLE and NOTWHOLE standing alone are ambiguous between their functions as a quality and a substantive, and so (NOTWHOLE BE) could be either type V or VI, whereas (NOTWHOLE KIND) can only be III and so ((NOTWHOLE KIND)BE) – by rules of type inclusion we shall come to – can only be interpreted as type V, a predication of a quality.

Two minor points should have emerged in passing. First, that any element can be negated by becoming the new atom with NOT as its first three characters, the rest staying the same. Not all elements are ever negated in fact and some of the case elements could not be interpreted if they were negated. Secondly, that many of the elements can function in more than one subformula or group, and so in more than one role – all substantives can also be qualifiers, for example, many action elements can be qualifiers. This is clarified by the tables attached to the full element list below.

Not all qualifier elements have a substantive function, for example, GOOD, MAL (male) are *only* qualifiers, they cannot be governors in type *IV*.

IV. Nominal (or Substantive) Subformulas

These subformulas are those whose governor is a substantive element like MAN, STUFF, THING:

$$(FEM\ MAN)$$

means a feminine human being, that is to say it has the function of "woman" in English. As the tables below will show elements like MAN can be governors only in type IV groups, so a subformula like the one above must be of type IV even if it functions as a dependent qualifier as in

$$((FEM\ MAN)KIND)$$

which is of type III and equivalent to "feminine" in English.

Three cases POSS (possession), WITH (accompaniment), and LIKE (is similar to) are dependents in type IV subformulas, rather than being dependents on actions as are the other cases.

There are also *conventional subformulas*, whose meaning could not be extracted from their structure, and which are two-element pairs of type IV that are kept on a special list, which includes:

(FLOW STUFF) liquid
(GET SIGN) money
(THRU PART) aperture.

It will be clear that these have a dependency structure in which case and action names appear to be dependents in type IV. However, the table below for the elements' functions will *not* give actions like FLOW and GET, nor cases like THRU, as possible dependents in type IV, since the conventional subformula dictionary will always be consulted for the presence of such pairs and therefore no participation information (for say GET in type IV) is required to parse the conventional subformulas.

V. Action Subformulas

Types V, VI, and VII all have primitive action elements as their governors – elements like DO, MOVE, TELL, STRIK, – and it is the nature of the dependents that determines the type of the subformula.

In type V the dependent is either another action

$$(CAN\ DO)$$

equivalent to "can" in English (since, see below, CAN cannot be the head of an action *formula*), or an action qualifier type I, as in

$$(TRUE\ TELL)$$

or an action complement, itself of type V, as in

$$(((\text{NOTWHOLE KIND)BE)CAUSE})$$

or a case subformula of type II, or, *if the action is BE*, the dependent can be a type III (qualifier) predication:

$$((\text{NOTWHOLE KIND)BE})$$

The relation of dependent on governor in this group is always one of qualification.

VI. Transitive Action Subformulas

In this subformula type the dependent is either an object case type II, as in

$$((\text{*PHYSOB OBJE)STRIK})$$

or is an assertion, of type VII, typically dependent on the governors CAUSE, THINK, FORCE, DROP or WANT.

It is important to note that objects of actions must be marked by the OBJE case: i.e. the dependent of VI must be or case-headed II and not IV (unless the action is BE) *unless* it is itself VI or a full assertion (VII) which need not be marked.[16]

VII. Assertions (or Full Clause) Subformulas

The dependent of this subformula type is normally an agent, which need not be marked, as in

$$(\text{*HUM MOVE})$$

meaning a human being, or beings, move. The governor may be a primitive action, or a type V or a type VI group as in

$$(\text{*HUM((*PHYSOBJ OBJE)STRIK)})$$

which will be made clear if the subformula types are appended at the last parenthesis of the group as follows

$$(\text{*HUM((*PHYSOBJ OBJE)STRIK)})$$

$$\text{II   VI VII}$$

---

[16] so, for example, the subformula ((MAN ((*PHYSOB OBJE) HAVE)) CAUSE) would be interpreted so that the whole "a human has a physical object" would be a type VII (full assertion, see below) and the object of CAUSE, though it is *not marked* as such, in that there is no additional OBJE element dominating the VII subformula.

If the governor is HAPN, a VII subformula can have a type VII dependent (unmarked as SUBJ) also.

We can now set out the mutual relations of the subformula types (that are not single elements) in a table which, together with the tables that follow for the *individual semantic elements*, plus any standard parsing algorithm, will yield an unambiguous labelling of the structure of any formula or subformula.In the table:

0 means cannot be a governor or dependent
1 means can be a dependent but not a governor
2 means can be a governor but not a dependent
3 means can be either a governor or a dependent.

Figure refers to the participation of the *column* type in the row type

	I	II	III	IV	V	VI	VII
I Adverbial	0	0	0	0	1	0	0
II Case	1	2^d	1^d	3^d	1	1^g	1^h
III Qualifier	1	0	0	1	1^e	0	0
IV Nominal	0	1	1	2	0	1^f	1
V Transitive	0	1^c	1	0	3	2	2
VI Transitive	0	1^c	1	1	1	0	2
VII Assertional	0	1^c	0	1	0	1^b	1^a

a   only if governor is HAPN.
b   only if governor is CAUSE, THINK, or WANT.
c   only if governor of II group is WAY, SUBJ, *TLOCA, GOAL or POSS.
d   only if governor of II group is POSS, WITH.
e   only if governor of V group is BE.
f   only if governor of VI group is BE.
g   only if governor of II group is OBJE.
h   only if governor of II group is SUBJ.

We are now in a position to give the list of semantic primitive elements in full, with their possibilities of participation in the seven types of subformula.

Group A: Nineteen Case Primitives

Element names preceded by a star/asterisk are equivalent to a class of other primitives, including themselves and the elements inset to the right below the corresponding class primitive. Following the seven place rows of the table above, the function of case primitives is given by

$$(0\ 2\ 0\ 0\ 1\ 0\ 0))$$

unless indicated otherwise.

*DIRE	the general *DIRECTION* case element	
TO	direction towards	
FROM	direction away from something	
UP	in an upwards direction	
THRU	direction through some other thing	
INST	the *INSTRUMENT* case, indicating the instrument used in some action	
FOR	the *RECIPIENT* case, indicating the normal recipient of an action	
*LOCA	the *SPATIAL LOCATION* case, indicating the place of an activity or thing	
IN	the *CONTAINMENT* case, indicating what contains some other thing	
*TLOCA	the *TIME LOCATION* case, indicating the time location of an activity	$(0\ 2\ 0\ 0\ 1\ 0\ 0)$
BEFO	indicating an action occurs before another	$(0\ 2\ 0\ 0\ 1\ 0\ 0)$
AFT	indicating an action occurs after another	$(0\ 2\ 0\ 0\ 1\ 0\ 0)$
SIMUL	indicating an action occurs at the same time as another	$(0\ 2\ 0\ 0\ 1\ 0\ 0)$
GOAL	the *PURPOSE* case, indicating the purpose of an activity	
SOUR	the *SOURCE* case, indicating the substance from which some object came	
WAY	the *MANNER* case, indicating the manner or method by which an activity was performed	
OBJE	the *OBJECTIVE* case, indicating the object of an action	$(0\ 2\ 0\ 0\ 0\ 1\ 0)$
SUBJ	the *AGENT* case, indicating the instigator of an action	$(0\ 2\ 0\ 0\ 0\ 0\ 1)$
	'subject' here being taken to refer to a semantic, rather than a surface, subject	
WITH	the *ACCOMPANIMENT* case, indicating the accompanier of an entity	$(0\ 2\ 0\ 1\ 0\ 0\ 0)$
POSS	the *POSSESSIVE* case, indicating who owns some thing	$(0\ 2\ 0\ 1\ 0\ 0\ 0)$
	Additionally, POSS indicates the preferred object to which a type III qualifier group applies, as in:	

((*ANI POSS)(WELL THINK) KIND))

meaning, say, "intelligent", where the initial type II subformula indicates that it is preferably predicated of animate entities. So POSS covers both the possession of entities by owners, *and* the possession of properties by entities; though not both situations lead inferentially to conclusions in terms of HAVE (see below).

LIKE   the *SIMILARITY* case, indicating that the object is like some other thing   (0 2 0 1 0 0 0)

Group B: Thirty Four Action Elements

*DO   a dumny element covering all the action elements except PDO and PBE.

It has the union of the vectors of all action primitives namely,

(0 0 0 0 2 2 2)

The elements below have the *same* participation vector as *DO unless otherwise specified.

CHANGE   changing the state of a substance or object

COUNT   computation or reckoning.

FEEL   having of emotional sensations.

GET   obtaining some thing or substance.

GIVE   yielding up some thing or substance.

GIVTEL   telling a story or any utterance, is the formula head of the English "tell". It has no *semantic* difference from TELL (see below), but as the *head* of a formula for verbs like "tell" it constitutes a cue for picking up the indirect object construction. GIVE above has the same property but, unlike GIVTEL, it can also function within subformulas that are not *formulas* (i.e. word senses). The TELL/GIVTEL distinction is necessary if the syntax of indirect objects is to be handled in a simple and uniform manner without a separate syntactic component or a surface case frame.

HAVE   possessing an object or substance.

MAKE   constructing an entity from substance or parts.

PICK   choosing from among alternatives.

PLEASE   causing good feeling in an animate entity.

SENSE   sensing via the physical faculties.

STRIK   striking some kind of blow.

USE   making use of.

TELL   telling a story or any utterance (functions as of the formula head for the English "say").

WRAP   enclosing or surrounding.

DROP   ceasing to do something. It takes a type VI but not type IV (nominal) object.

CAUSE[17]	causing something to happen (can take a V, VI or VII but not a IV object).
THINK	acting mentally in any way (as for CAUSE).
FORCE	*compelling* something, a physical thing or an event to happen (can take a VII or IV object).
WANT	DESIRING SOME THING OR STATE OF AFFAIRS (as for FORCE)
MOVE	self moving in space. It takes no object of any type in vector space VI. (0 0 0 0 2 0 2)
FLOW	freely moving as a liquid (0 0 0 0 2 0 2)
FUNC	FUNCTIONING AS OF A MACHINE (0 0 0 0 2 0 2)
HAPN	taking place. Its dependent in VII must itself be VII, expressing a state of affairs (0 0 0 0 2 0 2)
WILL	expresses futurity and can only be dependent of another action. The following five actions are of this "auxiliary" type. (0 0 0 0 1 0 0)
CAN	expresses ability to do something (0 0 0 0 1 0 0)
ASK	expressing interrogation (0 0 0 0 1 0 0)
LET	expresses allowing something to be done (0 0 0 0 1 0 0)
MAY	expresses possibility of something happening (0 0 0 0 1 0 0)
MUST	expresses necessity of something happening (0 0 0 0 1 0 0)
BE	equivalent and predicator (depending on type of object as explained above under subformula types V and VI) (0 0 0 0 2 2 0)
PDO	dummy pseudo-action functioning as the head of formulas for "action-oriented prepositions" like "to".
PBE	dummy pseudo-action functioning as the head of formulas for "static prepositions" like "with".

Group C: Nineteen Substantive Elements (Plus Twelve "Class Elements" Classifying Them)

All the substantive elements below, except SELF, can function as qualifiers too with an appropriate shift of interpretation. (i.e. be dependents in types III and IV). There are no *a priori* restrictions or agency imposed during the construction of subformulas, and hence all the substantives below, again excepting SELF, can be dependents in type VII. All the elements below, unless otherwise marked, have the participation vector: (0 1 3 3 0 1 1)

SELF	used to refer back to agent of next higher order action. Can appear only as dependent of case element or as agent of (a lower order) type VII. (0 1 0 0 0 0 1)
WHOLE	a totality of some kind.

---

[17] As noted above, the objects of CAUSE (and THINK, WANT, and FORCE) are not marked, if of types V, VI or VII, but agents *are*.

WORLD	the physical universe.
POINT	a place marking entity, spatial or temporal.
SIGN	symbols, thoughts and signs.
SPREAD	an extension, as in (WHERE SPREAD), a spatial extension.
STATE	a state of affairs.
STUFF	any substance.
BEAST	any non-human animal (BEAST is *not* above MAN on some Aristotelean tree).
THING	an inanimate physical object.
LINE	a physical line between two points.
MAN	a human being.
PART	a part of any of the *entities* listed (see *ENT below).
PLANT	any vegetable entity.
EVNT	an event.
ACT	an act, done by a conscious being.
GRAIN	any kind of structure.
FOLK	any human group.
THIS	an unidentified, but particular, entity of any type.
*ENT	any entity (i.e. covered by THIS, POINT, FOLK, MAN, GRAIN, PART, THING, BEAST, SIGN, SPREAD or LINE).
*ANI	any animate entity (i.e. THIS, MAN, FOLK, BEAST or SIGN).
*POT	any "potent" entity (i.e. *ANI, STATE, PART, ACT, PLANT).
*MAR	any "mark-like" entity (i.e. THIS, SIGN, ACT, STATE).
*ANIMAR*ANI*MAR	
*SOF	any "malleable" entity (i.e. THIS, PART, WHOLE, GRAIN, STUFF)
*PLA	any "place definer" (i.e. THIS, POINT, SPREAD, PART).
*AC	any "act definer" (i.e. THIS, ACT, EVNT).
*PHYSOB	any physical object (i.e. THIS, THING, MAN, BEAST, SPREAD,
*HUM	PLANT, PART).
*HUM	any human entity (i.e. THIS, MAN, FOLK).
*INAN	any inanimate entity (i.e. THIS, PART, GRAIN, STUFF, PART, THING, LINE, SPREAD).

Group D: Sixteen Qualifier Elements

These qualifiers, unlike group C, cannot also be substantives. Most can qualify only substantives (i.e. as dependents in type IV) and, unless indicated otherwise, all will be deemed to have the corresponding participation vector, namely:

$$(0\ 0\ 0\ 1\ 0\ 0\ 0)$$

| TRUE | qualifies only actions and implies *correctness* in the sense of conformity with reality. | $(1\ 0\ 0\ 0\ 1\ 0\ 0)$ |
| GOOD | morally correct or approved. | |

WELL	qualifies only actions and implies reaching some (non-moral) standard (1 0 0 0 1 0 0)
SEE	
TOUCH	qualify actions, normally SENSE, so as to specify which of the five
HEAR	human senses is intended (1 0 0 0 1 0 0)
SMELL	
TASTE	
MANY	qualify substantives: MANY qualifying entities and MUCH substances.
MORE	MORE is not a *relation* here, like "greater than". SAME is an
MUCH	identifier that relates the entity qualified to the similar entity at the
SAME	next level up.
WHEN	qualify, normally POINT, to indicate temporal or spatial entities or
WHERE	locations. Some of these are on the conventional subformula list, such as (WHERE STUFF) meaning "space".
MAL	indicate the sex of the entity qualified, so that (MAL MAN) is
FEM	equivalent to "man".

Two miscellaneous elements:

HOW	is, as explained, always the head of formulas that are of type I (2 0 0 0 0 0 0)
KIND	the head of formulas of type III is always this element (0 0 2 0 0 0 0)

Assembling and Interpreting Formulas: The Role of Trans-Group Rules

The participation vectors given for subformula groups and for individual semantic elements suffice for the construction of actual formulas for English word senses *and* for the parsing and interpretation of such formulas by any one of a number of simple algorithms. We shall now look in detail at the decomposition and interpretation of the formula for "break" given earlier, and in doing so set out the *transgroup rules* that are needed to make the process watertight in the situations where the full subformula that satisfies the vector has to be constructed inferentially. This process is quite clear and will be explained at the appropriate point in the discussion.

Interpretations can be constructed from the following general rules for the building and interpretation of formulas:

i) Each subformula in a formula is of one of the seven types and consists of a left member depending on a right member, and left or right may be either a single primitive element or another group. Thus, (*HUM SUBJ) is type II (case), known to be such because the rightmost member of its pair is the governor and SUBJ is a primitive element that can be governor of *only* the Agent case (i.e. it has a 2 or 3 only in the second place in its vector).

Similarly, within the GOAL-headed subformula, the vectors show that (NOTWHOLE KIND) must be III, and ((NOTWHOLE KIND)BE) must be V.

The type assignments to the principal subformulas can thus be written as Roman numerals after the corresponding closing parenthesis as follows:

((*HUM SUBJ)(*PHYSOBOBJ)((((NOTWHOLE KIND)BE)CAUSE)GOAL)THING INST)STRIK)

Now, the formula as written above, and as written earlier with the tree branches drawn in, is a slightly abbreviated form of the actual dictionary formula. In the diagram the main subformulas are shown as being all at the same level, with the tree branches corresponding to them connected directly to the top of the 'formula tree'. However, the formula is in fact a *binary tree*, and so contains the 'ghost brackets' drawn in below the formula above. The formula can now be fully parsed as follows: the (THING INST)II is dependent on STRIK to form a type V subformula – this is the only possible interpretation. see line II column V of the table and the vector for STRIK. Then, the GOAL-headed II depends on that V subformula to form another V – this must be unique since a II, not headed SUBJ, OBJE, POSS or WITH, can be dependent on an action only in a V. Consulting the table again shows that, going leftwards, we obtain next a VI and finally the VII which is the type of the whole formula.

Thus the full *binary* structure of the formula, each node labeled with its parsed subformula type is:

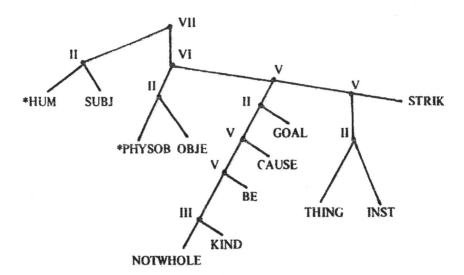

A reader might perhaps feel that the extra parentheses impose too much structure on the formula in that, if the whole system is implemented in LISP (as it in fact is), then that level of structure is expressed by LISP's own data structure because, for any formula or subformula F, its governor would be given by CADR F, and its type properties could be computed from that.

ii) The transgroup rules

If we turn back to the formula for "break" annotated by the type Roman numerals we shall see that, although the type V-dependent of GOAL is legitimate in that it is allowed by the table, nonetheless it does not obey the restriction specific to GOAL, namely that GOAL requires a whole assertion (type VII) as its dependent.

The same consideration applies to the V dependent of the CAUSE – headed type V formula. The restriction specific to CAUSE (as for THINK and other actions) is that its dependent be a full (type VII) assertion, whereas in this formula it is type V.

The full dependents can be constructed inferentially *when required* during later processing, as I shall now describe. But we should note that what has been done is to make the formula "habitable", as a coding system for human dictionary makers, by *compressing* it: making agents and objects function for more than one primitive action. Agents and objects of actions in a formula are normally sought to the left of the primitive action element. If the whole formula is for an action (as above for "break") the two leftmost subparts of the formula fwill always be the preferred agent and object of the head primitive, in that order (see below on "full formula" restrictions). For any actions *within the formula* (such as CAUSE in the formula for "break") its preferred agent and object are normally the *next agent and object to its left* – which of course, as in the case of "break", may turn out to yield the same entity as the preferred agent of the whole formula, though this need not be the case. Moreover, in the case of actions *within* a formula (i.e. not constituting the head) the agent need not be marked, though the object must be unless it is of type VII. Thus, within a formula a group like (MAN STRIK) is always interpreted as an *assertion* (type VII) group, MAN being an unmarked object to yield a (type VI) *action* group i.e. ((MAN OBJE)STRIK).

So, the general form of the transgroup rule for locating agents and objects (to satisfy restrictions peculiar to certain elements) is:

Search next left at levels higher up in the formula.[18]

Thus, the dependent of GOAL, as mentioned earlier, must be an assertion, whereas it is bracketed to only (((NOTWHOLE KIND)BE)CAUSE) which can only (during inference procedures called 'extraction' to be described later) become an assertion group by the addition of the next agent found to the left namely *HUM. CAUSE also requires a dependent object that is an assertion (hence (*PHYSOB

---

[18] As we noticed earlier, this method is also applied in type III (KIND-headed) formulas, where a type II (POSS-headed) subformula indicated the type of entity qualified but can also be interpreted as the agent of an included action by transgroup rules.

OBJE) will not do as its object taken alone) and can take, to fill that assertion group, an entity to its left marked either OBJE or SUBJ whichever is closest. Hence the dependent of ((NOTWHOLE KIND)BE) is *PHYSOB and the "real" dependent of CAUSE (found by inference) is (*PHYSOB ((NOTWHOLE KIND)BE)) and so the "real" dependent of GOAL is (*HUM((*PHYSOB((NOTWHOLE KIND)BE))CAUSE)).

This compression of expression can be argued to be "habitable" (Watt 1968) for a formula maker. It also avoids to a large extent the defect of other conceptual representations of this general type, pointed out by [32] that, if the entities like (*HUM SUBJ) are put into the representation many times but are intended to refer to the same human, then this must be indicated.

Where such identity must be specific in formulas, but that cannot be achieved by the above compressed expressions, it is obtained by means of the primitives SAME and NOTSAME : the same (or not), that is to say, as the next encountered token of the associated primitive when working leftwards inside the formula.[19]

Full formula rules

The types I-VII described earlier can, in general, be either whole formulas (representing the meaning of word senses in the dictionary) or subformulas at any level within a formula. Any binary structuring of elements, that obeys the syntax rules given earlier, is a subformula but not every subformula is a formula.
Below are listed rules *peculiar to formulas*.

  i) A type II subformula cannot be a formula.
 ii) If a type I subformula is a formula its head must be HOW.
iii) If a type III subformula is a formula its head must be KIND.
 iv) PDO, PBE, GIVTEL can be the heads of formulas but not of subformulas.
  v) Both the object *and the agent* of an action *formula* must be marked, and they must be respectively the CADR and CAR of the whole. During later processing a 'tense primitive' (not listed here) may be CONSed on as the CAR of the whole formula, but this does not appear in the dictionary version of an action formula.
 vi) In certain nominal (type IV) subformulas *that are formulas* the order of the head and of the OBJE/SUBJ markers may be reversed so as to yield a nominal, not a case head. For example, consider the following formula for "shepherded" (marked with types):

((((LINE THING)INST) (((THIS BEAST)OBJE)FORCE)) (SUBJ MAN))

     IV   II   IV   II   VI VI   II IV

---

[19] It may be noted that if the formula marker thought that the interpretation of *PHYSOB would be ambiguous, he could simply repeat it using SAME, so as to yield the subformula (((SAME*PHYSOB)((NOTWHOLE KIND)BE))CAUSE).

Here, the agent of forcing (of the sheep) is placed to the right of the associated action, and the reversal of the SUBJ and MAN elements cues an agent-seeking routine that the agent is to be found to the right of the action and not, as is normal, to its left. The reversal is also necessary so that the head of the whole formula shall be the appropriate MAN, and not the inappropriate SUBJ. It is also necessary therefore that the participation table allows II to be a governor of IV, and VI to be a dependent in IV.

It may be worth emphasizing that formulas are not in any straightforward sense transformable into the more conventional semantic net representations of natural language. The main reason is that those representations attempt to conflate (in an unclear way in the author's opinion) the representation of word senses, real world knowledge, and actual texts (or sentences). They are all represented in a uniform way in semantic nets with a bias towards the paradigm of "language-free-knowledge". In the present system, on the other hand, the bias is towards representation of texts, and of "knowledge" as coded forms of texts – these structures are the higher order structures of templates to be discussed later – but formulas represent the structure *of individual nodes in those representations. Thus the correspondence between formulas and conventional semantic nets is approximately that a formula for, say "shepherd" is the structure present at a node in a semantic net that would normally have just the atom "shepherd" attached to it.*[20] These, then, are radically different ways of seeing the representation of meaning and knowledge.

Any attempt to see formulas *directly* as nets (rather than as the structure of nodes in nets) will lead to trouble. If this were to be attempted, then the formula for "break" above would contain not only the net links:

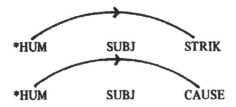

---

[20] A closer analogy exists between formulas and the "stack of slot names" form of word meaning in KRL (Bobrow and Winograd, in press). It is clear that a formula could be expressed as a stack of case names and the preferred type of their "fillers" as in

Give UNIT Specialization ...
object (a Thing)
giver (a Person)
recipient (a Person) etc.

Moreover, it appears that the slots in this "prototype" object for *give* are not simply *filled*, but rather that this object dictated *how slots are* to be filled in a copy of it elsewhere rather as formulas dictate how templates are to be constructed.

but also the quite *other type* of link

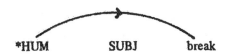

$$\text{*HUM} \qquad \text{SUBJ} \qquad \text{break}$$

which asserts that the preferred agent of breaking will be human. However, the top link must not be interpreted as saying that the *preferred agent* of the primitive STRIK is human, because that is not an assertion in the present system at all. All the top link can say is that the primitive action STRIK sometimes takes human agents. In some other formula, for another surface action whose underlying primitive was also STRIK, the preferred agent *might* be *ANI, a wider class. In this system there are not specific semantic restrictions on the dependents of the primitives, as in, say Schank (1973). Such restrictions could easily be imposed on the present system by fiat: by deeming, for example, that in any formula the agent of STRIK must be *ANI for the formula to be well formed. However, this is, I believe, premature at the present stage of things, and nothing would be gained from laying down such restrictions. They could, however, emerge *inductively* from a survey of a large body of real formulas. It might be argued, though, that specifying that, say, the object of CAUSE must be an assertion (type VII) subformula is already a step in this direction, although it would certainly be misleading to refer to that direction as the "semantics of formulas" – as opposed to a "syntax of formulas" governed by the table of participation. There is no difference of type *here* – all that is being discussed is the degree of restriction to be stated in terms of the substitutability of the elements and classes of them.

References

[1] Apostel, L. (1977). The Cognitive Point of View, in De Mey et. a. (eds.) *Proc. Internat, Workshop on the Cognitive Viewpoint* (Ghent: Univ. of Ghent).

[2] Bierwisch, M. (1970). Semantics, in Lyons (ed.) *New Horizons in Linguistics* (London: Penguin).

[3] Bobrow, D. (1975). Dimensions of Representation, in Bobrow and Collins (eds.) *Representation and Understanding* (New York: Academic Press).

[4] Bobrow, D. and T. WINOGRAD (in press). An overview of KRL, a Knowledge Representation Language. *Cognitive Studies*.

[5] Bobrow, D. et. al. (1973). Steps towards language understanding (Palo Alto: Xerox Corp.).

[6] Bolinger, D. (1965). The Atomization of Meaning. *Language*.

[7] Charniak, E. (1975a). Organization and Inference, in *Proc. Conf. on Theoret. Issues in Natural Language Processing*. (Cambridge, Mass.: BBN).

[8] Charniak, E. (1975b). A brief on case. Memo 22. (Castagnola: Inst. for semantic and cognitive studies).

[9] Charniak, E. and Y. Wilks (eds.) (1976). *Computational Semantics*. (Amsterdam: North Holland).

[10] Chomsky, N. (1972). *Studies on Semantics in Generative Grammar*. (The Hague: Mouton).

[11] Fillmore, C. (1968). The case for case, in Bach and Harms (eds.). *Universals in Linguistic Theory*. (New York: Holt, Rinehart and Winston).

[12] Goodman, N. (1951). *The structure of appearance*. (Cambridge, Mass.: Harvard Univ. Press).

[13] Hayes, P. (1974). Some issues and non-issues in representation theory, in *Proc. AISB Conference*. (Sussex: University of Sussex).

[14] Hayes, P. (1977). In defence of logic. unpublished ms.

[15] Heidrich, C. (1973). Should intensional logic be related to Generative Semantics? in Keenan (ed.) *The Formal Semantics of Natural Language*. (Cambridge: Cambridge University Press).

[16] Hobbs, J. and S. Rosenschein (1977). Making Computational Sense of Montague's Intensional Logic, Memo 11 (New York: Courant Institute, Dept. of Computer Science).

[17] Johnson–Laird, P. (1974). Memory for words. *Nature*.

[18] Johnson–Laird, P. and J. Quinn (1976). To define true meaning. *Nature*.

[19] Joshi, A. (1974). Factorization of verbs, in Heidrich (ed.) *Semantics and Communication*. (Amsterdam: North Holland).

[20] Katz, J. (1966?). *The Philosophy of Language*. (New York: Harper and Row).

[21] Katz, J. (1972). *Semantic Theory*. (New York: Harper and Row).

[22] Katz, J. and J. Fodor (1963). The structure of a semantic theory. *Language*.

[23] Lewis, D. (1972). General Semantics, in Davidson and Harman (eds.) *Semantics of Natural Language*. (Dordrecht: Reidel).

[24] Lyons, J. (1968). *Introduction to Theoretical Linguistics*. (Cambridge: Cambridge University Press).

[25] Morgan, J. (1969). On arguing about semantics. *Papers in Linguistics*, Vol. 1, No. 1.

[26] Miller, G. and P. Johnson–Laird (1976). *Language and Perception*. (Cambridge: Cambridge University Press).

[27] Norman, D. and D. Rummelhart (eds.) (1975). *Explorations in Cognition*. (San Francisco: Freeman).

[28] Postal, P. (1970). On the surface verb 'remind'. *Linguistic Inquiry*.

[29] Prior, A. (1960). The run-about inference ticket. *Analysis*.

[30] Putnam, H. (1970). Is semantics possible: *Metaphilosophy*.

[31] Sampson, G. (1975). *The form of language*. (London: Weidenfeld and Nicholson).

[32] Sandewall, E. (1972). PCF-2 – a first order calculus for expressing conceptual information. (Uppsala, Sweden: Dept. of Computer Science).

[33] Shafe, L. (1976). unpublished London University Ph.D. thesis.

[34] Schank, R. (1972). Conceptual Dependency. *Cognitive Psychology*.

[35] Schank, R. (ed.) (1975). *Conceptual Information Processing*. (Amsterdam: North Holland).

[36] Thalberg, I. (1975). When do causes take effect? *Mind*.

[37] Weinreich, U. (1966). Explorations in Semantic Theory, in Sebeok (ed.) *Current Trends in Linguistics*, Vol. 3 (The Hague: Mouton).

[38] Wierzbicka, A. (1972). *Semantic Primitives*. (Frankfurt: Athenäum Verlag).

[39] Wilks, Y. (1968). Computable semantic derivations. Memo 3017. (Santa Monica: Systems Development Corp.).

[40] Wilks, Y. (1972). *Grammar, Meaning and the Machine Analysis of Language.* (London: Routledge).

[41] Wilks, Y. (1973). Natural Language Inference. *Stanford University Memo AIM-211.*

[42] Wilks, Y. (1975). *An intelligent analyzer and understander of English. Comm. A.C.M.*

[43] Wilks, Y. (1976). Processing Case. *Amer. Jnl. Comp. Ling.*

[44] Wilks, Y. (1977). Making preferences more active. (Edinburgh: Dept. of Artificial Intelligence).

[45] Zwicky, A. (1973). Linguistics as Chemistry : the substance theory of semantic primes. in Anderson and Kiparsky (eds.) *Festschrift for Morris Halle.* (New York: Holt, Rinehart and Winston).

7

Making Preferences More Active

Yorick Wilks
University of Essex

Abstract: The paper discusses the incorporation of richer semantic structures into the Preference
Semantics system: they are called pseudo-texts and capture something of the information
expressed in one type of frame proposed by Minsky (q.v.). However, they are in a
format, and subject to rules of inference, consistent with earlier accounts of this system
of language analysis and understanding. Their use is discussed in connection with the
phenomenon of extended use: sentences where the semantic preferences are broken. It is
argued that such situations are the norm and not the exception in normal language use,
and that a language understanding system must give some general treatment of them.
A notion of sense projection is proposed, leading on to an alteration of semantic formulas
(word sense representations) in the face of unexpected context by drawing information
from the pseudo texts. A possible implementation is described, based on a new semantic
parser for the Preference Semantics system, which would cope with extended use by the
methods suggested and answer questions about the process of analysis itself. It is argued
that this would be a good context in which to place a language understander (rather
than that of question-answering about a limited area of the real world, as is normal)
and, moreover, that the sense projection mechanisms suggested would provide a test-
bed on which the usefulness of frames for language understanding could be realistically
assessed

7.1 Introduction

This paper is intended to suggest how we might deal with *extensions of word-sense*
in a language understanding system, one manipulating rich structures of meaning
and knowledge, and do so in a general and systematic manner. But two preliminary
points must be dealt with immediately. First, what I shall call new, or extended,
use is the *norm* in ordinary language use and so cannot be relegated to some mode
of special, but dispensible, treatment. Secondly, that simply to *accept* extended
uses, in the way I have shown that the Preference Semantics system does [21],
is not sufficient, and that we must seek ways to *interpret* those uses in an active
manner.

141

K. Ahmad, C. Brewster and M. Stevenson (eds.), Words and Intelligence 1, 141–166.
© 2007 *Springer.*

Suppose we look at some perfectly ordinary sentence of newspaper text chosen, I promise you, at random:

(1) "Mr Wilson said that the *line taken* by the Shadow Cabinet, that a Scottish Assembly should be *given no executive powers*, would *lead to the break up of the United Kingdom*."

The Times: 5 February 1976

The sentence presents no problem whatever to the normal reader with a general grasp of British politics, and yet, if we start from the point of view of "selection restrictions" [9] we notice that, at no less than four (italicized) places in a perfectly straightforward sentence, they are broken. That is to say, anyone setting out to write down the selection restrictions for the objects of the verb "take" would not want to write them in such a way that lines could be said to be taken, and so on for the other three actions in the sentence.

My first preliminary point is that, whether or not we want to call such usage "metaphorical", it is the *norm* in ordinary everyday language use, and cannot be relegated to the realm of the exceptional, or the odd, and so dealt with by considerations of "performance" in the sense of Chomsky [4]. On the contrary it is, I shall argue, central to our language capabilities, and any theory of language must have something concrete to say about it. Even if the newspaper usages above are "extended", I would suggest that anyone who could not grasp these extensions could not be said to understand English properly (given adequate knowledge *from which* to extend, and we shall come to that later).

No claims are being made here about the murky matter of language *learning* beyond saying that, given some grasp of word-senses and some knowledge representation, a language understanding system should have mechanisms for extending that repertory of senses in a systematic way, and this is a much weaker claim than any general one about language learning as such. For it is only a claim about how to extend the language *from some given starting point*.

An additional argument for some such facility, as a glance at any dictionary shows, is that yesterday's extended use is today's normal sense of a word: in other words, sense-extension is part of the fundamental process underlying language development, and a natural language cannot be contained within a fixed repertory of senses, in the way that a logical language can, and this is a fundamental point of difference between the two.

My second preliminary point concerns the difference between *acceptance and interpretation* of extended use. In previous papers describing a programmed system of natural language understanding (e.g. [22]) I have described how rules operate on semantic descriptions of word-senses so as to build up text descriptions. The rules for inserting the word-sense descriptions are what I have described as "preferential", in that they seek preferred entities but will *accept* those that do not satisfy the preferences. For example, the action of drinking can be said to prefer an animate agent and so will correctly select as the agent of

(2) The adder drank from the pool

the snake and not the machine. However, in the case of

(3) My car drinks gasoline

none of the senses available for "car" are animate, and so the system simply accepts what it is given. I contrasted this approach with that of selection restrictions, not so much as regards the content of the restriction (to animate in this case), nor the form of its coding, but as regards the form of the rule that operates on the restriction. I described a form of rule that would both make the discrimination required for (2) and accept (3), while the "selection restrictions" approach was specifically intended to *reject* (3).

However, it is clear that simply accepting the car as the agent of (3) is not enough, as far as "understanding the utterance" goes, which we may take as implying at least some of the structure derived for interpreting *later* stretches of text. In [18] I described a feature of an early LISP program in which the system did make an attempt to interpret "preference-breaking" utterances like (3): by finding a coded sense for some *other* word (in the same text) that *did* satisfy the preference under examination, and substituting that for the sense that did not fit. In that way the sense repertory of the non-fitting word (such as "car" in (3)) was extended by one new sense representation. However, that heuristic depended very much on the semantically dense structure of the particular texts under examination, and was almost certainly not of any general application. So, for example, in a text containing (3) there is no reason to believe that there would be another (animative) drinker mentioned in the same text, such that "car" could plausibly be said to be being used to mean that animate drinker. We could easily construct texts to which such a heuristic *would* apply, viz:

(4) Smith took the chair at the Board Meeting. Jones came in late, acknowledged *the chair* and crept to his seat

where the underlined phrase is used to indicate Smith, who *would* in this example be an appropriate type of object for the action "acknowledge". Nonetheless, there is no reason to believe that such a heuristic would be much use in dealing with everyday language like (1).

Clearly something more is required. Let us return to (3) briefly and ask what an intelligent program might be expected to make of it. First, it should see that non-animate entitles may be said to drink, and be prepared to revise its agent preference accordingly in the future.

Secondly, and more importantly, it should notice that cars can be said to drink *in virtue of something already known about cars*, namely that they have a fluid (petrol or gasoline) injected into them in order to make them run. That is to say, the program should have access to a sufficiently rich knowledge structure for "car", and be able to notice that cars stand in a consumption relation to a particular fluid, that is of the same semantic structure (in the sense of that phrase yet to be defined) as the relation in which a drinker normally stands to a liquid to be drunk. All this may sound obvious, but it must surely be that on that similarity the successful metaphorical force of (3) rests.

It will also come as no surprise to those acquainted with recent Artificial Intelligence (AI) literature to know that the knowledge structures proposed will be within the recent Minskyan paradigm for larger knowledge structures that are normally called "frames" [10]. However, the detailed structures to be proposed here are consistent with previous accounts of the preference semantics system (see [25]).

A final point to be noted about (3) is that its normal force in English is to suggest not only that the car consumes gasoline but also that it consumes *a great deal* of it. We might distinguish that element in the interpretation as the *idiomatic* element, in that there is no way in which a reasoned basis could be established for deducing it. Like all idioms it would have to be dealt with by crude listing of forms, just as we have to *learn* idioms in a foreign language simply because there is no way we could deduce them unless, by chance, they happen to match our own.

The next section is simply to recap the programmed form of the preference semantics system. A reader who is familiar with it should precede direct to the following section which is the nub of the present paper.

7.2 A Brief Recap of the Processes of the Preference Semantics System

The purpose of these general processes is to construct a unique semantic representation for a text. This representation, a *semantic block*, will consist of *template* structures tied together with various case, anaphora and inference ties. Each template structure corresponds to a phrase or clause of the surface text and expresses its gist. A template consists of a network *formulas* that represent word senses. Every structure in the system consists, directly or indirectly, of *semantic primitives* (drawn from a vocabulary of one hundred). In order to construct a unique semantic block for a text, that system may have had to make explicit semantic information not present in the surface text. This is done (see below) by inferring template-like objects (extractions) and adding them to the semantic block, even though they do not correspond to any surface clause in the text. This "deepening" of the representation is only done if necessary for the isolation of a unique representation.

The system assumes that every English *word-sense* in the dictionary has had a *formula* associated with it that expresses its meaning. Formulas are trees of semantic primitives. They consist, at the top level, of *case sub-formulas*. All dependency, within sub-formulas, and *of* sub-formulas on others, is left-on-right, with the result that the right-most primitive—the *head* of the formula becomes its principal category. (6) and (7) are two *action* formulas for two senses of the English "grasp", having heads THINK and SENSE respectively, and represent the senses of that word we would locate in:

(5) It took John four hours of practise to grasp how to grasp a golf-club.

Primitives like *ANI (animate) indicate with the asterisk that they are equivalent to a *class* of other primitives. The above formulas can be loosely explicated as follows (a full syntax of formulas is given in [27]):

(6) implies that grasping is a THINKing action, that the SAME SIGN is TRUE, an action preferably done by an ANImate agent to a SIGN (the same sign as earlier)

OBJect, and with an INSTrument that is a particular PART of a MAN (human, i.e. the brain or mind).

(7) implies that grasping is a SENSing action, TOUCH sensing, preferably done by an ANImate agent, and to a PHYSical OBJect, and again by an INSTrument that is a particular PART of a MAN (the hand this time).

Templates are the initial, shallow, semantic representations attached to clause or phrase-length fragments of text. They are networks of formulas consisting of at least an agent formula, an action formula and an object formula, where other formulas may depend on each of those three, and any one of the three may be only a dummy in any particular example.

(6)

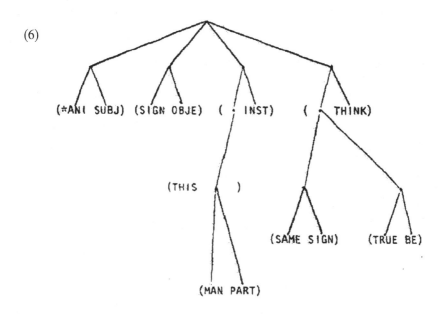

(7)

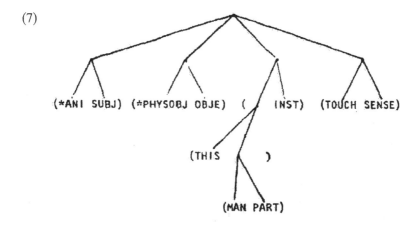

In what follows, square brackets enclosing English words will stand as shorthand for the above semantic formula trees and the template networks of them. Thus, [John] will indicate the formula for "John", and

(8) [John grasped the +idea]

will indicate the template (of three formulas) for "John grasped the idea".

The process that constructs the templates is the first operation of "preference" in the system: the formulas function as active objects, each seeking to specify what its *neighbouring* formulas in a template shall be. Thus the preference expressed by (6) for a SIGN (= symbolic) object is satisfied if (6) goes at the central (action) node of (8), but *not* if (7) goes there. The principle of preference is that the template structure is assigned to a fragment in which *the most such preferences are satisfied*. By this method "grasp" is correctly resolved in (8) to (6), not (7). However, preference-breaking templates are set up if there is no formula available to satisfy them.

Templates are then tied together by *paraplates*. These are structures, of no direct relevance to this paper (see [22] for details), with the form of an inference rule connecting two template skeletons. If the skeletons match two templates—one for a main clause, the other for a prepositional phrase—then whatever case name is attached to the inference arrow is the name of the case tie between the two templates in the semantic representation. Thus, the second phrase of "John grasped the idea in the lecture" would be tied to the first by a paraplate with a TLOCA (time location) inference arrow. But note that the paraplate is only a structure *by means of which* this case tie is assigned (and the ambiguity of "in" is resolved); it does not itself become part of the representation.

Pronoun ties, assigned on similar principles, complete this *basic mode* of the system. If a unique semantic block can be constructed in this way then that representation suffices, but in many cases it cannot and the representation must be *deepened*. For this, the system shifts to the *extended mode*. First, as many templates are *repacked* as possible, which means filling in their dummies by inference. So in the second template for "John drank the whisky from a glass", the dummy agent—prepositional phrase templates always have a dummy agent, with the preposition functioning as a "pseudo-action"—can be repacked by the formula [whisky], yielding a repacked template [whisky from a + glass] that is also a true inference. More importantly, the representation is enlarged with *extractions*: template-like entities, not represented in the original surface text, but which are appropriate inferences from the structure of the original, shallow, template representation.

In what follows, we extend the "short form" of templates (obtained by writing square brackets round English words, clustered at three nodes to show the distribution of formulas in the full template) by writing extractions as English words inside *double* square brackets.

Let us consider

(9) John fired at a line of stags with a shotgun

The *result* of matching this with templates, applying paraplates, and then performing case extractions can be written in summary form as follows:

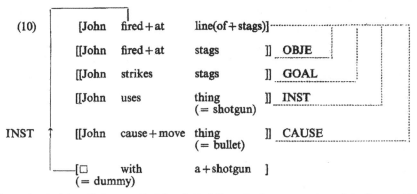

(10)

[John   fired + at   line(of + stags)]
[[John   fired + at   stags   ]] OBJE
[[John   strikes   stags   ]] GOAL
[[John   uses   thing   ]] INST
                        (= shotgun)
INST   [[John   cause + move   thing   ]] CAUSE
                                  (= bullet)
        ─[□   with   a + shotgun]
         (= dummy)

The extracted templates are tied by dotted lines to the source template from which they have been extracted, and the case name on the dotted line shows the case type of the extraction. The inferences cover both those that *must* be true (like the OBJE extraction, since to fire at a line of stags is necessarily to fire at stags) and those, like the GOAL extraction, that are only *likely*.

The extraction *mechanism* consists of a "specialist" (to use Winograd's term) for each case (and for CAUSE, which is treated as a semi-case during extraction). An extraction, resulting in a new double-square-bracketted template, as in (10) above, is made for each case (or CAUSE) sub-formula at the top level of the formulas of each source template.

Let us see how the extractions in (10) are actually obtained. This will require that we give more of the content of the first source template in (10), and in particular the formula for "fire + at". (11) may be considered a semi-full-form of template for

"John fired at a line of stags"

in that the centre mode has been expanded to its formula but the other two nodes are left in "short form".

(11)

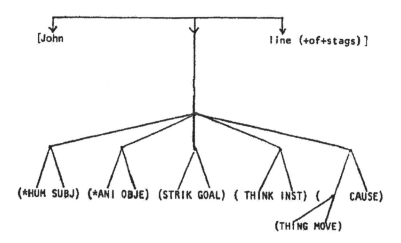

The dependent of OBJE case in (11) shows that "fire at" prefers an ANImate object, but the formula is in a template whose object is *not* animate (it is "line") and so we have a failed preference. However, an animate object (stags) is available as a dependent of the surface object in the template. The extraction process takes the form of filling *a new copy* of the source template, and *imposing* the available preferred animate object, to yield:

$$[[\text{John fired} + \text{at stags}]]$$

The repackings and extractions provided an extended or deeper representation and chains of *inference rules* are now constructed in order to resolve any outstanding pronoun or sense ambiguities. The inference rules, like paraplates, consist of two template skeletons and again like them do not become *part of* the representation into which they insert ties. But, unlike paraplates, they can be chained together, although the system always prefers the shortest inference chain it can construct between any two templates. An inference rule would typically express some inductive generalization such as "If a human entity wants some object then it will try to obtain it". This would tie the two templates representing "John wanted a bicycle. He went to get his money box".

One structural change to the system should be mentioned briefly. In [22] it was suggested that, since there is no *theoretical* difference of any sort between the semantic primitives and English words, then more specific entities could be put into the formulas if necessary, *provided that they too were in the dictionary and had their own formulas there*. This would have the effect of making the formulas more compact.

In [25] this notion was extended, and it was suggested that the formula dictionary should be thought of as imposing a *thesaurus* structure on the whole vocabulary.

A thesaurus, like Roget's, say, is a grouping of English words into semi-synonymous *rows*, usually having the same part of speech type. These rows are grouped under one of about a thousand *heads* (not to be confused in any way with "head" meaning the rightmost primitive of a formula), which are in turn grouped under about ten very general sections.

Thus, under the very general section # volition we would find the *head*, say 22, # propulsion and under that we would find a *subhead* # 221 *firer*, attached to some row of "firer" words:

(12) # 221 firer: gun, bow, rifle, howitzer. ...

Similarly, row "# 222 projectile", say, would name a row of projectiles.

This organization is imposed by the formulas in the following way (Fig. 7.1): each of the above is a word in the dictionary and has a formula, where the inclusion relations of the formulas *should reflect the head, subhead, rowmember*, relation. Thus "gun", "bow" etc. are co-members of a row, and should have a common part to their formulas (all are THINGS, all have a *goal* of hitting something) and this common part *should be the (simpler, more general) formula in the dictionary for that row's subhead name* "# *firer*" (which could also mean a person, of course, and ambiguous words will appear in the thesaurus under more than one head). This progressive generalization should extend right up the thesaurus to the general

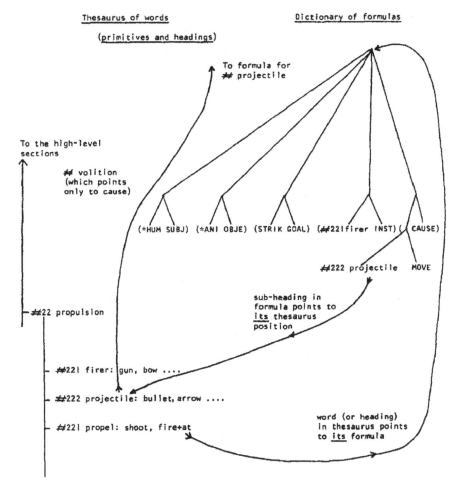

Thesaurus of words

(primitives and headings)

Dictionary of formulas

To formula for
projectile

To the high-level
sections

volition
(which points
only to cause)

(*HUM SUBJ) (*ANI OBJE) (STRIK GOAL) (#221firer INST) (CAUSE)

#222 projectile   MOVE

sub-heading in
formula points to
its thesaurus
position

#22 propulsion

#221 firer: gun, bow ....

#222 projectile: bullet, arrow ....

#221 propel: shoot, fire+at

word (or heading)
in thesaurus points
to its formula

Fig. 7.1.

section names (# volition, for example, would be associated only with the primitive elements GOAL and WANT).

Now, we see that the formula for "fire + at" in (11) could be made more specific if "# 222 projectile" replaced the rightmost THING in it, and "# 221 firer" replaced the leftmost THING, to yield (11).

These thesaurus subheads would have their own dictionary formulas, hence (11) would now express more information. They would also, implicitly, point to the thesaurus row each names, whose first member could, by convention, be an *even more explicit default*: "gun", say, for "# firer".

Thus in summary:

(i) A *formula* is a binary tree representing a word sense. It is a dependency tree all of whose terminal nodes are *semantic primitives* or *non-primitives*.

Primitives come from a list of 100 items with interpretations, and non-primitives from a hierarchical *thesaurus*. Interpretation rules specify what trees are well formed formulas and what their interpretations are.

(ii) A *template* is a network of formulas representing a clause or phrase of text. It normally has an agent, action and object formula (in that order), and other formulas depending on these three nodes, though any of the main formulas may be a dummy. Again, interpretation rules specify which such networks are wellformed templates.

(iii) A *semantic block* is a text representation consisting of a network of templates and *extractions*. The ties between the items of a semantic block may be imposed by *paraplates, inference rules*, or *extraction rules*.

(iv) *Paraplates* are relations between template pairs, and if a paraplate applies to a particular (usually contiguous) template pair it imposes a *case relation* between them. A paraplate consists of six predicates which must apply to the three major nodes of the two templates, if the relation is to hold.

(v) *Inference rules* are also relations between template pairs, of the same form as paraplates, but they impose a relation not of a particular case but of CAUSE, REASON or CONSEQUENCE.

(vi) An *extraction* is identical to a template, except that it does not necessarily correspond to any clause or phrase of surface text (it is inferred from a template).

(vii) *An extraction rule* produces, from any given template, a set of extractions. It corresponds to a particular case and produces an extraction for each occurrence of that case in any formula in a template to which it applies.

7.3 Preference-breaking Already Accommodated in the System

The function of this paper is to discuss *new* ways of accommodating preference breaking utterances, yet we should mention those preference breakers already dealt with by the processes described, and most particularly by the extraction process.

The standard ergative paradigm of verbs like "break" is dealt with in a uniform, though unconventional, manner. Utterances like

(13) The window broke

and

(14) The hammer broke the window

are well-formed English, but are preference breakers since "break" prefers an animated agent.

Thus (13), for example, yields *initially*:

(15) [the + window broke □]

Now, on extraction, the "SUBJ (agent) specialist" sees not only that

(a) the surface subject (window) does not satisfy the (* ANI SUBJ) preference of [break], but

(b) the same surface subject does satisfy the (*PHYSOB OBJE) preference of [break], which is filled by only a dummy in the source template (15). Thus the "SUBJ specialist" on extraction produces a copy template with the agency preference satisfied:

[[some + animate broke □]]

while "OBJE specialist" correspondingly produces:

[[□ broke window]]

and these are immediately conflated, on the general preferences [20] principle of producing the fullest representation possible, as the extraction:

(16) [[some + animate broke window]]

where the agent formula (now, of course, a true agent, not a surface subject) is *merely* (THIS * ANI), an extraction from the "break" formula. (14) is dealt with in a similar manner by the general extraction routine, with the added feature that [hammer] now cannot fit in the main template and will have to be inserted as object in the *INST*rument extraction from [break].

The standard type of extraction in the last example required the filling in a "new copy" template extracted from an *action* formula. Extractions are also made from substantive formulas (though only in the face of a preference violation) and these cover a range of examples like

(17) * John received a shock.

where [shock] is

(18)

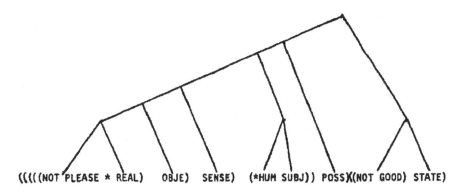

((((NOT PLEASE * REAL)   OBJE)   SENSE)   (*HUM SUBJ)) POSS)((NOT GOOD) STATE)

and so is not the physical object that "received" would prefer. It indicates a shock is a not-good state possessed by a human who senses a not-pleasing real entity (a wider class than physical object).

The head of [received] is the primitive GET, and the extraction specialist for POSS (in [shock]) cued by the relation of POSS and GET can write out a "copy template" from the formula [shock], namely:

(19) (*HUM) (SENSE) (NOTPLEASE *REAL)

whose agent, at least can be filled in from the context of the template for (17) to yield the extraction

(20) [[JOHN (SENSE) (NOTPLEASE *REAL)]]

where this entity (20) can now seek further specifications in the text, if present, to fill its action and object which now have only a very general primitive form. It is important to see that the extraction is cued by the relation of GET and POSS: it would *not* have been cued by

(21) John gave a shock to ....

since [give] does not have the head GET.

It should be remembered during what follows that an *extraction* is a new template-like object, not present in the surface, or source, text, and which is produced by inference using *case-specialists* when there is a preference-breaking in a source template. This is quite consistent with the methods of Wilks [23] in which extractions were also produced to deal with problems of word sense ambiguity.

7.4 Pseudo-texts: A Simple Projection System

We shall now define a new operation in the system, *projection*, which requires a new form of coded knowledge, *the pseudo-text* (PT).

A pseudo-text is a structure of factual and functional information about a concept or item, and is intended to fall broadly within the notion of *frame* in the sense of Minsky, Charniak and Schank [10, 3, 15].

Its form, in the terms developed so far, is simply that of a *semantic block*: a linear sequence of template forms tied by case ties, here taken to include CAUSE and GOAL (reason-for) ties inserted by the mechanisms of [26]. The linear order of the templates is taken by default to indicate normal time sequence. Thus a pseudo-text for "car" might start:

(22)

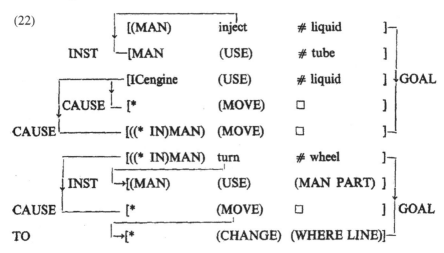

The first two lines refer to the insertion of fuel; the next three to the fact that the petrol using engine moves the car; and the last four to the way the driver turning the wheel changes the direction of the car.

This entity is pointed to by "car" which *also*, of course, points to the formula [car]; (23).

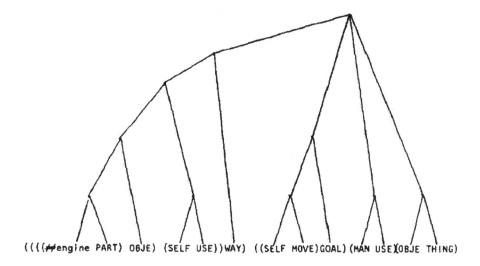

((((#engine PART) OBJE) (SELF USE))WAY) ((SELF MOVE)GOAL)(MAN USE(OBJE THING)

which says that a car is a thing that a person uses with the purpose of moving him-or herself, by means of an engine part. Here as in (12) # engine in (23) points to both a formula for "engine" and to a *thesaurus row* of types of engines:

(24) # engine: IC engine, turbine, electric motor ... etc (IC = internal com-combustion)

just as "car" points to both (22) and (23) from *its* place in some thesaurus row under subhead # vehicle, say.

The pseudo-text can be extended to taste to express as much detailed information about cars as is thought necessary, using exactly the same structure for text representation as was described in the earlier (recap) section, with the one addition that * indicates the formula [car] *from which we reached* this whole "pseudo-text", so that ((* IN)MAN) indicates "a person inside the car" (i.e. the driver or passenger).

The entities in the templates of the pseudo-text are either dummies ( ), primitive, elements (USE), formulas of primitive elements ((* IN)MAN), words which point to their own formulas in the thesaurus, such as "turn", or words preceded by a sharp sign # liquid, which point to their formula in the thesaurus where it is a head or sub-head formula. This notion will aid search in that it will indicate that the formula is not to be found at the bottom level of the thesaurus.

The pseudo-text could clearly have this same information about the function of an engine, and steering, expressed in a number of different ways at different levels. For example, the third template in (22) indicates that an IC (internal combustion) engine uses a liquid, where [IC engine] is a word formula, but [# liquid] is a very general formula (FLOW STUFF), since # liquid is a thesaurus subheading. It would have been possible to make the object of that template the more specific formula [petrol] or [gas] with an increase in specificity.

In general, these pseudo-texts are intended to be as *specific as possible*, but, and this is why they are called pseudo-texts, they have exactly the format of a text representation in preference semantics, and the intention is that *the processes that operate on such (dictionary) entities shall be identical with those operating on representations derived directly from surface texts*. The emphasis here is the reverse of the conventional one in this field: we stress the form of representation of *language* and seek to accommodate the representation of knowledge *to that*, rather than the reverse. And, of course, from a practical point of view it means that, with our parsing procedures, "pseudo-texts" could be input *as texts*.

Thus (22) is not a copy of a text representation, or even a script for a possible text about cars, it *is* the representation of some, rather general, text about the basics of driving a car. Notice too, that # vehicle, being a thesaurus sub-head above "car", will point to a pseudo-text more general than (22)—one we cannot assume is steered with a wheel, nor that is running by means of a liquid consuming engine—and so *the thesaurus imposes a hierarchy of pseudo-texts as well as the associated hierarchy of formulas*. That is to say that, just as the thesaurus row-members (as in (24)) stand in the row in virtue of the fact that their formulas have some common sub-formula (which should be also the formula for the sub-heading of the row itself), so should the pseudo-texts of co-row members be related. Thus, (22) as the pseudo-text for car may be expected to have some *strong structural resemblance* to the pseudo-texts for "truck", "railway train", "aeroplane", etc which are plausible co-row members with "car" in the row whose sub-heading is # vehicle.

However, the relation may be more complex than can be expressed by any "single common sub-pseudo-text" relation—as seemed possible with sub-formulas. Moreover, it may not be possible either to express the relation by saying that there are "slots" in the pseudo-text for # vehicle that are simply filled differently in the more specific pseudo-texts for the members of the # vehicle row, like "car". This has been suggested in [1], but, although one might express, say, the third line of (22) by

(Propellant: liquid)
(Motor   : IC engine)

where the right members could be replaced differently for "aeroplane", "railway engine" etc. It is not obvious that the whole content of (22) is easily captured by this format—though it may of course turn out that it is possible to do just that.

However, it is certainly possible to imagine the general structure of (22) being stored only *once* for the # vehicle row, and a specific repacking function being assigned to each row that would construct its pseudo-text when and only when required. Thus, in (22) all the lines given would appear in the pseudo-text for "aeroplane" except the sixth. Thus the repacking function for the row might well require that the row-members were *ordered* so that their pseudo-texts could be constructed from the one for the row sub-heading (like # vehicle) so that as much pseudo-text structure was "inherited" as possible as the repacking function was applied, let us suppose, rightwards along the row. It is not yet clear, however, that row members could be simply ordered in terms of the relative generality of their pseudo-texts in this way. There will also, of course, be more general "inheritances" of pseudo-texts down the thesaurus hierarchy, but that is not brought out from the # vehicle: car, etc. row because the head primitive of all the row-members' formulas is THING, whose *own* pseudo-text is pretty vacuous. However, the pseudo-text for the high level primitive (= thesaurus section) MAN would be highly complex. But note there is no "inheritance of property" problem in this system: the formula for "amputee" would have head MAN and would specify the loss of limbs and any inherited pseudo-text from MAN—asserting "two legs"—would be modified by [amputee].

Since pseudo-texts are text representations it must be assumed that it will be possible to "deepen" them by the *extraction* and other inference procedures described in [26].

In this paper we shall discuss a particular inference rule called projection that operates when extended use, in the sense of preference breaking, is encountered in the input surface text.

Projection results in the replacement of a template formula by a new one constructed by access to a pseudo-text. Projection is operated *only in the presence of preference breaking*, so as to avoid assigning peculiar interpretations to wholly conventional utterances.

The need for such specific information as (22) provides can be seen if we think at an intuitive level about the understanding of (3). I suggest that we can understand (3)—apart from its idiomatic element, noted already,—in two ways:

(i) We are made to feel that the car is in some way human-like as a drinker is.
(ii) We know, more importantly, that "drink" is equivalent to "use" *because that is what car engines do with gasoline.*

Element (i) of the meaning might be important to the understanding of:

(25) My car drinks gasoline. His thirst is never slaked,

where we might be helped to refer "his" to the car if we had simply projected the preferred (MAN) agent of [drink] as the head of [car]. In any case this requires no more mechanism than the corresponding *extraction* from (3), which would yield a form [[(MAN) drink gasoline]].

The important notion (ii) is captured by accessing the pseudo-text for "car" and *seeking the template in it with the closest match to the source template for* (3).

If we accept that that is the third one:

[IC Engine (USE) # liquid]

then we would expect to project the formula [*use*] *in place of* [drink] to obtain—as the new representation for (4):

(26) [my + car use gasoline]

But now we notice that we cannot have a rule that produces the "projected" representation (26) for sentence (3) *solely* in virtue of the partial match of the original template for (3) with the third template of pseudo-text (22), because that might lead to the same projection for "my car leaks gasoline" for which (26) would *not* be a suitable projected representation. So, the *general projection principle* of accommodating extended use with a pseudo-text is PROJECT SENSE ONTO ACTIONS FROM A PSEUDO-TEXT GIVING *WHAT WE NORMALLY* DO WITH THE ASSOCIATED OBJECT—but it must be modified somewhat in the light of "My car *leaks* gasoline".

We notice also that the template for (3) also matches the *first* line of (22), under an appropriate definition of match, in that [drink] and [inject] are both (MOVE CAUSE) formulas, but this is a weaker match than with the third line if we consider the agent and object terminals as yielding a stronger match given by *IC engine* being known as a car part from the structure of [car] (23) and # liquid being the sub-heading of the row containing "gasoline" (which is simply the *extensional* idiom for saying that [gasoline] can be seen to contain [liquid], because (FLOW STUFF) is their common sub-formula).

So, we may risk a new generalization: the projection represented by (26) is done in virtue of what I called the *general projection principle*, but requires confirmation by another weaker match, in the same pseudo-text, on action not object/agent terminals. This would prevent an undesirable projection on "My car leaks gasoline" (although it might well be argued that since that sentence involves no preference breaking we should not consider it as a problem for projection in any case, since this process, unlike extraction, would never be applied to it), as well as on the more distant "my car drinks *mud*" (which would not even achieve the agent/object terminal match), and "My car *chews* gasoline". The projected sense, "use" in (26) then, *carries over more than any alternative projection.*

A more complex case would be presented by a recent newspaper headline:

(27) Britain tries to escape Common Market.

We would have the possibility of simply projecting the preferences of [escape] for a human escaper and a prison-like object—onto the agent and object formulas. The difficult aspect would be to get the [escape] formula replaced by something like [disassociate from]. This could not be done by, say, simplifying [escape] to a [leave] component, because that is still *metaphorical*.

The interesting feature is that, although we might possibly have a historical pseudo-text about Britain *joining* the Common Market, we would not have one about *disassociation*. Mere facts are sometimes not enough, even when highly structured, as here.

We would in fact require a matching algorithm (as is argued for in [23]) that ignored negation in certain cases in favour of what one might call "mere relevance". That is, [joins] would have to be negated before being projected onto [escapes] as [disassociate from].

We would assume, too, that once having made a plausible projection in a text, the system should retain it, at least as a trial substitution, to other occurrences of the same word sense in the text.

In concluding this section, it is important to re-emphasize that it is anticipated that this projection rule will be required a great deal in the analysis of normal text, and not only for obscure examples. Those examples discussed here do have a non-standard quality, and were chosen for their interest. However, the very same procedures and pseudo-text would be required twice in so simple an example as "Johns new car runs on diesel, but it does 100 m.p.h. though" for the preference failures of "run on" and "do".

The reader should note ways in which the newly defined *projection* operation differs from that of *extraction*. Extraction adds new template-like forms to a text representation, "copying them out of" formulas in *source templates* which are those actually matched with surface text. But the source templates remain as part of the representation. Moreover, extraction operates not only in response to preference-breaking.

In projection, on the other hand, *at least one formula of a source template is replaced* by a new formula constructed, either by rule from formulas in the source templates, or by access to "pseudo-texts" and, as noted before, projection is operated *only in the presence of preference-breaking*.

Thus the two processes are distinct in the system though, as always with semantics the phenomena covered may not divide so neatly. Thus, in dealing with (17) "John received a shock" *by extraction*, we added extraction (20) [[John (SENSE) (NOTPLEASE * REAL)]] to the text. It *could* be argued here that this is equivalent to the replacement of [received] in the template for (17) by a minimal formula consisting only of the primitive SENSE. Thus, in certain cases, projection may produce the same inferential effect as extraction.

7.5 Some Control Issues

The fact that the proposals of this paper have not yet been implemented in a working program rather limits discussion of control issues. Some can be forseen but cannot be settled in advance: for example, any given preference-breaking template may contain a number of formulas pointing to pseudo-texts, and it would seem reasonable that the matching algorithms outlined in the last section should apply to all of them. This is only a particular example of a problem that arises in all "frame using" systems but has not yet, to my knowledge, been solved in any of them: many frames are called but few can be chosen, and preferably only one: If different pseudo-texts called by a given preference-break can yield rival projections, then some way will have to be found of choosing between them.

Again, the fact that the pseudo-texts are only accessed by preference breaking templates, and not by "normal" semantic structures, continues the "laziness" approach of the preference semantics system and remains a point of contrast with the frame systems of [17] and [3]. It is assumed that such structures should only be accessed when needed, and that a successful model of understanding will no more be able to tolerate "information overload" than we can. One specific aspect of that approach is that, although pseudo-texts contain specific knowledge, the system will try to work with the *most general* pseudo-text that it can.

Since it is intended that pseudo-texts for bottom-level formulas in the thesaurus, like [car], will be constructed from more general ones, like [# vehicle], this means that the system will see how far it can get with matching into a pseudo-text using only the one for the thesaurus sub-head, like # vehicle, and only construct the more specific pseudo-text if no adequate match is found in the general one. This approach need not be inconsistent with the assumption stated earlier that "projection rests on specific knowledge", since the more specific pseudo-text will in fact be *accessed via* the more general one, given the thesaurus structure.

It is important to all this that the thesaurus is not a "bad hierarchy", and it need not be, given that

(a) It avoids bad property inheritance in the construction of specific pseudo-texts, as indicated earlier, and

(b) the thesaurus contains *normal cross-referencing*, i.e. [knife] would appear under both [# tool] and [# weapon].

It is hoped that the "higher levels" of the thesaurus will play an important semantic role and explicate the obscure but important notion of what it might be to have the most specific possible information about very general concepts.

Let me give an example here:

In the course of discussing the present system of language understanding in connection with extended use Boden [2] draws attention to a class of examples like:

(27) I see what you mean

where we might say that "see" is being used in an extended sense, at least with respect to its central sense formula in which it would express a preference for *PHYSOB or *REAL objects. We must say "with respect to" here, as always, because the metaphor in (27) might be considered so dead, so normal, as to deserve its own dictionary entry in virtue of having been learned by our culture. But let us consider how the system proposed might deal with (27) on the assumption that the dictionary does *not* explicitly anticipate it.

We must postulate two initial operations on the second template for (27), i.e. for "what you mean". The action "mean" can by extraction impose on the (dummy) object for the head SIGN (since the formula for "mean" shows that it prefers a SIGN object). This operation is covered by a simple extension of the extraction procedures discussed already, namely that, in the presence of template dummies, formulas elsewhere in the template can impose their preferences on those dummies. Secondly, we must assume an operation for a relative clause template, like the one under discussion, in which the routines that tie templates together can postulate the head SIGN as equipollent with *the whole template*. This is a perfectly natural semantic analogue of the fact that the phrase "what you mean" is the object of "see" in (27).

The important difference here from preceding examples is that the object of "see" is now given to us only as the semantic primitive SIGN, and not as the name for an entity (like "car" in (3)). Hence there is no question of accessing a *specific* pseudo-text as we did for car, because there cannot be one.

If we wish to project an appropriate THINK head onto the formula for "see", in place of its normal SENSE, we shall have to use more general semantic procedures.

Now the *topmost* level of a thesaurus is that of the very general section names[1] equivalent to Human beings, Entities, etc., and these correspond directly to the primitives MAN, THING etc. of our system. I have argued elsewhere that there is no *essential* difference between primitives and words (see [24]): MAN is just an English word, even though it happens to have a fundamental *organizing role* in the present system of meaning representation. But what would be "pseudo-texts" for such general primitives?

It is in fact fairly clear what they would be: very general assertion forms, consisting wholly of heads, like:

MAN HAVE THING

MAN THINK SIGN

MAN WANT THING

These are *very* general expressions of human activity so general as to be almost vacuous. However, in the parsing procedures [18, 19, 22] of the present system these are the *bare template triples* which define the skeletons of well-formed templates. Yet it is here, as pseudo-texts for the primitives themselves that they "really belong" in the knowledge structure of the system.

In [10] he writes of the top levels of a frame being "always true" in the sense of analytic postulates about the world in question. Most of these 3-primitive forms would express assertions of that type.

Now what might they do for us here? Well, if we now apply to (27) *exactly the same processes* that we applied to "My car drinks gasoline" we shall access the "pseudo-text" of the preference-breaker and project from there. Here the preference-breaker is merely SIGN, and *its* "pseudo-text" will be a stack of bare templates that list the primitive actions normally done to SIGN, of which the top[2] of the list will of course be THINK, which would also have an agent MAN matching the "I" of (27), since thinking is what is normally done to and with SIGNS. This would enable us to project the desired THINK as the head of the (extended) "see" *using exactly the mechanisms we have already created for more specific knowledge examples.*

---

[1] In Roget's Thesaurus the general section names are different, but again very close to primitives in the system. Viz: # Abstract relations (GRAIN), # Space (WHERE), # Matter (STUFF), # Intellect (THINK), # Volition (GOAL) etc.

[2] "top" here is loose, and the procedures of the earlier section, applied here, might well locate more than one "bare template" under SIGN that would have Agent MAN, viz: MAN CAUSE SIGN as well as MAN THINK SIGN. We must presume upon other, natural, determinants of closeness that will result in THINK being projected first: for example, SENSE, THINK, FELL etc will already be grouped as the extension of a more general primitive *AFFEC (affections). These "high-order" primitives impose a tree-structure on the lower order ones.

7.6 An Environment for Implementing these Suggestions

Having made a number of suggestions in this paper for restructuring the preference semantics system, it may be appropriate to give by way of conclusion a very brief sketch of the proposed implementation environment.

An important feature will be the attempt to make use of both local and global context as necessary, where any frame-type information can be thought of as a *global context*, and intra-template preference as a paradigm of *local context*. It is well known that neither of these is adequate taken alone. In

(28) John went hunting with four bucks in his pocket.

we are misled about the sense of "buck" by using only the global context of "hunt". Conversely, in

(29) John licked the gun all over and the stock tasted good

we are misled about the sense of "stock" by taking the (local) preference of "taste" and ignoring the global context given by "gun". With a little ingenuity one can produce a total *deadlock* between the two influences, as with "stock" in:

(30) I licked the gun all over after the soup course when the stock tasted particularly
     good.

In the implementation local context will again be the operation of preference within and between templates via the operation of *paraplates* and *inference rules* [22, 23]. Global context will be the processes operating on the pseudo-texts, the use of the thesaurus in determining topic context and its minimal ability to express a more *dynamic* notion of frame (see [25]) than that dealt with here. The local and global context features will be, either directly or more likely by simulation, operated in parallel, so that they can independently, as it were, seek structures in the incoming text. But, as (30) shows there can be no *guarantee* of a general solution.

The aim in doing this is two-fold: first, to retain for the system the ability of doing *less than* all possible inference. If whatever problems of analysis the text presents can be settled without access to pseudo-texts and other frames, so much the better, in processing terms I have called this the operation of a lazy system.[3]

Secondly, retaining both local and global processing options, ideally in parallel, means that we can approach frames experimentally: to see what they do for us in practice. The ideal arrangement would be the facility in the HEARSAY [12]. Speech Understanding System, where one can switch off one branch of the analysis, such as local context, to see if that makes any difference. We cannot assume *in advance* that extended use, say, *must*[4] require access to frame-level knowledge. Our preliminary investigations in this paper suggest that sometimes it does and sometimes it doesn't.

Another feature of a desirable implementation will be some attempt to incorporate the sort of global rules of conversation investigated by Grice [8]. As we shall see in

---

[3] A feature now styled as "variable depth processing" [1].

[4] Though Fillmore seems to make this assumption about frames in [6].

the example that follows, such rules can over-ride frame-like knowledge in certain situations.

The actual environment for the implementation will be an interactive question-answering facility in English *about* the construction of a semantic text representation, including accommodating to "extended use". This methodology has the disadvantage that the *final semantic representation achieved*, though it remains available for some further task, is nevertheless in an internal linguistic representation rather than output in English.

However, it has the compensating advantage that the data base is non-trivial,[5] as is almost inevitable in the mini-world situations often chosen, and that the system will be that much more perspicuous if its semantic choices and inferences can be followed by a user.

Let us see, in sketch form, how such a system might work with a real example text: (*The Times*, April 6, 1975).

> (31) "An ambulance driver answering an emergency call, which turned out to be a hoax, went through red traffic lights and collided with a car, killing its driver...."

Readers of that sentence generally have no trouble seeing that the last mentioned driver is the car driver, and not the ambulance driver, though the inferences required to get that right are not easy to specify in any standard linguistic or logical terms. That professional language users sometimes use over-simple rules for noun-phrase reference is seen from the fact that the sentence appeared in *The Times* under the (wrong) headline: AMBULANCE DRIVER DIES IN HOAX CALL CRASH!

It will become clear that the understanding of the sentence requires inferences from both linguistic and real world knowledge. In the ideal dialogue that follows the user interventions are in upper case, and notes are preceded and followed by square brackets.

7.7 End of Text Input

1. An ambulance answering an emergency call
2. $ went through red traffic lights
3. and $ collided with a car
4. $ killing its driver
   [$ marks missing template agents in the four fragments the text has been cut into for ease of reference]
   All fragments match templates.
   Template 2 fails preference for agent.

---

[5] By that I mean no more than that question-answering implementations of frames *may* be no more than that question-answering implementations of frames *may* be no test of the analytic power of frames at all, but only of the *need of a data base*. That is, if you ask a system that has cinema-frames "what do I buy during the movie intermission" and get a suitable reply, you have not in any way shown the need for frames in *language understanding*.

Now repacking $ slots:

2. The *ambulance driver and ambulance* went through red traffic lights. WHY?
   A driver and ambulance are mobile, a call not.
3. *The ambulance driver* and ambulance collided with a car.

Suggest:

4. The ambulance driver killed ? its driver.
   [system unsure of $ in (4) 1: ?its is marked as a problem].
   WHY?
   Active agent preferred for *kill* (ambulance inanimate).
   But now re-inferring as follows:
   preference breaking in (2) drives inferences as follows:
   traffic lights are aperture (by extraction)
   or
   went through means passed (by projection).
   I select latter and *project* onto "went through"
   [straightforward extraction in (2), plus access to pseudo-text[6] for "traffic lights"]
   examining preferences in

4. $ killing ?its driver
   "It" is lights (number wrong)
   or
   call
   or
   car
   or
   ambulance
   Prefer car or ambulance for "it".
   [calls don't have drivers]
   Confirm

4. *ambulance driver* kills *car's* driver
   WHY?
   First:
   from traffic-lights pseudo-text:
   passing red traffic lights causes people hurt
   ["pass" has replaced "went through" by projection, remember].
   [pseudo-texts can have a "cause tied" template *pair* read out].
   this confirms kills both car *and* ambulance drivers.
   Second:
   Calling *pragmatic over-ride*
   its = cars

---

[6] Notice that the pseudo-text is being used to analyse the text here, though no *general claim* is being made, as in [15] that the frame can be used as a basis for parsing the text.

means "its" not twice coreferential.[7]
[a general Gricean-style pragmatics rule that maximizes information in the
fragment. If it = ambulance driver, writer would have used "killed himself"]
Confirm its = cars.
Representation complete.

The new point brought out of the hat at the end, as it were, shows the persistent
need for general pragmatic principles at the highest level, just as we need preference
at the lowest. The general interest here would be the possibility of two *clashing*
general principles in the analysis of a given text: that of preference, seeking, in some
sense, to minimize information (argued in [21]), and another seeking to maximize it.

7.8 Relation to Other Systems

There has been little attempt to cope with preference-breaking in recent literature
in Artificial Intelligence. Schank [16:p. 233] allows non-fitting items to be inserted
into his diagrams, marked with an asterisk, but gives no indication of how they
are accommodated. Bobrow and Winograd [1] write of "forcing a match" in their
KRL system, but give no description of how it is to be done, over and above
emphasizing that it would be a nice thing to do. An interesting thesis by Russell
[13] does tackle the problem. She describes a simple program, equipped with
Schanktype conceptual information augmented in an important way: she provides,
for the first time, conceptual coding of nouns for that system (what we here call
noun-formulas). Her program contains rules that attempt to draw inferences from
input examples of "extended use". So, for example, the program would output (INK
START BE IN CHAIR) from input (CHAIR DRINK INK), and quite properly
give no output for (HE CLOSE INK). The program appears to have only simple
conceptual structures, and to make no general claims over and above those contained
in the extraction procedures of this paper and [20, 23]. But some of its output
seems extremely interesting: divide the input–output pair: (HE CLOSE MIND), (HE
(IPART:MIND) STOP POSSIBILITY-OF START-THINK.) However, this would,
in the terminology of the present paper, almost certainly be *extraction* rather than
projection.

Another interesting program [7] tackles the different but related task of inferring
the sense of *unknown* words from semantic structures. However, it is not clear to
this reader, that his program does actually make use of script-like knowledge, since
almost all his inferences seem to be from conceptual content (i.e. formulas), as are
Weber's.

The pseudo-text proposals, as regards the structure itself rather than its application, will have many points of similarity with those of Schank and Charniak,

---

[7] A reader tempted to argue that "its" *must* refer to the car on syntactic grounds since it has
been mentioned while the ambulance has not should consider "A bicycle rider passing a
stationary truck swerved to avoid a dog and fell over buckling *its* wheel".

among others, who have also extended their "propositional representation" up one level to an *organization of* propositional representations (i.e. frames): for example, the case ties CAUSE and GOAL perform the same functions as Charniak's [3] COMES-FROM and LEADS-TO ties. Unlike Charniak, these proposals emphasize the relation to parsing yet, as should be clear, the relation proposed is not that envisaged by Schank's "expectational" methods.

The notion of perspective, much emphasized by Bobrow and Winograd [1] has always been present in the system as the possibility of multiple formulas for a word (such as "house as a point in space, a location, a destination" *and* "house as a container for people and their activities", where these two formulas do not correspond to a sense distinction), and is now made more general with the cross-referencing feature of the thesaurus where, as noted, a pseudo-text and formula for, say, knife can be pointed to from the rows subheaded [# tool], [# weapon] etc.

7.9 Discussion

This paper has not been a report on programs written nor on a working system of language understanding. It is however, based on considerable experience with such a system, and is intended to indicate extensions to it that will be implemented and tested as soon as possible. The aim here has been to develop extensions of meaning and knowledge representation in a way consistent with the earlier assumptions of the preference semantics system, and to sketch out the sort of practical developments in the program that would facilitate their testing. It is also clear that some test of these suggestions for dealing with extended use need not wait upon the arrival of usable parallel processing.

There has been a great deal of attention to examples in this paper, but there is intended to be a simple moral, or rather an (ultimately) testable maxim to the effect that much of what we call "understanding of language" may consist not merely in the correct and appropriate manipulation of precise knowledge—the "society of experts" view of knowledge and understanding—but in the manipulation of very general principles, possibly conflicting general principles, as here. Moreover, the ambulance driver example suggests that on occasions such principles may be needed *even where all possible detailed knowledge is available.*

It is a part of this view that the knowledge structures employed should, where possible, reflect language structure (hence the use of "pseudo-texts" here for the frame-like objects) and that the system using them should make general claims about the nature of language and knowledge—if it does not then no scientific phenomenon is being investigated and we have no claim to be scientists.

However, these general views can only be justified in the process of implementation and not by further general discussion. Moreover, a very important point will arise in such an implementation: the paper has emphasized both the role of *detailed* knowledge in projection (as in the *car* example) *and* the need to start at a general level in the hierarchy of pseudo-texts when seeking a match in projection. There is no contradiction here, but it leaves open the possibility that the rules as described will sometimes produce *very general* projections: in the Common Market example (27) the projection might produce a very *general* sense of "escape" as "exit from any enclosed space", rather than a fact-based one.

Again, it might, rather than replace [drink] by USE in the analysis of (3), project instead some very general sense such as "has fluid put into it". These will be matters to be worked out in practice, even though fundamental questions about meaning and understanding hang upon them. They will also require decisions on two other points:

(1) Are the senses produced by projection to be stored or not? Are they to be tried as possible senses for further uses of the same word in the same text?
(2) After projection has changed a template, should a copy of the original remain as part of the semantic block for the text, for fear that certain vital "surface" inferences will be blocked if it is not?

The last point is particularly important in connection with the issue of *how general* projections will turn out to be: the more general they are, the more it may be vital to keep a copy of the original template in the overall text representation.

Readers will also have remarked that the whole formula/pseudo-text distinction rests on some intuitive meaning/factual distinction that cannot be formally justified. Why keep it rather than go over to a uniform notation for both, as KRL would suggest? I think one can only say that the meaning/factual distinction, even if not philosophically sound, does have some role in our understanding. And in this system, the formulas are basic to parsing, and that that is a procedural role that should have some reflection in the system's structure.

In conclusion, one could hope that the above techniques might produce some small additional understanding of text in this almost unchartered area. But optimism is almost certainly out of place where imaginative writing is concerned. Consider:

The sad colonel did not have a nervous breakdown because he had a friend and because he was too unimaginative to admit defeat. He poured Rembrandt a glass of his friend. (Pownall 1974, p. 195)

The interpretation of the last word is, alas, both straightforward and totally beyond the scope of any system conceivable at the moment.

References

[1] Bobrow, D. and Winograd, T., K.R.L.—an overview of a knowledge representation language, *Cognitive Science* **1** (1977) 3–46.
[2] Boden, M., *Artificial Intelligence and Natural Man*. (Harvester Press, Hassocks, 1977).
[3] Charniak, E., A framed PAINTING: the representation of a commonsense knowledge fragment, *Cognitive Science* **1** (1977) 355–394.
[4] Chomsky, N., *Aspects of a Theory of Syntax* (M.I.T. Press, Cambridge, MA, 1965).
[5] Chomsky, N., *Language and Mind* (M.I.T. Press, Cambridge, MA, 1969).
[6] Fillmore, C., Scenes and frames semantics, in: Zampolli, ed., *Linguistics Structures Processes* (North-Holland, Amsterdam, 1977) 55–82.

[7] Granger, R. H., FOUL-UP, a program that figures out meanings of words from context, Dept. of Computer Science, Yale University (1977).

[8] Grice, H. P., Logic and Conversation, in: Cole and Morgan, eds., *Syntax and Semantics*, **3** (Academic Press, New York, 1975) 43–59.

[9] Katz, J. and Fodor, J., The structure of a semantic theory, *Language* **39** (1963) 170–210.

[10] Minsky, M., A frame-work for representing knowledge, in: Winston, ed., *The psychology of computer vision* (McGraw-Hill, New York, 1975) 211–277.

[11] Pownall, D., *The Raining Tree War* (Heinemann, London, 1974).

[12] Reddy, R. et al., The *Hearsay* speech understanding system, *Proc. Third Internat. Joint Conf. on Artificial Intell.* (Stanford, CA, S.R.I., 1973) 185–193.

[13] Russell, S., Computer understanding of metaphorical verbs, *Amer. Jl. Comput. Ling.* **44** (1976).

[14] Schank, R., ed., *Conceptual Information Processing* (North-Holland, Amsterdam, 1975).

[15] Schank, R., Using knowledge to understand (1975) as [24].

[16] Schank, R. and Colby, K., eds., *Computer Models of Thought and Language* (Freeman, San Francisco, 1973).

[17] Schank, R. and Abelson, R., *Scripts, Plans and Goals* (Erlbaum, New Jersey, 1977).

[18] Wilks, Y., *Computable Semantic Derivations*. Memo # SP-3017 (Systems Devel. Corp., Santa Monica, 1968).

[19] Wilks, Y., *Grammar, Meaning and the Machine Analysis of Language* (Routledge, London and Boston, 1972).

[20] Wilks, Y., *Natural Language Inference*, Memo # AIM–211 (Artificial Intelligence Lab., Stanford, 1973).

[21] Wilks, Y., Preference Semantics, in: Keenan, ed., *The Formal Semantics of Natural Language* (Cambridge U.P., Cambridge, 1975) 329–350.

[22] Wilks, Y., An intelligent analyzer and understander of English, *Comm. A.C.M.*, **18** (1975) 264–274.

[23] Wilks, Y., A preferential, pattern-matching semantics for natural language understanding, *Artificial Intelligence*, **6** (1975) 53–74.

[24] Wilks, Y., Primitives and words, in: *Theoret. Issues in Natural Language Processing* (B.B.N. Cambridge, MA, 1975) 27–31.

[25] Wilks, Y., De minimis: the archaeology of frames, in: *Proc. AISB Conf.* (Artif. Intell. Dept., Edinburgh, 1976) 111–126.

[26] Wilks, Y., What sort of taxonomy of causality do we need for natural language understanding? *Cognitive Science* **2** (1977) 235–264.

[27] Wilks, Y. Good and bad arguments for semantic primitives (Dept. of Artificial Intelligence Univ. of Edinburgh, 1977) Memo No. 42.

8

Providing Machine Tractable Dictionary Tools

Yorick Wilks, Dan Fass[1], Cheng-ming Guo[2], James E. McDonald,
Tony Plate[3] and Brian M. Slator[4]

New Mexico State University,
[1] *Simon Fraser University*
[2] *University College, Dublin*
[3] *University of Toronto*
[4] *Northwestern University*

Abstract: Machine readable dictionaries (MRDs) contain knowledge about language and the world essential for tasks in natural language processing (NLP). However, this knowledge, collected and recorded by lexicographers for human readers, is not presented in a manner for MRDs to be used directly for NLP tasks. What is badly needed are machine *tractable* dictionaries (MTDs): MRDs transformed into a format usable for NLP. This paper discusses three different but related large-scale computational methods to transform MRDs into MTDs. The MRD used is *The Longman Dictionary of Contemporary English* (LDOCE). The three methods differ in the amount of knowledge they start with and the kinds of knowledge they provide. All require some handcoding of initial information but are largely automatic. Method I, a statistical approach, uses the least handcoding. It generates "relatedness" networks for words in LDOCE and presents a method for doing partial word sense disambiguation. Method II employs the most handcoding because it develops and builds lexical entries for a very carefully controlled defining vocabulary of 2,000 word senses (1,000 words). The payoff is that the method will provide an MTD containing highly structured semantic information. Method III requires the handcoding of a grammar and the semantic patterns used by its parser, but not the handcoding of any lexical material. This is because the method builds up lexical material from sources wholly within LDOCE. The information extracted is a set of sources of information, individually weak, but which can be combined to give a strong and determinate linguistic data base

8.1 Introduction: The Value of MRDs

Dictionaries are texts whose subject matter is language. The purpose of dictionaries is to provide definitions of senses of words and, in so doing, supply knowledge about not just language, but the world. Researchers in computational linguistics and AI have viewed dictionaries with (1) theoretical interest as a means of investigating the semantic structure of natural language, and (2) with practical interest

K. Ahmad, C. Brewster and M. Stevenson (eds.), Words and Intelligence 1, 167–216.

as a resource for overcoming the knowledge acquisition bottleneck in AI: how to acquire formal meaning and knowledge representations automatically. Some researchers have recently begun to seek methods to overcome it, and have had some success. This difference in attitudes regarding the knowledge acquisition bottleneck is reflected in a long-standing difference between two alternative methods of lexicon building: the demo approach and the book approach [39, 5].

The demo approach, which has been the dominant paradigm in natural language processing (and AI in general) for the last two decades, is to handcode a small but rich lexicon for a system that analyzes a few linguistic phenomena. This is an expensive method as each entry in the lexicon is prepared individually. Every entry is constructed with foreknowledge of its intended use and hence of the knowledge it should contain. Being designed with only a specific purpose in mind, the knowledge representation runs into problems when scaled up to cover additional linguistic phenomena.

One alternative, the book approach, confronts the problem of knowledge acquisition directly. This approach attempts to develop methods for transforming the knowledge within dictionaries or encyclopedias into some format usable for CL and AI tasks, usually with the aim of covering as large a portion of the language as possible. The problem from a computational standpoint with dictionary and encyclopedia entries is that they are designed for human use.

Sparck Jones [59, 60] was an early proponent of the book approach but at the time her work was hindered by the absence of MRDs. More recently, interest in this approach has greatly expanded because a number of MRDs have become available, e.g., *The Merriam-Webster New Pocket Dictionary* [6, 3, 4], *Webster's Seventh New Collegiate Dictionary* [16, 13, 36, 7, 26], and *The Longman Dictionary of Contemporary English* [38, 61, 1, 10, 9, 69, 70].

The big advantage of MRDs is that both theoretical and practical concerns can now be investigated by large-scale computational methods. Some of the above research has been into the underlying semantic structure of dictionaries [e.g., 6, 3, 4, 13, 36, 7, 26]. The remainder of the research has sought to develop practical large-scale methods to extract syntactic information from MRD entries [e.g., 9] and transform that information into a format suitable for other users. This latter research has the effect of transforming an MRD into a limited MTD. We say "limited" because such an MTD has only syntactic information presented in a format usable by others; semantic information remains buried in the MRD, though this is the knowledge about language and the world that is needed as a resource for many CL and AI tasks. Therefore, the next step is to develop large-scale methods to extract both the syntactic and semantic information from MRD entries and present that information as a data base in a format acceptable to potential users.

Within the book approach there are a number of ways such an MTD can be constructed. One is to extract automatically the semantic information and build a full MTD. We firmly advocate automatic extraction. A second way is to extract the semantic information manually and handcode the entire MTD, as is being attempted in the CYC Project [31, 30]. The main problem here is the volume of effort required: the CYC Project aims to handcode one million encyclopedia entries, an estimated two person-centuries of work. We believe this approach is mistaken because it wastes precious human resources and makes dubious theoretical assumptions, despite Lenat's claims that their work is theory free (see Section 8.1.4).

Whichever form of the book approach is taken, there are two sets of issues that must be faced by those developing methods for the transformation of MRDs into MTDs: (1) nature of the knowledge in MRDs and (2) the design of the database format of an MTD. Both rest on understanding the structure and content of the knowledge that is both explicitly and implicitly encoded in dictionaries, but such understanding rests on certain crucial semantic matters. We examine some of these in the next section.

8.1.1 Background: The State of Semantic Theory

There are obstacles to the development of methods (whether manual or automatic for the transformation of semantic information in MRDs into MTDs; these obstacle are not present for those developing methods for syntactic analysis. The main obstacle is that, compared to syntactic theory, semantic theory is less advanced as shown by the lack of consensus about even the general underlying principle of semantics. Nevertheless, there is some understanding and local consensus on semantics that can allow work to proceed.

One's position on certain basic issues in semantics affects one's stance concerning what semantic information should be extracted from an MRD and represented in an MTD. In developing our own methods for the transformation of MRDs into MTDs, we have adopted a particular approach from computational semantics. Examples of this approach are Preference Semantics [64, 65, 66] and Collative Semantics [17, 18]. The main assumptions of this approach are that the problem of the *word sense* is inescapable and that *knowledge and language are inseparable.*

We believe that it is acceptable for a semantics to be based on the notion of word sense as used by traditional lexicography in constructing dictionaries. To put the matter another way, the inability of programs to cope with lexical ambiguity was a major reason for the failure of early computational linguistics tasks like machine translation. Yet, does it follow from that failure that the lexical ambiguity distinguished by conventional dictionaries has any real significance for CL, e.g., in the claim that a word such as *play* has eight senses that are then distinguished and described?

The point can perhaps be put most clearly by considering the suggestion that there never was lexical ambiguity until dictionaries were written in roughly the form we now have them, and that lexical ambiguity is no more or less than a product of scholarship: a social product, in other words. Translation between languages, as well as more mundane understanding tasks, had been going along for millenia before such scholarly products and therefore cannot require them.

This suggestion would be very much to the taste of certain formal semanticists who have never found the idea of lexical ambiguity interesting or important. For them, it is a peripheral phenomenon, one that can be dealt with by subscripting symbols as $play_1$, $play_2$, etc., (as Wittgenstein first did in his *Tractatus*) and claiming that there is, in any case, no real ambiguity in the world itself: Symbols designate disjoint classes of things and that fact can best be captured by disjoint (subscripted) symbols.

The answer to this position would be that when people translated "ambiguous words" before the advent of dictionaries, they went through a process that cannot be modeled by computer without some representation of lexical ambiguity. The subscripting position just presented, in parody form, is vacuous unless it also offers mechanical procedures for assigning the subscripts.

Another problem to be faced by those who make this last response (and who want to construct a lexical ambiguity data base, or customize an existing one) is the arbitrariness in the selection of senses for a word: different dictionaries may give 1, 2, 7, 34 or 87 senses for a single word and at first glance it seems that they cannot all be right. Byrd [11] has referred to this as the "mapping problem." This arbitrariness does not only appear between different dictionaries in their different sense ranges for the same word — it is also observable within a single dictionary when the sense-distinctions made for the definition of a word do not match the uses of that word in the definitions of other words in the dictionary. Worse yet, different dictionaries will segment usage into senses for a given word in non-comparable ways: Perhaps $play_3$ (the third of three) in dictionary A could not be associated with any one of the eight senses of 'play' in dictionary B. However, the way in which the different dictionaries "cannot all be right" is no different from the way in which different humans (with differing sense ranges for the same word) cannot all be right, even though none is clearly wrong. In short, they fail to agree but none of them is wrong.

The answer to the last problem is extensibility: A dictionary and sense-resolution algorithm are most plausible if they can extend so as to capture new senses, not already in the dictionary, on the basis of textual material presented. In that way differing dictionaries could, in principle, be tuned to "sense compatibility" (though it might serve no practical purpose), just as people can be if exposed to the same texts. The position defended here is that that phenomenon is utterly central for language understanding itself, and for the viability of machine dictionaries that start from different data bases.

Furthermore, any attempt to extract semantic information from a machine dictionary must acknowledge that the words used in dictionary entries may themselves be lexically ambiguous and must be disambiguated. When human readers see ambiguous words used in the definitions of real dictionaries, they appear to recognize those words as used in a particular sense, understand the intended senses of the words and hence disambiguate the words in the dictionary definitions. Three simple solutions then suggest themselves. The first is to mimic what humans appear to do and run a program on dictionary definitions and disambiguate those definitions when using them. The second solution is to remove beforehand the lexical ambiguity from the dictionary definitions and thus have definitions which contain only word-senses, a solution proposed by Quillian [45] and Amsler [3], among others. The third solution is to avoid the problem until it becomes essential that it be dealt with. In this paper we adopt two more subtle solutions. The first (part of what is called Method II below) is due to Guo and involves identifying "defining senses" of LDOCE words and cycles of redefinition based on them. It involves some handcoding followed by an automatic procedure, but is much less labor intensive than Amsler's method. Our other approach is almost circular, but not quite: we call it a "spiral method." A method of automatic network clustering, due to Plate and McDonald, is described below as Method I. This lexically disambiguates some of the words in LDOCE definitions, and the results are then used by Slator's LDOCE parser (Method III), which in turn disambiguates the full LDOCE definitions. This is a non-circular two-step procedure described in detail below.

Our position on the inseparability of knowledge and language is that this goes further than is normally thought and that particular language structures — text structures — are in fact a paradigm for knowledge structures [68] or, to put it very crudely, knowledge for certain purposes should be stored in text-like forms (as opposed to, say, predicate calculus-like ones). Examples of such knowledge structures include the planes of Quillian's Memory Model [45], pseudo-texts from Preference Semantics and sense-frames from Collative Semantics. Our position is that common principles underlie the semantic structure of text and of knowledge representations.

Given that the purpose of dictionaries is to provide definitions of words and their senses, it might well be expected that, of all forms of text, it would be in dictionaries that the semantic structure of language would be the most explicit and hence accessible for examination and comparison with the semantic structure of knowledge representations. And indeed, the semantic structure of dictionaries has been analyzed and compared to the underlying organization of knowledge representations, and similarities have been observed. Dictionary entries commonly contain a genus and differentia and the genus terms of dictionary entries can be assembled into large hierarchies [3, 13]. Likewise in the study of knowledge representation, a frame can be viewed as containing a genus and differentia and a semantic network is viewed as a hierarchy of terms.

These positions on semantics suggest the following for those engaged in transforming MRDs into MTDs. First, the problem of lexical ambiguity must be faced by any method seeking to extract semantic information from an MRD to build an MTD. Because lexical ambiguity exists in the language of dictionary definitions and in language generally, it follows that the language in MRD definitions needs to be analyzed at the word-sense level. Second, the format of the MTD, while being of principled construction, should be as language-like as possible.

Next, we focus attention on some basic issues in transforming MRDs, issues concerning the nature and accessibility of the knowledge in dictionaries.

8.1.2 The Analysis of MRDs

We hold that those who advocate the extraction (both manual and automatic) of semantic information from dictionaries (and even encyclopedias) have made certain assumptions about the extent of knowledge in a dictionary, about where that knowledge is located and how that knowledge can be extracted from the language of dictionary definitions. These are not assumptions about semantics but, rather, are assumptions about the extraction of semantic information from text. These assumptions are *methodological* because they underlie the decisions made in choosing one method for semantic analysis rather than another. These assumptions are about *sufficiency, extricability* and *bootstrapping*.

Sufficiency addresses the issue of whether a dictionary is a strong enough knowledge base for English, specifically as regards linguistic knowledge and, above all, the knowledge of the real world needed for subsequent text analysis. Sufficiency is of general concern, even for handcoding projects like CYC [30:1180].

Different positions have been taken within computational lexicography. Some researchers believe that there is not enough knowledge in dictionaries in principle [e.g., 25], i.e., that certain specific semantic information is not available anywhere in a dictionary and hence must be derived from another, outside, source. Other researchers believe that dictionaries do contain sufficient knowledge, though that knowledge may be implicit, but that it must be made explicit by using information from entries in other parts of a dictionary [eg., 3, 58, 9, 28]. We explain our position shortly.

Extricability is concerned with whether it is possible to specify a set of computational procedures that operate on an MRD and, without any human intervention, extract general and reliable semantic information on a large scale, and in a general format suitable for a range of subsequent NLP tasks.

Bootstrapping refers to the process of collecting the initial information that is required by a set of computational procedures for extracting semantic information from the sense definitions in an MRD. The initial information needed is commonly linguistic information, notably syntactic and case information, which is used during the processing of dictionary sense-definitions into an underlying representation from which semantic information is then extracted.

Bootstrapping methods can be *internal* or *external*. Internal methods obtain the initial information needed for their procedures from the dictionary itself and use procedures to extract that information. This is not as circular as it may seem. A process may require information for the analysis of some sense-definition (e.g., some knowledge of the words used in the definition) and may be able to find that information elsewhere in the dictionary. By contrast, external bootstrapping methods obtain initial information for their procedures by some method other than the use of the procedures themselves. The initial information may be from a source external to the dictionary or may be in the dictionary but impossible to extract without the use of the very same information. For example, the word *noun* may have a definition in a dictionary but the semantic information in that definition might not be extractable without prior knowledge of a sentence grammar that contains knowledge of syntactic categories, including what a noun is.

There are differences of opinion in computational lexicography regarding extricability and bootstrapping. Slocum and Morgan [58] are pessimistic about the use of machine readable dictionaries in machine translation. Others [e.g., 3, 9, 28] appear to believe that the semantic information in dictionaries can be extricated only with some external bootstrapping, that is, with some prior knowledge handcoded into an analysis program.

8.1.3 LDOCE: A Basic MRD

LDOCE, the MRD we use, is a full-sized dictionary designed for learners of English as a second language that contains more than 55,000 entries in book form and 41,100 entries in machine-readable form (a type-setting tape). We define an *entry* as a collection of one or more sense definitions that ends at the next head. The *head* is the word, phrase or hyphenated word defined by an entry. A *sense entry* is the sense definition, examples and other text associated with one sense of a head. If an entry includes more than one sense definition then each sense definition will have a number.

The preparers of LDOCE claim that entries are defined using a "controlled" vocabulary of about 2,000 words and that the entries have a simple and regular syntax. Table 8.1 shows some basic data derived from our analysis of the machine-readable tape of LDOCE (because of a tape error, words that follow alphabetically after *zone* have not been analyzed). The figure of 2,166 is arrived at as follows. The list of controlled vocabulary contains 2,219 words. We have removed 58 prefixes and suffixes that are listed as controlled vocabulary items and have removed 35 items that did not have heads. Furthermore, the analysis shows that some words are not part of the controlled vocabulary yet are used frequently in definitions; for example, the word *aircraft* is not part of the controlled vocabulary, yet it is used 267 times in sense definitions. About 30 such words have been added to the list of controlled vocabulary, giving 2,166 words. The criteria for adding a word were that it was used at least 13 times in definitions or examples without indication that it was a cross reference, and that at least one of these uses was outside of its definition. Most of these words added are compound words, such as *aircraft*.

The interesting thing to note from Table 8.1 is the extremely high number of senses for words belonging to the controlled vocabulary. Although there are only about 2,166 words in the controlled vocabulary, more than 24,000 of the 74,000 senses defined in LDOCE are senses of these words (including senses of phrases beginning with a word from the controlled vocabulary). To put this another way, controlled vocabulary items are roughly six times as ambiguous as non-controlled items: Words from the controlled vocabulary have an average of twelve senses while other words have an average of two.

The book and tape versions of LDOCE both use a system of grammatical codes of about 110 syntactic categories which vary in generality from, for example, *noun* to *noun/count* to *noun/count/followed-by-infinitive-with-TO*.

The machine readable version of LDOCE also contains "box" and "subject" codes that are not found in the book. The box codes use a set of primitives such as

Table 8.1. Head counts for words, entries and sense entries in LDOCE.

Heads	Words	Entries	Sense Entries
Controlled vocabulary	2,166	8,413	24,115
Non-controlled vocabulary	25,592	32,687	49,998
Totals	27,758	41,100	74,113

"abstract," "concrete" and "animate," organized into a type hierarchy. The primitives are used to assign type restrictions to nouns and adjectives, and type restrictions on the arguments of verbs.

The subject codes, referred to here as "pragmatic" codes to avoid confusion with the grammatical subject, use another set of primitives organized into a hierarchy. This hierarchy consists of main headings such as "engineering" with subheadings such as "electrical." These primitives are used to classify words by their subject area; for instance, one sense of *current* is classified as "geology-and-geography" while another is marked "engineering/electrical."

8.1.4 The Production of MTDs

One principal issue here concerns the format that MTDs should have. Certainly, the format must be versatile for a variety of consumers in CL and AI to use it. These consumers need a range of semantic information. To meet these needs MTD formats should be unambiguous and preserve much of the semantic structure of natural language, and should contain as much information as is feasible. However, this does not mean that the format of an MTD must consist of just a single type of representation, because it is possible that different kinds of information require different types of representation. For example, two kinds of information about word use are (1) the use of senses of words in individual dictionary sense definitions, and (2) the use of words throughout a dictionary, i.e., co-occurrence data. It is not clear that a single representation can record both (1) and (2): The former requires a frame-like representation of the semantic structure of sense definitions that records the distinction between genus and differentia, the subdivision of differentia into case roles, and the representation of sense ambiguity; whereas the latter requires a matrix or network-like representation of word usages that encodes the frequency of occurrence of words and of combinations of words. Hence, an MTD may consist of several representations, each internally uniform.

Given the arguments presented in Section 8.1.1, we believe that the first of these representations should be modeled on natural language though it should be more systematic and unambiguous. Hence, this component representation should be as text-like as possible and should distinguish word senses.

The other form of representation can be construed as a connectionist network based on either localist [e.g., 14, 62] or distributed approaches [e.g., 34, 48]. Like our position on semantics, connectionism emphasises the continuity between knowledge of language and the world, and many connectionist approaches have paid special attention to representing word senses, especially the fuzzy boundaries between them [e.g., 14, 62, 48]. Localist approaches assume symbolic network representations whose nodes are word senses and whose arcs are weights that indicate their relatedness.

An interesting new approach, described in Section 8.2, uses a network whose nodes are words and whose arc weights are derived from co-occurrence data for words. Although this approach initially appears to be localist, it is being used to derive more distributed representations which offer ways of avoiding some serious problems inherent in localist representations. Such frequency-of-association data do not appear in standard knowledge representation schemes, but are complementary to the knowledge in such schemes, and may be useful in their own right for CL tasks such as lexical ambiguity resolution.

8.1.5 Three Providers

We now move to describe three methods of extraction from LDOCE, which share some, but not all, of the principles advocated above. We shall argue that they yield different but consistent extractions from LDOCE, and at the end of the paper we discuss how to combine their separate "weak methods" [40] into a single strong source, to serve as a data base for a wide computational community. These three methods are extensions of fairly well established lines of research. The method in Section 8.2 is in the spirit of distributional analysis [24]. In Section 8.3, an attempt is made to develop an empirically motivated controlled vocabulary in the spirit of Amsler's, work [3] on the role of defining vocabulary in dictionaries. Section 8.4 describes the construction of a large-scale parser for the extraction of genus and differentia terms, expanding upon other similar work [e.g., 13, 1, 7].

All three methods pay special attention to the underlying methodological assumptions concerning the extraction of semantic information from dictionaries distinguished in Section 8.1.2 above. With respect to sufficiency and extricability, all three methods assume that dictionaries do contain sufficient knowledge for at least some CL applications, and that such knowledge is extricable. But the methods differ over bootstrapping, i.e., over what knowledge, if any, needs to be handcoded into an initial analysis program for extracting semantic information.

The three methods differ in the amount of knowledge they start with and the kinds of knowledge they produce. All begin with a degree of handcoding of initial information but are largely automatic. In each case, moreover, the degree of handcoding is related to the source and nature of semantic information required by that method.

- Method I, a statistical approach due to Plate and McDonald, uses the least handcoding; the co-occurrence data it generates is the simplest form of semantic information produced by any of the three.
- Method II, a compositional-reduction method due to Guo, derives a natural set of semantic primitives of about 2,000 "seed senses" (1,000 words) from LDOCE. These seed senses are used to construct an MTD that contains highly structured semantic information.
- Method III, a parsing of LDOCE dictionary entries due to Slator, requires handcoding a grammar and semantic patterns used by a parser, but not the handcoding of any lexical material. This is because the method builds up lexical material from sources wholly within LDOCE.

8.2 Method I: Statistical Lexical Disambiguation

In this section we explore the co-occurrence of words in LDOCE. We claim that co-occurrence data can provide an automatically-obtainable measure of the "semantic relatedness" of words. Also, we will investigate the possibility that statistics of co-occurrence of words in LDOCE can (1) give some empirical evidence for word sense distinctions, and (2), be used in conjunction with sense definitions to perform lexical disambiguation within LDOCE.

A semantic theory of language that treats word-senses as the basic unit of meaning makes a prediction about distribution of word senses. That prediction is that *two word-senses occurring in the same sentence will probably be semantically related.* This is because most sentences are coherent wholes, and in a coherent whole every item is involved in some relationship and every pair of items is linked by some chain of relationships. This prediction is weak, uncontroversial and essentially irrefutable. We make a much stronger claim, in three parts. First, the probability of a relationship between two word-senses occurring in the same sentence is high enough to make it possible to extract useful information from co-occurrence statistics. Second, the extent to which this probability is above the probability of chance co-occurrence provides an indicator of the strength of the relationship. Third, if there are more and stronger relationships among the word-senses in one assignment of word-senses to words in a sentence than in another, then the first assignment is more likely to be more correct.

So, we are interested in the possiblility of inferring semantic information from the observed distribution of words. However, there are two major obstacles to doing this. The first obstacle is that such statistics concern the distribution of words, whereas the semantic theory of distribution concerns the distribution of word-senses. In Section 8.2.3.2 we give an indication of how purely distributional statistics can indicate the presence of several word senses in a corpus. The network reduction technique we use to accomplish this separation of senses is one method for dealing with the obstacle that our distributional statistics are about words rather than senses. In our technique for lexical disambiguation we use another way to deal with this obstacle: we look up senses in the dictionary and use the definitions to provide information about them. In this technique we also have to deal with the same problem because the words in the definition of a sense are also ambiguous. We deal with this by allowing each word to contribute information from all of its senses and by considering that information contributed from several words is more informative: The irrelevant senses have less weight [32].

The second obstacle to extracting semantic information from co-occurrence statistics is that non-semantic factors can influence the choice of words and thus the distribution of sense-uses. Some of these factors, some of which overlap, are listed below.

- The pragmatic goal of avoiding ambiguity may lead to choosing the sense of one word rather than an equivalent sense of a different word to express an idea in a particular context.

- The distribution of topics in the sample of text will influence the distribution of sense-uses. This is further discussed in Section 8.2.4.2, on using LDOCE as a source of co-occurrence statistics.
- The style of the sample of text will affect the distribution of sense-uses. This too is discussed in Section 8.2.4.2.
- The social and cultural context of a text will influence the distribution of sense-uses in it.
- The collocability and idiomatic uses of words will influence the choice of senseuses.

The extent to which the above factors will prevent the collection of useful information from co-occurrence statistics is an empirical question. It may even be possible that some of the above factors, especially the last, may be useful things to have information about.

8.2.1 Obtaining Measures of Relatedness of Words from LDOCE

There are two aspects to obtaining measures of relatedness of words from LDOCE using co-occurrence statistics. One is the collection of statistics of co-occurrence of words in LDOCE. The other is the interpretation of those statistics, i.e. the function we use to compute measures of relatedness from statistics of co-occurrence.

8.2.1.1 Collecting Statistics of Co-Occurrence from LDOCE

Co-occurrence data record the frequencies of co-occurrence of pairs of words within some textual unit. All the co-occurrence data used in the experiments reported in this section were collected using the sense-entry as the textual unit. Sense-entries were chosen to be the textual units because they are moderately sized, coherent samples of text focused on one topic.

We have taken advantage of the controlled vocabulary of LDOCE in order to reduce the amount of co-occurrence data to be collected. Statistics were collected only for words in a version of the controlled vocabulary modified as described in Section 8.1.3; this version has no prefixes or suffixes and has 31 additional words.

The definition of *word* that has been used is as follows. Plurals of nouns are considered the same *word* as the singular form, and conjugations of verbs are considered the same *word* as the infinitive form. Some forms of words have more than one morphologically possible root; e.g., *rose* could be a flower or the past tense of *rise*. Such difficulties have been ignored and the root form has been chosen arbitrarily. So, for instance, *rose* is always taken to be the flower, even in a sentence such as *the sun rose*. This is only a problem for the very few words (*rise, rose, leaf,* and *leave*) which have derived forms that are identical to other words, or derived forms thereof, in the controlled vocabulary. In some cases two words derived from the same root but having different parts of speech are the same word, and in other cases they are not. For example, *quick* and *quickly* are considered to be the same word, but *beauty* and *beautiful* are not. LDOCE's controlled vocabulary was used to determine this — if a root form and a derived form of a word were included as separate items in the controlled vocabulary, then they were regarded as different words. If just the root form was included, then all derived forms were regarded as the same word as the root.

- For the purposes of this section, when *word* is used to refer to a word in the controlled vocabulary, it also refers to all variants of that word that do not appear separately in the vocabulary.
- The *textual unit* is the sense-entry, which is the definition and example text for one word sense. The number of textual units is N $(= 74, 113)$.
- The *frequency of co-occurrence* of two words x and y, f_{xy}, is the number of textual units (also referred to as *events*) in which both of those words occur.
- The *independent frequency of occurrence* of a word x, f_x, is the number of events in which it occurs.

8.2.1.2 Deriving Relatedness from Co-occurrence

If it is true that related words are more likely to occur together than unrelated words, then co-occurrence statistics should be able to provide some indication of the relatedness of words — related words will occur together more frequently than by chance. Co-occurrence data can also indicate negative relatedness, where the probability of co-occurrence is less than by chance. This has been determined to be uninteresting because initial investigation revealed that all negative relatedness occurred with closed-class words (e.g., *for* and *to*). Thus we seek exclusively to measure positive relatedness.

The problem is to find some function of frequencies of occurrence and co-occurrence that will rank the relatedness of pairs of words, i.e. a function that will indicate whether or not words x and y are more strongly related than words v and w. The easiest way of ranking is to have a function that maps to a point on a linear scale of relatedness, and such functions will be refered to as *relatedness functions*.

Relatedness functions should be unbiased and sensitive across the domain of independent frequencies; that is, for all possible independent frequencies of words, the frequency of co-occurrence that is expected by chance should map to minimum relatedness and the maximum possible frequency of co-occurrence should map to maximum relatedness. We are unsure as to whether relatedness functions should be symmetric. An argument in favor of symmetry is that it is not possible to tell from co-occurrence data that word x "causes" word y to appear more than word y "causes" word x to appear. Assymetry in a relatedness functions can only arise from differential independent frequencies of words x and y. An argument against symmetry is that assymetry might be useful and that the above argument is invalid because we are not measuring how much one word "causes" another to appear.

The relatedness functions used in the experiments are shown in Table 8.2 along with comments as to their bias, sensitivity, symmetry and motivation.

We had hoped to find a relatedness function which would give a low relatedness value to word pairs where one word was a closed-class word (especially determiners and very common prepositions). This would provide a principled way of ignoring such words, as they seem to provide very little information. The *sdd* function

Table 8.2. Relatedness functions

NAME	VALUE	COMMENTS
$cp(x, y)$	$\dfrac{f_{xy}}{f_y} \, (= Pr(x\|y))$	Conditional probability of x given y. Assymmetric. Insensitive and heavily biased for all f_x and f_y, except low, equal values. Same as f_{xy} for a given y. Included for comparison.
$dcp(x, y)$	$Pr(x\|y) - Pr(x)$	Deviation of cp. Difference between $Pr(x\|y)$ and $Pr(x)$. Assymmetric. More sensitive than cp but still biased and fails to map to full range for most values of f_x and f_y. An attempt to remove some of the bias of cp.
$dcp_{min}(x, y)$	$\min(dcp(x, y), dcp(y, x))$	Minimum of dcp in both directions. Symmetric. Sensitive if f_x and f_y are similar, but maps to zero if they are considerably different. An attempt to remove more of the bias of cp than dcp removes.
$iou(x, y)$	$Pr(x \text{ and } y\|x \text{ or } y)$	Intersection over union. Produced by dividing number of events in which both x and y occur by the number of events at least one of them occurs in. Attempt to remove bias from cp. More sensitive than dcp_{min} when f_x and f_y are different.
$dex(x, y)$	$\dfrac{f_{xy} - f_x \cdot f_y}{\min(f_x, f_y) - f_x \cdot f_y}$	Dependency extraction. Normalizes f_{xy} by mapping it to $[0,1]$ according to its scaled position between the minimum and maximum possible values. Symmetric. Fully sensitive for all f_x and f_y. Attempt at a sensitive, unbiased symmetric relatedness function.
$sdd(x, y)$	$\dfrac{f_x y - \dfrac{f_x \cdot f_y}{N}}{\sqrt{\dfrac{f_x f_y \cdot (N - f_x)(N - f_y)}{N^2 \cdot (N - 1)}}}$	Standard deviation distance. Based on Fisher's exact method for deciding whether two samples have identical distribution, which uses the hypergeometric distribution for co-occurrence of x and y, assuming that x and y are independent. Symmetric. We use a normal approximation to measure the number of standard deviations that the observed value of f_{xy} is from its expected value (assuming independence).

Table 8.3. Twenty words most strongly related to *bank* for each function

cp	*a, account, an, and, as, bank, be, by, for, from, have, in, money, of, on, or, river, the, to, which*
dcp	*a, account, as, at, bank, be, by, from, have, in, keep, money, of, on, pay, river, rob, the, to, water*
dcp_{min}	*account, bank, cheque, criminal, earn, flood, flow, lake, lend, money, pay, prevent, promise, rate, river, rob, rock, safe, sand, sum, thief*
iou	*account, bank, busy, cheque, criminal, earn, flood, flow, interest, lake, lend, money, overflow, pay, river, rob, safe, sand, thief, wall*
dex	*a, account, bank, be, by, cheque, clerk, dollar, in, messenger, money, of, overflow, participle, pay, river, rob, September, the, to*
sdd	*account, bank, busy, cheque, clerk, criminal, dollar, flood, international, keep, lake, lend, money, overflow, pay, river, rob, sand, thief, water*

seemed to do this reasonably well — *a* and *the* were the 27th and 51st words most strongly related to *bank* as measured by *sdd*. *dex* and dcp_{min} gave higher values for function words, but not as high as did *cp*. However, none of the functions produced significantly better results than *cp* in the lexical disambiguation task.

The types of words these relatedness functions select as highly related are shown in Table 8.3, which gives the 20 words most strongly related to *bank*, as measured by each of the relatedness functions. There are 21 words for dcp_{min} because of ties.

We have used all six of the above functions and raw frequency of co-occurrence as measures of relatedness in various experiments (but not all in all experiments). Despite the theoretical considerations, none was markedly superior; all worked reasonably well (given appropriate choices of other parameters). Surprisingly, raw conditional probability was slightly superior in the two experiments in which it was used, namely comparison with human judgments (Section 8.2.2.3), and lexical disambiguation using word sets (Section 8.2.3).

8.2.2 The Use of Co-Occurrence Information for Lexical Disambiguation

The ability to find sets of words related to a word allows us to formulate a technique for lexical disambiguation based on local context. The general idea behind this technique is to compare the local context of the word we want to disambiguate with the sense-entry for each of the senses of that word. For all of the experiments reported, the local context of a word was taken to be the sentence in which it appeared. The sense-entry that the local context is most similar to is likely to be the correct sense. This technique is not completely straightforward because the sense-entry of a particular sense, and a sentence in which a use of that sense appears, often have no words (in the controlled vocabulary) in common. For example, the definition of sense 4.1 of *bank* is shown below, with the words in the controlled vocabulary in parenthesis. Note that we use the convention of numbering the Mth sense in the Nth entry (homograph) for a word as 'sense$N.M$'. Homographs or senses unnumbered in LDOCE are labelled with '0'. Note also that for the purposes of the experiments described in this section the following words were omitted from the controlled vocabulary: *a, and, be, for, in, of, or, than, that, the this, those, to, what, when, where, which, who* and *with*.

bank[4] **1** a place in which money is kept and paid out on demand, and where
   related activities go on (*activity, demand, go, keep, money, on, out, pay, place, related*)

An example of the use of sense 4.1 of *bank* is (from the definition of 'savings account'):

> *BrE* any of various kinds of bank accounts earning higher interest than a
> DEPOSIT ACCOUNT (*account, any, earn, high, interest, kind, various*)

The context of the use of sense 4.1 of *bank* and its sense-entry have no words in common. This is not unexpected given the small number of words in the sense-entry. A consequence is that we cannot use the straightforward technique of looking for the sense-entry with maximum word overlap with the context.

Using relatedness functions we can expand contexts and sense-entries to included related words, making the technique of looking for maximum overlap more reliable. Lesk [32] reported a similar technique for performing sense disambiguation. In his technique definitions of words were used to find related words, rather than relatedness functions based on co-occurrence data, and only contexts were expanded. Sparck Jones [59] also presented a closely related technique, based on finding chains of synonyms that linked senses of words in the sentence. Sparck Jones's technique differs from the one presented here in that all words in the sentence were disambiguated at once. We have avoided doing this because of the problems of combinatorial explosion — for each word in a sentence the number of possible sense-assignments is multiplied by the number of senses that word has. For the sentence above there are 276,480 possible sense-assignments for the words listed in parenthesis alone. It is quite possible that better results could be got by disambiguating all the words in a sentence at once, but an efficient search technique would be required. Simulated annealing and genetic searching are potentially suitable search techniques for this.

8.2.2.1 Vectors for Words, Senses and Contexts

Using the co-occurrence data we can judge the similarity of sense-entries and contexts even though they might have no words in common, like the context and sense-entry in the example shown above. We do this by expanding sense-entries and contexts to include related words. It is then possible to judge their similarity by using some function that counts overlap.

We represent the expanded contexts and senses as vectors rather than sets because we want to have a weight associated with each word. The weight is used to record the number of words related to words in the context, or related to words in the sense definition, and to record the number of words further related to these recorded words. We do not use the relative values of relatedness functions to weight words: A word is judged as related just if it exceeds some threshold. For consistency we also represent the sets of words related to a word as vectors, though the only values in the word-vectors are zero and one.

Let the vector of related words for word x be denoted by the vector R^x, such that $R^x_y = 1$ if $f(x, y) > t$ (and if y is not one of the 20 words said just above to have been omitted), and 0 otherwise, where f is some relatedness function, and t is a threshold. Two methods for setting t were used. One was to fix its value so that it was the same for all word-vectors, and the other was to adjust t for each x so that the number of 1s in R^x, i.e. the number of words judged to be related, was near to some constant value s. It could not always be made exactly equal to s because of ties in relatedness function values.

We build a vector of words R^S for a sense-entry (a *sense-vector*) by summing the vectors of related words of each of the words, except for the word being defined, in the sense-entry. Similarly, we build a vector of words R^C for the context (a *context-vector*) of the word to be disambiguated by summing the vectors of related words of each of the words in the context, again with the exception of the word being disambiguated.

8.2.2.2 Judging the Similarity of Sense-Vectors and Context-Vectors

There are many ways one can judge the similarity of two vectors. All the functions we used can be seen as some measure of overlap. Some ignore the weights on words in word-vectors; others take them into account.

The following simple functions are used in the definitions of the vector similarity functions: $Z1$ maps vectors to vectors, non-zero elements are mapped to 1 and zero elements are mapped to 0. *SUM* maps vectors to scalars; its result is the sum of all the elements of the vector. The dot-product function '$\cdot$' maps two vectors to a scalar in the conventional way. The pairwise sum '$\oplus$' maps vector pairs to vectors.

The first vector similarity function treats the vector as a set, and computes the size of the intersection over the size of the union (hence the name *IOU*).

$$IOU(V, W) = \frac{Z1(V) \cdot Z1(W)}{SUM(Z1(V \oplus W))} \tag{1}$$

The second vector similarity function counts the "hits" of V in W (i.e., it sums the elements of W for which the corresponding element in V is non-zero) and divides this value by the sum of the elements in W.

$$HIT^{\rightarrow}(V, W) = \frac{Z1(V) \cdot W}{SUM(W)} \tag{2}$$

The third function takes the symmetric product of $HIT^{\rightarrow}$.

$$HIT^{\times}(V, W) = HIT^{\rightarrow}(V, W)HIT^{\rightarrow}(W, V) \tag{3}$$

The fourth is the normalized dot-product (the cosine of the angle between the two vectors)

$$NDP(V, W) = \frac{V \cdot W}{\sqrt{V \cdot V + W \cdot W}} \tag{4}$$

We tried all of the above functions and found $HIT^{\times}$ and NDP to produce the best results.

8.2.2.3 The Lexical Disambiguation Experiment

The disambiguation of the 197 occurrences of the word *bank* in LDOCE was attempted in the manner just described.[1] All the sentences were first disambiguated by hand by the authors and the occurrence of *bank* in each was labeled with a sense from the sense distinctions made in LDOCE. This was not an easy task, as some of the usages of *bank* did not seem to fit any of the definitions very well. The method was judged to have assigned the correct sense to a word in context if it chose the same sense as that represented by the hand-labeling.

Bank was chosen as a test case for a number of reasons. It has a moderate number of senses (13), and these senses can be split into two main groups: financial senses and earth or river senses. These two groups account for seven of the 13 senses and nearly all of the usages of *bank* in LDOCE. Within these two sense-groups there are finer distinctions, some semantic and some syntactic. For example, one of the three financial senses of bank is transitive and one is intransitive. As the method ignores syntactic information, we would not expect it to be able to make correct distinctions between the three financial senses of *bank*. We might also expect it to have difficulty distinguishing the earth senses of *bank* which have only fine semantic differences. However, we do expect it to do well in making gross semantic distinctions. Given these considerations, completely accurate performance on this task would be very strange and would indicate something wrong; a rate of not much more than 50% exactly correct is expected.

The 13 senses of *bank* listed in LDOCE are shown in complete form below. In order to judge how well the method makes grosser semantic distinctions, the 13 senses were allocated (by the authors' judgment) to six *sense-groups* (labeled (A), (B), etc.); the performance on assigning a usage to the correct sense-group was also measured. The number of times each sense was used in the dictionary, including the definitions and examples shown here, is given in square brackets at the end of each sense-entry.

All combinations of the six relatedness functions (*cp* was used in both directions, making a seventh), four vector similarity functions ($HIT^{\rightarrow}$ was used in both directions, making a fifth), and ten criteria for choosing word sets (five fixed sizes,

---

[1] *Bank* occurs slightly more often than this, but only in examples of use of its phrasal verb forms (defined separately in LDOCE and not shown here). These were omitted because they are easily identifiable and thus can be disambiguated by other means.

$n = 5, 10, 20, 40, 70$ and 100, and five fixed thresholds, which varied for each relatedness function) were tried. This was a total of 350 experiments.[2]

bank[1] **n1** (A) land along the side of a river, lake, etc. [32] **2** (A) earth which is heaped up in a field or garden, often making a border or division [5] **3** (A) a mass of snow, clouds, mud, etc.: *The banks of dark cloud promised a heavy storm* [2] **4** (B) a slope made at bends in a road or race-track, so that they are safer for cars to go round [0] **5** (A) SANDBANK: *The Dogger Bank in the North Sea can be dangerous for ships* [6]

bank[2] *v* (B) (of a car or aircraft) to move with one side higher than the other, esp. when making a turn — see also BANK UP [0]

bank[3] *n* (C) a row, esp. of OARS in an ancient boat or KEYS on a TYPEWRITER [0]

bank[4] **n1** (D) a place in which money is kept and paid out on demand, and where related activities go on — see picture at STREET [143] **2** (E) (*usu. in comb.*) a place where something is held ready for use, esp. ORGANIC products of human origin for medical use: *Hospital bloodbanks have saved many lives* [1] **3** (F) (a person who keeps) a supply of money or pieces for payment or use in a game of chance [2] **4** (F) *break the bank* to win all the money that the BANK4 (3) has in a game of chance [1]

bank[5] *v***1** (D) to put or keep (money) in a bank [0] **2** (D) to keep one's money (esp. in the stated bank): *Where do you bank?* [1]

After elimination of '— *see* ...' constructions, substitution of the definition of *sandbank* for the definition by cross reference of sense 1.5, and conversion to the root forms of the controlled vocabulary (minus the words listed at the beginning of Section 8.2.2), we have the following definitions with which the system works. These are presented in alphabetical order to emaphasize that all syntactic and morphological information has been removed.

Bank1.1 *along, lake, land, river, side*
Bank1.2 *border, division, earth, field, garden, heap, make, often, up*
Bank1.3 *cloud, dark, heavy, mass, mud, promise, snow, storm*
Bank1.4 *at, bend, car, go, make, race, road, round, safe, slope, so, they, track*
Bank1.5 *can, danger, ship, high, water, sand, north, sea*
Bank2.0 *aircraft, car, high, make, move, one, other, side, turn*
Bank3.0 *ancient, boat, key, on, row*
Bank4.1 *activity, demand, go, keep, money, on, out, pay, place, related*

---

[2] For interest's sake, note that if all the experiments were random, the probability of all 350 experiments producing 30 or less correct sense assignments would be 0.96. In fact, fewer than 145 of the 350 experiments produced 30 or less correct sense-assignments. Thus, the successes cannot be attributed to having a large enough number of random experiments.

Bank4.2 *have, hold, human, live, many, medicine, origin, place, product, ready,*
        save, something, use, organ, hospital
Bank4.3 *chance, game, keep, money, pay, person, piece, supply, use*
Bank4.4 *all, break, chance, game, have, money, win*
Bank5.1 *keep, money, put*
Bank5.2 *do, keep, money, one, state, you*

8.2.2.4 Results of the Lexical Disambiguation Experiment

The experiments with the top scores for sense-assignment and group-assignment
are shown in Table 8.4. For comparison, the results of doing lexical disambiguation
by computing overlap between context and sense-entry without expanding either
are also shown (relatedness function for this technqiue is equivalence: =.)

The most successful experiment has labeled *bank* with the correct sense in 45%
of the sentences. This was a large improvement on the result achieved (23%) when
senses and contexts were not expanded to include related words.

Labeling *bank* with the correct sense was a difficult task. In 38 of the 350 experiments *bank* was labeled with the correct sense at least 35% of the time. Labeling
with the correct sense group was a far easier task: In 120 of the experiments, *bank*
was labeled with the correct sense group at least 85% of the time. A less stringent
test of correct sense labeling was to label a word with the top three senses as
judged by the technique and to see if the correct sense was among those. In 36 of
the experiments, the correct sense was among the top three rated at least 85% of
the time.

The best relatedness and vector similarity functions were determined by
examining the top 20 scores for correct sense and correct sense group. To assign to
the correct sense (e.g., Bank 1.1, Bank 1.2, etc.), the best relatedness functions were
cp, *dcp*, and *sdd* and the best vector similarity functions were $HIT^{\times}$ and *NDP*. To
assign to the correct sense group (e.g., A, B, C, etc.) *dcp* was the best relatedness
function and $HIT^{\to}(R^C, R^S)$ was the best vector similarity function.

We also conducted experiments in which expanded only the contexts, but not the
sense. These experiments were conducted using only the *sdd* relatedness function.
The best of these experiments labeled *bank* with the correct sense 41% of the time.
In general, performance dropped very slightly (2% to 4%) compared to those cases
in which senses were also expanded. These experiments are more comparable to

Table 8.4. The parameters and results of some of the experiments

		$t = 0.1$	$t = 0.03$
Word-vector criteron			
Relatedness function	=	$cp(x, y)$	$dcp(x, y)$
Vector similarity function	NDP	$HIT^{\times}$	$HIT^{\to}(R^C, R^S)$
Assignment to correct sense	23%	45%	15%
Correct was in top 3	40%	85%	74%
Assignment to correct group	52%	79%	97%

the experiments done with the Pathfinder networks, as described in Section 8.2.4, because senses were not expanded in those experiments.

Experiments were also conducted with different sets of closed-class words being ignored. In one experiment the three prepositions were introduced back into the sense entries and word sets, and in another all the ignored words were re-introduced. The performance of the technique declined in both cases, but less (only five or ten hits lower for both cases) when the *sdd* relatedness function was used. This was expected because it was the function which seemed to draw the fewest closed-class words into word sets. The set of words we chose to ignore seems reasonably optimal in that the performance also declined when more prepositions were added to the set of words to be ignored.

8.2.2.5 Discussion of the Lexical Disambiguation Experiment

The technique was able to assign the correct sense in up to 45% of the test sentences, which is quite good performance for disambiguating the work *bank*. Precise assignment of the correct sense of *bank* was very difficult, if not impossible in some contexts. This is because syntactic information, including morphology, was ignored. *Bank* has both nominal and verbal forms of a very similar sense and it is unreasonable to expect any method that takes no notice of syntax to be able to distinguish these reliably. Additionally, *bank* has quite a few senses which are very close to each other. If the critereon for success was relaxed a little by requiring fewer close sense distinctions (i.e. assigning to a sense in the correct sense-group), then the hit rate increased to greater than 90%. However, to evaluate fully the value of this technqiue, experiments would have to be conducted for a number of words other than *bank*.

The technique of expanding contexts and sense entries to include related words (judged to be related by some relatedness function) was reasonably successful. Without expansion, the correct sense assignment was made 23% of the time, and with expansion the highest rate of correct sense assignment was 45%. The example given at the beginning of Section 8.2.2, of a sentence with no controlled vocabulary words in common with the definition correct of the correct sense of bank, was assigned the correct sense in a number of experiments, demonstrating that the technique can work for some more difficult cases.

The relative success of conditional probability as a relatedness function is surprising; it might indicate that the data in LDOCE is poor for all but the most frequent words.

There might be serveral ways to improve the technique. One way might be to disambiguate all the senses in a sentence at once, as discussed at the beginning of Section 8.2.2. Another would be to improve the sets of related words by combining this technique with the techniques of Lesk [32] and Sparck Jones [59]. Or the co-occurrence might be improved by collecting data over a larger corpus than LDOCE. Another possibility is to start to collect co-occurrence data for word senses rather than for words, using sentences that have been disambiguated by this technique.

8.2.3 Pathfinder Networks Based on Co-Occurrence Information

One of the problems with co-occurrence data is the sheer quantity of it. Co-occurrence data for words in the LDOCE controlled vocabulary contain nearly 2.5 million frequencies of co-occurrence (the triangle of a 2,200-by-2,200 matrix). This much data cannot be examined in raw form, and so the amount of information must be reduced. This must be done without eliminating large amounts of interesting or useful information. That is to say, a mechanism is needed to eliminate noise in the data without destroying useful information.

A technique for data reduction that has proved quite interesting is to use the Pathfinder algorithm [50, 51], which was developed to discover the network structure in psychological data. The algorithm takes a completely connected network as input and removes most of the links, leaving networks sufficiently concise to be viewed directly while still retaining much interesting information. The networks have interesting stucture, and the remaining links correspond quite well to intuitive ideas of which nodes should have relationships between them. We have also used Pathfinder networks to do lexical disambiguation in preliminary judgments of whether any useful information is discarded in reducing the amount of data using the Pathfinder algorithm.

8.2.3.1 The Theory of Pathfinder

Pathfinder is a psychometric scaling method based on the mathematical theory of graphs and networks [12, 23]. We use the terms *nodes* and *links* to describe the entities in a graph, and *weight* to describe the value on a link in a network. In our application of graphs, nodes represent words, links represent pair-wise relations between words and weights represent the strength of the relations.

Pathfinder is implemented as an algorithm based on the idea that a link should be present in an output network if and only if that link is a minimum weight path between the nodes. The weight, $W(P)$, of a path, P, is a function of the weights on links in the path computed using the Minkowski r-metric, as follows:

$$W(P) = (w_1^r + w_2^r + \ldots + w_k^r)^{1/r} \tag{5}$$

where k is the number of links in P, w_i is the ith link weight, and $r \geq 1$.

This use of the r-metric in path weight measurement allows Pathfinder to accommodate different assumptions about the level of measurement associated with distance estimates. Ordinal level measurement requires $r = \infty$, in which case $W(P)$ is equivalent to the maximum weight in the path. Ratio-level measurement allows any value of $r \geq 1$.

The other parameter used by the Pathfinder algorithm is q, the maximum number of links in searched paths. Limiting the number of links in a path can result in significant savings in computation time and space when working with large numbers of nodes.[3]

---

[3] The theory of Pathfinder is discussed in much greater depth in [51, 50].

8.2.3.2 Pathfinder Networks of Co-occurrence Data

Pathfinder analyses were performed on a conditional probability matrix for 2,177 of the 2,187 words in the constrained vocabulary. The ten most frequent words, all of which were function words, were omitted. Retaining these was found to reduce the usefulness of the resulting network because these words provided meaningless pathways between many pairs of words. The weights on the links were computed according to the function $1 - iou$.[4] Because of the nature of this transformation, the most that can be assumed is that the data have ordinal properties. Therefore, the Pathfinder r parameter was always set at infinity in the analyses reported here. The q parameter was varied from 2 to 32, resulting in networks that ranged from 16,955 links to 2,204 links. When the q parameter was set to 5, the resulting network had 3,136 links. A subnetwork of this network is shown in Figure 8.1a. This subnetwork contains all the nodes (and links among them) that were within three links of the node for *bank* in that network. This subnetwork required spatial organization to make it readable, but the link structure is unaltered.

These networks demonstrate how pure distributional statistics can be used to show that a word has several different meanings (senses), something which some linguists, e.g., Lyons [33:613], have claimed is impossible. In Figure 8.1a, two distinct clusters can be observed, each corresponding to one of the two main senses of the word *bank*. These two clusters correspond to the two dominant senses of *bank* (senses 1.1 and 4.1 in Section 8.2.2.3), which account for 91% of the uses of the word in LDOCE. Thus we would not expect any other of its senses to be represented in this network. However, if the data did include more senses, it is not certain that clusters for the other senses would take shape as distinctively as the clusters in Figure 8.1a, since the other senses are less intuitively different.

A hierarchical cluster analysis [27] on the words in Figure 8.1a, (minus the word *bank*), is shown in Figure 8.1b. For the cluster analysis, the distance between words was also computed according to *iou*, and the distance between clusters was the minimum of the distance between any two words in each cluster. This cluster analysis shows more objectively the two distinct clusters for two senses of *bank*; the words in the lower cluster are exactly those in the lower half of the Pathfinder network. The word *bank* was omitted because once it became a member of one cluster, all other clusters quickly became clustered with that cluster. This is not surprising in that all the words were chosen because of their strong relationship to *bank*.

8.2.3.3 Using Pathfinder for Lexical Disambiguation

The networks that result from the Pathfinder were used to select the related-word sets for each word. Related sets were formed by selecting words that were directly linked to each word in the network. The number of links connected to each word

---

[4] The Pathfinder algorithm uses "distances," whereas *iou* is a similarity measure.

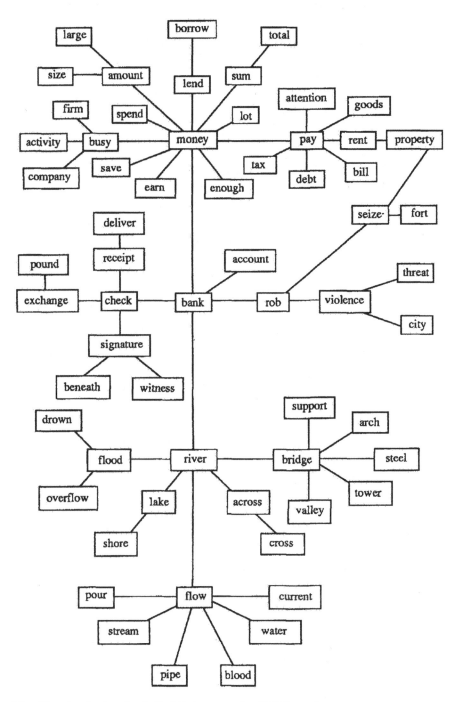

Fig. 8.1a. A subnetwork of a Pathfinder network of 2,177 words

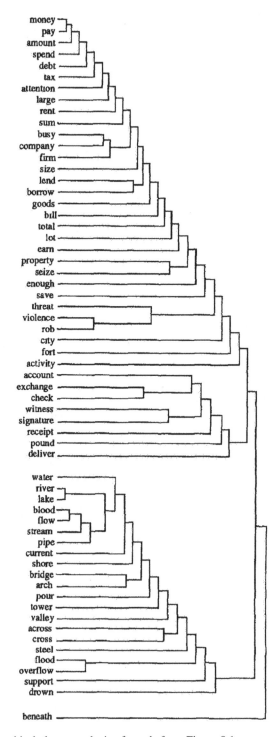

Fig. 8.1b. Hierarchical cluster analysis of words from Figure 8.1a

varies, depending on the extent to which other words consistently co-occur with it. This means that related-sets also varied in size.

Sense sets were formed for the test word by combining the related-word sets for the words in each sense entry. The union of the related-word sets was used in the experiments described here, although schemes which differentially weight words in the sense sets might be valuable.

As with the sense sets, the context set was formed from the related-word sets for the words in the context sentence. However, our approach here has been progressively to expand the size of the context set by increasing the number of links, or network distance, used in determining relatedness. This is analogous to causing activation to spread from the words in the context sentence until all of the words in the sense sets are contacted, although in practice a fixed distance is used.

Finally, a measure of match was computed for each sense entry at each distance from the context set. Several measures have been considered, but two are examined in these experiments: (1) the ratio of the number of items in the intersection of the sense-sets and the context-set divided by the number of items in the union of these two sets (intersection over union), and (2) the ratio of the number of items in the intersection divided by the number of items in the definition set.

8.2.3.4 Results and Discussion of the Experiments with Pathfinder Networks

We compared three Pathfinder networks (Q2 = 16, 955 links; Q5 = 3, 136 links; Q32 = 2, 204 links) for their utility in identifying the correct sense of the word *bank* in the 197 example sentences from LDOCE. In these tests the sense definition sets contained only the words in the definitions themselves (i.e. no related words and no weights). The context set was progressively expanded by including words directly connected to the words in the context set (Step 1), then to words related to the related words (Step 2), etc. At each step the evaluation function was used to compute a measure of strength for each of the sense definitions. Although several evaluation functions were compared, we will report results using the function *iou*.

The results of these comparisons are relatively straightforward. In terms of absolute performance, the network with the fewest links (Q32) performed best, allowing bank to be correctly sense-tagged in 104 of the 197 example sentences (53%). Maximum performance occurred when the context set had been expanded to include items three links away (average context set size = 102). Performance with the Q5 network was next best (91 hits at Step 2; average context-set size = 81) and worst with Q2 (82 hits at Step 1; average context-set size = 91). Although all of the networks were superior to Step 0 performance i.e., using only the words in the context sentence, the performance of the Q32 network is particularly surprising and encouraging (see Figure 8.2).

Selecting the correct sense from a large set of highly similar senses (there are 13 senses for *bank*) may be too stringent a test. Therefore, we also examined performance with the Q32 network when only the four homograph entries for *bank* were considered. The hit rate improved to 85% (167 out of 197), a far more useful result. Furthermore, several modifications to our methodology offer the potential of improved performance; these include using different probability functions as the

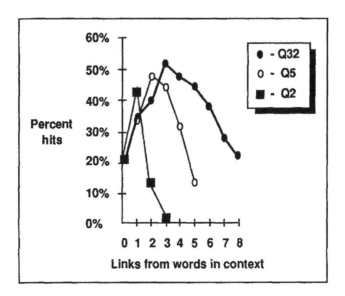

Fig. 8.2. Sense-labeling performance for different networks

basis for network computation, weighting the context and sense definition set words in terms of importance, etc. At present, it appears that Pathfinder is able to capture the important relationships in the co-occurrence data without losing anything of value, at least for our application.

8.2.4 General Discussion and Conclusion

Lexical disambiguation using co-occurrence data is possible. The Pathfinder algorithm seems to be a good way of reducing the amount of information about the co-occurrence of words that must be stored in order to do lexical disambiguation.

Frequencies of co-occurrence of pairs of words in a text and frequencies of word occurrence are only some of the distributional statistics that can be collected about words in a text. Other statistics, such as frequencies of co-occurrence of triples of words, or frequencies of contiguous co-occurrence of pairs of words, are potentially additional sources of distributional statistics.

8.2.4.1 Combining with Other Methods and Iterative Improvement

This technique for lexical disambiguation could be classified as a "weak method." As such, it might be quite suitable for combining with other methods for processing LDOCE entries, and language in general. For example, Slator's method, presented in Section 8.4, uses syntactic information and classifies words by part of speech, among other things. These classifications could be used to constrict the judgments of the technique presented in this section, resulting in more accurate sense labeling. Sampson [49], presented a statistical technique for assigning part-of-speech labels;

this also would be an excellent candidate for combination with the technique presented in this section.

Another type of potentially useful distributional statistic is the co-occurrence of words in particular syntactic relationships, e.g., an adjective with a noun that it modifies. Collection of these statistics would be possible if either of the two techniques just mentioned, or other syntactic techniques, were used in combination with this type of work.

Further possibilities for combining our technique with others are discussed in Section 8.5, where we indicate how our technique and Slator's might be used in a "spiral" of improvement.

8.2.4.2 Sources of Co-Occurrence Data

LDOCE is theoretically a good source of co-occurrence data for a number of reasons, some of which have to do with the factors contributing to the distribution of sense uses which were discussed in Section 8.2.1. The distribution of topics in LDOCE is broad, covering most concepts expressible in a word or short phrase. The style of LDOCE is of short textual units with a single topic (although examples sometimes diverge). Another aspect of the style is the controlled vocabulary, which makes co-occurrence data easier to collect. Only a limited number of the senses of words in the controlled vocabulary are used in the dictionary, and co-occurrence data will not reflect relationships between words where the relationships are based on unused senses. Another consequence of the controlled vocabulary appears to be that LDOCE contains relatively few defintions by synonym compared to other dictionaries.

The topics chosen for examples also affect the co-occurrence data. For example, bank-robbery is a surprisingly common theme: 24 of 143 uses of sense 4.1 of *bank* had to do with bank robberies, and this is reflected in the Pathfinder network for *bank*.

There is more information in LDOCE which could probably be used to improve the relatedness judgments of senses and words. The box codes and pragmatic codes discussed in Section 8.4 contain potentially useful information. It may also be useful to restrict the gathering of co-occurrence information to more syntactically close words, e.g., the genus and differentia terms in a definition.

Co-occurrence data could be collected from other texts. One could look just for co-occurrences of words from Longman's controlled vocabulary, or for co-occurrences of all words (if one had a powerful enough computer). The practical value of co-occurrence data from other texts would need to be verified.

8.2.4.3 Word Senses in LDOCE

The senses defined for *bank* in LDOCE do not seem very good; they do not even adequately cover the uses of *bank* in the dictionary. For example, the definition of Dam2.0 is "a wall or bank built to keep back water." But it is not clear whether the sense of *bank* used here is 1.1 or 1.2 — neither seems to describe the usage very well. It and similar uses were decided by the authors to be sense 1.1 (see Page 184).

This is likely to be a problem for any technique for automatically extracting information from an MRD. The only solution will be to have some technique for extending the coverages of sense definitions in LDOCE, or for creating new ones. The former alternative is likely to be easier, and should fall naturally out of an iterative improvement scheme such as that outlined above.

8.3 Method II: Constructing an MTD from LDOCE

This section discusses another method for constructing an MTD from LDOCE. The MTD under construction is intended to be a basic facility for a whole spectrum of natural-language processing tasks. The goal of this approach is the derivation of a natural set of semantic primitives from LDOCE and the use of these primitives in the construction of an MTD. Consistent with the semantic-primitive approach is a set of well-defined construction procedures; among these is a very specialized bootstrapping process.

Inductive learning systems often assume the existence of a set of hierarchically-arranged primitives that allows new concepts, new rules and new domain theories to be generalized [71, 15]. Such primitives take the form of semantic primitives [67] in an inductive learning system that acquires knowledge from natural language text. There are two alternative approaches to the development of a set of semantic primitives: the *prescriptive* approach and the *descriptive* approach. In the prescriptive approach, a set of primitives is defined, or *prescribed*, prior to or in the course of designing and developing a system. An example of a prescribed set of semantic primitives is the set of semantic features used as "box codes" in the electronic version of LDOCE. The descriptive approach [67:198] on the other hand, allows a natural set of semantic primitives to be derived from a natural source of data, such as a dictionary.

The MTD has two components, a lexical base and a knowledge base. The lexical base contains the same lexical information as LDOCE about each word sense, except that the definition of the word sense is given in terms of numbered word senses instead of words. The knowledge base consists of a network of semantic relations among the word senses defined in the lexical base. These semantic relations include case relations (agent, patient, recipient, time, location, goal, cause and reason), part/whole relations, class/membership relations and other schematic relations.

Important to this study is the distinction of four types of words and "word senses" contained in LDOCE. Each type of word and word sense is a subset of the next set of words and word senses given below. The four types are as follows.

Seed senses are the semantic primitives derived from the dictionary. The words that the seed senses are senses of are called *seed words*.

Controlled words are words from the list of the "controlled vocabulary" given at the back of the LDOCE dictionary. LDOCE uses the controlled vocabulary words in all its word sense definitions and usage examples. All the word senses of the controlled words defined in LDOCE are *controlled senses*.

Defining words are used to define the meanings of all the controlled words in their sense definitions. Note that not every controlled word is used in the definitions

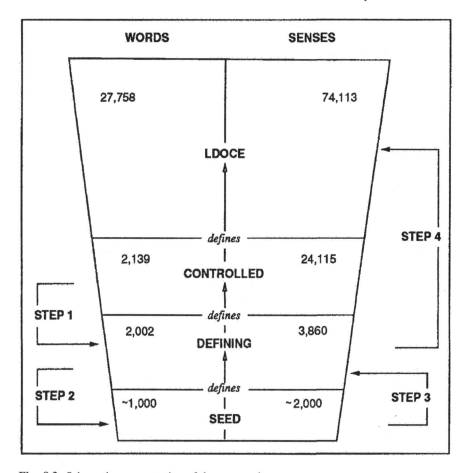

Fig. 8.3. Schematic representation of the MTD project

of the controlled words themselves. "*Defining senses*" are individual word senses of the defining words that are actually found used in the definitions of the meanings of the controlled words.

Any word contained in LDOCE is an LDOCE *word*. Any word sense of any LDOCE word is an LDOCE *sense*.

The subsetting relationship between the four types of words and word senses is shown in Figure 8.3.

8.3.1 Overview of Construction Procedures

The construction of the MTD proceeds in the following four steps:

Step 1: Determination of the defining senses of LDOCE, i.e., those word senses used in the definitions of 2,139 controlled words of LDOCE. The words defined by the defining senses constitutes the set of defining words of the dictionary. LDOCE defining words constitute a subset of the controlled words. There are 2,002 defining words in LDOCE.

Step 2: Derivation of a natural set of semantic primitives from LDOCE. These semantic primitives are, in fact, the seed senses of LDOCE. Seed senses are a subset of the defining senses of the 2,002 defining words, which are sufficient to define the set of defining senses of Step 1. There are approximately 2,000 seed senses in LDOCE. The words which the seed senses are senses of constitute the set of seed words of the dictionary. There are approximately 1,000 seed words in LDOCE.

Step 3: Handcrafting the lexical and the knowledge bases for the natural set of semantic primitives derived from LDOCE.

Step 4: Constructing a MTD for the rest of the controlled words and the rest of the LDOCE words by means of bootstrapping from the initial, handcrafted lexical and knowledge bases. The bootstrapping process is a process of knowledge acquisition from dictionary definition text.

Figure 8.3 illustrates the four-step project.

8.3.2 Step 1: Derivation of the Defining Senses of LDOCE

Of LDOCE's 2,139 controlled words, we found that 137 do not participate in defining the word senses of the controlled words. This leaves a reduced set of 2,002 controlled words. In this study, this reduced set is called the "defining words" of LDOCE. The word senses of the defining words that are used in the definition of the

aunt (0, 1):	the sister of one's father or mother, the wife of one's uncle, or a woman whose brother or sister has a child
by (1, 16):	having (the stated male animal, esp. a horse) as a father
get (0, 17):	to become the father of | BEGET
grandfather (0, 0):	the father of someone's father or mother
grandmother (0, 0):	the mother of someone's father or mother
parent (0, 1):	the father or mother of a person
uncle (0, 1):	the brother of one's father or mother, the husband of one's aunt, or a man whose brother or sister has a child
uncle (0, 3):	a man who takes the place of a father, especially in relation to the children of a woman who is or was married to someone else

2,139 controlled words are the defining senses of LDOCE. Because of inadequate computational techniques, human judgment is used in determining which sense(s) of the defining words are the defining senses in LDOCE. For each of the 2,139 controlled words, a file is created of all the occurrences of the word in the definition text of the controlled words, using Tony Plate's "thruld" program [see 69]. Those word senses that are found to be used in defining the meanings of the controlled words are recorded as the defining senses of those words. Below is an example of a file of all occurrences of the word *father* in the definition text of the 2,139 controlled words.

The word *father* can be either a noun or a verb. LDOCE provides eight senses for *father* as a noun. Among them are "male parent" and "priest." In the above example, only the "male parent" sense of *father* is used to define the word senses of other controlled words. Hence "a male parent" (father (1, 1), i.e., the first sense of the first homograph of *father*) is recorded as the defining sense of the word in LDOCE. This process repeats itself until the defining senses of all the defining words are determined. Now 3,860 word senses of the 2,002 defining words constitute the defining senses of LDOCE. Also, 1,051 defining words have single defining senses; 526 have two defining senses; and 425 have three or more defining senses.

8.3.3 Step 2: Derivation of a Natural Set of Semantic Primitives from LDOCE

To derive the seed words for LDOCE after Step 1, we proceed as follows:

1. Obtain a "hunch set" for the seed words using frequency of occurrence criteria. The seed words of LDOCE are generated from an initial hunch set of some 400 words. The words of the initial hunch set are the intersection of three basic lexicons: the 4,000 most frequently used words in all sense definitions in LDOCE [70]; the 850 words of basic English [41]; and the 500 most common words in The Brown Corpus [29]. The underlying assumption here is that a large portion of that subset of the English vocabulary which may function as the seed words in LDOCE is highly likely to appear in all the above-mentioned word lists.

2. Test the hunch set in terms of its ability to account for all the controlled words accounted for within three or four defining cycles. 'Defining cycle' refers to the process of one group of words defining another in a dictionary, resulting in the other group of words being defined. At the end of a defining cycle, those words whose defining senses have been defined then join the words that define their meanings, so to define more words at the next defining cycle. The first of such defining cycles starts with the hunch set and the last ends with the meanings of all the LDOCE words defined. For all practical purposes, this means that the defining senses should be accounted for within two or three defining cycles. A defining sense is accounted for if its definition text contains only words from the hunch set and/or words whose defining senses have been accounted for.

According to our studies, the first defining cycle in LDOCE starts with a set of some 1,200 seed words. At the end of the first defining cycle, about 700 more controlled words join the seed words to define more words at the next defining cycle. The second defining cycle defines another 200 or so controlled words. By the end of the third defining cycle, all the controlled words are defined. It takes another one or two defining cycles to have all LDOCE words defined. Note that the results reported here, on the seed words of LDOCE, are preliminary. Research is under way to pin down the exact number of the seed words and seed senses. The number of LDOCE seed words is expected to be about 1,000, with about 2,000 seed senses.

3. If the hunch set proved to be capable of accounting for all the senses of the controlled words accounted for within three or four defining cycles, the hunch set becomes the seed words. Otherwise revise the hunch set and go back to 2.

To test the hunch set, we first test whether it is able to account for the 3,860 defining senses within two or three defining cycles. The testing is carried out by a computer program. The program looks at each word in the definition text of each of the defining senses to see whether it is a word from the hunch set. If all the words in the definition text of a defining sense are from the hunch set, the defining sense becomes a candidate to be entered into a "success file." This file keeps a record of all words that have been accounted for. Note that the success file holds words, not word senses. For a word to be included in the file, all its defining senses must have been accounted for. The word senses that are not accounted for enter a "fail file." This file also keeps a record of the words that cause word senses to be unaccounted for. These words are called "problematic words." At the end of first defining cycle, words recorded in the success file join the hunch set to start the next defining cycle. Notice that our hunch set remains unchanged at this point. Our program starts checking again for the second defining cycle. This time the program examines the definition text of the yet-unaccounted defining senses to see whether the words are from the initial hunch set and/or the set of words that has just been added. It builds another success file and another fail file. Since the 3,860 defining senses are not all accounted for at the end of the second defining cycle, we keep revising the hunch set.

An issue involved in the revision of the hunch set is the size we would like it to be. We could add all words recorded in the fail file. The maximum number of words that can thus be put in the hunch set equals the number of the defining words. Or we could add words that are more problematic than others, i.e. more frequently recorded in the fail file as problematic. This latter approach is adopted. A computer program examines the problematic words in the fail file and picks out those that occur more often than others. These words become candidate words to be added to the hunch set.

Before we actually add any words to the hunch set, we make sure that no candidate words to be added have been recorded in the success files. Hence we delete any candidate words that are found in the success files after previous defining cycles. The deletion helps to reduce the size of the seed words without causing any word sense to be left unaccounted for at the end of three or four cycles. The process of deriving the seed words for LDOCE is an empirical process of much trial and error. However, each time we revise the hunch set, the chance increases of confirming it as the set of seed words.

A final remark on the derivation of the seed words for LDOCE concerns some 70 words from the definition text of the controlled words which are not found in the 2,139-word controlled vocabulary list. Among these words are *hole, tendency, success* and *American*. These 70-odd words are simply put into the hunch set and become part of the seed words.

Our hunch set gradually climbs from 400 to about 1,200 items, when it is finally confirmed as the set of LDOCE seed words. About half of these have one defining sense, one quarter have two defining senses, and those in the remaining quarter have three or more defining senses. Our preliminary studies produced a set of some 2,000 seed senses as the natural set of semantic primitives derived from LDOCE.

The discovery of the seed senses greatly reduces the amount of handcrafting needed for bootstrapping, topics to be discussed in the next two subsections.

8.3.4 Step 3: Handcrafting the Initial Lexical and Knowledge Bases

Lexical information concerning the seed senses derived from LDOCE is handcoded into the initial lexical base. Explicit word-sense numbers are manually attached to each word in the definition text of each semantic primitive. For the initial knowledge base, informants are asked to name a semantic relation they perceive to exist between pairs of LDOCE semantic primitives. These relations may include case relations, part/whole relations, ISA relations, or other schematic relations. The elicited information is then handcoded into the knowledge base. Efforts are being made to reduce the number of judgments that have to be made by humans. The ideal situation occurs when only critical pairs of semantic primitives are examined. According to a related study, critical pairs of primitives can be reduced to 1% of all possible pairs using Pathfinder network techniques [51].

8.3.5 Step 4: Knowledge Acquisition and the Bootstrapping Process

The acquisition of lexical and world knowledge from dictionary definitions for the rest of the controlled words (and the rest of the entire LDOCE vocabulary) involves a carefully controlled bootstrapping process.

The process acquires lexical and world knowledge from dictionary definition text using two processes: language analysis and semantic relation designation. Analysis of definitions is both syntactic and semantic. The result of the analysis is a parse tree with numbered word senses. These parse trees replace the original word-sense definition, thus expanding the lexical base of the MTD. Semantic relation designation involves assigning semantic relations to a pair of related word senses in the parse tree. For example, the semantic relation between the head noun of the subject and the head verb of the predicate could be "agent/action."

Bootstrapping requires the pre-existence of a lexical base and a knowledge base. The process proceeds in accordance with a "bootstrapping schedule" that fits the defining cycles of the dictionary. This schedule determines which word senses are to be processed first and which later. The bootstrapping schedule is needed because both lexical and world knowledge about words used in the definition of a word sense have to be present in the MTD before the definition text of that particular word sense can be analyzed and new lexical and world knowledge acquired. Lexical information is found in the lexical base where word-sense definitions are given in word senses instead of words. World knowledge information is in the network of semantic relations among the word senses defined in the lexical base. Lexical and world knowledge acquired from analyzing the definition text of a word sense from an earlier defining cycle assists the analysis of the definition text of word senses at later defining cycles. The success files discussed earlier are records of which word senses are defined at which defining cycle. These files provide an adequate basis for the establishment of an accurate bootstrapping schedule. The bootstrapping process terminates when an MTD is built for all word senses defined in LDOCE.

Following is an example from the electronic version of LDOCE showing the general process of bootstrapping associated with the three noun senses of *nurse*. (The definitions are in the form of Prolog assertions.)

Sense 1

```
(nurse,n,1,[a,person,typically,a,woman,who,is,trained,to,
           take,care,of,sick,hurt,or,old,people,esp,as,
           directed,by,a,doctor,in,a,hospital]).
```

Sense 2

```
(nurse, n,2,[a,woman,employed,to,take,care,of,a,young,child]).
```

Sense 3

```
(nurse,n,3,[wet,nurse]).
```

Cross-reference

```
(wet_nurse, n, 0, [a, woman, employed, to, give, breast, milk,
           to, another, woman's, baby]).
```

The bootstrapping process produces the following as part of the lexical information to be included in the lexical base of the MTD. Note that the word sense definitions are now given in word senses with explicit word sense numbers attached.

Sense 1

```
(nurse,n,1,[a1,person1,typically1,a1,woman1,who2,is2,
      trained2,to1,take_care_of1,sick1,hurt1,
      or2,old1,people1,especially2,as5,directed3,
      by5,a1,doctor2,in1,a1,hospital1]).
```

Sense 2

```
(nurse,n,2,[a1,woman1,employed1,to1,take _ care _ of1,a1,young1,
      child2])
```

Sense 3

```
(nurse,n,3,[wet_nurse1]).
```

Cross-reference

```
(wet_nurse,n,1,[a1,woman1,employed1,to1,give5,breast1,
        milk1,to9,another2,woman1's,baby1]).
```

Table 8.5 summarizes how the word senses involved in defining the three noun senses of *nurse* are themselves defined. Most of these senses are seed senses. Information concerning these word senses is handcoded into the lexicon. They can be identified by a '+' sign in the 'SEED SENSE' column. Some are defined at

Table 8.5. Summary of bootstrapping process for three noun senses of *nurse*.

WORD SENSE	SEED SENSE	FIRST DC	SECOND DC	THIRD DC
a1	+	−	−	−
another2	+	−	−	−
as5	+	−	−	−
baby1	−	+	−	−
breast1	−	− two	+	−
by5	+	−	−	−
child2	+	−	−	−
directed3	+	−	−	−
doctor2	−	− attend to	+	−
employed1	+	−	−	−
especial1	−	+	−	−
give5	+	−	−	−
hospital1	−	− cure	+	−
hurt1	+	−	−	−
in1	+	−	−	−
is2	+	−	−	−
milk1	+	−	−	−
old1	+	−	−	−
or2	+	−	−	−
people1	+	−	−	−
person1	+	−	−	−
sick1	−	+	−	−
to1	+	−	−	−
to9	+	−	−	−
take_care_of1	−	− responsible	+	−
trained2	+	−	−	−
typically1	−	+	−	−
who2	+	−	−	−
woman1	+	−	−	−
young1	+	−	−	−

the "first defining cycle", i.e., by the seed words. They are 'baby1', 'especially2', 'sick1' and 'typically1', indicated by a '+' sign in the table's 'FIRST DC' column. Others are defined at the "second defining cycle", i.e., by the seed words plus words defined at the first defining cycle. 'Breast1' and 'take_care_of1' belong to this group. Note that the word given after a '−' sign in the table is the word that keeps the word sense in question from being defined at a particular defining cycle, e.g., the word *cure* that appears in the definition text of the first word sense of *hospital* ('hospital1') keeps the word sense from being defined until the second defining cycle.

8.4 Method III: A Lexicon-Provider

A lexicon-provider system is outlined in this section. The system provides text-specific lexicons from selected MRD definitions from LDOCE. The input to this system is unconstrained text; the output is a collection of lexical semantic objects, one for every *sense* of every word in the text. Each lexical-semantic object in this lexicon contains grammatical and subcategorization information, often with general (and sometimes specific) grammatical predictions; most of these objects also have semantic selection codes, organized into a type hierarchy; and many have encoded contextual (pragmatic, LDOCE subject code) knowledge as well. As a natural by-product of the lexicon construction, a relative contextual score is computed for each object that bears such a pragmatic code; these scores provide a simple metric for comparing competing word senses for text-specific contextual coherence, and so directly address the problem of lexical ambiguity resolution. Besides exploiting those special encodings supplied with the dictionary entries, the text of selected dictionary definitions are analyzed, further to enrich the resulting representation. This lexicon-providing subsystem takes LDOCE as a database and produces a structured (and much smaller) knowledge base of lexical semantic objects organized by pragmatic context. Figure 8.4 shows an overview of the lexicon-providing system and the lexicon-consumer, a Preference Semantics parser for text [54].

8.4.1 Constructing the Lexicon

The lexicon-providing subsystem includes the program for constructing lexical-semantic knowledge bases. This program takes online MRD entries and, first, produces corresponding basic lexical-semantic objects (frames), as follows:

```
(technician
 (POS . n)
 (SENSE-NUM . 0)
 (GRAMMAR
  ((C) . N/Count)))
 (PRAGMATIC
  (ON (Occupations)))
 (TYPE
```

```
((H) (RESTRICTION . Human/Sex-Unspecified)))

(current
 (POS . n)
 (SENSE-NUM . 3)
 (GRAMMAR
  ((C) . N/Count))
 (PRAGMATIC
  (EGZE (Engineering/Electrical)))
 (TYPE
  ((T) (RESTRICTION . Abstract))))

(measure
 (POS . v)
 (SENSE-NUM . 1)
 (GRAMMAR
  (or
   ((I) . V/Intransitive)
   ((T1) . V/Transitive/N+-or-PRON+-Follows)))
 (PRAGMATIC nil)
 (TYPE
  ((H T -)
   (SUBJECT . Human/Sex-Unspecified)
   (OBJECT1 . Abstract)
   (OBJECT2))))

(ammeter
 (POS . n)
 (SENSE-NUM . 0)
 (GRAMMAR
  ((C) . N/Count)))
 (PRAGMATIC
  (EGZE (Engineering/Electrical)))
 (TYPE
  ((J) (RESTRICTION . Solid/Movable)))
```

This program is straightforward and provides a useful and consistent knowledge base for parsing [69, 70]. These basic frame-objects are further manipulated in two ways: (1) they are organized into a hierarchical contextual structure and (2) they are *enriched* by means of further processing of the texts of the dictionary definitions themselves, as described below. Consider, for example, the following short text:

(1) Current can be measured.
    The technician measures alternating current with an ammeter.

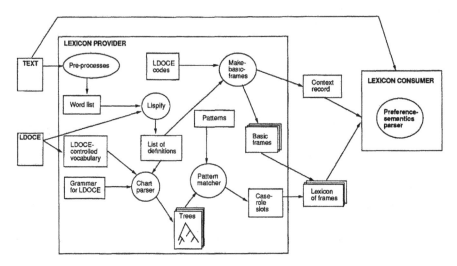

Fig. 8.4. The lexicon-provider subsystem.

The basic lexicon for this text contains 30 frames for content words[5] (not counting 18 senses of the infinitive *be* and ten senses of the auxiliary *can*). Each basic frame has five slots:

POS or part of speech, the top level of the GRAMMAR hierarchy.

SENSE-NUM, the sense number.

GRAMMAR slots, which are filled with category code information (such as transitive for V, count for N, etc.) and predictions from the LDOCE grammar for English with its 110-odd members [46, 47].

PRAGMATIC slots, which are filled with contextual domain terms like *engineering* or *religion*.

TYPE slots, which are filled, in the case of nouns and adjectives, with selection restrictions like solid, human or abstract and, in the case of verbs, with selection restrictions on the functional arguments to the verb such as human subject and abstract direct object.

8.4.1.1 Contextual Structure

The system for constructing the lexicon also establishes the conceptual domain of texts. In the basic lexicon construction process, all word senses for all parts of speech of all words in the text are looked up, giving a text-specific lexicon. Along the way, an ordered list of pragmatic (subject) codes is collected for a "content

---

[5] These 30 frames are *alternate* (three adjective senses, one verb sense), *ammeter* (one noun sense), *can* (two nouns, two verbs), *current* (three adjectives, four nouns), *measure* (eight nouns, three verbs, one adjective), *technician* (one noun sense), and the phrase *alternating current* (one noun sense). LDOCE defines about 7,000 phrases.

assessment" procedure [61] where lists of frequently occurring LDOCE pragmatic codes are compiled by simply counting up the instances found in the various senses of the words in the text). The LDOCE pragmatic coding system divides the world into 124 major subject categories ranging from "aeronautics" and "agriculture" to "winter sports" and "zoology." Many of these subjects are further subcategorized (for example, under "agriculture" is "soil-science" and "horticulture," and under "zoology" is "entomology," "ornithology" and "ichthyology"), so there are 369 different subject codes in the LDOCE pragmatic system. However, the LDOCE hierarchy is flat (only two layers deep), and the 124 major categories have equal and unrelated status; for example, business and economics are both at the top of the tree and are unconnected; the same is true of science and zoology (Figure 8.5).

The lexicon-providing subsystem relates these codes through a manually restructured hierarchy, making communication, economics, entertainment, household, politics, science and transportation the fundamental categories. Every word sense defined with a pragmatic code therefore has a position in the hierarchy, attached to the node for its pragmatic code. Every node in the hierarchy is assigned a value by the lexicon-provider according to the number of words in the original text that bear that code; values lower in the structure are propagated by summing upwards towards the root. At the end of this process a single pragmatic code for one of the seven fundamental categories, high in the hierarchy and therefore general in nature, asserts itself as the domain description term for the text. The result is a structure for lexical ambiguity resolution because this process also yields a set of preferred word senses that cohere with the subject domain of the text (in the sense that a set of, say, engineering terms is coherent with respect to engineering). The implication of discovering a global domain description term for a text is that the global domain description term carries with it an entire sub-hierarchy of more specific pragmatic codes. The Preference Semantics parsing algorithm strongly prefers these word

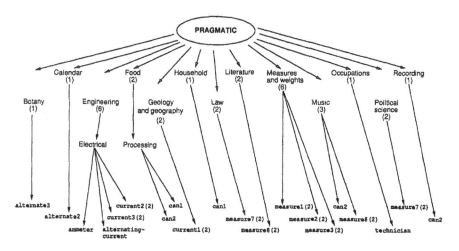

Fig. 8.5. The LDOCE Pragmatic Hierarchy (with words from (1)). The parenthetical numbers are from the 'Before Restructuring' column of Table 8.6.

senses coherent with (i.e., in the same subject area with) the domain description term established for the text; the more specific the word sense (the lower in the restructured pragmatic hierarchy), the higher the preference.

The scheme implemented here imposes deeper structure onto the LDOCE pragmatic world (Figure 8.6), relating pragmatic categories in a natural way, in order to discover important relationships between concepts within text. This particular restructuring is not one to be defended point by point; there has been, for instance, an arbitrary division made at the highest level. What *can* be defended is the notion that, for example, words classified under botany have pragmatic connections to words classified as plant names, as well as connections with other words classified under science (connections *not* made by the LDOCE pragmatic hierarchy as given), and that these connections are useful to exploit when attempting to determine the subject matter of a text, or when attempting to choose the correct sense of polysemous words.

To illustrate, again consider the text of (1).

(1) Current can be measured.
    The technician measures alternating current with an ammeter.

Without context, the correct sense of *current* in the first sentence cannot be selected until after the second sentence is processed; with context, a strong candidate can be preferred.[6]

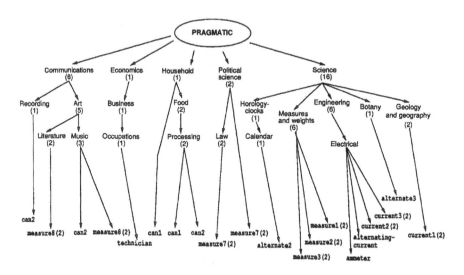

Fig. 8.6. The LDOCE Pragmatic Hierarchy (with words from example (1).) The parenthetical numbers are from the 'After Restructuring' column of Table 8.6.

---

[6] It would be natural to expect this process to work better on longer text, the longer the better, and indeed this appears to be true in tests we have run. However, good results can be got even with these relatively short fragments.

Table 8.6. Pragmatic codes and domain descriptors for example (1)

CODE	BEFORE RESTRUCTURING	Score	CODE	AFTER RESTRUCTURING	Score
MS	measures, weights	6	SI	science	16
EGZE	engineering/electrical	6	CM	communications	6
MU	music	3	MS	measures, weights	6
PL	political-science	2	EG	engineering	6
LT	literature	2	EGZE	engineering/electrical	6
LW	law	2	AF	art	5
GO	geology, geography	2	PL	political-science	4
FOZP	food/food-processing	2	MU	music	3
ON	occupations	1	HH	household	3
RE	recording	1	LT	literature	2
HH	household	1	LW	law	2
BO	botany	1	GO	geology, geography	2
CA	calendar	1	FO	food	2
	...		FOZP	food/food-processing	2
			EC	economics	1
			BZ	business	1
			ON	occupations	1
			RE	recording	1
			BO	botany	1
			HR	horology-clocks	1
			CA	calendar	1

In Table 8.6, the BEFORE RESTRUCTURING column is compiled simply by counting up the LDOCE pragmatic codes found in the various senses of the words in the text (as in content assessment). The AFTER RESTRUCTURING column gives the scores resulting from the deeper pragmatic structure. Note that descriptors like 'economics' and 'science' have been introduced, and that the status of 'science' as a domain descriptor for the text only asserts itself after restructuring. Beforehand, 'science' is not on the list and 'engineering/electrical', 'measures-and-weights', etc. are of equal and unrelated status. This is clearly an over-compartmentalized view of the world. The deeper hierarchy gives a far better intuitive ordering of the important concepts in each text than the given LDOCE hierarchy, and using these orderings as a word-sense selection heuristic is computationally useful.

8.4.2 Enriching Frames

The basic frames (as given in Section 8.4.1) are a large step towards the knowledge required for parsing by a lexicon-consumer operating over non-dictionary text [54]. However, there is a hidden wealth of further information within the genus and differentia of the text of the definitions. When the needs of a knowledge-based parser increase beyond this initial representation (as is the case of, say, resolving lexical ambiguity or making non-trivial attachment decisions), the frame representations are enriched by appeal to parse trees constructed from the dictionary entries of the relevant word senses. That is, the text of the definition entry itself is analyzed to extract genus and differentia terms [4]. This additional information further enriches the semantic structures.

A chart parser has been developed that accepts LDOCE definitions as Lisp lists and produces phrase-structure trees. The grammar is still being tuned, but it currently covers the language of content-word definitions in LDOCE, achieving a 95% success rate in a test of 1,200 entries. This chart parser is not, we emphasize, a parser for English — it is a parser for the sub-language of LDOCE definitions (Longmanese), and in fact only for the open-class or content word portions of that language. LDOCE sense definitions are typically one or more complex phrases composed of zero or more prepositional phrases, noun phrases and/or relative clauses. The syntax of sense definitions is relatively uniform, and developing a grammar for the bulk of LDOCE has not proven to be intractable. Chart parsing was selected for this system because of its utility as a grammar testing and development tool. The chart parser is driven by a context-free grammar of more than 100 rules and has a lexicon derived from the 2,219 words in the LDOCE core vocabulary. The parser is left-corner and bottom-up, with top-down filtering (taken from [57]), producing phrase-structure trees. The context-free grammar driving the chart parser is unaugmented and, with certain minor exceptions, no procedure associates constituents with what they modify. Hence, there is little or no motivation for assigning elaborate or competing syntactic structures since the choice of one over the other has no semantic consequence [43]. Therefore, the trees are constructed to be as "flat" as possible. The parser also has a "longest string" (fewest constituents) syntactic preference. A tree interpreter extracts semantic knowledge from these phrase-structure definition trees [56].

8.4.2.1 The Tree Interpreter

The output of the chart parser, a phrase-structure tree, is passed to an interpreter for pattern matching and inferencing. The tree interpreter first picks off the dominating phrase and, after restructuring it into GENUS and FEATURE components by reference to the currently active grammar version, inserts it into the current basic frame under a GENUS slot.[7] Further strategies for pattern-matching are being developed to extract more detailed differentia information.

The relationship between a word and its definition can trivially be viewed as an ISA relation; for example, an ammeter *is* "an instrument for measuring ... electric current." The frame created for each word-sense from its definition, then, represents the *intension* of that word-sense. This observation motivates the assumption that portions of this intensional material can be isolated and given a label for eventual preference matching. For example, by noting that an ammeter is "for measuring" it becomes reasonable to create a slot in the 'ammeter' frame that is labeled PURPOSE

---

[7] If the grammar is modified, the restructuring rules change automatically.

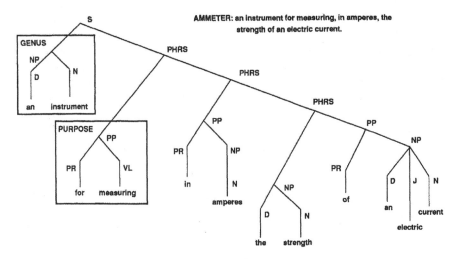

Fig. 8.7. Pattern matching against tree constituents

and filled with 'measuring'. This kind of knowledge is precisely what is needed to compute case roles and preferences (Figure 8.7):

Consider once again this sentence from (1): *The technician measures alternating current with an ammeter.*

The pattern 'for <verb>-ing' in the differentia of a noun strongly predicts a PURPOSE case role for that noun, and the preposition *with* in English predicts various case roles for its noun-phrase object, principally ACCOMPANIMENT ("a man ate a meal with a friend"), POSSESSION ("a man ate a fish with many bones") and INSTRUMENT ("a man ate a fish with his fingers"). In this instance, the definition for *ammeter* contains a pattern indicating it is a constituent that prefers to fill a PURPOSE and, in particular, prefers to be *for measuring*. In cases like this a parser should prefer the INSTRUMENT reading over both the ACCOMPANIMENT case relation and the POSSESSION noun phrase complement alternatives because the object of the *with* preposition (*ammeter*), has a PURPOSE case-role marker (filled with *measuring*), that suggests an INSTRUMENT attachment. Other case roles that appear extractable from LDOCE differentia, but still subject to further investigation, include PART-OF, MEMBER-OF, MEANS-OF and MEASURE-OF.

8.4.3 Comparison to Other Work

The most closely related pragmatic work, and that from which the ideas for this scheme arose, is by Walker and Amsler [61] who used the LDOCE pragmatic (subject) coding system to do content assessment on wire service stories from The New York Times News Service. The focus of that work was to arrive at a list of codes that, taken together, would reflect the subject matter of each story. Their work differs from ours in that they accepted the LDOCE pragmatic hierarchy as given, getting good results because their texts, while arguably general, were by nature highly coherent.

The pragmatic hierarchy scheme has roots in a far older tradition, one that dates to the days of "mechanical translation." Wilks [63] describes a system for word-sense disambiguation used by the Cambridge Language Research Unit [37]. The idea was to choose the correct senses for the words in a sentence by looking them all up in a thesaurus, finding the thesaural heads for each, and then determining which thesaural heads were held in common. Then the sets of words found under the common thesaural heads for each word were themselves compared for commonality, and any that were in the intersection of these sets became sense descriptors for that particular instance of the word in the sentence. This method worked remarkably well, and its major shortcoming was that it failed to take into account word usage that was other than the most "coherent"; therefore, the only sense of *mass* discovered in a physics text would be "mass as weight" and a phrase like "a mass of data" in a physics text would have the wrong sense assigned to it [59, 60]. The pragmatic hierarchy scheme is essentially equivalent to this older idea (although their thesaurus, like LDOCE as given, was only two layers deep and so was not well able to discriminate between competing senses).

Little machine-readable dictionary work has focused on the dictionary as a language resource for semantic, knowledge-based parsing. Approaches to extracting semantic knowledge from machine-readable sources, such as "sprouting" [13], or employment of paid "disambiguators" [6, 3], typically labor to construct taxonomies from an unconstrained definition vocabulary, such as in Webster's Seventh. The LDOCE work that we know of, principally at Cambridge University, has mainly concentrated on explicating the grammar codes for use with unification-based parsing [2, 9]. Other efforts at extracting semantic information from machine-readable sources include recent work on locating meaningful patterns in definition text using LDOCE at Cambridge [1]; searching for and explicating the so-called "defining formulas" of definitions using Webster's Seventh [36]; and recent work at IBM that has taken an approach to interpreting definition parse trees by applying a pattern matcher and a rule-based inference mechanism to assign MYCIN-like probabilities [52] to attachment alternatives (the numbers arrived at by intuition and tuning), again using Webster's Seventh as a knowledge base [7, 26].

8.5 Conclusion and Future Directions

The tools produced by the methods described in this paper all take as input the forms of information given on the LDOCE tape (English definitions, syntax codes, subject and pragmatic codes) and provide either:

- From Method I, a clustered network of LDOCE words whose clusters correspond to empirically derived senses.
- From Method II, a formalized set of definitions of sense entries in a nested predicate form, where the predicates are a "seed set" of senses, half the size of the existing controlled vocabulary of LDOCE.

- From Method III, frame-like structures containing a formalization of the English definitions using predicates that are (initially) English words (not senses) from the controlled vocabulary, as well as the given LDOCE codes.

Let us now consider two intended extensions to the three methods, which would have the effect, we claim, of combining these separate "weak" sources of semantic and syntactic information so as to provide stronger tools for text analysis.

8.5.1 The SPIRAL Procedure

This procedure would be one that cycled information between Slator's (Method III) LDOCE parser and Plate and McDonald's (Method I) distributional-network so as to yield a sense-tagging of the words in the frames Slator outputs from parsing LDOCE; at the same time it would provide a filter for the networks so as to reduce the search space required. It also gives senses (rather than words) at the network nodes. This passing of material between the provider modules (shown in Figure 8.8) is not circular but a spiral that yields, from a combination of weak sources, a stronger semantic data base.

In the following stages, the numerals 1, 2 and 3 index the integer labels in Figure 8.8.

Stage 1: Slator's LDOCE parser passes part-of-speech disambiguated words to the network algorithm, thus filtering its work by a large factor.

Stage 2: The network procedures give sense-tagging to the words in the LDOCE definitions.

Stage 3: The LDOCE parser now parses the sense-tagged entries in the dictionary, and passes the result back again to the network system, enabling the nodes in the network to be sense-tagged.

8.5.2 The ARC Procedure

In the ARC procedure, the arcs of Plate and McDonald's networks can be labeled automatically with either predicates (yielding a conventional semantic net) or with numerical values (yielding a connectionist network [34]). The latter would follow fairly directly from Pathfinder techniques, but the former presents a great challenge. ARC can be thought of as a fourth stage of the SPIRAL procedure and our initial approach to it will be to extend stage 3 of the SPIRAL technique of the previous section.

The first phase of ARC is driven from the frames already obtained from Slator's Method III: For each appropriate predicate in a frame that has two word-senses s1 and s2 as its arguments, we seek nodes n1 and n2 in a Plate and McDonald network corresponding to those senses. When found, we label the connecting arc with the predicate from the frame. This method simply transfers information from the frames to the networks.

A second phase now begins from the networks: For any two nodes in a network n1 and n2, both representing English word senses, and not already connected by a labeled arc, we seek their occurrence in LDOCE entries, immediately linked by plausible predicate and case forms (e.g. IS, ON, USED-FOR, PART-OF, etc.) and in senses that Slator's LDOCE parser asserts are the appropriate ones. If the occurrences in the entire dictionary are consistent, that is, are like:

```
hand (=bodyhand)  IS-A-PART-OF  body (=human body)
```

with no other predicate appearing where PART-OF does in any LDOCE entry, then that label could be attached, at that point, to an arc of the network. This is only one of a range of empirical possibilities that we shall explore in extending this work. Naturally, many of the co-occurences of the two word-senses in the body of LDOCE will be in forms for which Slator's parser may not provide a predicate unless augmented with inferential techniques: For instance, if we seek co-ocurrences of 'bridge' and 'tower' in the text, a form like 'tower bridge' will not, without deeper analysis of the kind developed within noun-phrase analysis systems, provide any

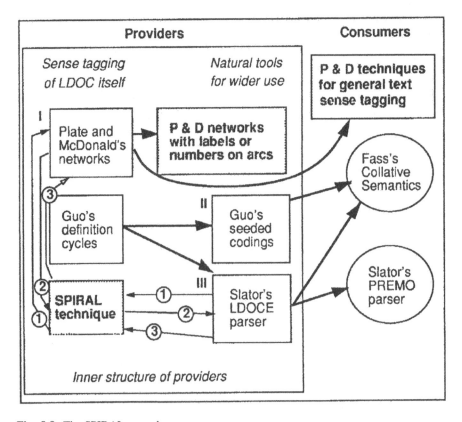

Fig. 8.8. The SPIRAL procedure

linking predicate, showing the type of linkage of the two concepts. Of course, we hope to provide this level of analysis in our work.

An interesting empirical question, after the application of the SPIRAL and ARC techniques, will be whether the sense-tagged frames (from Method III and augmented by methods I and II) and the labeled network (of Method I augmented by Method III) will then be equivalent, consistent or even contradictory "strengthened" semantic data bases, each formed from a different combination of the same weak methods. Notice that, in the two phases of ARC as described above, that since the second but not the first phase ranges over the examples in the dictionary text, the two sorts of information may be expected to be different, though, it is to be hoped, consistent.

References

[1] Alshawi, Hiyan. 1987. Processing Dictionary Definitions with Phrasal Pattern Hierarchies. *Computational Linguistics*, 13: 203–218.

[2] Alshawi, H., B. Boguraev and T. Briscoe. 1985. Towards a Dictionary Support Environment for Real Time Parsing. Proceedings of the 2nd European Conference on Computational Linguistics, Geneva, 171–178.

[3] Amsler, R.A. 1980. The Structure of the *Merriam-Webster Pocket Dictionary*. Technical Report TR-164, University of Texas at Austin.

[4] Amsler, R.A. 1981. A Taxonomy of English Nouns and Verbs. Proceedings of ACL-19, Stanford, 133–138.

[5] Amsler, R.A. 1982. Computational Lexicology: A Research Program. AFIPS Conference Proceedings, 1982 National Computer Conference, 657–663.

[6] Amsler, R.A., and J.S. White. 1979. Development of a Computational Methodology for Deriving Natural language Semantic Structures via Analysis of Machine-Readable Dictionaries. NSF Technical Report MCS77-01315.

[7] Binot, J.-L., and K. Jensen. 1987. A Semantic Expert Using an Online Standard Dictionary. Proceedings of IJCAI-87, Milan, 709–714.

[8] Boguraev, B.K. 1987. The Definitional Power of Words. Proceedings of the 3rd Workshop on Theoretical Issues in Natural Language Processing (TINLAP-3), Las Cruces, 11–15.

[9] Boguraev, B.K., and T. Briscoe. 1987. Large Lexicons for Natural Language Processing: Exploring the Grammar Coding System of LDOCE. *Computational Linguistics* 13: 203–218.

[10] Boguraev, B.K., T. Briscoe, J. Carroll, D. Carter and C. Grover. 1987. The Derivation of a Grammatically Indexed Lexicon from the Longman Dictionary of Contemporary English. Proceedings of ACL-25, Stanford, 193–200.

[11] Byrd, R.J. 1989. Discovering Relationships Among Word Senses. In Proceedings of the 5th Conference of the UW Centre for the New OED (Dictionaries in the Electronic Age). Oxford, 67–79.

[12] Carre, B. 1979. Graphs and Networks. Clarendon Press: Oxford.

[13] Chodorow, M.S., R.J. Byrd and G.E. Heidon. 1985. Extracting Semantic Hierarchies from a Large On-Line Dictionary. In Proceedings of ACL-23, Chicago, 299–304.

[14] Cottrell, G.W., and S.L. Small. 1983. A Connectionist Scheme for Modelling Word-Sense Disambiguation. *Cognition and Brain Theory* 6: 89–120.

[15] Dietterich, T.G., and R. Michalski. 1981. Inductive Learning of Structural Descriptions. *Artificial Intelligence* **16**:257–294.

[16] Evens, M., and R.N. Smith. 1983. Determination of Adverbial Senses from Webster's Seventh Collegiate Definitions. Paper presented at Workshop on Machine Readable Dictionaries, SRI-International, April 1983.

[17] Fass, D.C. 1986. Collative Semantics: An Approach to Coherence. Memorandum in Computer and Cognitive Science, MCCS-86-56, Computing Research Laboratory, New Mexico State University, Las Cruces.

[18] Fass, D.C. 1988a. Collative Semantics: A Semantics for Natural Language Processing. Memorandum in Computer and Cognitive Science, MCCS-88-118, Computing Research Laboratory, New Mexico State University, Las Cruces.

[19] Fass, D.C. 1988b. Metonymy and Metaphor: What's the Difference? In Proceedings of COLING-88, Budapest, 177–181.

[20] Fass, D.C. 1988c. An Account of Coherence, Semantic Relations, Metonymy, and Lexical Ambiguity Resolution. In S.L. Small, G.W. Cottrell and M.K. Tanenhaus (Eds., Lexical Ambiguity Resolution in the Comprehension of Human Language. Los Altos: Morgan Kaufmann, 151–178.

[21] Fass, D.C., and Y.A. Wilks. 1983. Preference Semantics, Ill-Formedness and Metaphor. *American Journal of Computational Linguistics* **9**: 178–187.

[22] Guo, C. 1987. Interactive Vocabulary Acquisition in XTRA. In Proceedings of IJCAI-87, Milan. 715–717.

[23] Harary, F. 1969. Graph Theory. Reading, MA: Addison-Wesley,

[24] Harris, Z. 1951. Structural Linguistics. Chicago: University of Chicago Press.

[25] Hobbs, J.R. 1987. World Knowledge and World Meaning. In Proceedings of the 3rd Workshop on Theoretical Issues in Natural Language Processing (TINLAP-3), Las Cruces, 20–25.

[26] Jensen, K., and J.-L. Binot. 1987. Disambiguating Prepositional Phrase Attachments by Using On-Line Dictionary Definitions. *Computational Linguistics* **13**: 251–260.

[27] Johnson, S.C. 1967. Hierarchical Clustering Schemes. *Psychometrika* **32**: 241–254.

[28] Kegl, J. 1987. The Boundary Between Word Knowledge and World Knowledge. In Proceedings of the 3rd Workshop on Theoretical Issues in Natural Language Processing (TINLAP-3), Las Cruces, 26–31.

[29] Kucera, H., and W.N. Francis. 1967. Computational Analysis of Present-Day American English. Providence, RI: Brown University Press.

[30] Lenat, D.B., and E.A. Feigenbaum. 1987. On The Thresholds of Knowledge. In Proceedings of IJCAI-87, Milan, 1173–1182.

[31] Lenat, D.B., M. Prakash and M. Shepherd. 1986. CYC: Using Common Sense Knowledge to Overcome Brittleness and Knowledge Acquisition Bottlenecks. *AI Magazine* **7** (4): 65–85.

[32] Lesk, M.E. 1986. Automatic Sense Disambiguation Using Machine Readable Dictionaries: How to Tell a Pine Cone from an Ice Cream Cone. In Proceedings of the ACM SIGDOC Conference, Toronto, 24–26.

[33] Lyons, J. 1977. Semantics, Volume 2. Cambridge: Cambridge University Press.

[34] McClelland, J., D.E. Rumelhart and the PDP Research Group (Eds.). 1986. Parallel Distributed Processing: Explorations in the Microstructure of Cognition. Two Volumes, Volume 2: Psychological and Biological Models. Cambridge, MA: MIT Press/Bradford Books.

[35] McDonald, J.E., T. Plate and R.W. Schvaneveldt. Forthcoming. Using Pathfinder to Analyse a Dictionary. In R. Schvaneveldt (Ed.), untitled.

[36] Markowitz, J., T. Ahlswede and M. Evens. 1986. Semantically Significant Patterns in Dictionary Definitions. In Proceedings of ACL-24, New York, 112–119.

[37] Masterman, M. 1957. The Thesaurus in Syntax and Semantics. *Mechanical Translation* **4**: 1–2.

[38] Michiels, A., J. Mullenders and J. Noel. 1980. Exploiting a Large Data Base by Longman. In Proceedings of COLING-80, Tokyo, 374–382.

[39] Miller, G.A. 1985. Dictionaries of the Mind. In Proceedings of ACL-23, Chicago, 305–314.

[40] Newell, A. 1973. Artificial Intelligence and the Concept of Mind. In R.C. Schank and K.M. Colby (Eds.), Computer Models of Thought and Language. San Francisco: W.H. Freeman, 1–60.

[41] Ogden, C.K. 1942. The General Basic English Dictionary. New York: W.W Norton.

[42] Procter, P. et al, (Eds.). 1978. Longman Dictionary of Contemporary English. Harlow, Essex: Longman.

[43] Pulman, S.G. 1985. Generalised Phrase Structure Grammar, Earley's Algorithm, and the Minimisation of Recursion. In K. Sparck Jones and Y.A. Wilks (Eds.), Automatic Natural Language Parsing. New York: John Wiley and Sons, 117–131.

[44] Pustejovsky, J., and S. Bergler. 1987. The Acquisition of Conceptual Structure for the Lexicon. In Proceedings of AAAI-87, Seattle, 556–570.

[45] Quillian, M.R. 1967. Word Concepts: A Theory and Simulation of Some Basic Semantic Capabilities. *Behavioral Science* **12**: 410–430. Reprinted in R.J. Brachman and H.J. Levesque (Eds.), Readings in Knowledge Representation. Los Altos: Morgan Kaufmann, 1985, 98–118.

[46] Quirk, R., S. Greenbaum, G. Leech and J. Svartik. 1972. A Grammar of Contemporary English. Harlow, Essex: Longman.

[47] Quirk, R., S. Greenbaum, G. Leech and J. Svartik. 1985. A Comprehensive Grammar of English. Harlow, Essex: Longman.

[48] St. John, M.F., and J.L. McClelland. 1986. Reconstructive Memory for Sentences: A PDP Approach. Ohio University Inference Conference.

[49] Sampson, G. 1986. A Stochastic Approach to Parsing. In Proceedings of COLING-86, Bonn, 151–155.

[50] Schvaneveldt, R.W., and F.T. Durso. 1981. Generalized Semantic Networks. Paper presented at the meeting of the Psychonomic Society, Philadelphia.

[51] Schvaneveldt, R.W., F.T. Durso and D.W. Dearholt. 1985. Pathfinder: Scaling with Network Structure. Memorandum in Computer and Cognitive Science, MCCS-85-9, Computing Research Laboratory, New Mexico State University, Las Cruces.

[52] Shortliffe, E.H. 1976. Computer-Based Medical Consultation: MYCIN. New York: Elsevier.

[53] Slator, B.M. 1988a. Lexical Semantics and a Preference Semantics Parser. Memorandum in Computer and Cognitive Science, MCCS-88-116, Computing Research Laboratory, New Mexico State University, Las Cruces.

[54] Slator, B.M. 1988b. PREMO: the PREference Machine Organization. In Proceedings of the Third Annual Rocky Mountain Conference on Artificial Intelligence, Denver, 258–265.

[55] Slator, B.M. 1988c. Constructing Contextually Organized Lexical Semantic Knowledge-Bases. Proceedings of the Third Annual Rocky Mountain Conference on Artificial Intelligence, Denver, CO, 142–148.

[56] Slator, B.M., and Y.A. Wilks. 1987. Toward Semantic Structures from Dictionary Entries. In Proceedings of the Second Annual Rocky Mountain Conference on Artificial Intelligence, Boulder, CO, 85–96. Also, Memorandum in Computer and

Cognitive Science, MCCS-87-96, Computing Research Laboratory, New Mexico State University, Las Cruces.

[57] Slocum, J. 1985. Parser Construction Techniques: A Tutorial. Tutorial held at the 23rd Annual Meeting of the Association for Computational Linguistics, Chicago.

[58] Slocum, J., and M.G. Morgan. Forthcoming. The Role of Dictionaries and Machine Readable Lexicons in Translation. In D. Walker, A. Zampolli and N. Calzolari (eds.), Automating the Lexicon: Research and Practice in a Multilingual Environment. Cambridge: Cambridge University Press.

[59] Sparck Jones, K. 1964. Synonymy and Semantic Classification. Ph.D. Thesis, University of Cambridge.

[60] Sparck Jones, K. 1986. Synonymy and Semantic Classification. (Ph.D. thesis with new Foreword.) Edinburgh Information Technology Series (EDITS). Edinburgh: Edinburgh University Press.

[61] Walker, D.E., and R.A. Amsler. 1986. The Use of Machine-Readable Dictionaries in Sublanguage Analysis. In R. Grishman and R. Kittredge (Eds.), Analyzing Language in Restricted Domains. Hillsdale, NJ: Lawrence Erlbaum, 69–84.

[62] Waltz, D.L., and J.B. Pollack. 1985. Massively Parallel Parsing: A Strongly Interactive Model of Natural Language Interpretation. *Cognitive Science* **9**: 51–74.

[63] Wilks, Y.A. 1972. Grammar, Meaning, and the Machine Analysis of Language. Routledge and Kegan Paul: London.

[64] Wilks, Y.A. 1973. An Artificial Intelligence Approach to Machine Translation. In R.C. Schank and K.M. Colby (Eds.), Computer Models of Thought and Language. San Francisco: W.H. Freeman, 114–151.

[65] Wilks, Y.A. 1975a. A Preferential Pattern-Seeking Semantics for Natural Language Inference. *Artificial Intelligence* **6**: 53–74.

[66] Wilks, Y.A. 1975b. An Intelligent Analyser and Understander for English. *Communications of the ACM* **18**: 264–274.

[67] Wilks, Y.A. 1977. Good and Bad Arguments about Semantic Primitives. *Communication and Cognition* **10**: 182–221.

[68] Wilks, Y.A. 1978. Making Preferences More Active. *Artificial Intelligence* **10**: 75–97.

[69] Wilks, Y.A., D.C. Fass, C. Guo, J.E. McDonald, T. Plate and B.M. Slator. 1987. A Tractable Machine Dictionary as a Resource for Computational Semantics. Memorandum in Computer and Cognitive Science, MCCS-87-105, Computing Research Laboratory, New Mexico State University, Las Cruces. To appear in B. Boguraev and T. Briscoe (Eds.), Computational Lexicography for Natural Language Processing. Harlow, Essex: Longman.

[70] Wilks, Y.A., D.C. Fass, C. Guo, J.E. McDonald, T. Plate and B.M. Slator. 1988. Machine Tractable Dictionaries as Tools and Resources for Natural Language Processing. In Proceedings of COLING-88, Budapest, 750–755.

[71] Winston, P.H. 1975. Learning Structural Descriptions from Examples. In P.H. Winston (Ed.), The Psychology of Computer Vision. New York: McGraw-Hill.

9

Belief Ascription, Metaphor, and Intensional Identification

Afzal Ballim[1], Yorick Wilks[2] and John Barnden[2]

[1] *University of Geneva, Switzerland*
[2] *New Mexico State University*

Abstract: This article discusses the extension of *ViewGen*, an algorithm derived for belief ascription, to the areas of intensional object identification and metaphor. ViewGen represents the beliefs of agents as explicit, partitioned proposition sets known as environments. Environments are convenient, even essential, for addressing important pragmatic issues of reasoning. The article concentrates on showing that the transfer of information in metaphors, intensional object identification, and ordinary, nonmetaphorical belief ascription can all be seen as different manifestations of a single environment-amalgamation process. The article also briefly discusses the extension of ViewGen to speech-act processing and the addition of a heuristic-based, relevance-determination procedure, and justifies the partitioning approach to belief ascription

9.1 Introduction

An AI system that takes part in discourse with other agents must be able to reason about the beliefs, intentions, desires, and other propositional attitudes[1] of those agents, and of agents referred to in the discourse. This is especially so in those common situations where the agents' beliefs differ from the system's. Thus, the question of how to represent and reason about propositional attitudes is central to the study of discourse.

Clearly, this question is really about the beliefs, and so forth, that the system *ascribes* to the agents, on the evidence presented by the discourse itself and by context and prior information, because persons have no direct access to each other's mental states. We view the ascription problem as being a fundamental one.

---

[1] We use the term "propositional attitude" to cover beliefs, intentions, and so on, without intending to imply any specific philosophical view, such as one in which a state of belief (say) is a relationship between an agent and a "proposition."

K. Ahmad, C. Brewster and M. Stevenson (eds.), Words and Intelligence 1, 217–253.
© 2007 *Springer.*

It has been the focus of our past work on propositional attitudes [4, 5, 6, 8, 9, 10, 11, 12, 13, 14, 15, 16, 65, 66, 67, 68, 69, 70]. Ascriptional reasoning is profoundly dependent on the communicative context, general information that the system has about the world, and special information the system has about the agents at hand. Moreover, there are major pragmatic features of discourse, such as speech acts, metaphor, and the determination of the intensional entities in play in a discourse, that any system for ascribing beliefs to agents must address. We would go further, and assert that even the most apparently superficial aspects of natural language understanding depend on belief ascription: such as prepositional phrase attachment. Anyone hearing a sentence with the all-too-familiar structure:

He told his mother about the murder in the park.

will interpret it differently according to whether he believes that the speaker believes there was a murder in a park and whether the speaker believes that the hearer believes it too. The function of our basic program *ViewGen* is to create, or as we shall call it, *ascribe*, environments into which appropriate beliefs can be segregated so that parsing and reasoning can be done in that limited environment.

We have described the basic algorithm in ViewGen in the publications above, and we address basic parsing issues seen as belief phenomena elsewhere. Here, our purpose is simply to review the basic ascription mechanism and then show its extension to the pragmatic phenomena in the title of the article.

In interpreting an utterance by an agent, the system must ascribe a speech act to that agent; and doing this is a matter of ascribing specific intentions, beliefs, desires, expectations and so on to the agent. Thus, speech-act ascription is an important special case of ascriptional reasoning. That speech-act considerations make reasoning about propositional attitudes essential for the computational modeling of discourse has been established at least since the work of Perrault and his colleagues [e.g., 51]. A major difference between that work and ours is that they took the content of belief environments to be already established, whereas our approach is based on the real-time computation of the contents of such belief environments.

As for metaphor, to consider it at all in a study of propositional attitudes might initially seem unmotivated or overly ambitious. However, we are among those who hold that metaphor is central, not peripheral, to language use, and indeed, cognition in general [for related positions see, e.g., 17, 32, 33, 35, 38, 39]. We believe, in particular, that metaphor is *inextricably* bound up with propositional attitude processing for three main reasons:

1. A key aspect of a metaphorical view of a topic is seeing it *as something else*: even in such simple, conventionalized cases as *John caught a cold*, where a cold is seen as a missile or other object. This, we suggest, is no more than a special case of an *agent's view* of a topic, in the sense of a set of beliefs.

2. Many, if not most, beliefs arising in ordinary discourse and reasoning are at least partly metaphorical in nature. Consider, for instance, the beliefs that *Terrorism is creeping across the globe, Sally's theory is threatened by the experiment,* and

Prussia invaded France in 1871, all of which are, in a broad sense, metaphorical. As an example of the difficulties that such beliefs raise, notice that the last one cannot in general be adequately represented by any literal sense representation for *Prussia*, since it may be important to take into account exactly how the believer may be viewing the invasion:

- as a matter of the army of Prussia doing something,
- of the Prussian government doing something,
- or of the Prussian people as a whole doing something, and so on.

The simple predicate notations commonly used in belief research lead us to overlook such basic representational issues.

3. People commonly (if not universally) think of minds and mental functioning in highly metaphorical terms—for instance, as physical containers of ideas, beliefs, intentions, and so on—those contents themselves being viewed metaphorically as active or passive physical objects of some sort. Thus, in a sentence like, *Mike believes that George believes that P*, we confront the issue of possible metaphorical views Mike may hold of George's beliefs. This issue, which is an important special case of (2), is studied by Barnden [14, 15, 16], but for reasons of space is not addressed here.

The similarity in (1) is the main topic of this article. Note also that Davidson [24] said that metaphor "is simply false belief." Our aim could be said to show that this is correct, but in a surprising and computationally realizable way. Our previous work was based on the use of *explicit belief environments*. Each of these is a group of propositions, manipulable as an explicit entity in the system, and which can, in ways we shall show, be thought of as *nested* within other such entities. The relation of nesting or containment represents the intuitive notion of a believer (an outer proposition group) having beliefs about other entity (the inner group). Our belief environments are akin to the belief spaces and other types of cluster or partition discussed more recently by authors such as Fauconnier [29] and Dinsmore [25]. We also share a general belief in the primacy of intensional representation with Shapiro and Rapaport [58] and their SNePS system. However, SNePS does not have any natural analogue of partitions or nestings of belief sets (the boxes that appeared in diagrams in [53], just being a notational convenience), and so lacks a crucial feature of what we propose.

Maida's work [42, 43] shared many of the current concerns here: Maida linked belief ascription to analogical reasoning, and his diagrammatic representations of nested beliefs were isomorphic to those of Wilks and Bien [69] and Shadbolt [56]. Maida's concerns were with the problem of shared reasoning strategies between believers and how, for example, it could be established that a dialogue partner also used *modus ponens*. We argue, on the contrary, that this phenomenon is best handled by general default assumptions, as are the concrete contents of beliefs. No finite set of dialogue observations could ever establish conclusively that another believer was using *modus ponens*. That being so, concentration on such issues that are not susceptible to proof seems, to us, only to delay the central issue, which is how to infer heuristically the actual beliefs of other believers. Maida [41] was also concerned with the very important, and we believe quite separable issue, of a heuristic rule for identifying intensional individuals under different descriptions. Konolige's [37] work had strong similarities to that just noted; Konolige considered what he called views, for which he wrote, for example, $v = John, Sue, Kim$ to mean *John's view of Sue's view of Kim's beliefs*. But he had no effective construction for the content of such views. Rather, Konolige was concerned with giving an account of limited deduction in such views, an important process, but not relevant to issues of constructing individuals' views. Dinsmore [25] was concerned with what he termed the "algebra of belief spaces" but, although the term is highly general, the focus of his attention was always, in fact, the notions of presupposition and counterfactuals, which are not notions we treat explicitly here, and his treatment of them may well be compatible with our own general approach.

Our work has been closer in spirit to that of Perrault and others [e.g., 19, 51]; though without their (then) commitment to the language of speech-act theory and, most importantly, without their key assumption that the partitions among beliefs are all present at the beginning of the speech-act reasoning procedures. Our work makes no such assumption: For us, nested beliefs are not merely accessed, but constructed and maintained in real time, a position we find both computationally and psychologically more plausible. The Gedankenexperiment here is to ask yourself if you aready know what Mr. Gorbachev believes the U.S. President believes about Colonel Qaddafi. Of course you can work it out, but how plausible is it that you already have precomputed such nested viewpoints, in advance of any such consideration?

In general, our work has been, since that of Wilks and Bien [69, 70], to construct a formalism and programs (some would not abstain from the word "theory" here, but that difference of taste need not detain us, or see [64]) that capture the heuristic belief ascriptions that individuals actually perform in the process of understanding and participating in dialgoue: That is to say, concrete beliefs and not merely meta-beliefs about the reasoning architecture of others, activities we suspect are rarely, if ever, undertaken. Thus, we have been less concerned with the general expressive powers of particular notations and demonstrations of their adequacy (as has been the central feature of most work on propositional attitude representation) than with the *content* of belief ascription. We suspect that the procedures we offer here could be applied to a large range of representational systems already available in the field.

The plan of this article is as follows: Sections 9.2 to 9.3 describe ViewGen, our present belief ascription system based on explicit proposition groups known as *environments*, and present justifications for the use of explicit environments. Section 9.4 discusses two issues that are important both for belief ascription and reasoning in general. The first is the notion of relevance, which is essential to realistic processing; the second is the intensional identification of objects, which, among other things, has a strong bearing on determining relevant beliefs. Section 9.5

forms the core of the article: It explains some profound connections that we see between belief ascription and metaphor, and describes how our current system is being extended to embody these connections. Section 9.6 considers the bearing of these issues on the processing of speech acts. Section 9.7 contains a general discussion, and Section 9.8 is the conclusion.

9.2 ViewGen: The Basic Belief Engine

A computational model of belief ascription is described in detail elsewhere [5, 8, 65, 69, 70] and is embodied in a program called ViewGen. The basic algorithm of this model uses the notion of default reasoning to ascribe beliefs to other agents unless there is evidence to prevent the ascription. Perrault [49, 50] and Cohen & Levesque [20] also recently explored a belief and speech-act logic based on a single explicit default axiom. As our previous work showed the default ascription is basically correct, but the phenomena are more complex (see the following) than are normally captured by an axiomatic approach.

ViewGen's belief space is divided into a number of topic-specific partitions (topic environments). These environments can be thought of as a less permanent version of *frames* [18, 48], or more suitably, in terms of Wilks [62], as "pseudotexts." In effect, a pseudotext is a set of unsorted, unrefined items of knowledge. These pseudotexts are general items, and can be not only about individual objects, but also about abstract ideas and groups of things. The hierarchical and inheritance relations of pseudotexts are discussed in Wilks [62] and Ballim & Wilks [8]. We jusify the general notion of explicit environment in the next section.

ViewGen also generates a type of environment known as a *viewpoint*. A viewpoint is some person's beliefs about a topic. Within ViewGen, all beliefs are ultimately beliefs held by the system (e.g., the system's beliefs about France, what the system believes John believes about cars, etc.) and so, trivially, lie within the system's viewpoint. The system's view of some topic (say, atoms) is pictorially represented as in Figure 9.1.

This diagram contains two types of environments: First, there is the box labeled with "system" at the bottom. This is a "believer environment" or "viewpoint." Viewpoints contain "topic environments," such as the box labeled with "atom" at the top of it. A topic environment contains a group of propositions about the "topic." So, for example, the diagram in Figure 9.1 conveys that the system believes that atoms are light and small. Topic boxes are motivated by concerns of limited

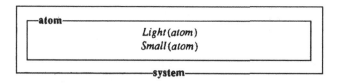

Fig. 9.1. The system's view of an atom.

reasoning (see Section 9.4.1 on relevance, and also [70]). In short, it is envisaged that reasoning takes place "within" a topic environment, as if it were the environment of a procedure in a programming language.

Within ViewGen, environments are dynamically created and altered. ViewGen's "knowledge base" can be seen as one large viewpoint containing a large number of topic environments, with each topic environment containing a group of "beliefs" that the system holds about the topic. The reader should note that each proposition in a topic environment has at least one symbol identical to the name of the topic. Each such proposition is, therefore, *explicitly* about the topic. There are, however, implicit ways in which a proposition can be "about" (or "relevant to") a topic. The simplest cases are generated by inheritance in the usual way: For example, if John is a man, then any proposition in a "man" topic environment is implicitly or indirectly about John. However, we choose not to put such a proposition in the John topic box, and will justify that decision in Section 9.4.1 on relevance. Again, the same proposition can occur in more than one box, as would the expression asserting that an elephant was larger than an atom, for it is about both atoms and elephants, and should appear under both topics.

If the topic of a topic environment is a person then the topic environment may contain, in addition to the beliefs about the person, a viewpoint environment containing particular beliefs held by that person about various topics. Normally, and for obvious reasons of efficiency, this is only done for those beliefs of a given person that are, as some would put it, reportable, which often means beliefs that confict with those of the system itself. For example, suppose the system had beliefs about a person called John who believes that the Earth is flat. (This is pictorially represented as in Figure 9.2.)

The John viewpoint, shown as the box with "John" on the lower edge, is a *nested viewpoint*, as it is enclosed within the system viewpoint shown (through an intervening topic environment about John, shown as the box with "John" on its upper edge). For simplicity, in the diagram of a nested viewpoint we often leave out propositions that are not in the innermost topic box: In this example, we would leave out the beliefs that John is a man, and that he is six feet tall. Further simplifying this, we often omit all but the innermost topic box, leaving only it

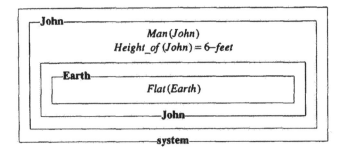

Fig. 9.2. The organization of beliefs about and of John.

and the viewpoint boxes. Hence, the diagram in Figure 9.2 would be simplified as in Figure 9.3.[2]

The system stores its own beliefs, and the beliefs of other agents that differ from the system's own beliefs. Others' viewpoints are generated on demand a position we find both computationally and psychologically more plausible than the "prestored nesting" view mentioned in Section 9.1. The process of generating a viewpoint can be regarded as an *amalgamation* mechanism that ascribes beliefs from one viewpoint to another (or, "pushing one environment down into another"): ascribing certain beliefs, transforming some, and blocking the ascription of others.

The simplest form of this algorithm, described in Wilks and Bien [69, 70], is that a viewpoint should be generated using a default rule for ascription of beliefs. The default ascriptional rule is to assume that another person's view is the same as one's own *except where there is explicit evidence to the contrary*. An important special case of such examples is when the topic is the same as the agent, and we can illustrate with that. Suppose that at a certain stage in dialogue, the system, acting as a medical diagnostician, has the view that John is not healthy, and is six feet tall, although John believes himself to be healthy. This basic situation is represented pictorially in Figure 9.4. The more complex environment for the system's view of John's view of himself can be generated by trying to ascribe the beliefs from the system's topic enviornment about John to the topic environment about John within John's viewpoint (where, as always, the last expression must be glossed as "the system's view of.."). One of the two beliefs survives the attempt but the other is blocked, giving the state in Figure 9.5. This can be pictured in the simplified (or as we shall call it, *compressed*) manner as in Figure 9.6.

We see that in examples of this sort, where the topic is also the agent into whose environment as ascription is being attempted, propositions in an outer topic environment E are *pushed inwards* into a topic environment (for the same topic)

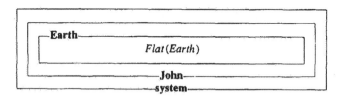

Fig. 9.3. The system's view of John's view of the Earth.

---

[2] We do not discuss here the issue of different mental descriptions under which John might have beliefs about the Earth. A case in which, say, John believes that a certain planet is flat, describing it mentally as the third planet from the Sun, can be handled in our system by having a complex topic-environment label, on the lines of the complex labels used on some occasions later in the article. Also, our techniques allow John to fail to realize that the third planet from the Sun is Earth (see 4.2.2).

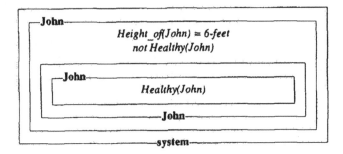

Fig. 9.4. Beliefs pertinent to John.

within a viewpoint nested within E.[3] Such inward pushing is central to our later observations of intensional identification and metaphor.

The example just outlined demonstrates the basic ascription algorithm and a simple case of ascriptions being blocked. However, belief ascription is a far more complex phenomenon, and the key to our method is the delimitation and treatment of cases where the default algorithm is incorrect. But even the default algorithm requires, for its operation, a notion of blocking beyond that of explicit contradiction: For example, the proposition *Healthy(John)* should be able to block *Sick(John)*, if *Sick* and *Healthy* are known to be incompatible predicates. Similarly, we appeal later to blocking that arises from incompatible function values, as in the blocking

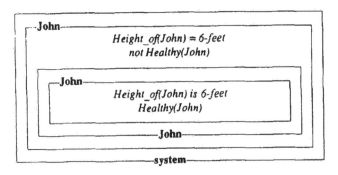

Fig. 9.5. Generating John's beliefs about himself.

---

[3] In our example we do take John to be having beliefs which he recognizes as being about *himself*. There are also unusual cases in which it is appropriate to take John's concept of himself to differ from that concept of his that most closely corresponds to the system's concept of him. (For example, he may be an amnesiac who has forgotten who he is, but nevertheless has beliefs involving a person that the system would say was he; c.f. [53]). Such cases can easily be handled within the approach to intensional objects in Section 9.4.2.2, below, basically by having two environments on the topic of John within John's viewpoint.

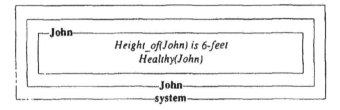

Fig. 9.6. Simplified form of Figure 9.5.

of *Eye-color(Frank) = Green* by *Eye-color(Frank) = Blue*. The more significant complication is that there is an entire class of beliefs that require the opposite of the default-ascription rule given above. We call these *atypical beliefs* and they include technical expertise, self-knowledge (itself a form of expertise), and secrets. For example, beliefs that I have about myself, such as how many fillings I have in my teeth, are beliefs that I would not normally ascribe to someone else *unless I had reason to do so* (if, say, the person, to whom I was ascribing the belief was my dentist). A representation based on lambda expressions is used in dealing with atypical beliefs, and is described elsewhere [5, 8, 65], and follows a suggestion originally made by McCarthy and Hayes [47]. This combination of a basic default ascription rule, augmented by a mechanism for dealing with atypical belief, is an original algorithm and has not, to our knowledge, been described or tested elsewhere in the literature.

The essential feature of this notation is that lambda expressions, as in the following example

$$(\exists X).\{X = (\lambda y(Cure\text{–}for\ y)tuberculosis)\}$$

can only be evaluated by qualified believers (e.g., physicians or informed lay people in this case) in appropriate environments. Yet, anyone can believe the Fregean triviality expressed by the above sentence when it is unevaluated (and it is vital that they can) but a nontrivial interpretation can only be placed on it by those who can evaluate the lambda expression in an environment. In a crude sense therefore, the lambda expressions correspond to intensional representations, and their evaluations correspond, when available, to extensions, or at least other intensions in those situations where the evaluation of such an expression produces yet another lambda expression (see also [41]).

The above expressions, for example, might evaluate to another lambda expression using a predicate *Sulfonamide-drug*, for whose evaluation a particular drug might be appropriate. Each evaluation would require an environment whose "holder" was qualified to perform it. It is really this possibility of successive evaluations of expressions that justifies the abstraction capacity of the lambda notation, because it could well result in expressions, such as a conjunction of predicates, for which there is no single predicate that deals with the problem of the over-application of the main default rule of ascription, since the ascription of unevaluable expressions, about, say, the number of my own teeth, to you does not lead to undesirable results.

It should be noted that in blocking the ascription of a proposition, from one environment to another, we often need to consider not just whether it contradicts a proposition in the target environment, but also whether some combination of propositions in the source environment contradict some propositions in the target environment. This is considered in more detail in Ballim and Wilks [8].

While on the subject of ascription blocking, we should mention that, in principle, a proposition P should not be ascribed from an environment $E1$ to an environment $E2$ if some presuppositions used in deriving P are blocked from being ascribed to $E2$. Thus, in principle, the issues addressed by truth-maintenance systems arise for us, although they are not yet addressed by ViewGen.

9.3 Why Explicit Environments?

In a realistic discourse, the system has to make rapid decisions about the sets of propositions believed by the agents. Now, ascription can involve a significant amount of work in modifying an existing proposition before ascribing it, or in checking that there is no contrary proposition blocking the ascription [8, 65]. Therefore, it is beneficial to minimize the number of propositions ascribed (as long as the techniques for minimization do not themselves take up too much time). One technique for limiting the ascription is to ascribe only those propositions that are deemed relevant according to some set of efficient relevance-determination heuristics (see Section 9.4.1).

Suppose the system has already constructed its own topic environment R, containing system beliefs about Reagan. The "default-ascription rule" used in ViewGen to construct or expand John's topic environment JR concerning Reagan is then just to push propositions in R down into JR. The pushing of a proposition may be blocked, because, for instance, it is explicitly contradicted by a proposition in JR, or because it is political expertise which should not be ascribed to the politically inexpert John. Also, propositions may need to be modified rather than blocked [65]. Therefore, the pushing process as applied to R does require separate processing of individual propositions in R. However, the explicitness of R as a *group* is nevertheless important because R is likely to be the result of a significant amount of *knowledge-intensive, relevance-determination work* (see Section 9.4.1). This work may have involved the processing of system beliefs that are not about Reagan in any directly obvious, explicit way. Once the system has created R for the purposes of its own reasoning about Reagan, R is immediately available to help in constructing environments such as JR, for the purposes of the system's reasoning about various other agents' reasoning about Reagan. If beliefs were not parceled up in explicit environments, the ascription beliefs about Reagan to those agents would be likely to involve essentially *duplicated* relevance-determination work similar to what is necessary to create R. In sum, one justification for environments—proposition groups that are explicit in the above sense—is that they serve to reduce the amount of work dictated by considerations of relevance.

Also, the pushing down of system beliefs about Reagan into John's view-point could involve the conjoint examination of several such beliefs, rather than examination of them one at a time. It makes it especially important for the system to be able to determine *quickly* which of its beliefs are relevant to Reagan. A similar observation holds for pushing of beliefs at deeper levels of nesting, as in the attempted pushing down of John's beliefs about Reagan into a Bill viewpoint nested within John's.

People talk explicitly or implicitly about *sets* of beliefs (and other propositional attitudes) held by agents. For instance, someone might say "John's beliefs about New Mexico are confused." This sentence is best interpreted as conveying that John's beliefs are, as a set, inconsistent in some sense, rather than as conveying something about individual beliefs of John. Explicit topic environments and viewpoints give us a handle on dealing with such cases.

Work by other researchers tends to support the importance of explicit environments. Fauconnier's [29] mental space theory used environment-like entities to explore a number of the same issues as in this and previous articles, from a linguisitic perspective. Although Fauconnier's account was not procedural in nature, there are certainly analogies between our default-ascription mechanism and his notion of "maximizing similarity" in a belief space, using notions like "in the absence of explicit contrary stipulation," and so on. This is very similar to our own statements of the default rule [e.g., 69], although it does not capture the sort of work we have described here and elsewhere on the strong limitations to the applicability of that rule in conditions of atypical belief [5, 8, 65]. The main point to note is that Fauconnier made great headway with difficult issues such as counterfactuals, presuppositions, and ambiguities of propositional attitude reports by applying an environment-like "mental space" idea.

Of similar relevance is Johnson-Laird's [36] use of explicit, nested groups of representational items in an application of his mental-model theory of human commonsense reasoning to propositional attitudes. In a different vein, there is a growing amount of work emanating from the modal-logic tradition that is bringing in notions of belief clusters to make the belief logics more accurately reflect commonsense views of belief. See, for example, Fagin and Halpern's [26] local reasoning logic. It is, however, strange that in this logic it is only in the *semantics* that any notion of clusters is made at all explicit, as "frames of mind." What is important for *reasoning processes* is, of course, clustering made explicit in the representational expressions.

The propositions in John's Reagan environment are not necessarily the ones (about Reagan) that John is aware of, in any sense of "aware" that is closely linked to the ordinary notion of conscious awareness. We are reacting here against the use of the term "awareness" in Fagin and Halpern [26]. The propositions in a belief environment have no necessary relationship to "explicit beliefs" as used by, say, Levesque [40], because no clear idea is given, by authors using the term, of exactly what explicitness is meant to capture. However, insofar as other authors' explicit-belief notions seem to get at the idea of beliefs agents actually use in reasoning, those notions are exactly our notion of propositions within a belief environment. Our orientation is different, though: We are not interested in massaging modal logic so as to give an appropriate deductive logic of explicit and implicit belief, but rather in devising plausible commonsense-reasoning mechanisms for constructing the explicit-belief sets in the first place.

9.4 Extensions to ViewGen: The Belief Engine Firing on all Cylinders

This section reports progress on two extensions to the ViewGen approach: relevance and intensional object identification. Both of these are complex issues that we have not fully resolved, but we can say enough about them to illuminate various other considerations in this article. The relevance subsection gives an idea of the envisaged complexity of relevance determination, and this complexity was appealed to in the earlier section justifying the use of explicit environments. The intensional identification subsection, together with a later section on metaphor, supports the notion that intensional identification, belief ascription, and metaphoric information transfer are three corners of one hat.

It should be noted that, in what follows, we make no firm distinction between beliefs about meaning and beliefs about matters of fact. Hence,

John believes Thalassemia is a province of Greece

reports just another belief (false in this case). Representational consequences follow from this such as that word meanings should also be considered propositional in form, so that they, too, can take part in all the belief-ascription processes we describe. That is no more shocking than noticing that conventional frame representations of meaning can easily be considered to consist of propositions like *Animate(human)*, as can any standard form of net representation, linked by set membership and inclusion arcs. And such propositions are clearly about meaning, in some sense, since the fact that humans are animate is hardly a fact about the physical world. As will be seen in Section 9.7, in treating metaphor we cannot separate issues of fact and meaning.

There would be a considerable philosophical trade-off if we could do away with this conventional distinction: (1) a Quinean one (in the sense of wanting to substitute talk about beliefs and sentences for talk about word meaning; [52]) where we let the representation of meaning be a function of belief representation, even though this is the inverse of the conventional view; and (2) neo-Quinean, in the sense of aligning ourselves with some current AI-oriented philosophers (e.g., Schiffer, at least in 1972, if not now) who have adopted the view that a self-contained theory of meaning is vacuous, and that such a theory cannot be had independently of a theory of belief and action.

9.4.1 Relevance

An ascriptional reasoning system must address the issue of relevance simply because, in ascribing a belief or other attitude to an agent, a system should seek to ensure that the belief is relevant to the discourse interpretation needs of the moment.

This can involve considerable complexity for a variety of reasons, as will be seen later. Relevance is a complex, variegated notion that has received intense study in its own right, for instance in formal logic [e.g, [2]], discourse theory [30, 59, 63], AI problem solving [60], and elsewhere closer to the present work [57, 46]. Our general strategy, at present, is to seek simple, powerful heuristics that will provide a useful basis for the environment-generation processes that are our current focus.

In the following, we consider the fate of a proposition, P, entering the system through the interpretation of natural language input. We assume this proposition is to be taken as a belief of some agent, A. We consider the question of whether the proposition should be inserted into a topic environment E, for some topic T, within A's viewpoint, because of being construed as being relevant to T. We assume that, initially, P is placed at the top level within A's viewpoint, that is, not inside any particular topic environment. Notice that if P is placed inside E, it may later be a candidate for pushing into some other environment, and so on.

The overarching strategic question about the role of relevance in our system is about *when* relevance determination is done: To what extent should the determination be "zealous" or "lazy"? A totally zealous approach would consider inserting P in E as soon as P arrives. A totally lazy approach would leave all relevance to be determined on demand; that is, during the course of reasoning about A's view of T, certain beliefs in A's viewpoint (but outside E) would be determined to have become relevant, and therefore to have become candidates for pushing into E.

Our approach will be zealous at least to the extent of having a basic rule which zealously deems as relevant those propositions that explicitly mention the topic. Thus, if T is John, then the proposition **seriously-ill(wife-of(John))** is relevant. This explicit-mention rule has been the basis of our initial approach to relevance. The presently reported extensions will only account for a limited portion of the full relevance capability that a complete environment-generating system should have. However, they present interesting and significant problems in themselves. A significant problem to be addressed is that of deciding what other manageable and useful types of zeal should be added.

One source for additional zeal is equality statements. Suppose T is John, E contains a proposition stating that John is Peter's father, and P says that Peter's father is seriously ill. Then, surely, P is relevant to John and is a candidate for being pushed into E zealously, just as much as the proposition stating directly that *John* is seriously ill would be.

Another possible addition of zeal involves inheritance down taxonomic links. Suppose again that John is the topic. Let E state that John is a (medical) patient, and let P say that patients are afraid of the disease thalassemia. Should P be deemed relevant zealously? We suggest that (usually) it should not be, because of the possibly large number of general propositions about patients (and superordinate categories). On the other hand, if the topic were a joint one involving patients in general, as well as John, then P would stand to be deemed relevant anyway, simply by the basic explicit-mention rule. In this specific example we could also consider the possibility of P's being marked as medical expertise, so that it would only be deemed relevant if the agent A in whose viewpoint E lies was believed to be expert on medical matters. Such attention to agent-relative extent of expertise is a feature of the current ViewGen program.

A special case of the taxonomic issue is when, instead of a proposition like the above P—saying patients are afraid of thalassemia—we consider a proposition P that is itself taken to be taxonomic, such as one saying that patients are clients. It may be that such taxonomic information indirectly related to the given topic (John) should be zealously deemed as relevant. The question of how zealously the relevance processing should traverse taxonomic chains is a matter we are investigating.

Inheritance down taxonomies is traditionally concerned with *(quasi-) universal* statements about categories of objects, for example, *all* (or *most*) patients are afraid of thalassemia. However, *existential* statements about categories could also come into play in the relevance issue. Consider a proposition P saying that *some patient or other* in a particular hospital ward is afraid of thalassemia, and suppose John is held to be in that ward. Then P is, in principle, relevant to John (though it need not zealously be deemed to be), because it lends a nontrivial amount of support to the hypothesis that John is afraid of thalassemia. Separate work on *belief convictions* [7] will eventually allow investigation of existential statements.

9.4.2 Intensional Objects and Their Identification

It is natural in a system of partitioned environment notation to treat environments as intensional objects: to treat the Jim-object, pushed down into the Frank-object, as not just yielding by computation an environment that is Frank's-view-of-Jim, but also as a sort of intensional object we might call Jim-for-Frank.[4] Consider now two simple cases of intensional objects to see how the basic default algorithm deals with them:

Case 1 (or Two-for-me-one-for-you): The system believes that Frank and Jim's father are two people, but that Mary, whose point of view is being computed, believes them to be the same person.

Case 2 (or One-for-me-two-for-you): Mary believes Frank and Jim's father to be separate people, whereas the system believes them to be the same individual.

Scenarios such as these are common, and arise over such mundane matters as believing or not believing that John's house is the same as the house-on-the-corner-of-X-and-Y-streets.

---

[4] The names and descriptions attached to environments correspond to the names and descriptions in play in constituent propositions, but we should resist any tendency to think of the environments as being a meaning or referent of the expressions they are named for. The environment names, as far as their meanings go, are simply derivative: dependent, in the best Fregean tradition, on whatever meanings the environment names are assigned on the basis of their participation in the (contained) propositions.

9.4.2.1 Two-for-me-one-for-you

Processing of the first case will begin with the system having three topic environments: for Frank, Jim's father, and Mary. Two questions that arise are: What intensional object(s) (i.e., environments) should Mary's viewpoint contain? And what should be the beliefs about those intensional objects? Let us say that the system has beliefs about Frank and Jim's father as shown in Figure 9.7.

The first question can be rephrased as "given certain intensional objects in one viewpoint (the system, in this case), what are the corresponding intensional objects in the system's version of another viewpoint (Mary's)?" Extending the normal default rule for belief ascription to cope with intensional object ascription, we would say, naturally enough, that intensional objects in one environment directly correspond to identically named (or described) intensional objects in another environment, *unless there is counter evidence to believing this.* This notion of correspondence of intensional objects between environments can be expressed as beliefs, but these beliefs must be of a different type from those previously discussed.

There are two reasons for this: (a) they are beliefs about *intensional (mental) objects*[5] that (b) express the believed relationship between intensional objects in one space and intensional objects in another space. We represent such beliefs by a predicate called *co-ref.* An occurrence of such a predicate, in an environment about an agent (say, agent X), indicates a correspondence between certain objects in the belief space of the agent (say agent Y) holding the beliefs about agent X,

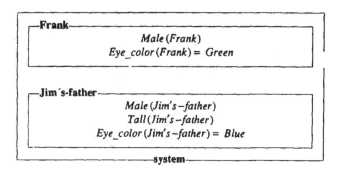

Fig. 9.7. System beliefs about Frank and Jim's-father.

---

[5] Beliefs about co-reference are special. Consider the following belief: "John Believes tall(Mike)." This belief expresses that John believes about *the person Mike,* that he is tall. However, the belief "John believes co-ref(Mike, Jim's-father)" expresses a relationship between two intensional descriptions, *not the things of which they are a description.*

and objects in agent X's belief space. The predicate expresses that the intensional object mentioned for the first person, correspond (as a set) to the intensional objects mentioned for the second person. We are only interested (here) in one-to-one, one-to-many, and many-to-one correspondences. Note that (by default) we assume a one-to-one correspondence. In Section 9.4.3, we discuss the relationship of co-ref to the more standard "equality" predicate. It should be noted that the correspondence of intensional objects between belief spaces was discussed previously by Fauconnier [29], Maida [43,44] Wiebe and Rapaport [61], and Ballim [5].

In the case at hand (Case 1), Mary's viewpoint ends up containing a single intensional object O (a topic environment) corresponding both to the system's Frank object (topic environment) and to the system's Jim's-father object (topic environment). The question now is to decide what should be put inside the environment O. One possibility is to combine the information in the system's Frank and Jim's-father objects *symmetrically*, removing any conflicting information. In the present case, this would result in O stating that Frank/Jim's father is male and tall, but stating neither that he has blue eyes nor that he has green eyes. However, we claim that *in realistic situations it will often be more appropriate to take an asymmetrical view*, in which we choose to give precedence either (a) to the information in the system's Frank object over the information in the system's Jim's-father object, or (b) vice versa. Choice (a) reflects the presumption that there is a stronger or closer correspondence between Mary's idea of Frank and the system's idea of Frank than there is between her idea of Frank and the system's idea of Jim's father. This difference of closeness would be plausible, for instance, if the system regarded Mary's view of Frank as being essentially the same as its own except in making the (presumed) mistake of taking Frank to have the property of being Jim's father. Choice (b) reflects the converse presumption, which would be most likely to arise from a hypothesis that Mary is focussing on the person-description "father of Jim," and that she happens to hold that this description identifies Frank. Our claim is that in realistic situations there is more likely to be a reason for making one of these choices than for taking the symmetrical approach.

As an example of such asymmetrical situations arising in discourse, consider the following fragment, in which the boy referred to is Jim.

> Mary was listening to what Frank was saying to the boy. It led her to
> conclude that he was the boy's father.

With reasonable assumptions about the discourse context, it would be apparent that Mary, to some degree, was already knowledgeable about Frank, and was adding to her knowledge the notion that he was the boy's father. This corresponds to asymmetry choice (a) above. To see the potential force of this asymmetry, suppose that the system takes the boy's father to be German, but Frank, American. Then, the asymmetry we are proposing makes the system take the reasonable course of ascribing the "American belief" to Mary, rather than the "German belief." On the other hand, consider the following fragment.

Mary had met Jim's father on several occasions, although he had never told
her his name. Under the mistaken impression that he was Frank Timson,
she...

It is plausible in this case that Mary was in some respects knowledgeable about
the person she thought of as the boy's father, and was augmenting her knowledge
with the proposition that this person was Frank. This corresponds to asymmetry
choice (b) above. If, again, the system takes Frank to be American, and Jim's father
to be German, the asymmetry leads to the reasonable ascription of the "German
belief" to Mary.

With either choice of asymmetry, what happens can be affected by the presence
of beliefs, that, on the basis of other evidence, the system takes Mary to have
had. For instance, if, in the case of asymmetry choice (b), the system has already
decided that Mary believed Frank Timson was French, then the imposition of the
intensional identification in question should not generally lead to the system going
back on its decision. That is, the "French belief" blocks the ascription of both the
"American belief" and the "German belief."

The influences on choices of ascription in such examples are more complex
than is implied by this brief discussion, but the examples serve to suggest that
asymmetry in a particular direction will be well-motivated in many realistic
examples.

We handle the asymmetrical choices as follows. For choice (a), the system
constructs an intensional object O called "Frank-as-Jim's-father" inside Mary's
viewpoint.[6] This object is so-called because it is, so to speak, "the Jim's-father view
of Frank" (according to Mary). Notice that this phrase does *not* say that the object
is the view of Frank that Jim's father *holds* (according to Mary); rather, the object
is a view of Frank that is colored by the idea that he is Jim's father. This way of
regarding Mary's intensional object O is directly reflected in the proposed process
for constructing O, as will be seen in a moment. Mary's Frank-as-Jim's-father
object, O, arises in two stages, as follows (see Figure 9.8).

Stage 1: The *system's* view of Frank as Jim's father is created. This view is created
as a topic environment O' inside the system's viewpoint. The creation occurs in
three substages:

1a. Initially, a copy of the system's Frank object (topic environment) is placed
   inside the Jim's-father object (topic environment). Intuitively, the idea so far
   is that we have not yet tried to identify Frank as Jim's father, but have merely
   established a view of Frank that is, so to speak, in the context of Jim's father.
   That context does not have an effect until Substage 1b.

1b. We now respect the required identification of Frank as Jim's father. We try to
   push the beliefs in the system's Jim's-father object *inwards* into the Frank object
   embedded within it, *using the ordinary default rule*, with the slight modification
   that *Jim's father* is replaced by *Frank* in a pushed belief. Thus, the beliefs that

---

[6] There may already be such an object, as we note later.

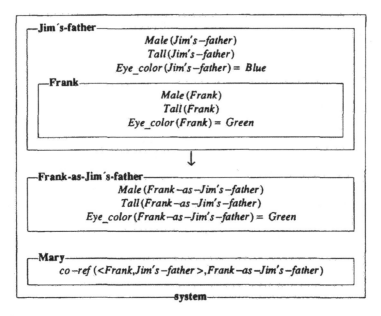

Fig. 9.8. Forming the Frank-as-Jim's-father environment.

Jim's father is male and is tall are successfully pushed *inwards* (although the former happens to duplicate a belief already in the embedded-Frank object), but the belief that Jim's father has blue eyes is blocked by the green-eye belief already in the embedded-Frank object.

1c. The final substage in constructing the system's Frank-as-Jim's-father object O' is to pull out the Frank object that is embedded within the Jim's-father object, making it into an object (topic environment) O' at top level within the system's viewpoint. In doing this we replace the "Frank" topic-name by the name "Frank-as-Jim's-father," and similarly change the *Frank* symbols inside the environment to *Frank-as-Jim's-father*. The diagram in Figure 9.8 shows the result, with the arrow notation indicating the pull-out process.

Stage 2: We now ascribe the system's beliefs about Frank as Jim's father, that is, the beliefs inside O', to Mary, *once again using the ordinary default rule*. On the assumption that there is no prior information about Mary's view of Frank/Jim's father (e.g., that his eyes are brown), all that will happen is that a copy O of O' will be created inside the Mary viewpoint, giving the revised Mary viewpoint shown in Figure 9.9. If we had had prior information from discourse input that Mary believes the person's eyes to be brown, then there would already have been a Frank-as-Jim's-father object (topic environment) O inside Mary's viewpoint, and the beliefs in O' would all have been pushed into that object except for the green-eye belief.

If the sytem had decided to give precedence to the Jim's-father information rather than to the Frank information in doing the intensional identification (that is, if it had

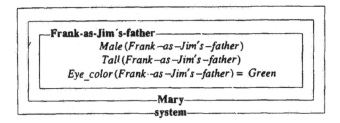

Fig. 9.9. Ascribing the new environment to Mary.

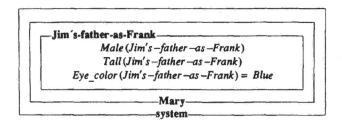

Fig. 9.10. Analogous ascription, with precedence to Jim's father.

made choice (b) above) then it would have generated the state shown in Figure 9.10 by an analogous process.

It might be thought that a symmetric intensional object, with the feature differences appearing as disjunctions (e.g., Eye_color Blue OR Green) would be appropriate as a construct for the Mary environment. We suggest that this is, in fact, psychologically less plausible, and that subjects do construct stronger, and more refutable, hypotheses.

An important thing to notice about the process just described is that the crucial pushing of information from the Jim's-father environment into the embedded-Frank environment (or vice versa) is exactly the type of "inward" pushing used in a particular class of examples with which we illustrated basic belief ascription in Section 9.2. That was the class where the topic was identical to the believer to whom beliefs were being ascribed. In Sections 9.5 and 9.7, we seek to show that belief ascription (e.g., Jim's-father's-view-of-Frank), intensional identification (e.g., Frank-as-Jim's-father), and even metaphor are all different forms of a single fundamental computational process.

The issue of relevance, in the sense discussed in the earlier section, interacts with that of intensional identification in at least two ways. First, if, in the previous example touching upon the ascription of a German or American nationality belief to Mary, it so happened that nationality was irrelevant to the current concerns of the discourse-understanding process, then there would be no need even to address the conflict between nationalities of Frank and Jim's father. This elementary point underscores the importance of devising a good treatment of relevance.

The second point is more complex and remains a matter for further investigation, hinging as it does on the degree of zealousness adopted in dealing with inheritance of potentially relevant information down taxonomic links. We touched upon this type of zealousness in our earlier discussion of relevance. Consider again the choice (b) case of a Frank/Jim's-father situation. Under choice (b), precedence is asymmetrically given to the system's Jim's-father object. Suppose that the system believes that fathers are usually responsible citizens and there is nothing in the system's beliefs about Jim's father that suggests that he is an exception, but on the other hand the system believes that Frank is not a responsible citizen. Assume also that societal attributes are in focus during the discourse understanding. If the system acted zealously with regard to inheritance, it would adopt the explicit belief that Jim's father is a responsible citizen. The system would then ascribe to Mary the belief that Frank/Jim's father is a responsible citizen because of the choice (b) asymmetry.

However, one might argue that intensional identification using specific beliefs, such as that Frank is not a responsible citizen, should be done first, and only then should inheritable defaults be considered. In this example, the belief just mentioned about Frank would be ascribed to Mary, because there would be nothing in the system's beliefs about Jim's father to block it; and, if the system *now* did inheritance, the possible belief that Jim's father is a responsible citizen would no longer be ascribable to Mary.

Under the latter procedure the system could still have proceeded zealously, as long as it had marked its beliefs that Jim's father was a responsible citizen as having been derived by inheritance. It could therefore have been barred from taking part in the specific-belief part of the intensional identification. We suspect that a full treatment of intensional identification will have to pay careful attention to the different types of origin of beliefs.

9.4.2.2 One-for-me-two-for-you

In the second case, where the system believes in one individual but Mary two, the natural computation of Mary's view either of Frank or Jim's father is simply to push the system's single representation, changing "Frank" to "Jim's father" as necessary. This is shown in Figure 9.11.

These are not merely aliases, but are best thought of as dual ascriptions, performed by making two identical copies. Further information about Mary's beliefs would then presumably cause the contents of the two environments to differ, because she presumably has at least some differing beliefs about what she believes to be distinct individuals.

9.4.2.3 Discussion

Neither Case 1 nor Case 2 turns out to be particularly problematic, and the situation is no different if the entities about whose identity there is dispute are nonbelievers rather than believers. Those would be like the classic but natural cases such as

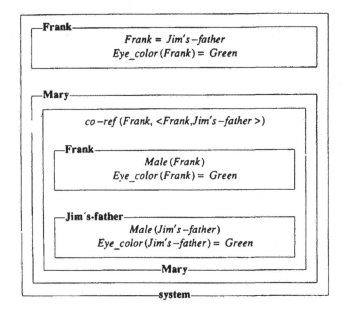

Fig. 9.11. Treatment of CASE 2 on the Frank/Jim's-father example.

a difference between dialogue participants as to whether Tegucigalpa and Capital-of-Honduras are, or are not, the same, or as to whether Rome or Avignon should be identified with City-of-the-Popes.

More difficult cases, which bring in all the panoply of philosophical distinction and discussion, are those conventionally discussed under the *de re/de dicto* distinction. One type is the following: The system reasonably believes Feynman to be a famous physicist but encounters Frank who, on the strength of a single appearance on the TV screen, believes Feynman to be a famous TV performer. For the sake of this example, it is essential to accept that the two occupations are incompatible. Suppose the discussion now forces the system to construct its view of Frank's view of Feynman. Now, there will be no point at all in performing that computation unless the system believes Frank's beliefs to be *de re*. Frank no doubt considers his own beliefs *de re*, as we all do. The crucial thing is that the system believe this, and the test would be some proposition in the Frank environment, and ABOUT Frank, equivalent to *("Feynman" names Feynman)*. If that is not present, the system should infer that Frank has another person in mind: that his beliefs are *de dicto* FOR THE SYSTEM, and hence any push-down computation would be pointless.

Consider the relation of this example to the former, simpler cases, where the system can identify or separate distinct environments. This last case would be similar if the system knew which non-Feynman individual Frank was confusing Feynman with, perhaps Johnny Carson. In that case, the system could perform a push down, even though it believed Frank's beliefs to be *de dicto* as far as Feynman was concerned, for they would be *de re* with respect to Johnny Carson. The system could then push Carson into Frank, while changing the resulting environment's name to "Feynman." To summarize, the absence of *("Feynman" names Feynman)* in the Frank environment is only a reason for not pushing down Feynman, but leaves open the possibility of some other *de re* push down.

9.4.3 Co-reference versus Equality

A special point about intensional identification (and relevance) arises from the issue of equality versus co-reference, where the former is the deeming of referents as identical and the latter the deeming of (different) intensional descriptions as co-referential. Our use of environments corresponds naturally to the use of intensional entities deemed co-referential, and hence, to the implicit use of a co-reference (rather than equality) operator. In that sense our assumptions are very like those of the CASSIE group [45, 58] except that we see no need to make any strong claim, as they do, that only co-reference will ever be used, and that all entities in the system are intensional. The crucial point in our system is that the environment notation moves, as it were, the belief predicate, at any level of nesting, out to the environment boundary or partition, and so, within an environment, we have *precisely the conditions of a belief space that sanction substitution of co-referents without problems,* as in the *de dicto/re* examples above.

The use of co-reference statements linking terms denoting intensions, as in **co-ref (Father-Of(Peter), Boss-Of(Jim))**, has a well-known advantage over the use of equality statements linking the corresponding ordinary terms, for example, **father-of(peter) = boss-of(jim)**.[7] The advantage is that the co-reference statements allow more controlled separation of inference about a thing under different descriptions than the equality statements do; and the separation gives us, in turn, an extra, *explicit* handle on relevance (Section 9.4.1). Since co-reference statements do not sanction substitution in the way that equality statements do, we could have the expression **Strict-Boss(Boss-Of(Jim))** without being automatically tempted to produce the expression **Strict-Boss(Father-Of(Peter))**. (**Strict-Boss** is a function that takes a person-concept and delivers a concept of that person being a strict boss.)

We could view all this as having special axioms that sanction co-reference-based substitutions only under certain conditions, rather than having to adopt a nonstandard meaning for the equality predicate or having knowledge-intensive, behind-the-scenes heuristics that limit the application of equality-based reasoning. For instance, we could have an axiom schema of the (very rough) form:

$$P(T) \text{ and co-ref}(T, U) \text{ and } C - P(U)$$

---

[7] Here we are appealing to the notation of Creary [23], where the noncapitalized symbols denote ordinary subjects, functions and predicates in the domain, whereas the capitalized symbols denote intensional objects and functions. For instance, **Boss-Of** is a function that takes a person-concept and delivers a concept of that person's boss as such.

provided that: *P* is an "intensional predicate" in a domain *D*1, *T* is an intensional term describing something using the resources of *D*1, *U* is an intensional term describing something using the resources of some domain *D*2, and *C* is a formula stating that the system is currently considering cross-inferences between *D*1 and *D*2.

If *D*1 and *D*2 are the employment and family domains respectively, then an example of *P*, *T* and *U* could be **Strict-Boss, Boss-Of(Jim)**, and **Father-Of(Peter)**. What we would need behind the scenes is a single heuristic giving lower priority to equality-based reasoning than to co-reference-based reasoning.

However, there is no need for such an axiom schema if we know our inferences are limited to the appropriate environments; that is precisely what our partitioning provides, as, in principle, do all systems that look back to [31] partitioned networks, although his work, of course, provided no analogue of belief ascription.

9.5 Metaphor: Shifting the Belief Engine to a Higher Gear

Metaphor is normally explicated, formally or computationally, by some process that transfers properties by some structural mapping from one structure (the vehicle) to another (the tenor). A classic example in AI would be the work of Falkenhainer, Forbus and Gentner [27], and Indurkhya [34]. All these authors were concerned, as we are, with metaphor and analogy viewed as some form of structural mapping; the difference between what they offered and what we offer here is the linkage between that process and those of intensional identification and belief ascription. Some would object here about the issue of transferring properties versus transferring structure, but we shall not enter this argument here because, although the following examples transfer properties within propositional beliefs, it will be clear from the discussion in Section 9.7 that we consider our current representation inadequate and only illustrative, and that a fuller representation would display mapping of more complex structures. Again, in this section we shall play fast and loose with the metaphor versus metonymy and the metaphor versus analogy distinctions. For our purposes here, those distinctions affect nothing.

We are exploring the possibility of applying our basic belief algorithm to metaphor, as an experiment, to see if it gives insight into the phenomenon. That should not be as surprising as it may sound: Metaphor has often been viewed, in traditional approaches, as "seeing one thing as something else," a matter of viewpoints, just as we are presenting belief. We propose that propositions in the topic environment for the vehicle of a metaphor be "pushed inward" (using the standard algorithm, presented before), into an embedded environment for the tenor, to get the tenor seen through the vehicle, or the view of the tenor-as-vehicle. This process was already described in Section 9.4.2 on intensional identity.

The key features here are:

1. One of the conceptual domains is viewed as a "pseudobeliever".
2. The pseudobeliever has a metaphorical view of a topic or domain.
3. The generation of such a view is not dissimilar from ascribing beliefs by real believers.

4. Explicating this by pushing or amalgamating environments yields new intensional entities after an actual transfer of properties.

So, in the classic historical case of atom-as-billiard-ball, given the environments for atom and billiard ball as shown in Figure 9.12, we generate the environment for atoms as billiard balls as follows. The environment for atoms is nested within the environment for billiard balls, and then the contents of the billiard ball environment are pushed down into the nested-atom environment, replacing the term "billiard ball" by "atom" wherever it occurs in propositions being pushed. The overriding of properties would follow in the same way as for standard beliefs: For example, **Light(atom)** overrides the incoming **Heavy(billiard ball)**. However, **Round(billiard ball)** would survive as the property **Round(atom)**—correctly for the original analogy—because there would be no preexisting shape property in the system's belief set for atoms. Then, the nested-atom environment is pulled out to form a new environment "atom-as-billiard-ball," replacing such occurrence of "atom" with "atom-as-billiard-ball." This new environment is the metaphoric view of atoms as billiard balls. Figure 9.13 uses an arrow, as before, to illustrate the process. Similarly, in

Jones threatened Smith's theory by reimplementing his experiments.

we would know we had a preference-breaking, and potentially metaphorical, situation from the object-feature failure on "threaten" (which expects a person object). Or, rather, Wilks [62] argued that metaphors could be identified, procedurally at least, with the class of preference-breaking utterances (where, in a wide sense, assertions relating two generic classes, as in "An atom is a billiard ball" or "Man is an animal," can be preference breaking). The awkward cases for that broad delimitation are forms like "Connors killed McEnroe," which breaks no verb preferences but is read metaphorically by some as "beat soundly at tennis." Here, one might consider taking the classic Marcus escape and using our procedural definition to rule this example out of court as a "garden-path metaphor." However, as we shall see in later discussion (Section 9.7), there is a deeper way in which preferences and metaphor are linked.

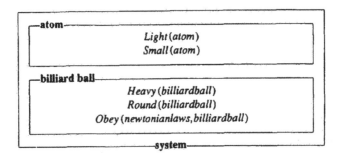

Fig. 9.12. System beliefs about atoms and billiard balls.

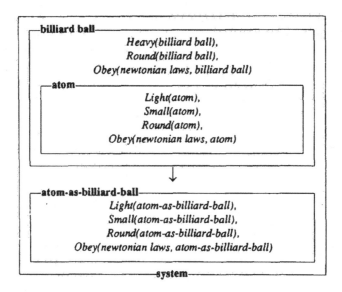

Fig. 9.13. Forming the atom-as-billiard-ball environment.

We could now plausibly form a metaphoric view of theory-as-person using the same process as above, and using the assumption that the basic preferences of the concept "threaten" [62] are for a person as agent and as object (if that is not accepted, a metaphorical push down can begin from whatever such preferences an objector would be prepared to assign to the action.) Figure 9.14 shows possible system environments for theory and person, and the resulting theory-as-person environment.

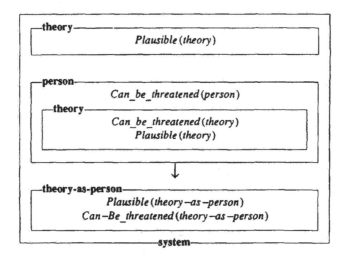

Fig. 9.14. Forming a theory-as-person environment.

By this maneuver, a new and complex metaphorical property of theories is derived. It might be, of course, that this procedure of belief overriding as a basis for metaphor would produce no different a set of plausible properties transferred than any other system [e.g., 27]; that would be, again, an experimental question. But its importance or originality would lie in the fact that it was further application of an algorithm designed to explicate another phenomenon altogether (i.e., belief) and, therefore, yield a procedural connection between the notions, one that has other intellectual justifications, as will be shown in a moment.

In principle, the method should extend to other phenomena widely considered to be metaphorical [22] but with a quite different grammatical basis, such as "rubber duck." Here, we can envisage the push down of environments (duck and rubber object), after which properties like animacy from the DUCK environment would be canceled by the pre-existing property (alias belief) "inanimate" within the RUBBER environment so that we did not end up with rubber ducks (alias rubber-as-a-duck) being animate. Cohen and Margalit argued that there could be no principled basis for property transfer in metaphor explication, but, in a sense, all computational accounts, including this one, consider this an empirical claim, one which AI researchers believe is false. Here, the principled basis would fall back on a relevance algorithm (see Section 9.4.1) supplemented by the default-belief algorithm. The intuitive support for what we propose comes from a deep connection between belief and metaphor: taking metaphor-as-false-belief [24] seriously, in that metaphors for a particular believer are just special beliefs, ones which can, of course, become more generally believed (e.g., Men are beasts! Women are cats!).

There is a further interesting aspect to the connection between belief and metaphor. We have stressed a procedural connection that may seem improbable to some people. There is also the important but neglected phenomenon of the content of belief being inherently metaphorical, and in a way that conventional theorists totally neglect by their concentration on simplistic belief examples like "John loves Mary." A far more plausible candidate might be a truth such as:

Prussia threatened France before invading it successfully in 1871.

What are we to say of this historically correct belief? What are the entities referred to by "Prussia" and "France"? Simple translation into some first-order expression like **Invade(Prussia, France, 1870)** just obscures the real problem, one for which the semantics of first-order logic are of no help at all. Are the entities referred to somehow metaphorically the Prussian people, or army, or a part of the army?

Following the approach described earlier, we might expect to detect breaking of linguistic preferences of the verb "threaten" and perform a trial push down of properties of the "people" environment (given by the conventional preferences of "threaten") into an environment for Prussia (= a land mass, the basic representation). An important safeguard, which there is no space to discuss here, would be that we examine our inventory of representations to see if we have one for "Prussia" that already expressed the (dead) metaphor of a country-name-as-a-polity (some would insist that this was a metonymy, but we decided not to make this a significant issue in this article).

The possibility of a metaphorical belief belonging to some agent other than the system itself underscores the benefits of our method of unifying metaphorical transference with belief ascription. Suppose that (according to the system) Bill has a certain metaphorical belief B, perhaps the Prussia/France one if we assume that it does indeed involve a country-as-person metaphor. Suppose, now, that the system takes Bill to attribute this belief B to Sally in the ordinary default way (subject to the check that, according to Bill, Sally is "qualified" to have beliefs about European history). Here we have a combination of metaphorical transference (from the person domain to the country domain) and belief ascription: A combination that could, of course, appear at any level of nesting of belief. These processes essentially work by the same mechanisms in our method. This obviates the need that would otherwise exist to create a suitable interface between mechanisms for belief ascription and (previously unrelated) mechanisms for metaphorical transference.

Furthermore, we may anticipate a point we make later about fuzziness of the distinction between intensional identification and metaphor. Our method allows the system to be neutral as to whether a belief B of an agent Bill is viewed *by him* as being metaphorical or not. If it is, then the environment manipulation involved in constructing, say, a country-as-person environment is consistent with the system taking Bill to be thinking metaphorically. On the other hand, if Bill does not regard B as metaphorical, then the same environment manipulation is consistent with the system taking Bill to be (partially) confusing the notion of a country with the notion of a person, and thus performing an intensional identification (albeit one between general concepts rather that concepts of individuals). With our method, there is simply no need for the system to have to adjudicate on whether Bill is engaged in metaphorical thinking or not.

Notice, finally, that in the environment-based processing of metaphor there is an asymmetry of available push down, much as with the construction of intensional entities in an earlier section. This asymmetric duality of metaphor is exactly that of the alternative treatments of:

My car drinks gasoline.

in Wilks [62], where one can consider the statement as being a car-as-drinker metaphor OR as a drinking-as-using metaphor, and only overall coherence with a database of cases and knowledge structures will tell one which is right. In that work, the model was not one of beliefs, but (in the spirit of its age) of framelike structures expressing dictionary information. But the underlying point is the same: Preference violations are the cues or triggers for metaphorical processes but do not settle which metaphor (depending on the directionality of the preferences) should establish itself in the context. That is a matter for other, more general inference processes and the coherence of what they produce. In the examples here, we have simplified the matter by considering only a single push down for each example.

9.6 Towards a General Theory of Speech Acts

Much work has been done in recent years in developing natural language processing (NLP) systems that interpret sentences in terms of speech acts[8] [1, 21, 49]. As noted earlier, the relation of our basic belief-ascription method to that work is that those authors assumed some partition of the beliefs needed for understanding into viewpoints and to any required depth of nesting. That is to say, they assumed those environments were already in existence as a database before speech-act computations were done. In our view, this is psychologically and computationally unrealistic and, for us, the creation and maintenance of nested viewpoints is the primary computational and theoretical task. Seen in that way, we are not so much building on their work as providing a foundation for it, by building a processing model of their key assumption.

Our approach can thus be seen as (a) a demand for more realistic complexity in belief-environment computation and, at the same time, (b) a reaction against the complexities of speech-act analysis in, for example, the work at the University of Toronto (and we believe that [50], made this latter move, too). If we treat belief less simplistically, we get a simpler treatment of speech acts as a reward. But our main assumption in treating speech acts is similar to that of the other approaches mentioned: We locate a belief environment, usually of the beliefs of the system about the beliefs of another agent about the system itself, within which reasoning is done so as to make sense of otherwise incomprehensible dialogue input. This most general assumption also serves to link the treatment of speech acts to that of metaphor: A belief environment is created that "makes sense" of otherwise anomalous input. However, by including speech acts in this article, we intend only this connection of ideas, and not that speech acts are phenomena that, like metaphor and intensional identification, can be seen as modeled by the same process as belief ascription.

As many commentators have pointed out, the construction of plans corresponding to speech acts on each occasion they are encountered is implausible. For example, it would be inefficient to work out that the surface interrogative:

Can you give me your departure time?

was a request *each time it was encountered*. In our view such "speech-act interpretation shifts," which do not undergo significant changes over time in a language, are best seen as stored, learned wholes.

All this is purely programmatic, but we are concerned here with establishing that speech acts are part of a family of notions, along with intensional identification, metaphor, and belief itself that are inseparably linked. It is not only that speech acts rest upon some belief calculus for their formal expression, but that speech-act phenomena themselves are not always separable from metaphor, say.

---

[8] See [3] and [55].

A real and interesting murder case in Britain in the 1950s concerned robbers called Craig and Bentley. Craig shot and killed a policeman on a roof, but was 16 and not hanged. Bentley was hanged for shouting at Craig "Let him have it." His (unsuccessful) defense at this trial was that he intended by those words that Craig should give the policeman the gun but was misunderstood. Guilt being (in theory) based on intention rather than causality, that was a reasonable defense, whether or not it was honest. It was part of his defense that he intended the literal meaning of the words and not the (conventionalized or dead) metaphor "shoot." Clearly, both alternatives admit of similar speech-act analysis, but the interesting issue relevant here is under what conditions the beliefs in an environment lean towards an interpretation of input as metaphorical (by some such methods as we have discussed) because that would be a determination prior to any determination of what speech act was in play.

9.7 The General Issue of Belief, Intensional Identification, and Metaphor

The goal of this article has been the application of notions derived for belief to the explication and modeling of intensional entities and metaphor understanding. In this section we recap our views both on this idea and on the other fundamental links between belief processing and metaphor. First, we summarize our views on the question of how, in our view, intensional identification fits with both belief ascription and metaphor.

9.7.1 Belief Ascription and Intensional Identification

Intensional identification intrinsically involves some sort of combination of two or more bodies of information, whether or not one follows our environment-based approach. We also claim that intensional identification is likely to have an asymmetrical quality as a matter of fact, and this makes the asymmetric aspect of belief ascription a plausible technique for constructing the intensional entities. In the Mary example, this might be because Mary's Frank/Jim's-father idea is likely to corres-pond more closely to one of our two person-ideas than to the other, and we might also expect there to be dialogue clues from which we could infer Mary's presumed direction of conflation. This is not to deny the possibility of more complex situations where there is no clear precedence, but the approach is a heuristically plausible one.

9.7.2 Intensional Identification and Metaphor

The identification of intensional objects A and B (done with bias towards A) is a matter of taking A as B. We hold that this "as" is the same as in taking a metaphorical target A as the vehicle B of the metaphor (e.g., atom as billiard ball). In both cases, one view is imposed upon another (information about B is imposed upon A). This correspondence does not amount to saying that there are no differences between typical intensional identification and typical "metaphorizing." Certainly, the latter is likely to involve more unusual, unexpected, or category-crossing impositions of information. Nevertheless, the two processes are similar, both conceptually and from the procedural point of view of the detailed computational processes taking place. Moreover, in cases where someone uses a phrase like "God the Father," we might not be able to say whether that was an example of the conflation of two (independent) intensional entities, or a metaphor. The method of this article suggests that, if the basic computational technique were the same for treating both, we would not have to decide that question.

9.7.3 Belief and Metaphor

Here we return to the core idea of this article, namely, that representational and processing notions derived for belief can usefully be applied to the explication and modeling of metaphor understanding. The core idea has a general force derived from the fact that metaphor has often, in the literature, been seen as a point-of-view phenomenon, or "seeing something as something else." But all that is very general support: The crucial idea here has been the application of a precise notion of computational belief ascription to metaphor, and transferring properties (expressed as believed propositions) by our standard algorithm in order to create a metaphorical point of view of an entity.

One type of analogy that can be drawn in mundane discourse is between different people's states of mind or belief frameworks. Consider, for instance, the discourse fragment "Bill is a chauvinist … John is like Bill." Assuming there is no interruption of coherence here, the reported analogy between John and Bill is one of belief framework. That is, chauvinist beliefs of Bill's can be trans-ferred (by default) to John. What we have here is straightforward belief ascription that is *also* a case of analogical tranference, which is essentially the same thing as metaphorical transference. This intersection provides considerable additional support to the basing of metaphorical transference on the extended belief-ascription mechanism.

However, we also wish to mention, although there is no space here to defend it fully, the force and generality of the converse notion: *Belief ascription, as a funda-mental psychological and computational process, is also logically and empirically dependent on metaphor.*

In one sense, that claim is trivial, because all computational approaches to propositional attitudes ultimately rest on underlying metaphors: Most commonly, metaphors that bring in the idea of "possible worlds" or "situations," or others that cast the mind as holding, possessing, or being otherwise related to abstract objects akin to natural language sentences or logical formulae. Our approach rests on a metaphor in the latter class, namely the mind-as-container metaphor, under which the minds and belief sets of others are seen as porous containers that can be nested like buckets or jars. This metaphor carries with it the explicit grouping idea emphasized in Section 9.3.

But we intend something much more general here, independent of any particular prevalent metaphor for the mind or belief states. First, consider the precept that, in plausibly hypothesizing what some agent X believes on some topic T, one proceeds largely by trying to ascribe one's own beliefs about T to X, perhaps failing to do so because of contrary beliefs about T one already knows X to have. What we are now suggesting is that this activity is very much like metaphorizing: the process of "ascribing" information from the metaphor vehicle to the tenor, perhaps failing to do so because of contrary existing tenor information that one wishes to preserve. Specifically, in a belief-ascription activity *one uses one's current belief state about the topic T as the vehicle of a metaphor, the target being the other agent's belief state*. In brief: One uses one's own state of mind as a metaphor for other people's. This has a general similarity to Maida's [43] view.

A second very general aspect of the dependence of belief processing on metaphor can be seen by considering the unexamined assumption we have made throughout this article, which is also one that virtually all AI researchers and logicians use for discussing beliefs: Beliefs can be conveniently expressed as simple propositions, which contain predicates, which unfortunately look like words, but, in fact (so the assumption goes), univocally denote entities that are concepts or world referents.

Everyone knows that this assumption, underlying all modern formal semantics as it does, is a claim of highly dubious content, and it is particularly so if we consider the fact—always cited in the research of (e.g.,[62]) on preference semantics—that many, if not most English sentences in real texts like newspapers, are preference breaking: That is to say, the concepts contained in them are used out of their dictionary-declared contexts of constraint, as in "Prussia attacked France." This is no more than a repetition of the now common observation that much normal discourse is "metaphorical" in a broad sense, but what is not so often concluded, as it must be, is that this has strong and destabilizing consequences for any formal semantic representation of language [35, 38], and for belief ascription in particular.

In the face of such observations, the notion of univocal predicates as the basis of formal representations of a natural language, freed from the contamination of languages like English, becomes hard to sustain, and the problem is in no way solved by allowing for non-univocality (i.e., indexing predicates for particular dictionary word senses; e.g., POST1 and meaning only a stick) because the ubiquity of metaphor or preference-breaking use suggests that a natural language is used normally and comprehensibly even when no such indexing to conventional senses can be done. And, it should not need adding, this difficulty is not alleviated at all by those who say things like "we do not use predicates, only axiomatic structures, or sets of n-tuples." To them, the answer is simply that the only way they have of knowing which set or axiom is which must be by means of the associated predicate name, and then the above problems return unsolved.

If we now return to our central theme and consider that those comprehensible sentences, containing non-sense-indexible metaphorical uses, are the stuff of beliefs also, and that they must also be ascribed by believer to believer, then what trust can we put in the sorts of naive representations used in this and every other article on the subject? The short answer is none, unless we can at least begin to see how to move to a notion of representation of meaning for belief ascription that also takes the metaphoricity of beliefs and language as basic.

At present, we can do little more than draw attention to this phenomenon, so that we cannot, in the future, be accused by our successors of more naivety than necessary. However, we believe we know where to look, and what other aspects of current research to draw into work on belief ascription. One essential for the future is to link the present work fundamentally to work on meaning that is both dictionary based and shows how to extend beyond that, so that new usages can be represented, usually within networks of associations as the basis of discrete senses [28, 71, 72]. Another essential is that the sorts of explorations we have carried out here on explicating the notion of metaphor via belief ascription be boot-strapped back into the belief-ascription process, so that we can ascribe a belief from believer A to believer B that "Smith attacked Jones's notion of continuity" in such a way as to assume that the metaphorical content of "attack" here also transfers from environment to environment (saving here the assumption that culturally similar believers may be assumed to have the same metaphorical processing mechanism, just as they do the same belief-ascription mechanism. But those assumptions, too, might have to be relaxed in certain situations). Such transfers are central to work by Barnden [14, 15, 16].

One interesting class of cases of this phenomenon will be those where a system believes that another believer has false (as opposed to metaphorical) beliefs about word meaning. To return to the believer who thinks Thalassemia is a province of Greece, he is confronted by the input phrase "The cure for Thalassemia." A system might predict that, faced with what should be a radical preference violation, the believer will give up and ask for help, and so the system might wait and see and make no ascriptions. But a plausible zealous strategy would be to ascribe the results of a metaphorical push down (based, in the system's own view, on wholly false beliefs about meaning). Anyone who considers this implausible should consider the locution, heard recently on American television, "The cure for Panama."

If we can escape from the basic representational assumption, made here and everywhere else (because it is so hard to think of anything else!) that the predicates in the (ascribed) representation for belief are sense-determinate in some simple denotational way, then the problem may be soluble, and require, as we noted, only some method of metaphor processing (by belief-like methods such as those we propose here) during the belief-ascription process.

An alternative, and lazier, possibility is that we move to a representational phase where we make no strong referential assumptions about the meanings of the predicates in beliefs ascribed from believer to believer (just as one can assume that if natural languages are very close, like Dutch and German, we may not need to sense-resolve words transferred between them, allowing the target understander to do the work). Then we could use a process like the metaphor processor described here only on demand, when required to push an interpretation below/beyond its metaphorical expression. This again is consistent with certain strong and plausible assumptions about human processing. Whichever of these alternatives is ultimately chosen, both require recognition of the intimate dependence of belief ascription on the metaphoricity of language and belief representations.

9.8 Conclusion

This article advocates a highly "pragmatic" approach to propositional attitudes. Rather than being concerned with traditional issues such as devising an elegant axiom set, satisfying semantics, or adequate proof procedure for a belief logic, we believe that concern should be focused on a commonsense plausible reasoning schema about propositional attitudes. In particular, we are interested in ascriptional reasoning about attitudes. We claim that for ascriptional reasoning, it is important to concentrate on environments: groups of propositions that can be manipulated as explicit units, rather than as implicit groups arising only behind the scenes.

Our main concern has been to demonstrate some of our reasons for thinking that belief processing and metaphorizing are strongly interdependent, and indeed very similar in some respects. The essence of metaphorizing is assimilable into a generalization of the environment-manipulation procedures we originally devised for handling ordinary belief ascription. Conversely, belief ascription is, in large measure, assimilable into metaphorizing, in that one's ascriptional activities use one's states of mind as metaphors for other people's states of mind. Moreover, Barnden [14, 16] argued that metaphors for the mind, which are commonly used by people in ordinary discourse, have to be given a central role in representational approaches to propositional attitudes. Our ViewGen work already observes this to a useful extent by adopting, via environments, the prevalent mind-as-container metaphor.

We have also presented our reasons for perceiving deep connections between intensional identification on the one hand, and both belief ascription and metaphorizing on the other. Part of our view is a claim about intensional identification being typically asymmetrical. A corollary of these connections is a strengthening of the bond between belief processing and metaphor. We are investigating the extension of our approach to deal with speech acts, and the incorporation of a sophisticated but heuristically restricted treatment of relevance. The expense of relevance processing is one reason for wanting to use explicit groupings of beliefs. Finally, we resist the possible objection that our linkage of belief to metaphor requires the problem of metaphor to be fully solved first: a huge task. Rather, research on metaphor to date can serve as a basis for useful progress with belief processing, and vice versa.

Acknowledgement

We are indebted to Gerald Gazdar, Brian Slator, Nigel Shadbolt, Dan Fass, Louise Guthrie, and Sylvia Candelaria de Ram for thoughtful discussions. The errors are, as always, our own.

References

[1] Allen, J.F., & Perrault, C.R. (1978). Participating in dialogue understanding via plan deduction. *Proceedings of the Second National Conference of the Canadian Society for Computational Studies of Intelligence.* Toronto, Canada.

[2] Anderson, A., & Belnap, J. (1975). *Entailment: The logic of relevance and necessity.* Princeton, NJ: Princeton University Press.

[3] Austin, J.L. (1962). *How to do things with words.* Oxford, England: Oxford University Press.

[4] Ballim, A. (1986). Generating points of view. In *Memoranda in computer and cognitive science* (Tech. Rep. No. MCCS-86-68). Las Cruces: New Mexico State University, Computing Research Laboratory.

[5] Ballim, A. (1987). The subjective ascription of belief to agents. In J. Hallam & C. Mellish (Eds.), *Advances in artificial intelligence.* Chichester, England: Wiley & Sons..

[6] Ballim, A. (1988a, July). A language for representing and reasoning with nested belief. *Proceedings of the First Annual Irish Conference on Artificial Intelligence and Cognitive Science.* Dublin, Ireland.

[7] Ballim, A. (1988b). *Belief convictions, quantification, and default reasoning.* Unpublished manuscript.

[8] Ballim A., & Wilks, Y. (in press). *Artificial believers.* Hillsdale, NJ: Erlbaum.

[9] Barnden, J.A. (1983). Intensions as such: An outline. *Proceedings of the 8th International Joint Conference on Artificial Intelligence* (pp. 347–353). Los Altos, CA: Morgan Kaufman.

[10] Barnden, J.A. (1986). Imputations and explications: Representational problems in treatments of propositional attitudes. *Cognitive Science, 10,* 319–364.

[11] Barnden, J.A. (1987a). Interpreting propositional attitude reports: Towards greater freedom and control. In B. du Boulay, D. Hogg, & L. Steels (Eds.), *Advances in artificial intelligence-II.* Amsterdam: Elsevier (North-Holland).

[12] Barnden, J.A. (1987b). Avoiding some unwarranted entailments between nested attitude reports. In *Memoranda in computer and cognitive science* (Tech. Rep. No. MCCS-87-113). Las Cruces: New Mexico State University, Computing Research Laboratory.

[13] Barnden, J.A. (1988). Propositional attitudes, commonsense reasoning, and metaphor. *Proceedings of the 10th Annual Conference of the Cognitive Science Society* (pp. 347–353). Hillsdale, NJ: Erlbaum.

[14] Barnden, J.A. (1989a). Towards a paradigm shift in belief representation methodology. *Journal of Experimental and Theoretical Artificial Intelligence, 1,* 131–161.

[15] Barnden, J.A. (1989b). Belief, metaphorically speaking. *Proceedings of the First International Conference on Principles of Knowledge Representation and Reasoning* (pp. 21–32). San Mateo, CA: Morgan Kaufmann.

[16] Barnden, J.A. (1990). Naive metaphysics: A metaphor-based approach to propositional attitude representation. In *Memoranda in computer and cognitive science* (Tech. Rep. No. MCCS-90-174). Las Cruces: New Mexico State University, Computing Research Laboratory.

[17] Carbonell, J.G. (1982). Metaphor: An inescapable phenomenon in natural language comprehension. In W. Lehnert & M. Ringle (Eds.), *Strategies for natural language processing.* Hillsdale, NJ: Erlbaum.

[18] Charniak, E. (1978). On the use of knowledge in language comprehension. *Artificial Intelligence, 11,* 225–265.

[19] Cohen, P., & Levesque, H. (1980). Speech acts and recognition of shared plans. *Proceedings of the Third Biennial Conference of the Canadian Society for Computational Studies in Intelligence* (pp. 263–271).

[20] Cohen, P., & Levesque, H. (1985). Speech acts and rationality. *Proceedings of the 23rd Annual Meeting of the Association for Computational Linguistics* (pp. 49–60). University of Chicago.

[21] Cohen, P.R., & Levesque, H.J. (1987, July). Intention = Choice + Commitment. *Proceedings of the Sixth National Conference on Artificial Intelligence*, 410–415. Seattle.

[22] Cohen, J., & Margalit, A. (1972). The role of inductive reasoning in the interpretation of metaphor. In D. Davidson & G. Harman (Eds.), *Semantics of natural language*. Dordrecht, Holland: Reidel.

[23] Creary, L.G. (1979). Propositional attitudes: Fregean representation and simulative reasoning. *Proceedings of the Sixth International Joint Conference on Artificial Intelligence* (pp. 176–181). Los Altos, CA: Morgan Kaufmann.

[24] Davidson, D. (1978). What metaphors mean. *Critical Inquiry, 5,* 31–48.

[25] Dinsmore, J. (1987). Mental spaces from a functional perspective. *Cognitive Science, 11,* 1–21.

[26] Fagin, R., & Halpern, J.Y. (1987). Belief, awareness and limited reasoning. *Artificial Intelligence, 34,* 39–76.

[27] Falkenhainer, B., Forbus, K., & Gentner, D. (1986). The structure-mapping engine. *Proceedings of the Fifth National Conference on Artificial Intelligence* (pp. 272–278). Los Altos, CA: Morgan Kaufmann.

[28] Fass, D.C. (1987). Collative semantics: An overview of the current Meta 5 program. In *Memoranda in computer and cognitive science* (Tech. Rep. No. MCCS-87-112). Las Cruces: New Mexico State University, Computing Research Laboratory.

[29] Fauconnier, G. (1985). *Mental spaces: Aspects of meaning construction in natural language*. Cambridge, MA: MIT Press.

[30] Grosz, B.J. (1977). The representation and use of focus in a system for understanding dialogs. *Proceedings of the Fifth International Joint Conference on Artificial Intelligence* (pp. 67–76). Los Altos, CA: Morgan Kaufmann.

[31] Hendrix, G.G. (1979). Encoding knowledge in partitioned networks. In N.V. Findler (Ed.), *Associative networks*. New York: Academic.

[32] Hobbs, J.R. (1983a). Metaphor interpretation as selective inferencing: Cognitive processes in understanding metaphor (Part 1). *Empirical Studies of the Arts, 1,* 17–33.

[33] Hobbs, J.R. (1983b). Metaphor interpretation as selective inferencing: Cognitive processes in understanding metaphor (Part 2). *Empirical Stuidies of the Arts, 1,* 125–141.

[34] Indurkhya, B. (1987). Approximate semantic transference: A computational theory of metaphor. *Cognitive Science, 11,* 445–480.

[35] Johnson, M. (1987). *The body in the mind*. Chicago: Chicago University Press.

[36] Johnson-Laird, J.N. (1983). *Mental models*. Cambridge, MA: Harvard University Press.

[37] Konolige, K. (1983). A deductive model of belief. *Proceedings of the Eighth International Joint Conference on Artificial Intelligence* (pp. 377–381). Los Altos, CA: Morgan Kaufmann.

[38] Lakoff, G. (1987). *Women, fire, and dangerous things: What categories reveal about the mind*. Chicago: University of Chicago Press.

[39] Lakoff, G., & Johnson, M. (1980). *Metaphors we live by*. Chicago: Chicago University Press.

[40] Levesque, H. (1984). A logic of implicit and explicit belief. *Proceedings of the Fourth National Conference on Artificial Intelligence* (pp. 198–202). Los Altos, CA: Morgan Kaufmann.

[41] Maida, A.S. (1983). Knowing intensional individuals. *Proceedings of the Eighth International Joint Conference on Artificial Intelligence* (pp. 382–384). Los Altos, CA: Morgan Kaufmann.

[42] Maida, A.S. (1984). Belief spaces: Foundations of a computational theory of belief (Tech. Rep. No. CS-84-22). University Park: Pennsylvania State University, Department of Computer Science.

[43] Maida, A.S. (1986). Introspection and reasoning about the beliefs of other agents. *Proceedings of the Eighth Annual Conference of the Cognitive Science Society* (pp. 187–195). Hillsdale, NJ: Erlbaum.

[44] Maida, A.S. (1988). A syntactic approach to mental correspondence. *Proceedings of the Canadian Society for Computational Studies of Artificial Intelligence* (pp. 53–58). Edmonton, Alberta.

[45] Maida, A.S., & Shapiro, S.C. (1982). Intensional concepts in propositional semantic networks. *Cognitive Science, 6,* 291–330.

[46] Martins, J., & Shapiro, S. (1988). A model for belief revision. *Artificial Intelligence, 35,* 25–79.

[47] McCarthy, J., & Hayes, P. (1969). Some philosophical problems from the standpoint of artificial intelligence. In B. Meltzer & D. Michie (Eds.), *Machine Intelligence 4.* Edinburgh, U.K.: Edinburgh University Press.

[48] Minsky, M. (1975). A framework for representing knowledge. In P.H. Winston (Ed.), *The psychology of computer vision.* New York: McGraw-Hill.

[49] Perrault, R. (1987). Invited presentation. *Meeting of the Association for Computational Linguistics.* Stanford, CA.

[50] Perrault, R. (1990). An application of default logic to speech act theory. In P. Cohen, J. Morgan, & M. Pollack (Eds.), *Plans and intentions in communication and discourse.* Cambridge, MA: MIT Press.

[51] Perrault, R., & Allen, J. (1980). A plan-based analysis of indirect speech acts. *American Journal of Computational Linguistics, 6,* 167–182.

[52] Quine, W.V.O. (1960). *Word and object.* Cambridge, MA: MIT Press.

[53] Rapaport, W. (1986). Logical foundations for belief representation. *Cognitive Science, 10,* 371–422.

[54] Schiffer, S. (1972). *Meaning.* Oxford, U.K.: Oxford University Press.

[55] Searle, J. (1969). *Speech acts, an essay in the philosophy of language.* Cambridge: Cambridge University Press.

[56] Shadbolt, N. (1983). Processing reference. *Journal of Semantics, 2,* 63–98.

[57] Shapiro, S. (1976). *The relevance of relevance.* Indiana University, Computer Science Department, Bloomington.

[58] Shapiro, S.C., & Rapaport, W.J. (1986). SNePS considered as a fully intensional propositional semantic network. *Proceedings of the Fifth National Conference on Artificial Intelligence* (pp. 278–283). Los Altos, CA: Morgan Kaufmann.

[59] Sperber, D., & Wilson, D. (1986). *Relevance, communication and cognition.* Oxford, England: Basil Blackwell.

[60] Subramanian, D., & Genesereth, M.R. (1987). The relevance of irrelevance. *Proceedings of the 10th International Joint Conference on Artificial Intelligence* (pp. 416–422). Los Altos, CA: Morgan Kaufmann.

[61] Wiebe, J., & Rapaport, W. (1986). Representing de re and de dicto belief reports in discourse and narrative. *Proceedings of IEEE, 74,* 1405–1413.

[62] Wilks, Y. (1977). Making preferences more active. *Artificial Intelligence, 8*, 75–97.

[63] Wilks, Y. (1986). Relevance and beliefs. In T. Myers, K. Brown, & B. McGonigle (Eds.), *Reasoning and discourse processes*. London: Academic.

[64] Wilks, Y. (1990). Models and theories in artificial intelligence. In D. Partridge & Y. Wilks (Eds.), *The foundations of artificial intelligence: A sourcebook*. Cambridge: Cambridge University Press.

[65] Wilks, Y., & Ballim, A. (1987). Multiple agents and the heuristic ascription of beliefs. *Proceedings of the 10th International Joint Conference on Artificial Intelligence* (pp. 118–124). Los Altos, CA: Morgan Kaufmann.

[66] Wilks, Y., & Ballim, A. (1988). Shifting the belief engine into higher gear. In T. O'Shea & V. Sgurev (Eds.), *Proceedings of the International Conference on AI Methodology and Systems Applications*. Amsterdam: Elsevier Publications.

[67] Wilks, Y., & Ballim, A. (1989a). Belief systems: Ascribing belief. In T. Christaller (Ed.), *Kunstliche intelligenz* (pp. 386–403). Berlin: Springer-Verlag.

[68] Wilks, Y., & Ballim, A. (1989b). The heuristic ascription of belief. In N.E. Sharkey (Ed.), *Models of cognition: A review of cognitive science* (pp. 1–23). Norwood, NJ: Ablex.

[69] Wilks, Y., & Bien, J. (1979). Speech acts and multiple environments. *Proceedings of the Sixth International Joint Conference on Artificial Intelligence* (pp. 968–970). Tokyo, Japan.

[70] Wilks, Y., & Bien, J. (1983). Beliefs, points of view, and multiple environments. *Cognitive Science, 8*, 120–146.

[71] Wilks, T., Fass, D., Guo, C-M., McDonald, J., Plate, T., & Slator, B. (1989). A tractable machine dictionary as a resource for computational semantics. In B.K. Boguraev & T. Briscoe (Eds.), *Computational lexicography for natural language processing*. Harlow, U.K.: Longmans.

[72] Wilks, Y., Fass, D., Guo, C-M., McDonald, J., Plate, T., & Slator, B. (in press). *Providing machine tractable dictionary tools*. In J. Pustejousky (Ed.), *Semantics and the lexicon*. Hingham, MA: Kluwer.

10

Stone Soup and the French Room

Yorick Wilks
University of Sheffield

Abstract: The paper argues that the IBM statistical approach to machine translation has done rather better after a few years than many sceptics believed it could. However, it is neither as novel as its proponents suggest nor is it making claims as clear and simple as they would have us believe. The performance of the purely statistical system (and we discuss what that phrase could mean) has not equaled the performance of SYSTRAN. More importantly, the system is now being shifted to a hybrid that incorporates much of the linguistic information that it was initially claimed by IBM would not be needed for MT. Hence, one might infer that its own proponents do not believe "pure" statistics sufficient for MT of a usable quality. In addition to real limits on the statistical method, there are also strong economic limits imposed by their methodology of data gathering. However, the paper concludes that the IBM group have done the field a great service in pushing these methods far further than before, and by reminding everyone of the virtues of empiricism in the field and the need for large scale gathering of data

10.1 History

Like connectionism, statistically-based machine translation is a theory one was brought up to believe had been firmly locked away in the attic, but here it is back in the living room. Unlike connectionism, it carries no psychological baggage, in that it seeks to explain nothing and cannot be attacked on grounds of its small scale as connectionist work has been. On the contrary that is how it attacks the rest of us.

> It is well known that Western Languages are 50% redundant. Experiment shows that if an average person guesses the successive words in a completely unknown sentence he has to be told only half of them. Experiment shows that this also applies to guessing the successive word-ideas in a foreign language. How can this fact be used in machine translation? [7].

Alas, that early article told us little by way of an answer and contained virtually no experiments or empirical work. Like IBM's approach it was essentially a continuation of the idea underlying Weaver's original memorandum on MT: that foreign languages were a code to be cracked. I display the quotation as a curiosity, to show that the idea itself is not new and was well known to those who laid the foundations of modern representational linguistics and AI.

255

K. Ahmad, C. Brewster and M. Stevenson (eds.), Words and Intelligence 1, 255–265.
© 2007 *Springer.*

I personally never believed Chomsky's arguments in 1957 against other theories than his own any more than I did what he was for: his attacks on statistical and behaviorist methods (as on every thing else, like phrase structure grammars) were always in terms of their failure to give explanations, and I will make no use of such arguments here, noting as I say that how much I resent IBM's use of "linguist" to describe everyone and anyone they are against. There is a great difference between linguistic theory in Chomsky's sense, as motivated entirely by the need to explain, and theories, whether linguistic/AI or whatever, as the basis of procedural, application-engineering-orientated accounts of language. The latter stress testability, procedures, coverage, recovery from error, non-standard language, metaphor, textual context, and the interface to general knowledge structures.

Like many in NLP and AI, I was brought up to oppose linguistic methods on exactly the grounds IBM do: their practitioners were uninterested in performance and success at MT in particular. Indeed, the IBM work to be described here has something in common with Chomsky's views, which formed the post-1957 definition of "linguist". It is clear from Chomsky's description of statistical and Skinnerian methods that he was not at all opposed to relevance/pragmatics/semantics-free methods – he advocated them in fact – it was only that, for Chomsky, the statistical methods advocated at the time were too simple a method to do what he wanted to do with transformational grammars. More recent developments in finite state (as in phrase structure) grammars have shown that Chomsky was simply wrong about the empirical coverage of simple mechanisms.

In the same vein he dismissed statistical theories of language on the ground that sentence pairs like:

$$\text{I saw a} \begin{cases} \text{the.} \\ \text{triangular whole.} \end{cases}$$

are equally unlikely but utterly different in that only the first is ungrammatical. It will be clear that the IBM approach discussed here is not in the least attacked by such an observation.

10.1.1 Is the Debate about Empiricism? No.

Anyone working in MT, by whatever method, must care about success, in so far as that is what defines the task. Given that, the published basis of the debate between rationalism and empiricism in MT is silly: we are all empiricists and, to a similar degree, we are all rationalists, in that we prefer certain methodologies to others and will lapse back to others only when our empiricism forces us to. That applies to both sides in this debate, a point I shall return to.

An important note before continuing: when I refer to IBM machine translation I mean only the systems referred to at the end by Brown et al. IBM as a whole supports many approaches to MT, including Mc Cord's [10] prolog-based symbolic approach, as well as symbolic systems in Germany and Japan.

10.1.2 Is the Debate about How we Evaluate MT? No.

In the same vein, I shall not, as some colleagues on my side of the argument would like, jump ship on standard evaluation techniques for MT and claim that only very special and sensitive techniques (usually machine-aided techniques to assist the translator) should in future be used to assess our approach.

MT evaluation is, for all its faults, probably in better shape than MT itself, and we should not change the referee when we happen not to like how part of the game is going. Machine-aided translation (MAT) may be fine stuff, but IBM's approach should be competed with head on by those who disagree with it. In any case, IBM's method could in principle provide, just as any other system could, the first draft translation for a translator to improve on line. The only argument against that is that IBM's would be a less useful first draft *if a user wanted to see why certain translation decisions had been taken*. It is a moot point how important that feature is. However, and this is a point Slocum among others has made many times, the evaluation of MT must in the end be economic not scientific. It is a technology and must give added value to a human task. The ALPAC report, it is often forgotten, was about the economics of contemporary MT, not about its scientific status: the report simply said that MT at that time was not competitive, quality for quality, with human translation.

SYSTRAN won that argument later by showing there was a market for the quality it produced at a given cost. We shall return to this point later, but I make it now because it is one that does tell, in the long run, on the side of those who want to emphasize MAT. But for now, and for any coming showdown between statistically and non-statistically based MT – where the latter will probably have to accept SYSTRAN as their champion for the moment, like it or not – we might as well accept existing "quasi-scientific" evaluation criteria, Cloze tests, test sets of sentences, improvement and acceptability judged by monolingual and bilingual judges, etc. None of us in this debate and this research community are competent to settle the economic battle of the future, decisive though it may be.

10.2 Arguments Not to Use Against IBM

There are other well known arguments that should not be used against IBM, such as that much natural language is mostly metaphorical and that applies to MT as much as any other NLP task and statistical methods cannot handle it. This is a weak but interesting argument: the awful fact is that IBM cannot even consider a category such as metaphorical use. Everything comes out in the wash, as it were, and it either translates or it does not and you cannot ask why. Much of their success rate of sentences translated acceptably is probably of metaphorical uses. There may be some residual use for this argument concerned with very low frequency types of deviance, as there is for very low frequency words themselves, but no one has yet stated this clearly or shown how their symbolic theory in fact gets such uses right (though many of us have theories of that). IBM resolutely deny the need of any such special theory, for *scale* is all that counts for them.

10.3 What is the State of Play Right Now?

Away with rumor and speculation; what is the true *state of play* at the moment? In recent reported but unpublished DARPA-supervised tests the IBM system CANDIDE did well, but significantly worse than SYSTRAN's French-English system over texts on which neither IBM nor SYSTRAN had trained. Moreover, CANDIDE had far higher standard deviations than SYSTRAN, which is to say that SYSTRAN was far more consistent in its quality (just as the control human trans-lators had the lowest standard deviations across differing texts). French-English is not one of SYSTRAN's best systems but this is still a significant result. It may be unpleasant for those in the symbolic camp, who are sure their own system could, or should, do better than SYSTRAN, to have to cling to it in this competition as the flagship of symbolic MT, but there it is. IBM have taken about 4 years to get to this point. French-English SYSTRAN was getting to about IBM's current levels after 3–4 years of work. IBM would reply that that they are an MT system factory, and could do the next language much faster. We shall return to this point.

10.4 What is the Distinctive Claim by IBM About How to Do MT?

We need to establish a ground zero on what the IBM system is: their rhetorical claim is (or perhaps was) that they are a pure statistical system, different from their competitors, glorying in the fact that they did not even need French speakers. By analogy with Searle's Chinese Room, one could call theirs a French Room position: MT without a glimmering of understanding or even knowing that French was the language they were working on! There is no space here for a detailed description of IBM's claims (see [2, 3]). In essence, the method is an adaptation of one that worked well for speech decoding [8].

The method establishes three components: (a) a trigram model of English sequences; (b) the same for French; (c) a model of quantitative correspondence of the parts of aligned sentences between French and English. The first two are established from very large monolingual corpora in the two languages, of the order of 100 million words, the third from a corpus of *aligned* sentences in a parallel French-English corpus that are translations of each other. All three were provided by a large machine-readable subset of the French-English parallel corpus of Canadian parliamentary proceedings (Hansard). (1) and (2) are valuable independent of the language pair and could be used in other pairings, which is why they now call the model a *transfer* one. A very rough simplification: an English sentence yields likeliest equivalences for word strings (sub-strings of the English input sentence), i.e., French word strings. The trigram model for French re-arranges these into the most likely order, which is the output French sentence. One of their most striking demonstrations is that their trigram model for French (or English) reliably produces (as the likeliest order for the components) the correct ordering of items for a sentence of ten words or less.

What should be emphasized is the enormous amount of pre-computation that this method requires and, even then, a ten word sentence as input requires an additional hour of computation to produce a translation. This figure will undoubtedly reduce with time and hardware expansion but it gives some idea of the computational intensity of IBM's method.

The facts are now quite different. They have taken in whatever linguistics has helped: morphology tables, sense tagging (which is directional and dependent on the properties of French in particular), a transfer architecture with an intermediate representation, plural listings, and an actual or proposed use of bilingual dictionaries. In one sense, the symbolic case has won: they topped out by pure statistics at around 40% of sentences acceptably translated and then added whatever was necessary from a symbolic approach to upgrade the figures. No one can blame them: it is simply that they have no firm position beyond taking what ever will succeed, and who can object to that?

There is then no theoretical debate at all, and their rhetorical points against symbolic MT are in bad faith. It is Stone Soup: the statistics are in the bottom of the pot but all flavor and progress now come from the odd trimmings of our systems that they pop into the pot.

They are, as it were, wholly pragmatic statisticians: less pure than, say, the Gale group (e.g., [6]) at AT&T: this is easily seen by the IBM introduction of notions like the one they call "informants" where a noun phrase of some sort is sought before a particular text item of interest. This is an interpolation of a highly theoretically-loaded notion into a routine that, until then, had treated all text items as mere uninterpreted symbols.

One could make an analogy here with localist versus distributivist sub-symbolic connectionists: the former, but not the latter, will take on all kinds of categories and representations developed by others for their purposes, without feeling any strong need to discuss their status as artifacts, i.e., how they could have been constructed other than by handcrafting.

This also makes it hard to argue with them. So, also, does their unacademic habit of telling you what they've done but not publishing it, allegedly because they are (a) advancing so fast, and (b) have suffered ripoffs. One can sympathize with all this but it makes serious debate very hard.

10.5 The Only Issue

There is only one real issue: is there any natural ceiling of success to *PURE* statistical methods? The shift in their position suggests there is. One might expect some success with those methods on several grounds (and therefore not be as surprised as many are at their success):

- There have been substantial technical advances in statistical methods since King's day and, of course, in fast hardware to execute such functions, and in disk size to store the corpora.

- The redundancy levels of natural languages like English are around 50% over both words and letters. One might expect well-optimized statistical functions to exploit that to about that limit, with translation as much as another NLP task. One could turn this round in a question to the IBM group: how do they explain why they get, say, 40–50% or so of sentences right, rather than 100%? If their answer refers to the well-known redundancy figure above, then the ceiling comes into view immediately.

  If, on the other hand, their answer is that they cannot explain anything, or there is no explaining to do or discussions to have, then their task and methodology is a very odd one indeed. Debate and explanation are made impossible and, where that is so, one is normally outside any rational or scientific realm. It is the world of the witch-doctor: Look – I do what I do and notice that (sometimes) it works.

- According to a conjecture I propounded some years ago, with much anecdotal support, *any theory whatever no matter how bizarre will do some MT.* Hence my surprise level is always low.

10.6 Other Reasons for Expecting a Ceiling to Success with Statistics

Other considerations that suggest there is a ceiling to pure statistical methods are as follows:

1. A parallel with statistical information retrieval may be suggestive here: it generally works below the 80% threshold, and the precision/recall tradeoff seems a barrier to greater success by those methods. Yet it is, by general agreement, an easier task than MT and has been systematically worked on for over 35 years, unlike statistical MT whose career has been intermittent. The relationship of MT to IR is rather like that of sentence parsers to sentence recognizers. A key point to note is how rapid the early successes of IR were, and how slow the optimization of those techniques has been since then!

2. A technical issue here is the degree of their reliance on alignment algorithms as a pre-process: in ACL91 they claimed only 80% correct alignments, in which case how could they exceed the ceiling that that suggests?

3. Their model of a single language is a trigram model because moving up to even one item longer (i.e., a quadgram model) would be computationally prohibitive. This alone must impose a strong constraint on how well they can do in the end, since any language has phenomena that connect outside the three item window. This is agreed by all parties. The only issue is how far one can get with the simple trigram-model (and, as we have seen, it gives a basic 40%), and how far can distance phenomena in syntax be finessed by forms of information caching. One can see the effort to extend the window as enormously ingenious, or patching up what is a basically inadequate model when taken alone.

10.7 The Future: Hybrid Approaches

Given the early success of IBM's methods, the most serious and positive question should be what kinds of *hybrid* approach will do best in the future: coming from the symbolic end, plus statistics, or from a statistical base but inducing, or just taking over, whatever symbolic structures help? For this we can only watch and wait, and possibly help a little here and there. However, there are still some subsidiary considerations.

10.7.1 IBM, SYSTRAN, and the Economics of Corpora

In one sense, what IBM have done is partially automate the SYSTRAN construction process: replacing laborious error feedback with statistical surveys and lexicon construction. And all of us, including SYSTRAN itself, could do the same. However, we must always remember how totally tied IBM are to their Hansard text, the Rosetta Stone, one might say, of modern MT. We should remember, too, that their notion of word sense is only and exactly that of correspondences between different languages, a wholly unintuitive one for many people.

The problem IBM have is that few such vast bilingual corpora are available in languages for which MT is needed. If, however, they had to be constructed by hand, then the economics of what IBM has done would change radically. By bad luck, the languages for which such corpora are available are also languages in which SYSTRAN already has done pretty well, so IBM will have to overtake, then widen the gap with, SYSTRAN's performance a bit before they can be taken seriously from an economic point of view. They may be clever enough to make do with less than the current 100 million word corpora per language, but one would naturally expect quality to decline as they did so.

This resource argument could be very important: Leech has always made the point, with his own statistical tagger, that any move to make higher-level structures available to the tagger always ended up requiring much more text than he had expected.

This observation does not accord with IBM's claims, which are rather the reverse, so an important point to watch in future will be whether IBM will be able to obtain adequate bilingual-corpora for the domain-specialized MT that is most in demand (such as airline reservations or bank billings). Hansard has the advantage of being large but is very very general indeed.

10.7.2 Why the AI Argument About MT Still Has Force

The basic AI argument for knowledge-based processing does not admit defeat and retreat, it just regroups. It has to accept Bar Hillel's old anti-MT argument [1] on its own side – i.e., that as he said, good MT must in the end need knowledge representations. One version of this argument is the primitive psychological one: humans do not do translation by exposure to such vast texts, because they simply have not had such exposure, and in the end how people do things will prove important. Note that this argument makes an empirical claim about human exposure to text that might be hard to substantiate. This argument will cut little ice with our opponents, but there may still be a good argument that we do need representations for tasks in NLP related to MT: e.g. we cannot really imagine doing summarization or question answering by purely statistical methods, can we? There is related practical evidence from message extraction: in the MUC competitions [9], the systems that have done best have been hybrids of preference and statistics, such as of Grishman and Lehnert, and not pure systems of either type.

There is the related argument that we need access to representations *at some point* to repair errors. This is hard to make precise but fixing errors makes no sense in the pure IBM paradigm; you just provide more data. One does not have to be a hard line syntactician to have a sense that rules do exist in some linguistic areas and can need fixing.

10.7.3 Hard Problems Do Not Go Away

There remain, too, crucial classes of cases that seem to need symbolic inference: an old, self-serving, one will do such as "The soldiers fired at the women and I saw several fall" [11].

I simply cannot imagine how any serious statistical method (e.g., not like "pronouns are usually male so make "several" in a gendered translation agree with soldiers"!) can get the translation of "several" into a gendered language right (where we assume it must be the women who fall from general causality). But again, one must beware here, since presumably any phenomenon whatever will have statistically significant appearances and can be covered by some such function if the scale of the corpus is sufficiently large. This is a truism and goes as much for logical relations between sentences as for morphology. It does not follow that that truism leads to tractable statistics or data gathering. If there could be 75,000-word-long Markov chains, and not merely trigrams (which seem the realistic computational limit) the generation of whole novels would be trivial. It is just not practical to have greater-than-three chains but we need to fight the point in principle as well!

Or, consider the following example (due to Sergei Nirenburg):

PRIEST IS CHARGED WITH POPE ATTACK
(Lisbon, May 14)

A Spanish priest was charged here today with attempting to murder the Pope. *Juan Fernandez Krohn*, aged 32, was arrested after *a man armed with a bayonet* approached the Pope while he was saying prayers at Fatima on Wednesday night.
According to the police, *Fernandez* told the investigators today he trained for the past six months for the assault. He was alleged to have claimed the Pope 'looked furious' on hearing *the priest's* criticism of his handling of

the church's affairs. If found guilty, *the Spaniard* faces a prison sentence of 15–20 years.

(*The Times* 15 May 1982)

The five italicized phrases all refer to the same man, a vital fact for a translator to know since some of those phrases could not be used in any literal manner in another language (e.g. "the Spaniard" could not be translated word-for-word into Spanish or Russian). It is hard to imagine multiple identity of reference like that having *any* determinable statistical basis.

10.8 Is the Pure Statistics Argument What is Being Debated? No

Everything so far refers to the *pure statistics argument*, from which IBM have now effectively backed off. If the argument is then to be about the deployment of hybrid systems and exactly what data to get from the further induction of rules and categories with statistical functions (e.g., what sort of dictionary to use) then there is really no serious argument at all, just a number of ongoing efforts with slightly differing recipes. Less fun, but maybe more progress, and IBM are to be thanked for helping that shift.

10.8.1 IBM as Pioneers of Data Acquisition

I can add a personal note there: when I worked on what I then called Preference Semantics [11] at McCarthy's Stanford AI Lab, McCarthy always dealt briefly with any attempt to introduce numerical methods into AI – statistical pattern-matching in machine vision was a constant irritation to him – by saying "Where do all those numbers COME from?" I felt a little guilty as Preference Semantics also required at least link counting. One could now say that IBM's revival of statistical methods has told us exactly where some of these numbers come from! But that certainly does not imply that the rules that express the numbers are therefore useless or superseded.

This touches on a deep metaphysical point: I mentioned above that we may feel word-sense is a non-bilingual matter, and that we feel that there *are* rules that need fixing sometimes, and so on. Clearly, not everyone feels this. But it is our culture of language study that tells us that rules, senses, metaphors, representations etc. are important and that we cannot imagine all that is just a cultural artifact. An analogy here would be Dennett's recently restated theory of human consciousness [5] that suggests that all our explanations of our actions, reason, motives, desires etc. as we articulate them may be no more than fluff on the underlying mechanisms that drive us.

IBM's work induces the same terror in language theorists, AI researchers and linguists alike: all their dearly-held structures may be just fluff, a thing of schoolmen having no contact with the reality of language. Some of us in AI, long ago, had no such trouble imagining most linguistics was fluff, but do not want the same argument turned round on us, that *all* symbolic structures may have the same status.

Another way of looking at this is how much good IBM are doing us all: by showing us, among other things, that we have not spent enough time thinking about how to acquire, in as automatic a manner as possible, the lexicons and rule bases we use. This has been changing lately, even without IBM's influence, as can be seen from the large-scale lexical extraction movement of recent years. But IBM's current attempts to recapitulate, as it were, in the ontogeny of their system, much of the phylogeny of the AI species is a real criticism of how some of us have spent the last twenty years.

We have not given enough attention to knowledge acquisition, and now they are doing it for us. I used to argue that AIers and computational linguists should not be seen as the white-coated laboratory assistants of linguistic theorists (as some linguists used to dream of using us). Similarly, we cannot wait for IBMers to do this dirty work for us while we go on theorizing. Their efforts should change how the rest of us proceed from now on.

10.9 Conclusion: Let Us Declare Victory and Carry on Working

Relax, go on taking the medicine. Brown et al.'s retreat to incorporating symbolic structures show the pure statistics hypothesis has failed. All we should be haggling about now is how best to derive the symbolic structures we use, and will go on using, for machine translation.

Acknowledgments

In acknowledgement of contributions from James Pustejovsky, Bob Ingria, Bran Boguraev, Sergei Nirenburg, Ted Dunning and others in the CRL natural language processing group.

References

[1] Bar-Hillel, Y., "The present status of automatic translation of languages", in J. Alt (ed.), *Advances in Computers* 1, Academic Press, New York, 1960.
[2] Brown, P.F., J. Cocke, S. Della Pietra, V. Della Pietra, F. Jelinek, J. Lafferty, R. Mercer, P. Roossin, "A statistical approach to machine translation", in *Computational Linguistics*, 16, 1990, 79–85.
[3] Brown, P.F., J. Lai, R. Mercer, "Aligning sentences in parallel corpora", in *Proceedings 29th Annual Meeting of the Association for Computational Linguistics*, Berkeley, CA, 1991, 169–176.
[4] Chomsky, N., *Syntactic Structures*, Mouton and Co., The Hague, 1957.
[5] Dennett, D., *Consciousness Explained*, Bradford Books, Cambridge MA, 1991.

[6] Gale, W., K. Church, "Poor estimates of context are worse than none", in *Proc. 1990 DARPA Speech and Language Meeting*, Hidden Valley, PA, 1990.

[7] King, G. "Stochastic methods of mechanical translation", in *Mechanical Translation*, 3, 1956.

[8] Jelinek, F., R. Mercer, "Interpolated estimation of Markov source parameters from sparse data", in *Proceedings of the Workshop on Pattern Recognition in Practice*, North Holland, Amsterdam, The Netherlands, 1980.

[9] Lehnert, W., B. Sundheim, "A performance evaluation of text analysis technologies", *AI magazine*, 12, 1991.

[10] McCord, M., "A new version of the machine translation system LMT", *Literary & Linguistic Computing*, 4, 1989.

[11] Wilks, Y., "A preferential pattern-matching semantics for natural language understanding", *Artificial Intelligence*, 11, 1975.

11

Senses and Texts

Yorick Wilks

University of Sheffield

Abstract: This paper addresses the question of whether it is possible to sense-tag systematically, and on a large scale, and how we should assess progress so far. That is to say, how to attach each occurrence of a word in a text to one and only one sense in a dictionary – a particular dictionary of course, and that is part of the problem. The paper does not propose a solution to the question, though we have reported empirical findings elsewhere [5, 22, 21], and intend to continue and refine that work. The point of this paper is to examine two well-known contributions critically: The first [13], which is widely taken to show that the task, as defined, cannot be carried out systematically by humans and, secondly [25], which claims strikingly good results at doing exactly that

11.1 Introduction

Empirical, corpus-based, computational linguistics has reached by now into almost every crevice of the subject, and perhaps pragmatics will soon succumb. Semantics, if we may assume the sense-tagging task is semantic, has shown striking progress in the last five years and, in Yarowsky's most recent work [25], has produced very high levels of success in the 90s%, well above the key bench-mark figure of 62% correct sense assignment, achieved at an informal experiment in New Mexico about 1990, in which each word was assigned its *first* sense listed in LDOCE (Longman Dictionary of Contemporary English).

A crucial question in this paper will be whether recent work in sense-tagging has in fact given us the breakthrough in scale that is now obvious with, say, part-of-speech tagging. Our conclusion will be that it has not, and that the experiments so far, however high their success rates, are not yet of a scale different from those of the previous generation of linguistic, symbolic-AI or connectionist approaches to the very same problem.

A historian of our field might glance back at this point to Small et al. [16] which surveyed the AI-symbolic and connectionist traditions of sense-tagging at just the moment when corpus-driven empirical methods began to revive, but had not been published. All the key issues still unsettled are discussed there and that collection showed no naivety about the problem of sense resolution with respect only to existing lexicons of senses. It was realised that that task was only meaningful against an assumption of some method for capturing new (new to the chosen lexicon, that is) senses and, most importantly, that although existing lexicons differed, they did

K. Ahmad, C. Brewster and M. Stevenson (eds.), Words and Intelligence 1, 267–279.
© 2007 *Springer.*

not differ arbitrarily much. The book also demonstrated that there was also strong psychological backing for the reality of word senses and for empirical methods of locating them from corpora without any prior assumptions about their number or distribution (e.g. in early versions of Plate's work, published later in Wilks et al. [20]; see also Jorgensen [12]).

Our purpose in this paper will be to argue that Kilgarriff's negative claims are wrong, and his errors must be combated, while Yarowsky is largely right although we have some queries about the details and the interpretation of his claims. Both authors, however, agree that this is a traditional and important task: one often cited as being a foundational lacuna in, say, the history of machine translation (MT), because of the inability of early NLP systems to carry it out. It was assumed by many, in that distant period, that if only word-sense ambiguity could be solved, by the process we are calling sense-tagging, then MT of high quality would be relatively straightforward. Like many linguistic tasks, it then became an end in itself, like syntactic parsing and, now that it is, we would claim, firmly in sight (despite Kilgarriff) it is far less clear that its solution will automatically solve a range of traditional problems like MT. But clearly it would be a generally good tool to have available in NLP and a triumph if this long-resistant task of CL were to yield.

11.2 The Very Possibility of Sense-Tagging

Kilgarriff's paper [13] is important because it has been widely cited as showing that the senses of a word, as distinguished in a dictionary such as LDOCE, do not cover the senses actually carried by most occurrences of the word as they appear in a corpus. If he can show that, it would be very significant indeed, because that would imply that sense-tagging word occurrences in a corpus by means of any lexical data based on, or related to, a machine-readable dictionary or thesaurus is misguided. I want to show here that the paper does not demonstrate any such thing. Moreover, it proceeds by means of a straw-man it may be worth bringing back to life!

That straw-man, Kilgarriff's starting point, is the 'bank model' (BM) of lexical ambiguity resolution, which he establishes by assertion rather than quotation, though it is attributed to Small, Hirst, and Cottrell as well as the present author. In the BM, words have discrete meanings, and the human reader (like the ideal computer program) knows immediately which meaning of the word applies [13:367], "given that a word occurrence always refers to one or the other, but not both" of the main meanings that a word like 'bank' is reputed to have. In the BM, the set of senses available for a word does not depend on which particular dictionary you start with, but is somehow abstractly fixed. The main argument of Kilgarriff's paper is to distinguish a number of relationships between LDOCE senses that are not discrete in that way, and then to go on to an experiment with senses in a corpus. But first we should breathe a little life back into the BM straw-man: those named above can look after themselves, but here is a passage from Wilks [18:12] "...it is very difficult to assign word occurrences to sense classes in any manner that is both general and determinate. In the sentences "I have a stake in this country" and "My stake on the last race was a pound" is "stake" being used in the same sense or not? If "stake" can be interpreted to mean something as vague as "Stake as any kind of investment in any enterprise" then the answer is yes. So, if a semantic dictionary contained only two senses for "stake": that vague sense together with "Stake as a post", then one would expect to assign the vague sense for both the sentences above. But if, on the other hand, the dictionary distinguished "Stake as an investment" and "Stake as an initial payment in a game or race" then the answer would be expected to be different. So, then, word sense disambiguation is relative to the dictionary of sense choices available and can have no absolute quality about it".

QED, one might say, since the last sentences seem to show very much the awareness (a quarter of a century ago, but in the context of a computer program for sense tagging) that sense choice may not be exclusive if defined, as it must be, with respect to a particular dictionary. Hence, in my view, BM is no more than a straw man because writers of the dark ages of CL were as aware as Kilgarriff of the real problems of dictionary senses versus text occurrences.

In general, it is probably wise to believe, even if it is not always true, that authors in the past were no more naive than those now working, and were probably writing programs, however primitive and ineffective, to carry out the very same tasks as now (e.g. sense-tagging of corpus words). More importantly, the work quoted, which became an approach called preference semantics, was essentially a study of the divergence of corpus usage from lexical norms (or preferences) and developed in the Seventies into a set of processes for accommodating divergent/non-standard/metaphorical usage to existing lexical norms, notions that Kilgarriff seems to believe only developed in a much later and smarter group of people around 1990, which includes himself, but also, for example, Fass whose work was a direct continuation of that quoted above. Indeed, in Wilks [18] procedures were programmed (and run over a set of newspaper editorials) to *accommodate* such "divergent" corpus usage of one word to that of an established sense of a different word in the same text, while in [19] programmed procedures were specified to accommodate such usage by constructing completely new sense entries for the word itself.

A much more significant omission, one that bears directly on his main claim and is not merely an issue of historical correctness, is the lack of reference to work in New Mexico and elsewhere [e.g. 5] on the large-scale sense tagging of corpora against a machine readable dictionary (MRD) derived lexical data base. These were larger scale experiments whose results directly contradict the result he is believed to have proved. I shall return to this point in a moment. The best part of Kilgarriff's paper is his attempt to give an intuitive account of developmental relations between the senses of a word. He distinguishes Generalizing Metaphors (a move from a specific case to a more general one) from Must-be-theres (the applicability of one sense requires the applicability of another, as when an act of matricide requires there to be a mother) from Domain Shift, as when a sense in one domain, like "mellow" of wine, is far enough from the domain of "mellow" (of a personality) to constitute a sense shift.

It is not always easy to distinguish the first two types, since both rest on an implication relationship between two or more senses. Again, the details do not matter: what he has shown convincingly is that, as in the earlier quotation, the choice between senses of a given word is often not easy to make because it depends on their relationship, the nature of the definitions and how specific they are. I suspect no one has ever held a simple-minded version of the BM, except possibly Fodor and Katz, who, whatever their virtues, had no interest at all in lexicography.

The general problem with Kilgarriff's analysis of sense types is that he conflates:

I. text usage different from that shown in a whole list of stored senses for a given word e.g. in a dictionary, (which is what his later experiment will be about) with

II. text usage divergent from some "core" sense in the lexicon.

Only the second is properly in the area of metaphor/metonymy or "grinding" [4] work of the group in which he places himself, and it is this phenomenon to which his classification of sense distinctions summarized above properly belongs. This notion requires some idea of sense development; of the senses of a word extending in time in a non-random manner, and is a linguistic tradition of analysis going back to Givon [8]. However, the straw-man BM, and the experiment he then does on hand-tagging of senses in text, all attach to the first, unrelated, notion which does not normally imply the presence of metonymy or metaphor at all, but simply an inadequate sense list. Of course, the two types may be historically related, in that some of the (I) list may have been derived by metaphorical/metonymic processes from a (II) word, but this is not be so in general. This confusion of targets is a weakness in the paper, since it makes it difficult to be sure what he wants us to conclude from the experiment. However, since we shall show his results are not valid, this distinction may not matter too much.

One might add here that Kilgarriff's pessimism has gone hand in hand with some very interesting surveys he has conducted over the Internet on the real need for word-sense disambiguation by NLP R&D. And one should note that there are others [e.g. 11] who have questioned the practical usefulness of data derived at many sites from MRDs. Our case here, of course, is that it has been useful, both in our own work on sense-tagging [5, op. cit.] and in that of Yarowsky, using Roget and discussed below.

Kilgarriff's experiment, which what has been widely taken to be the main message of his paper, is not described in much detail. In a footnote, he refuses to give the reader the statistics on which his result was based even though the text quite clearly contains a claim (p. 378) that 87% of (non-monsemous) words in his text sample have at least one text occurrence that cannot be associated with one and only one LDOCE sense. Hence, he claims, poor old BM is refuted, yet again.

But that claim (about word types) is wholly consistent with, for example, 99% of text usage (of word tokens) being associated with one and only one dictionary sense! Thus the actual claim in the paper is not at all what it has been taken to show, and is highly misleading.

But much empirical evidence tells also against the claim Kilgarriff is believed to have made. Informal analyses [9] by Georgia Green suggested that only some 20% of text usage (i.e. to word tokens) could not be associated with a unique dictionary sense. Consistent with that, too, is the use of simulated annealing techniques by Cowie et al. [5] at CRL-New Mexico to assign LDOCE senses to a corpus. In that work, it was shown that about 75%–80% of word usage could be correctly associated with LDOCE senses, as compared with hand-tagged control text. It was, and still is, hoped that that figure can be raised by additional filtering techniques.

The two considerations above show, from quite different sources and techniques, the dubious nature of Kilgarriff's claim. Wierzbicka [17] following Antal [1] has long argued that words have only core senses and that dictionaries/lexicons should express that single sense and leave all further sense refinement to some other process, such as real world knowledge manipulations, AI if you wish, but not a process that uses the lexicon.

Since the CRL result suggested that the automatic procedures worked very well (nearer 80%) at the homograph, rather than the sub-sense, level (the latter being where Kilgarriff's examples all lie) one possible way forward for NLP would be to go some of the way with Wierzbicka's views and restrict lexical sense distinctions to the homograph level. Then sense tagging could perhaps be done at the success level of part-of speech tagging. Such a move could be seen as changing the data to suit what you can accomplish, or as reinstating AI and pragmatics within NLP for the kind of endless, context-driven, inferences we need in real situations.

This suggestion is rather different from Kilgarriff's conclusion: which is also an empirical one. He proposes that the real basis of sense distinction be established by usage clustering techniques applied to corpora. This is an excellent idea and recent work at IBM [2] has produced striking non-seeded clusters of corpus usages, many of them displaying a similarity close to an intuitive notion of sense.

But there are serious problems in moving any kind of lexicography, traditional or computational, onto any such basis. Hanks [10] has claimed that a dictionary could be written that consisted entirely of usages, and has investigated how those might be clustered for purely lexicographic purposes, yet it remains unclear what kind of volume could result from such a project or who would buy it and how they could use it. One way to think of such a product would be the reduction of monolingual dictionaries to thesauri, so that to look up a word becomes to look up which row or rows of context bound semi-synonyms it appears in. Thesauri have a real function both for native and non-native speakers of a language, but they rely on the reader knowing what some or all of the words in a row or class mean because they give no explanations. To reduce word sense separation to synonym classes, without explanations attached would limit a dictionary's use in a striking way.

If we then think not of dictionaries for human use but NLP lexicons, the situation might seem more welcoming for Kilgarriff's suggestion, since he could be seen as suggesting, say, a new version of WordNet [14] with its synsets established not a priori but by statistical corpus clustering. This is indeed a notion that has been kicked around in NLP for a while and is probably worth a try. There are still difficulties: first, that any such clustering process produces not only the clean, neat, classes like IBM's [2] (Hindu Jew Christian Bhuddist) example but inevitable monsters, produced by some quirk of a particular corpus. Those could, of course, be hand weeded but that is not an automatic process.

Secondly, as is also well known, what classes you get, or rather, the generality of the classes you get, depends on parameter settings in the clustering algorithm: those obtained at different settings may or may not correspond nicely to, say, different levels of a standard lexical hierarchy. They probably will not, since hierarchies are discrete in terms of levels and the parameters used are continuous but, even when they do, there will be none of the hierarchical terms attached, of the sort available in WordNet (e.g. ANIMAL or DOMESTIC ANIMAL). And this is only a special case of the general problem of clustering algorithms, well known in information retrieval, that the clusters so found do not come with names or features attached.

Thirdly, and this may be the most significant point for Kilgarriff's proposal, there will always be some match of such empirical clusters to any new text occurrence of a word and, to that degree, sense-tagging in text is bound to succeed by such a methodology, given the origin of the clusters and the fact that a closest match to one of a set of clusters can always be found. The problem is how you interpret that result because, in this methodology, no hand-tagged text will be available as a control since it is not clear what task the human controls could be asked to carry out. Subjects may find traditional sense-tagging (against e.g. LDOCE senses) hard but it is a comprehensible task, because of the role dictionaries and their associated senses have in our cultural world. But the new task (attach one and only one of the classes in which the word appears to its use at this point) is rather less well defined. But again, a range of original and ingenious suggestions may make this task much more tractable, an senses so tagged (against WordNet style classes, though empirically derived) could certainly assist real tasks like MT even if they did not turn out wholly original dictionaries for the book buying public.

There is, of course, no contradiction between, on the one hand, my suggestion for a compaction of lexicons towards core or homograph senses, done to optimize the sense-tagging process and, on the other, his suggestion for an empirical basis for the establishment of synsets, or clusters that constitute senses. Given that there are problems with wholly empirically-based sense clusters of the sort mentioned above, the natural move would be to suggest some form of hybrid derivation from corpus statistics, taken together with some machine-readable source of synsets: WordNet itself, standard thesauri, and even bilingual dictionaries which are also convenient reductions of a language to word sets grouped by sense (normally by reference to a word in another language, of course). As many have now realised, both the pure corpus methods and the large-scale hand-crafted sources have their virtues, and their own particular systematic errors, and the hope has to be that clever procedures can cause those to cancel, rathr than reinforce, each other. But all that is future work, and beyond the scope of a critical note.

In conclusion, it may be worth noting that the BM, in some form, is probably inescapable, at least in the form of what Pustejovsky [15] calls a "sense enumerative lexicon", and against which he inveighs for some twenty pages before going on to use one for his illustrations, as we all do, including all lexicographers. This is not hypocrisy but a confusion close to that between (I) and (II) above: we, as language users and computational modellers, must be able, now or later, to capture a usage that differs from some established sense (problem (II) above), but that is only loosely connected to problem (I), where senses, if they are real, seem to come in lists and it is with them we must sense-tag if the task is to be possible at all.

11.3 Recent Experiments in Sense-Tagging

We now turn to the claims in Gale et al. [7], abbreviated to GCY, see also Yarowsky [23, 24, 25] that:

1. That word tokens in text tend to occur with a smaller number of senses than often supposed and, most specifically,
2. In a single discourse a word will appear in one and only one sense, even if several are listed for it in a lexicon, at a level of about 94% likelihood for non-monosemous words (a figure that naturally becomes higher if the monosemous text words are added in).

These are most important claims if true for they would, at a stroke, remove a major excuse for the bad progress of MT; make redundant a whole sub-industry of NLP, namely sense resolution, and greatly simplify the currently fashionable NLP task of sense-tagging texts by any method whatever [e.g. 5, 3].

GCY's claim would not make sense-tagging of text irrelevant, of course, for it would only allow one to assume that resolving any single token of a word (by any method at all) in a text would then serve for all occurrences in the text, at a high level of probability. Or, one could amalgamate all contexts for a word and resolve those taken together to some pre-established lexical sense. Naturally, these procedures would be absurd if one were not already convinced of the truth of the claim.

GCY's claims are not directly related to those of Kilgarriff, who aimed to show only that it was difficult to assign text tokens to any lexical sense at all. Indeed, Kilgarriff and GCY use quite different procedures: Kilgarriff's is one of assigning a word token in context to one of a set of lexical sense descriptions, while GCY's is one of assessing whether or not two tokens in context are the same sense or not. The procedures are incommensurable and no outcome on one would be predictive for the other: GCYs procedures do not use standard lexicons and are in terms of closeness-of-fit, which means that, unlike Kilgarriff's, they can never fail to match a text token to a sense, defined in the way they do (see below).

However, GCYs claims are incompatible with Kilgarriff's in spirit, in that Kilgarriff assumes there is a lot of polysemy about and that resolving it is tricky, whereas GCY assume the opposite.

Both Kilgarriff and GCY have given rise to potent myths about word-sense tagging in text that I believe are wrong, or at best unproven. Kilgarriff's paper, as we saw earlier, has some subtle analysis but one crucial statistical flaw. GCY's is quite different: it is a mush of hard to interpret claims and procedures, but ones that may still, nonetheless, be basically true.

GCY's methodology is essentially impressionistic: the texts they chose are, of course, those available, which turn out to be Grolier's Encyclopaedia. There is no dispute about one-sense-per-discourse (their name for claim (2) above) for certain classes of texts: the more technical a text the more anyone, whatever their other prejudices about language, would expect the claim to be true. Announcing that the claim had been shown true for mathematical or chemical texts would surprise no one; encyclopaedias are also technical texts.

Their key fact in support of claim (1) above, based on a sense-tagging of 97 selected word types in the whole Encyclopaedia, and sense tagged by the statistical method described below, was that 7569 of the tokens associated with those types are monosemous in the corpus, while 6725 are of words with more than two senses. Curiously, they claim this shows "most words (both by token and by type) have only one sense" I have no idea whether to be surprised by this figure or not but it certainly does nothing to show that [op. cit., 1992] "Perhaps word sense disambiguation is not as difficult as we might have thought". It shows me that, even in fairly technical prose like that of an encyclopaedia, nearly half the words occur in more than one sense.

And that fact, of course, has no relation at all to mono- or poly-semousness in whatever base lexicon we happen to be using in an NLP system. Given a large lexicon, based on say the OED, one could safely assume that virtually all words are polysemous. As will be often the case, GCY's claim at this point is true of exactly the domain they are dealing with, and their (non-stated) assumption that any lexicon is created for the domain text they are dealing with and with no relation to any other lexicon for any other text. One claim per discourse, one might say.

This last point is fundamental because we know that distinctions of sense are lexicon- or procedure-dependent. Kilgarriff faced this explicitly, and took LDOCE as an admittedly arbitrary starting point. GCY never discuss the issue, which makes all their claims about numbers of senses totally, but inexplicitly, dependent on the procedures they have adopted in their experiments to give a canonical sense-tagging against which to test their claims.

This is a real problem for them. They admit right away that few or no extensive hand-tagged sense-resolved corpora exist for control purposes, So, they must adopt a sense-discrimination procedure to provide their data that is unsupervised. This is where the ingenuity of the paper comes in, but also its fragility. They have two methods for providing sense-tagged data against which to test their one-sense-per-discourse claim (2).

The first rests on a criterion of sense distinction provided by correspondence to differing non-English words in a parallel corpus, in their case the French-English Canadian Hansard because, as always, it is there. So, the correspondence of "duty" to an aligned sentence containing either "devoir" or "impot" (i.e. obligation or tax) is taken as an effective method of distinguishing the obligation/tax senses of the English word, which was indeed the criterion for sense argued for in Dagon and Itai [6]. It has well known drawbacks: most obviously that whatever we mean by sense distinction in English, it is unlikely to be criterially revealed by what the French happen to do in their language.

More relevantly to the particular case, GCY found it very hard to find plausible pairs for test, which must not of course SHARE ambiguities across the French/English boundaries (as interest/interet do). In the end they were reduced to a test based on the six (!) pairs they found in the Hansard corpus that met their criteria for sense separation and occurrence more than 150 times in two or more senses. In GCYs defence one could argue that, since they do not expect much polysemy in texts, examples of this sort would, of course, be hard to find. Taking this bilingual method of sense-tagging for the six word set as criterial they then run their basic word sense discrimination method over the English Hansard data. This consists, very roughly, of a training method over 100 word surrounding contexts for 60 instances of each member of a pair of senses (hand selected) i.e. for each pair $2 \times 60 \times 100 = 12,000$ words. Notice that this eyeballing method is not inconsistent with anything in Kilgarriff's argument: GCY selected 120 contexts in Hansard for each word that DID correspond intuitively to one of the (French) selected senses. It says nothing about any tokens that may have been hard to classify in this way. The figures claimed for the discrimination method against the criterial data vary between 82 and 100% (for different word pairs) of the data for that sense correctly discriminated.

They then move on to a monolingual method that provides sense-tagged data in an unsupervised way. It rests on previous work by Yarowsky [23] and uses the assignment of a single Roget category (from the 1042) as a sense-discrimination. Yarowsky sense-tagged some of the Grolier corpus in the following way: 100-word contexts for words like "crane" (ambiguous between bird and machinery) are taken and those words are scored by (very roughly, and given interpolation for local context) which of the 1042 Roget categories they appear under as tokens. The sense of a given token of "crane" is determined by which Roget category wins out: e.g. 348 (TOOLS/MACHINERY) for the machinery contexts, one hopes, and category 414 (ANIMALS/INSECTS) for the bird contexts. Yarowsky [23] claimed 93% correctness for this procedure over a sample of 12 selected words, presumably checked against earlier hand-tagged data.

The interpolation for local effects is in fact very sophisticated and involves training with the 100 word contexts in Grolier of all the words that appear under a given candidate Roget head, a method that they acknowledge introduces some noise, since it adds into the training material Grolier contexts that involve senses of a category 348 word, say, that is not its machinery sense (e.g. crane as a bird). However, this method, they note, does not have the sense-defined-by-language2 problems that come with the Hansard training method.

In a broad sense, this is an old method, probably the oldest in lexical computation, and was used by Masterman (reported in [18]) in what was probably the first clear algorithm ever implemented for usage discrimination against Roget categories as sense-criterial. In the very limited computations of those days the hypothesis was deemed conclusive falsified; i.e. the hypothesis that any method overlapping the

Roget categories for a word with the Roget categories of neighbouring words would determine an appropriate Roget category for that word in context.

This remains, I suspect, an open question: it may well be that Yarowsky's local interpolation statistics have made the general method viable, and that the 100-word window of context used is far more effective than a sentence. It may be the 12 words that confirm the disambiguation hypothesis at 93% would not be confirmed by 12 more words chosen at random (the early Cambridge work did at least try to Roget-resolve all the words in a sentence). But we can pass over that for now, and head on, to discuss GCY's main claim (2) given the two types of data gathered.

Two very strange things happen at this point as the GCY paper approaches its conclusion: namely, the proof of claim (2) or one-sense-per-discourse. First, the two types of sense-tagged data just gathered, especially the Roget-tagged data, should now be sufficient to test the claim, if a 93% level is deemed adequate for a preliminary test. Strangely, the data derived in the first part of the paper is never used or cited and the reader is not told whether Yarowsky's Roget data confirms or disconfirms (2).

Secondly, the testing of (2) is done purely by human judgement: a "blind" team of the three authors and two colleagues who are confronted by the OALD main senses for one of nine test words, and who then make judgements of pairs of contexts for one of the nine words drawn from a single Grolier article. The subjects are shown to have pretty consistent judgements and, of fifty-four pairs of contexts from the same article, fifty-one shared the same sense and three did not.

Notice here that the display of the OALD senses is pointless, since the subjects are not asked to decide which if any OALD sense the words appear in, and so no Kilgarriff-style problems can arise. The test is simply to assign SAME or NOTSAME, and there are some control pairs added to force discrimination in some cases.

What can one say of this ingenious mini-experiment? Lexicographers traditionally distinguish "lumpers" and "splitters" among colleagues: those who tend to break up senses further and those who go for large, homonymic, senses, of which Wierzbicka would be the extreme case. Five GCY colleagues (one had to be dropped to get consistency among the team) from a "lumper" team decided that fifty-one out of fifty-four contexts for a word in a single encyclopaedia article (repeated for eight other words) are in the same sense. Is this significant? I suspect not very, and nothing at all follows to support the myth of discovery that has grown round the paper: the team and data are tiny and not disinterested. The Grolier articles are mini-texts where the hypothesis would, if true, surprise one least. Much more testing is needed before a universal hypothesis about text polysemy enters our beliefs. Of course, they may in the end be right, and all the dogma of the field so far be wrong.

More recently, Yarowsky [24, 25] has extended this methodology in two ways: first, he has established a separate claim he calls "one sense per collocation", which is quite independent of local discourse context (which was the separate "one-sense-per-discourse" claim) and could be expressed crudely by saying that it is highly unlikely that the following two sentences (with the "same" collocations for "plants") can both be attested in a corpus:

Plastic plants can fool you if really well made (=organic)
Plastic plants can contaminate whole regions (=factory)

One's first reaction may be to counter-cite examples like "Un golpe bajo" which can mean either a low blow in boxing, or a score one below par, in golf, although "golpe" could plausibly be said to have the same collocates in both cases. One can dismiss such examples (due to Jim Cowie in this case) by claiming both readings are idioms, but that should only focus our mind more on what Yarowsky does mean by collocation.

That work, although statistically impressive, gives no procedure for large-scale sense-tagging taken alone, since one has no immediate access to what cue words would, in general, constitute a collocation sufficient for disambiguation independent of discourse context. An interesting aspect of Yarowsky's paper is that he sought to show that on many definitions of sense and on many definitions of collocation (e.g. noun to the right, next verb to the left etc.) the hypothesis was still true at an interesting level, although better for some definitions of collocation than for others.

In his most recent work [25] Yarowsky has combined this approach with an assumption that the earlier claim ((2) = one-sense-per-discourse) is true, so as to set up an iterative bootstrapping algorithm that both extends disambiguating collocational keys [24] and retrains against a corpus, while at the same time filtering the result iteratively by assuming (2): i.e. that tokens from the same discourse will have the same sense. The result, on selected pairs (as always) of bi-semous words is between 93 and 97% (for different word pairs again) correct against handcoded samples, which is somewhat better than he obtained with his Roget method (93% in 1991) and better than figures from Schuetze and Pederson (1995) who produce unsupervised clusterings from a corpus that have to be related by hand to intelligible, established, senses.

However, although this work has shown increasing sophistication, and has the great advantage, as he puts it, of not requiring costly hand-tagged training sets but instead "thrives on raw, unannotated, monolingual corpora – the more the merrier", it has the defect at present that it requires an extensive iterative computation for each identified bisemous word, so as to cluster its text tokens into two exclusive classes that cover almost all the identified tokens. In that sense it is still some way from a general sense-tagging procedure for full text corpora, especially one that tags with respect to some generally acceptable taxonomy of senses for a word. Paradoxically, Yarowsky was much closer to that last criterion with his 1991 work using Roget that did produce a sense-tagging for selected word pairs that had some "objectivity" predating the experiment.

Although Yarowsky compares his work favorably with that of Schuetze and Pederson in terms of percentages (96.7 to 92.2) of tokens correctly tagged, it is not clear that their lack of grounding for the classes in an established lexicon is that different from Yarowsky, since his sense distinctions in his experiments (e.g. plant as organic or factory) are intuitively fine but pretty ad hoc to the experiment in question and have no real grounding in dictionaries.

11.4 Conclusion

It will probably be clear to the reader by now that a crucial problem in assessing this area of work is the fluctuation of the notion of word sense in it, and that is a real problem outside the scope of this paper. For example, sense as between binary oppositions of words is probably not the same as what the Roget categories discriminate, or words in French and English in aligned Hansard sentences have in common.

Another question arises here about the future development of large-scale sense-tagging: Yarowsky contrasts his work with that of efforts like Cowie et al. [5] that were dictionary based, as opposed to (unannotated) corpus based like his own. But a difference he does not bring out is that the Cowie et al. work, when optimized with simulated annealing, did go through substantial sentences, mini-texts if you will, and sense-tag all the words in them against LDOCE at about the 80% level. It is not clear that doing that is less useful than procedures like Yarowsky's that achieve higher levels of sense-tagging but only for carefully selected pairs of words, whose sense-distinctions are not clearly dictionary based, and which would require enormous prior computations to set up ad hoc sense oppositions for a useful number of words.

These are still early days, and the techniques now in play have probably not yet been combined or otherwise optimised to give the best results. It may not be necessary yet to oppose, as one now standardly does in MT, large-scale, less accurate, methods, though useful, with other higher-performance methods that cannot be used for practical applications. That the field of sense-tagging is still open to further development follows if one accepts the aim of this paper which is to attack two claims, both of which are widely believed, though not at once: that sense-tagging of corpora cannot be done, and that it has been solved. As many will remember, MT lived with both these, ultimately misleading, claims for many years.

Acknowledgements

Work referred to was supported by the NSF under grant #IRI 9101232 and the ECRAN project (LE-2110) funded by the European Commission's Language Engineering Division. The paper is also indebted to comments and criticisms from Adam Kilgarriff, David Yarowsky, Karen Sparck Jones, Rebecca Bruce and members of the CRL-New Mexico and University of Sheffield NLP groups. The mistakes are all my own, as always.

References

[1] Antal, L. *Question of Meaning*. Mouton: The Hague, 1963.
[2] Brown, P. F., S. A. Di Pietra, V. J. Di Pietra and R. L. Mercer. "Word Sense Disambiguation Using Statistical Methods". In *Proc. ACL-91*, 1991.

[3] Bruce, R. and J. Wiebe. "Word-Sense Disambiguation Using Decomposable Models". In *Proc. ACL-94*. Las Cruces, New Mexico, 1994, pp. 139–145.

[4] Copestake, A. and T. Briscoe. "Lexical Operations in a Unification-Based Framework". In *Proc. ACL SIGLEX Workshop*. Berkeley, 1991.

[5] Cowie, J., L. Guthrie and J. Guthrie. "Lexical Disambiguation Using Simulated Annealing". In *Proc. COLING-92*, 1992, pp. 359–365.

[6] Dagon, I. and A. Itai. "Word Sense Disambiguation Using a Second Language Monolingual Corpus". *Computational Linguistics*, 20 (1994).

[7] Gale, W., K. Church, and D. Yarowsky. "One Sense Per Discourse". In *Proc. DARPA Speech and Natural Language Workshop*. New York: Harriman, February 1992, pp. 233–237.

[8] Givon, T. *Transformations of Ellipsis, Sense Development and Rules of Lexical Derivation*. Technical Report SP-2896, Sta Monica, CA: Systems Development Corp., 1967.

[9] Green, G. *Pragmatics and Natural Language Understanding*. Hillsdale, NJ: Erlbaum, 1989.

[10] Hanks, P. Personal communication, 1994.

[11] Ide, N. and J. Veronis. "Have We Wasted Our Time?" In *Proc. of the International Workshop on the Future of the Dictionary*. Grenoble, 1994.

[12] Jorgensen, J. "The Psychological Reality of Word Senses". *Journal of Psycholinguistic Research*, 19 (1990).

[13] Kilgarriff, A. "Dictionary Word Sense Distinctions: An Enquiry into Their Nature". *Computers and the Humanities* (1993).

[14] Miller, G. "WordNet: A Dictionary Browser". In *Proceedings of the First International Conference on Information in Data*. Canada: Waterloo OED Centre, 1985.

[15] Pustejovsky, J. *The Generative Lexicon*. MIT Press, 1995.

[16] Small, S., G. Cottrell and M. Tanenhaus, editors. *Lexical Ambiguity Resolution: Perspectives from Psycholinguistics, Neuropsychology and Artificial Intelligence*. San Mateo, California: Morgan Kaufmann, 1988.

[17] Wierzbicka, A. *Semantics, Culture and Cognition*. Oxford: Oxford University Press, 1989.

[18] Wilks, Y. *Grammar, Meaning and the Machine Analysis of Language*. London: Routledge, 1972.

[19] Wilks, Y. "Making Preferences More Active". *Artificial Intelligence*, 11 (1978).

[20] Wilks, Y., D. Fass, C. M. Guo, J. McDonald, T. Plate and B. Slator. "A Tractable Machine Dictionary as a Basis for Computational Semantics". *Journal of Machine Translation*, 5 (1990).

[21] Wilks, Y. and M. Stevenson. "Sense Tagging: Semantic Tagging with a Lexicon". In *Tagging Text with Lexical Semantics: What, Why and How?* Proc. ANLP, Washington, DC, 1997.

[22] Wilks, Y. A., B. M. Slator and L. M. Guthrie. *Electric Words: Dictionaries, Computers and Meanings*. MIT Press, 1996.

[23] Yarowsky, D. "Word-Sense Disambiguation Using Statistical Models of Roget's Categories Trained on Large Corpora". In *Proc. COLING-92*, 1992.

[24] Yarowsky, D. "One Sense Per Collocation". In *Proceedings ARPA Human Language Technology Workshop*, 1993, pp. 266–271.

[25] Yarowsky, D. "Unsupervised Word-Sense Disambiguation Rivaling Supervised methods". In *Proc. of ACL-95*, 1995, pp. 189–196.